BROADCAST PROGRAMMING

BROADCAST PROGRAMMING

*Strategies for Winning Television
and Radio Audiences*

Susan Tyler Eastman
Temple University

Sydney W. Head
Temple University

Lewis Klein
Temple University
Gateway Communications, Inc.

Wadsworth Publishing Company
Belmont, California
A Division of Wadsworth, Inc.

Senior Editor: Rebecca Hayden
Production Editor: Diane Sipes
Designer: Janet Wood
Copy Editor: Norma Traylor

Printed in the United States of America

1 2 3 4 5 6 7 8 9 10—85 84 83 82 81

Library of Congress Cataloging in Publication Data

Eastman, Susan Tyler.
  Broadcast programming, strategies for winning television and radio audiences.

  Bibliography: p.
  Includes indexes.
  1. Television programs—Planning—Addresses, essays, lectures. 2. Radio programs—Planning—Addresses, essays, lectures. I. Head, Sydney W., joint author. II. Klein, Lewis, 1927–   joint author. III. Title.
PN1992.55.E18   791.44'0973   80-16791
ISBN 0-534-00882-8

Preface

Hitherto there has not been a broadcasting book devoted exclusively to the all-important subject of programming strategies. There are plenty of books about programs themselves, individually and collectively; about the production of programs (what we regard as the tactics rather than the strategies of programming); and about management, in which programming has its place. But no one has focused on the distinctive role of the programming executive. A scholar who researched the considerations that enter into programmers' decision making deplored this lack:

> Unseen, and seldom sung, the television program director is the power behind the TV set in hundreds of communities. His are the decisions that change the copy in those millions of program guides week after week; he gets the blame, though seldom the praise. And oddly enough, the articles, studies, and books on the business focus on his job no more than the cameras do. Television programming gets a chapter in a textbook or one of the few books on management, while many chapters are devoted to production, direction, and performance. [1]

This gap in the literature of radio and television broadcasting is understandable when one considers the bewildering variety of situations in which broadcast programmers find themselves—ranging from the small radio station in a single-station market to the primetime network programmer responsible for the material seen by tens of millions of viewers every night. Only on the most generalized level can one make statements about programmers and their functions that apply equally to all sorts of programming situations. We do in fact start with such generalizations because all types of broadcasting ultimately share certain common attributes, no matter how diverse the surrounding circumstances. But the heart of our book is the testimony of actual practitioners in varied programming situations.

One caveat should be made at the outset: we do not attempt to evaluate programming except in the pragmatic sense that programmers themselves use—its ability to attract targeted audiences. This does not mean that we discount the importance of program quality or absolve broadcasters from responsibility for taking quality into consideration. We feel, however, that there is sufficient critical literature available. Our task was to examine objectively how programming decisions are actually made, whatever the wider artistic implications of those decisions might be.

One of the more perplexing problems we faced at the start was the decision as to what we meant by programming and hence what types of program decision makers we should include. It was tempting, for example, to think in terms of program genres and therefore to seek out experts in such specializations as sports, children's, and feature film programming. We were also tempted to call upon specialists in the making of programs, such as the package producers who are responsible for fashioning most of the network television entertainment programming.

We needed some defining principle that would impose limits and logical coherence on the selection of authors and the subjects of the chapters. In the end, we decided that we should confine the book to situations in which program executives are responsible not only for choosing and shaping individual programs or program segments but also for organizing such separate program items into coherent program *services*. It is universally recognized that an important—in some situations even the most important—part of the broadcast programmer's job is *scheduling*. Significant though producing organizations such as those of Norman Lear or Mary Tyler Moore are in the creative aspects of the medium, such organizations have no responsibility for designing entire program services. Instead, they focus their energies narrowly on turning out specific program series, leaving it to broadcast programmers to decide if, when, and how to use these programs in designing the continuous sequences that constitute broadcast or pay-cable services. We therefore selected authors who had responsibility for the design of entire network, station, or cable services.

The book divides into four major sections: Part One introduces a framework for evaluating the contents of the remaining chapters; Parts Two, Three, and Four look at programming strategy for television stations, television networks, and radio from the authors' perspectives as industry programming experts. Notes and annotated readings from periodicals appear at the close of each chapter. The readings are articles from current trade publications and scholarly journals that support, complement, or contrast with the contents of the chapters.

A list of abbreviations and acronyms appears near the end of the book. Words in **boldface** in the text appear in the glossary. An annotated bibliography of books, guides, reports, theses, and dissertations on programming follows. References appearing in the periodical readings are not repeated in the bibliography; readers should consult both the bibliography of books and reports and the additional periodical readings at the end of each chapter for items on specific topics. The general index at the end of the book is preceded by an index of the television and radio program titles and films mentioned in the text.

We want to thank warmly the individuals and organizations that assisted us. Robert Bernstein of March Five Inc.; Frederick Breitenfeld of Maryland Public Television; Joel Chaseman of Post-Newsweek Stations; Seymour Horowitz of ABC-owned stations, New York; Lee Tenebruso of Showtime; and Daniel T. Pecaro and Harry D. Trigg of WGN-TV, Chicago, made useful suggestions that aided in the formation of specific chapters. Christopher Sterling of Temple University assisted substantively with the bibliography. Rebecca Hayden of Wadsworth supported and counseled us with seemingly effortless expertise. Charles R. Bantz of the University of Minnesota, David Eshelman of Central Missouri State University, Donald G. Godfrey of the University of Washington, Daniel E. Gold of Comcast, Ralph L. Smith of Illinois State University, Jacob J. Wakshlag of Indiana University, and Robert D. West of Kent State University commented beneficially on the manuscript in draft. Tammy Dennis and Daw Ming Lee, Temple University students, assisted us with research. We are grateful to all these people for their help, to the National Association of Television Program Executives for sustaining a survey of its members, and to the Department of Radio-Television-Film at Temple University for its encouragement and support.

Susan Tyler Eastman
Sydney W. Head
Lewis Klein

NOTE

[1]J. David Lewis, "Programmer's Choice: Eight Factors in Program Decision-Making," *Journal of Broadcasting* 14 (Winter 1969–70): 72.

Contents

Foreword

Les Brown

As television/radio correspondent for the New York Times
*since 1973, (after fourteen years covering the broadcasting beat for
the trade magazine* Variety*), Les Brown gained a unique perspective on the business and institutional aspects of the media. In
1980 he left the* New York Times *to found his own television
magazine,* Channels of Communication, *funded by the Markle
Foundation. In addition to professional writing for the press, he
has taught at Columbia College in Chicago, Hunter College and
the New School for Social Research in New York, and Yale University in New Haven, Connecticut, and lectured at other universities and numerous broadcasting industry and public interest
forums. He is the author of* Television: The Bu$iness Behind
the Box *(Harcourt Brace Jovanovich, 1971),* Electric Media
(Harcourt School Division, 1977) and the New York Times
Encyclopedia of Television *(Times Books, 1977)—an invaluable factual guide to the television industry in terms of programs,
people, and concept. His most recent publications are* Keeping
Your Eye on Television *(Pilgrim Press, 1979) and a revised
edition of the* New York Times Encyclopedia *(1980). Among
his awards are a Special Award for Reporting from the National
Association of Television Program Executives in 1977, two fellow-
ships at Yale University in 1977 and 1978, and a presidential
fellowship at the Aspen Institute for Humanistic Studies since
1978. He is presently a member of the editorial board of* Television Quarterly. *With his characteristic flare for cutting through
to the heart of a story, Les Brown singles out, in his foreword to
this book, the form of programming that has by far the widest
circulation and hence, presumably, the most influence—
commercial network television. His analysis of the direct and
indirect roles played by advertisers in programming strategies is a
realistic rather than a cynical assessment that provides a counterpoint to the balance of this book.*

The editors of this book have my sympathy. They have taken on
no easy job in attempting to analyze the entire range of broadcast
programming in terms of universal common denominators. There is, of
course, a vast lore of programming wisdom, much of it self-
contradictory because what works well at one time or place may not
work at all at another time or place. The fact is, however, that one
particular branch of the programmer's art has overwhelming importance
from the point of view of sheer audience impact. There has never been
anything in the field of popular arts as massive and single-minded as

commercial network television programming, and so I will confine my remarks to that segment of the total programming spectrum. Once we understand the basic assumptions of commercial network programmers, we understand the most important facts about the strategies of American broadcast programming.

The commercial television program is surely the strangest phylum of the popular arts. Unlike phonograph recordings, books, comic strips, or movies, it is shaped, one way or another, by the imperatives of advertising. It exists to capture viewers, because audience is what commercial broadcasters sell to their client, the advertisers. A program survives or fails not on unit sales or box office admissions but on an index of attention paid it as expressed in audience ratings—digits representing an estimate of the percentage of television households that tuned in. Moreover, the television program is born not so much in a creative spirit as in a combative one, since the primary aim of each is to destroy two or more programs that compete with it in its time slot.

A television program, in the broadest of definitions, is anything that can be shown on a television screen if a broadcaster but chooses to put it there. It can be an opera from the stage of Italy's La Scala, a local town meeting, a national tap-dancing contest, a lecture in marine biology, a stand-up comedian doing a turn. Practically everything lends itself to a television presentation or coverage by the cameras—religion, education, business, science, history, politics, theater, dance, cabaret, concerts, movies, sporting events, and current events.

The possibilities for form are unlimited. A program may be fixed in as small a format as one minute, which proved suitable for *Bicentennial Minutes* and *Newsbreak,* or may run on indefinitely, like the coverage of a baseball game or some syndicated talk shows of the 1950s, David Susskind's *Open End* or Irv Kupcinet's *At Random.* A single program may even span an entire broadcast day or several consecutive days if it involves a national or local emergency or, as has happened, the assassination of a president.

But in the practical definition—the one applicable to what broadcasters like to call "the real world"—a television program is a preproduced show that runs somewhere from a half hour to 2 hours and falls into one of a limited number of categories: situation comedy, adventure melodrama, variety show, soap opera, quiz or game show, talk show, made-for-television movie, miniseries, documentary, or newscast. Commercial television in the United States has become so circumscribed because the narrow scope manifestly serves the business purposes of broadcasters.

The advertiser's role in television has evolved from pronounced to subtle. Television came on so rapidly after World War II that it had no time to develop an economic system of its own. Since most television licensees were already in the radio business, it became natural for them to adopt radio's commercial scheme, as well as many of its programs.

The important difference, where programs were concerned, was that those that ran 15 minutes on radio needed a half hour for an equivalent episode on television, while the half hour radio program translated into a 1-hour television show. Television gave the lie to the myth that a picture is worth a thousand words; the addition of the picture, in fact, doubled the time required to tell the story.

Advertisers' early involvement was in radio as the sponsors. This meant, in effect, that advertisers either owned or controlled time periods and could dictate what kind of programs would be broadcast. Often advertisers developed the programs and produced them to their specifications. They avoided controversy, since advertisers spent huge amounts of money strictly for the purpose of making friends and not of making enemies. And they excised from scripts anything, however petty, that might reflect unfavorably on their products. Thus an early television play sponsored by Chevrolet had to delete dialogue containing the phrase "fording a stream" because it evoked the name of a competing automobile. The American Gas Association deleted references to gas chambers in a program that dealt with the Nazis' technique for exterminating Jews. And as recently as 1970 Coca-Cola ordered a few frames of film clipped from an entertainment special that showed people in a cabaret drinking something that was not its product.

But these acts of commercial censorship were relatively minor penalties for television to pay for allowing advertisers to run the show. The crisis came in the late 1950s when the sponsors of certain popular primetime quiz shows ordered them rigged—to the extent of giving answers in advance to the most appealing contestants—in order to keep the ratings up. Since the networks were held responsible for practicing such deceptions on the audience and were upbraided by the Federal Communications Commission and members of Congress, they became wary of entrusting program decisions to advertisers and looked for ways to assume full control over programming. They were aided by rising program costs and the high rate of program failure, which by 1965 made it impractical for advertisers to bet entire national advertising budgets on single program series.

What evolved was a television version of the magazine advertising concept: The networks developed, selected, and scheduled their own shows, and advertisers bought a scattering of spots in a number of programs, in much the way that they purchased pages in magazines— with no direct identification with the surrounding textual material and no voice in the content. This became even more refined in the computer age. An advertiser now establishes with the network what will be paid per thousand viewers, the computer kicks out a schedule of spots based on that agreement, and, if the ratings should fail to equal the projections, the network makes up the shortfall of viewers with additional spots at no additional cost.

The advertisers no longer may decide which shows go into the schedule, but the rates an advertiser will pay still govern the programming decisions that are made at the networks and the stations. Beyond that, there is a consensus in the advertising community that governs the structure of a television schedule. It was for the convenience of advertisers, for example, that the children's hour in television was shifted from early-evening time periods to Saturday mornings. Young children could be corraled there more cheaply than in primetime and as a relatively "pure" audience, demographically speaking.

Programs survive in network television if they are able to carve out at least a 30 percent share of the audience; usually they are canceled if they do not. The ground rules appear bizarre to those of us who consider a book a best-seller if it sells 100,000 copies or a recording a smash hit if it sells a million. On the network level, a primetime program is a failure if it reaches only 20 million viewers—an audience that would keep an average-sized Broadway theater filled to capacity every performance for a quarter century.

The nature of the competition makes television programming a kill-or-be-killed proposition, and this inevitably affects the creative process. Always there is a sense of a network or station looking over its shoulder to see who might be gaining on another channel. The fear that a program may be paced too slowly or that it may be found boring by viewers who have other options on the television dial has caused American producers to put plot situations ahead of character development—in other words, to favor melodrama over drama. Consider how different television programs would be if there were only one national network instead of three. A network with no competition could set its own pace and decide for itself what programs are appropriate for the audience, at what intellectual level they should be pitched, and how many weeks or years any series should run.

In fact, the British Broadcasting Corporation had just such a luxury until 1956, when a competing commercial network was authorized in the United Kingdom. As a result, British television viewers were conditioned differently from those in the United States and came to have a greater tolerance for character drama and documentaries. Moreover, the commercial programs differ from the American brand in that they may not be interrupted for commercials; instead, the advertisements are segregated in clusters before and after the programs.

What most sets the American television program apart from those of most other countries is its accommodation to advertising. Programs in this country are built around the commercial breaks. And these must occur approximately at the quarter hour.

The advertising breaks are sacred and come first, their positions fixed in the schedule before the programs are even conceived. They govern form in American television. Half-hour situation comedies must be written in two acts of more or less equal length, followed optionally by a 1- or 2-minute epilogue. The hour-long adventure dramas have to be written in four acts of equal length, even though they are never identified as acts on the screen. Each act, moreover, must end with a climax, a surprising development, or some manner of heightened intrigue to keep the viewer in suspense through the period of commercials. Thus the American television writer works from a blueprint that provides a prepartitioned space.

The character of American television has been shaped more by the dictates of the commercial break than by any other force. It is by now engraved in the American television watcher's sensibility that heightened action comes at the quarter hour. Most made-for-television movies never rise above being ersatz motion pictures for the reason that they answer too well the peculiar structural mechanics of commercial television. These films play more neatly on television than do pictures made originally for theatrical distribution, but they remain different from real movies—from cinema—because they have been crafted modularly, with the commercial breaks in mind.

But it is in the nature of art to overcome the restrictions of form. Poets purposely set themselves a handicap when they choose to write a sonnet, and painters pose their own challenges with the size and shape of the canvas selected.

Television canvas has been cut to precise sizes by commerce. When you think about it, for all the mediocrity that broadcasting has fostered, it is amazing how often and how splendidly the limitations of form have been vaulted.

PART ONE
The Framework of Programming Strategies

In the first three chapters, the author lays the groundwork for conceptualizing the essential nature of the programming function. Despite the tremendous variety of programming situations that occurs in broadcasting, the author suggests in Chapter 1 that the medium itself has certain intrinsic attributes that underlie all programming strategies. From these shared attributes can be deduced programming principles that all levels of broadcasting have in common. All programmers therefore face similar fundamental problems, which can best be seen as constraints on the individual programmer's freedom of choice. Some of these constraints tend to be relatively fixed—beyond the programmer's immediate control. These the author defines as "nonnegotiable" constraints. Other constraints leave latitude for the exercise of the programmer's skills, learned and innate. Characterized as "negotiable" constraints, they can be overcome or modified by the use of appropriate programming strategies.

Chapter 2 focuses on the people who do programming, the research they use, and the kinds of constraints affecting them. Chapter 3 reviews regulatory constraints, showing how industry codes, legal requirements, and pressure groups influence programming decisions. The author looks at the priorities programmers assign to specific constraints and provides an overview of the influence of the Federal Communications Commission.

Together, these three chapters provide a broad framework within which to consider the more specialized problems dealt with by programming experts in the fourteen chapters that follow. Written by experienced practitioners of the programmer's art, the remainder of the chapters represents case studies of how basic strategies are modified to suit typical programming situations. Chapters 4 through 17 can be analyzed in terms of (1) the physical attributes characterizing each part of the system; (2) the programming strategies used in each situation; and (3) the specific regulatory constraints applying to each chapter's topic.

1 *Programming Principles*

Sydney W. Head

Sydney W. Head brings to the first three chapters of this book a lifetime of experience with broadcasting, both as a practitioner and as an academic. He was technical director of the university theater at the University of Colorado and full professor and chairman of the Department of Radio-Television-Film he founded at the University of Miami (Florida) and has been a senior faculty member at Temple University in Philadelphia since 1970. He headed teams advising the governments of the Sudan and Ethiopia on radio broadcasting development between 1961 and 1970. He wrote and produced many radio and television programs and, in addition to numerous journal articles, is author of Broadcasting in America: A Survey of Television and Radio *(Houghton-Mifflin, 1976), which is going into its fourth edition, and editor of* Broadcasting in Africa: A Continental Survey *(Temple University Press, 1974). His awards include a 1952 Kaltenborn Fellowship, the Academy of Television Arts and Sciences Fellowship in 1960, and a Fulbright senior lectureship at the University of Ghana in 1976–77. In this chapter he introduces the subject of this book—programming—and defines broadcasting by delineating its major attributes as they relate to programming. From these attributes, he develops five programming principles that apply to the wide variety of programming situations existing at commercial and noncommercial stations, at pay-television services, and at networks.*

PROGRAMMING AS STRATEGY

The program we see at any given moment on our television screens or hear on our radios is there for two reasons: first, someone planned an entire schedule of which this program is part; second, someone executed the program plans and put the schedule on the air. The seemingly obvious distinction between these two functions— *programming* and *production*—is important but often overlooked.

This oversight arises for understandable reasons: in the first place, production is much easier to define, teach, and practice than is programming. The production end product is visible, audible, observable, assessable. Programming, however, is far more elusive. It cannot be practiced unless one has on-air access to an actual station and perhaps a year to await results. Production, on the other hand, can be practiced with modest facilities, and the results can be recorded for instant analysis and evaluation.

A second reason for confusion about the respective roles of programming and production arises from the fact that in small stations people have to wear several hats. The person whose job at one moment is programming becomes a producer at the next moment and after that perhaps a salesperson or copywriter.

Third, the generally recognized divisions of **station** and **network** operations fall into four functional departments: (1) general/ administrative, (2) technical, (3) sales, and (4) program. This last lumps programming and production under the same heading.

Finally, the programming function varies so much in the scope and nature of its operations from one programming situation to another that it is difficult to discern what, if anything, all these situations have in common.

These are some of the reasons why textbook discussions of programming almost invariably get sidetracked into discussions of production—discussions not about how programming is done but rather about how programs are made. In this book we focus on programming—first by defining it in a way that clearly differentiates it from production, and second by showing that all broadcast programming does, in fact, have common underlying principles, despite its infinite variety. Our first task, therefore, is to differentiate between programming and production.

The difference can be expressed in terms of the contrast between strategy and tactics. *Strategy* refers to the planning and directing of large-scale operations with long-term goals in mind. *Tactics* refers to methods used to carry out the operations and reach the goals that strategy has defined. The boxer and his manager plan strategy back in the training camp, long before the bout. Once the fighter enters the ring, it is too late for strategy; now it is all tactics, an attempt to put strategy into practice in the heat of the encounter.

Programming is strategy. It deals with the advance planning of the program schedule as a whole. It involves searching out and acquiring program materials and planning a coherent sequence, a program service. Production is tactics. It deals with arranging and maneuvering the people and things needed to put programming plans into action. It selects and deploys the means for achieving program plans on the air.

Programming, as seen from this perspective, can therefore be defined as *the strategies involved in first searching out and acquiring program materials and then fitting them into a coherent service.* Once programs have been selected and the schedule set up, production takes over and makes the innumerable day-to-day tactical decisions needed to get the intended results.

Suppose a station management decides that it would be good

strategy to lengthen a locally produced program from a half hour to a full hour. A program executive gets the go-ahead, along with budget authorization and whatever stipulations management wants to impose. The programmer would then mandate the conditions under which the change is to be made—how the approved budget is to be spent, the nature of the additional content, the types of new personnel that may be hired. Many other details might be considered of strategic importance and therefore handed down to production as "givens" along with the basic change. These details might include even nit-picking items like a performer's hairdo or the color of a set—matters ordinarily left to production, but in a particular case (perhaps on advice of a program consultant) treated as having strategic importance.

Having received instructions from programming about the changes, production deals with the tactical problems of implementation. A production manager reschedules facilities and talent, orders new graphics and copy, and supervises the daily coordination of the work of writers, directors, graphic artists, performers, and others.

This hypothetical (and very simplified) example illustrates the practical difference between programming as strategy and production as tactics; it also shows how subjects for decision can shift back and forth between the two. Because the example concerns only one program, however, it fails to bring out the second element in the definition of programming: fitting program materials into a coherent service. This aspect of programming needs special emphasis because it supplies one of the programmer's most important strategic tools, and yet its significance is easily overlooked.

A program service is much more than the sum of its parts. Decisions about how to combine programs, or program elements, into an effective whole are just as important as decisions about which program items to accept or reject. Programming, in other words, is not simply a matter of collecting so many bricks and throwing them into a pile. Instead, the bricks must be put in place one by one, according to an overall plan, so that in the end they form a structure, not just a meaningless jumble. Creating this structure is the role of scheduling.

This definition of programming as strategy also fails to bring out the extent to which programming deals in future prospects rather than present facts. Programmers look further ahead than the next day's operational log. They try to anticipate changes in the social climate and in the strategies of competing stations. While producers are putting the programmers' past insights into effect in the current program schedule, programmers are already foreseeing strategic changes to be made on down the line—weeks, months, and even a year or so into the future. Indeed, a good programmer might be defined as a good futurist: one who by a combination of logic, research, and insight anticipates changing public tastes, the rise and fall of fashions, the emergence of new trends, the probable point of decline of current fads and preoccupations.

DIVERSITY OF PROGRAMMING SITUATIONS

Broadcast programming takes place under fantastically varied circumstances. At one extreme is the situation of the small-town radio station operator in a one-station market. The manager (who may well also function as a salesperson, a **disc jockey**, and a bookkeeper) has only a very limited range of programming decisions to make. Let us imagine, for example, a husband-and-wife team as joint owners of a small-market Class IV radio station (local channel, 250 watts of power) as they face each other across their front-to-front plywood desks.

One must understand that programmers of radio stations, especially small stations, are not concerned with individual programs. They plan the entire day, or at least major segments of the day (**dayparts**) according to a formula, usually one built around a specific type of popular recorded music. The entire schedule is one continuous program. The music tastes and personality traits of the music presenters, the DJs, are important elements in both the design and execution of a small-station formula. Once the basic formula has been adopted, the act of hiring a DJ to cover a daypart is a major programming decision as well as a personnel decision.

The husband and wife can hardly see each other between the stacks of mail, promotional pieces, equipment catalogs, give-away discs, tapes, cartridges, unanswered mail, old commercial copy, and trade journals. They sip coffee from battered mugs as they go over the pros and cons for the umpteenth time. At last the couple reaches a decision. They agree they will hire the best of the dozen applicants they have already interviewed to take over the 10:00 A.M. to 3:00 P.M. DJ shift. This will free the husband to give his wife more help with the sales as well as bring a fresh personality to the lineup.

At the other extreme might be the situation of a television **primetime network** programmer. We can imagine him in a luxuriously decorated executive office high above Manhattan's midtown traffic. Expensively tailored, he lounges at a marble-topped table that takes the place of a desk. He is conferring with several equally well turned out colleagues. Several weeks of close study and earnest debate have preceded this showdown meeting. They are about to arrive at a momentous decision. One of their **sit-coms**, now scheduled at 8:30 Thursday nights, will be shifted to 8:00 Saturday nights!

The common denominator in these two absurdly disparate scenes is that in each case a broadcast programmer's function is being performed. In each case a strategic decision is made about programming. Program executives are placing bets on the outcome of changes in their respective program services. The network decision may affect the viewing habits of 60 million viewers. Millions of dollars in gross revenue may be affected by the outcome of the change. Some 200 television stations will feel the repercussions. Thousands of stockholders of affiliated station companies as well as the network's own stockholders may eventually sense the shock waves. On the other hand, the radio station decision will affect at most about 6,000 local radio listeners, the immediate fortunes of one disc jockey, and the credit-and-loss statement of a family business that grosses on the order of $100,000 a year. The network decision concerns only one aspect of one specific television program series, namely, its placement in the network's overall weekly primetime pattern. The radio decision concerns the midday output of a radio station, Monday through Friday.

So different are the programmers' jobs in the scenes just described that they might be considered totally different occupations. The business of broadcast programming is indeed immensely varied. It demands skills and knowledge specific to particular programming situations—whether the situation of a small-market or a large-market station; whether radio or television; if radio, whether AM or FM; if television, whether VHF or UHF; whether an individual station or a network; whether a network **affiliate** or an **independent** station; whether a commercial or a noncommercial station or a network; and so on.

No one person can reasonably be expected to combine the experience and know-how specific to all these diverse programming situations. That is why in this book we have asked individuals with personal experience in a variety of programming situations to speak from the vantage point of their specialized practical knowledge.

First, however, it should be helpful to analyze broadcasting in terms of its unifying elements. What are the attributes of the medium that all stations and networks share? What are the underlying program principles that these attributes imply?

INHERENT ATTRIBUTES OF BROADCASTING

When people talk about programming, they usually take as their point of departure the existence of certain well-established formats: "news," "serial drama," "game shows," and the like, or programs defined in terms of the special target audiences (children, for example). Such ways of categorizing broadcasting are universal. But in the present context, we are interested in probing beyond these specific manifestations. What do all established formats have in common? What underlying principles apply just as much to sports as to serial drama, just as much to programs for women as to those for children?

In search of common denominators, we need to look first at the nature of the medium. Certain attributes peculiar to the medium of

over-the-air broadcasting contribute to the makeup of its unique character. If we identify broadcasting's unique attributes, we should be able to
deduce from them programming principles of universal application.

Wirelessness

The attribute of *wirelessness* clearly sets broadcasting apart from
other media of communication. Because of its wirelessness, broadcasting can reach larger numbers of people simultaneously than any other
medium. Moreover, unlike other major media, broadcasting benefits
from the fact that its own audience invests directly in the essential
physical equipment of the medium: broadcast receivers. This means
that, within the coverage area of a given station's transmitter, it costs
the station no more to reach a million people than it costs to reach only
one person.

It also means that, in order to take advantage of this potential,
programmers must motivate people to buy, to maintain, and to use
receiving sets. The implication for programming is obvious: people will
make this investment of time and money only to the extent that they
find the programs they are able to pick up worthwhile in their own
terms—not in terms of other people's standards or ideal standards.

Accessibility

A second special attribute of broadcasting, closely related to the
first, is its universal *accessibility* to listeners and viewers. Broadcast audiences need no preparation to participate in the act of broadcast communication. They do not have to learn to read, buy a ticket, get dressed, or
assemble at a designated place outside their home or other personal
environment.

Thus broadcasting can reach a wider, more varied spectrum of
consumers than any other medium. It can reach the young and the old,
the rich and the poor, the rural and the urban, the educated and the
dropouts, the shut-ins and the travelers, the blue collars and the white,
minorities and majorities. Accessibility depends, of course, on the distribution of receivers, but in the United States at least, both radio and
television receivers are essentially universally available.

Continuousness

A third attribute of broadcasting is its *continuously unfolding* nature. A book, a newspaper, a magazine, or a movie in a theater is a
separate entity, complete in itself. Broadcasting, however, exists from
moment to moment, always "there" yet always imminent. Something
else is always about to happen, and we can never be entirely certain
what that something else is going to be. Even the most routine program

might be interrupted for an unscheduled, possibly vitally important, message. The slight, subconscious tension this attribute creates is unique to broadcasting.

In an address to the International Institute of Communication, Les Brown, the *New York Times* television correspondent, spoke of the probable impact of the new technologies—cable, pay-television, home video recording, and the rest—on broadcasting. He concluded that over-the-air broadcasting will remain viable "because it has the potential to go live at any minute and to plug in the viewer to the outside world." He went on:

> Every time the television set is switched on, the household becomes implicitly connected to the unseen news operations of the networks and stations—the telephones, news tickers, microwaves, telegraph, mobile units, minicams, satellites, and other paraphernalia that enable people to keep contact with the community and the world. . . . Whatever range of programs it may offer, the video disc cannot interrupt itself for a news bulletin. It may present the outside world, but it is not plugged into it.[1]

Realism

A fourth broadcasting attribute is its potential for *realism*, its ability to deliver the actual sounds and sights of events directly and instantaneously to audiences. This attribute should not be confused with literary realism, which makes fictional or "re-created" characters and events in dramatic presentations seem "real." Realism here refers to broadcasting's ability to convey actuality in the very process of occurring. This unique ability, unmatched by any other medium, is responsible for some of broadcasting's most striking achievements.

Social Impact

The preceding four attributes, though described separately for purpose of analysis, work in combination. Together they give broadcasting what must be counted as its most significant attribute—its unique *social impact*. Its uniqueness arises from the facts that broadcasting comes directly into the home, is so readily accessible to children, reaches nearly the entire population, and takes up so much of people's time. No other medium has this combination of physical and psychological advantages.

Government regulation and industry self-regulation, based on this perception of broadcasting influence, seek to encourage practices thought to have prosocial effects and to discourage practices thought to have antisocial effects. Programmers therefore cannot avoid taking into consideration the possible social impact of programs, whether real or imagined. On the negative side, they may avoid subject matters and treatments that are likely to cause an outcry because of their antisocial effect, actual or alleged. On the positive side, they may be influenced to choose programs and treatments that they believe will have beneficial social effects.

DEDUCING PROGRAMMING STRATEGIES

If broadcasting has the foregoing attributes, programmers can hardly afford to ignore the potential they imply. Failure to capitalize fully on broadcasting's potential can arise not only from bad programming judgments but also from "circumstances beyond our control."

For example, the attribute of realism suggests that it would be a good idea to program live events. Some of the most outstanding programming is precisely that. But because picking up live events can be very costly, not every station can afford the luxury of capitalizing fully on this attribute of broadcasting. One of the penalties of scheduling frequent real events is that their timing cannot be controlled. Constant disruption of planned schedules to insert unplanned live events can be counterproductive. Moreover, too much realism can in itself be objectionable. For example, excessive realism in news pickups could violate a provision of the news section of the National Association of Broadcasters volunteer program code: "Morbid, sensational or alarming details not essential to the factual report, especially in connection with stories of crime or sex, should be avoided."[2]

In short, any programming strategy must be evaluated in context and used with moderation. With this proviso in mind, let us consider some of the principal strategies of programming that can be deduced from the inherent attributes of the medium.

Compatibility

Broadcast programming can be structured to coincide with and to complement what people are doing throughout their daily cycle of personal activities. This is compatibility strategy, the source of one of the medium's most powerful holds over audiences. Compatibility strategy is possible because of the continuously unfolding nature of the medium. Capitalizing on this attribute, programmers adapt their program service to changing audience activities as the day progresses. Programmers study life-styles of the people in their service areas, finding out how they divide their days into periods of sleeping, eating, personal toilet, relaxing, socializing, commuting, working, and so on. Broadcasting alone among the media has the capacity to adjust its own style to suit audience needs and interests from hour to hour throughout the day.

Compatibility strategies affect the choice of program types, subject matters, and scheduling. The programmer takes into consideration both who is available in each daypart and what the available audience members are most likely to be doing at that time.* Thus we have programming compatible with getting up in the morning and preparing for the day's activities, for driving to work, for doing the morning household chores, for the luncheon period, for the afternoon lull, for the ingathering of children in the late afternoon, for the reaccelerated tempo of home activities as the day draws to a close, for the relaxed family-oriented atmosphere of early primetime, for the more exclusively adult interests of later primetime and late **fringe** hours, and for the small hours of the morning before the whole cycle begins again. When the weekday cycle gives way to the weekend, the compatibility principle calls for adaptation to the changed schedule of activities.

Habit Formation

The power of the compatibility principle acquires even more leverage from the fact that audience members form personal listening and watching habits. Thus the programmer uses compatibility strategies to fit into people's living habits while at the same time using habit-formation strategies to reinforce the hold that programming acquires over audience attention. Scheduling programs for strict regularity and predictability (along with promotional efforts to make people aware of a station and its programs) establishes tuning habits that become automatic. Indeed, people go to extraordinary lengths to avoid missing the next episode in a favorite series. Programmers discovered this principle in the earliest days of radio when, for example, the *Amos 'n' Andy* habit became so strong that movie theaters of the 1930s found it necessary to shut down the picture and hook a radio into the sound system at 7:15 P.M. when *Amos 'n' Andy* came on.

Television program series are scheduled daily (Monday through Friday—called **stripping** or across-the-board scheduling), on alternate days (**checkerboarding**), or weekly. From the habit-formation point of view, daily scheduling is no doubt the most effective, but it would be too expensive to build up a sufficient backlog of high-cost first-run programs to enable scheduling such programs that often.

Daytime series (being by definition low in cost) are stripped. Primetime series are scheduled weekly, but when they are released for sale in the open market, the cost comes down enough to permit daily scheduling. The networks have another reason for scheduling their

---

*The usual television station weekday breakdown (EST) is: daytime—9 A.M. to 4:30 P.M.; early fringe time—4:30 P.M. to 7 P.M.; access hour—7 to 8 P.M.; primetime—8 to 11 P.M.; late fringe—11 P.M. to 1 A.M.; and "all other." The usual radio daypart breakdown is: morning drivetime—6 to 10 A.M.; midday—10 A.M. to 3 P.M.; afternoon drivetime—3 to 7 P.M.; evening—7 P.M. to midnight; and overnight—midnight to 6 A.M. Dayparting as a verb means altering a radio format in different periods of the day for compatibility reasons.

valuable primetime shows on a weekly basis: it gives them more maneuvering room for competitive schedule-change strategies. If a network stripped its three primetime hours with six half-hour shows, that would mean only six pawns to maneuver in the schedule battle. On the other hand, if each half-hour slot were occupied by a different show each weekday night, that would give the option of thirty different schedule changes.

Like all rules of programming, those concerning habit formation may be subjected to selective violation. The most brilliant of the early television strategists, Sylvester "Pat" Weaver, president of NBC, recognized that too much predictability can beget boredom. In the 1950s he invented the **spectacular** (nowadays called the **special**). Although at the time it seemed like a potentially destructive maneuver, Weaver boldly broke the established pattern of routine scheduling in primetime with one-time **blockbuster** programs, usually much longer than the normal programs they temporarily displaced. The interruption itself was an attention getter, a peg on which to hang special **promotional** campaigns.

By the 1970s, network specials themselves had become almost routine, with scores of them scheduled each season. Programmers were encouraged to take the risk of violating the habit-formation principle by the discovery that **demographics** had something to do both with public awareness of innovations and with the willingness to try something new. Research indicated that audience members with the most purchasing power (those in the middle range of ages) were the very ones most likely to be attracted by specials. The more habit-bound viewers were in the younger and older age ranges, of less interest to primetime advertisers.

As so often happens, a good programming idea got transformed into a bad idea as a result of overenthusiastic adoption. Network programmers, carried away by the attention-getting potential of abrupt primetime changes, developed a whole repertoire of schedule moves that came to be called **stunting**. Among the strategies of stunting are creating special one-time **long-form** versions of standard-length series for the season's kickoff, a holiday, or the week when national rating surveys are being made; shifting programs rapidly back and forth in the schedule; and devising **crossover** appearances by characters from one program to another. According to Les Brown, the *New York Times* business-of-broadcasting writer, stunting "succeeds chiefly in confusing the issue of which network had the most potent schedule."[3] By the end of the 1970s, when network affiliates began complaining about what they regarded as excessive stunting, the fad began to subside.

Freedom of Choice

Broadcasting's attributes of wirelessness and accessibility combine to give the listener/viewer unprecedented freedom of choice. This freedom is not just a matter of being free to make a go/no-go decision, such as deciding whether to buy a book, subscribe to a newspaper, or attend a movie or concert. Broadcast consumers can instantaneously switch back and forth among optional programs at will—in a sense doing their own stunting, if that is what they want.

For programmers, the freedom-of-choice principle means that they cannot count on a captive audience. Even the slight self-constraint that keeps a book buyer reading a book or a moviegoer watching a movie so as not to waste the immediate investment, even the social restraint that keeps a bored lecture audience in its seats, cannot be counted on by broadcasters. They strive to hold the attention of the media's most tenuously committed audience. Audience members take flight to other stations or other activities at the smallest provocation. Boredom or unintelligibility acts like a sudden shot into a flock of birds.

In consequence, one of the major scheduling strategies in the programmer's repertoire is to avoid abrupt switches in mood so as to keep the audience from using its freedom to choose. Programmers see the junctures between programs as extremely critical: those are the moments when audience members will either flow through to the next program on the same station, flow away to other stations, or (God forbid!) turn off the set entirely. **Block programming**—scheduling a succession of situation comedies or other single-note programs for an entire daypart—is supposed to ensure flow-through. Programmers also count on what they consider to be an inherent audience tendency: tuning inertia. This is a tendency for some viewers to leave the set tuned the way it is in the absence of any forceful reason for change.

Based on these concepts, a number of specific rules of strategy have become embedded in programming lore. Here are three examples:

1. Schedule a strong children's program just before adult programs begin in the early evening, counting on adults to leave the set tuned to the station the children selected.

2. Avoid scheduling a low-rated program between two strong programs because the drop-off caused by **audience flow** during the "saddle" between the two strong shows will never be regained.

3. Call the "saddle" a **hammock** and use it to support a new show by giving the untried program a good **lead-in**.

In radio, a program **formula** seeks, as one of its main objectives, to avoid striking false notes that will clash with the station's carefully tailored "sound." A formula ensures adherence to a combination of content and style that keeps the listener satisfied and away from the dial. There are exceptions, of course. For example, the all-news radio formula aims not at keeping listeners continuously tuned in but rather constantly coming back. With music formulas the listener can tune in and out mentally without touching the dial, but for most listeners the all-news sound is too repetitive to be left on constantly.

The strategic principle derived from the freedom-of-choice factor is that programming must always please, entertain, and be easily understood. Much criticism of the quality of broadcasting arises from the programmer's need to deal realistically with the democratic nature of the medium. Some critics of American broadcasting find it hard to grant the masses such influence over programming—more than they have in most foreign countries by far. Some have suggested forced feeding, for example, requiring all networks to carry certain worthwhile but not very popular programs at the same time (as the British do at election time). But nothing can force audiences to choose what is good for them rather than what they like, just as in democratic politics voters sometimes stubbornly insist on electing unworthy candidates, ignoring the opportunity to vote for worthy ones.

It could be argued that the validity of the democratic-choice principle is refuted by the fact that broadcasting succeeds in undemocratic countries. However, this argument misses the point that we are not claiming that programmers must follow the ideal strategies. We are merely saying that its inherent nature gives broadcasting certain *potentials*. Broadcasting organizations live up to (or take advantage of) these potentials in varying degrees. Broadcasting still works even if they are ignored, but not as well as it might if they were skillfully used. That undemocratic use of broadcasting amounts to this kind of unskillful use is evident from the fact that authoritarian countries have difficulty in motivating people to buy receivers and in preventing those who have receivers from tuning to stations beyond their borders.

Frugality

Broadcasting is notorious for burning up program materials faster than any other medium—an inevitable consequence of its attribute of continuousness. For that reason, frugality in the dispensing of valuable program resources is an essential principal strategy of programmers. A popular fallacy holds that innumerable workable new network program ideas and countless usable new scripts by embryonic writers are waiting to be discovered; only the perversity or shortsightedness of program executives keeps this treasure trove of new material off the air. The fact is, the national talent pool, even in a country the size of the United States (and even for the superficial, imitative programming that makes up much of the primetime schedule), is not infinitely large. It takes a certain unusual talent to create programs capable of holding the attention, week after week, of 25 million people—the minimum number said to be needed to justify a primetime entertainment television series.

Sometimes audience demands and frugality happily coincide, as when the appetite for a new popular hit song demands endless replays and innumerable rearrangements. Eventually, however, obsolescence sets in, and the song becomes old hat. Broadcasting is truly a striking exemplar of our throw-away society. Even the most massively popular and brilliantly successful program series eventually lose their freshness. Sooner or later they begin to seem like old-fashioned automobiles with tailfins. They end up finally on the cancellation junk heap, often when there are still many miles of use left in them. Also like cars, some programs come back to life again in revivals, taking a new lease on life as "classics"—nostalgic reminders of an idealized past. Radio is old enough to have entered this nostalgic phase as early as the 1950s, but it was only beginning for television in the 1970s.

Programmers, therefore, must constantly search out stratagems designed to extend the usefulness of any given body of program material. Methods vary from the use of repeatable material (recorded music, feature films, news stories, **syndicated** series) to the adoption of stretchable formats (soap operas); from the development of **spinoffs** from successful programs (as when a character in *All in the Family* spins off into a new series, *Maude*) to the creation of sequels to successful first ventures (*Roots: The Next Generation*).*

Toward the end of the season, primetime **reruns**—repeat showings of episodes in series first seen earlier in the season—begin. Former primetime weekly programs may turn up on the originating network in the afternoon, scheduled across-the-board instead of once a week. These same programs eventually leave the networks to go into **off-network syndication**. They crop up not only on unaffiliated stations but also on stations affiliated with rival networks, on **pay-cable**, and even on affiliates that first ran the shows as network originals. Even public television airs a limited number of programs previously used as commercial vehicles. The more enduring series such as the *Lucy* shows are played over and over again in the same markets. In the meantime, of course, they also have been shipped overseas and seen throughout the world.

Frugality must be practiced at every level and in every aspect of programming. Consider how often one sees or hears "the best of so-and-so," a compilation of bits and pieces from previous programs; news actualities broken into many segments to be parceled out one by one over a period of several hours or even days; the annual return of successful special-occasion programs of the past; the documentaries

---

*A *Time* cover story on Fred Silverman pointed out that this master of the stratagem achieved the "ultimate spinoff" when he created a new series, *Mrs. Columbo,* based on the wife of the detective in the *Columbo* series, despite the fact that Mrs. Columbo had never once appeared as an onstage character in the parent series. "The Man With the Golden Gut: Programmer Fred Silverman Has Made ABC No. 1," *Time,* September 5, 1977, p. 3.

patched together out of stock footage; the weather report broken down into separate little packets labeled "marine forecast," "shuttle-city weather," "long-term forecast," "weather update," "aviation weather," "U.S. Weather Bureau report," and so on and on . . . and on.

No small part of the programmer's job, then, is devising ingenious ways to get the maximum mileage out of each program item, to develop formats that require as little new material as possible for the next episode or program in the series, to invent ingenious justifications for repeating old programs over and over again. It is significant that the first programming coup of Fred Silverman, the most acclaimed television network program executive of recent times, was nothing more than the invention of a new framework within which overused old theatrical films could be shown once again with an appearance of freshness. Soon after getting his master's degree from Ohio State University, Silverman was hired by the program department of WGN-TV in Chicago. His simple but effective stratagem for reviving the old films was to incorporate them under a high-sounding series name, Family Classics, and to hire an attractive presenter to introduce them in an impressive-looking library setting.[4]

An old saw of radio's golden age is illustrated by the story about a neophyte writer enthusiastically bringing a brand new program idea to a jaded program executive. The young writer begins outlining the first episode in the series when the programmer interrupts. "Don't bother to tell me about the first program. Tell me what happens in the twenty-sixth." William Paley, who as president and later chairman of CBS Inc. since 1928 has had more top-level programming experience than any other broadcaster, made the same point in his autobiography: " 'What are you going to do for the next ten shows?' we might ask a writer. . . . What we really want to find out is how well the writer can handle his material over the long run."[5] Any tyro could design a winning schedule for a single week; a professional has to plan for the attrition that inevitably sets in as weeks stretch into the indefinite future.

Mass-Appeal Principle

The costs of setting up and operating a broadcasting station can be justified economically only if the station reaches a relatively large number of people. The threshold number varies, of course, with the type of station, market, and program format. A commercial station has a well-defined optimum target: the maximum number of listeners or viewers it can attract within the limits imposed by its coverage, market characteristics, and program format. The minimum acceptable number is reached when income begins to fall near or below operating costs. In the case of noncommercial broadcasting, the target is less precisely defined, but a cost-effectiveness formula can still be applied. The attribute of wirelessness means that it costs no more to reach the total target population than any fraction of it, so the incentive to maximize audience is inherent in the nature of the medium. Of course, special circumstances can justify uneconomic broadcasting operations. To take an extreme example, the Canadians provide a radio service in Eskimo to a very thinly dispersed population in their far northern territory. This must be extraordinarily uneconomic, but social and political incentives outweigh cost considerations.

This is not to say that all broadcasting need be addressed to all people. Even primetime network television entertainment generally reaches no more than about 20 percent of the United States households. Most programmers are content to reach far smaller audiences. All programs have a push-pull effect, attracting some people but repelling others. This effect is particularly conspicuous in the case of **formula** radio, which, by definition, limits its programming appeals to well-defined minority audiences. Followers of the "Jesus rock" format stick by a favorite station devotedly, but its music may well nauseate other segments of the audience that have markedly different tastes.

The programmer's goal, nevertheless, is to pull in as many potential audience members as possible, conceding that the potential is limited in the first place to the minority that could conceivably be interested by the type of programming offered. A programmer who schedules a show designed for children six to nine years of age would like to attract *all* available children in that age group in the station's service area. Moreover, the programmer also hopes that some older and younger children—and even some adults—might be attracted to the program and thus yield an extra dividend.*

Broadcasting's attributes of wirelessness and accessibility come to the programmer's aid in maximizing audience size. Radio and television tend to cut across class, age, educational, sex, income, and other social dividing lines more freely than any other medium. Broadcasting attracts a more heterogeneous range of people than might ever be expected to assemble in a stadium, theater, concert hall, or lecture room, or to engage in the less social act of reading a newspaper, magazine, or book.

Many programming strategies arise from this principle of potential mass appeal. One way of maximizing mass appeal is to reduce programming to a low common denominator of audience interests—a necessary stratagem for nationally distributed programming, critics to the contrary notwithstanding. The wary programmer tries, however, to avoid the trap of watering down content to the point of being not only

---

*One of the complaints from children's programming critics is that broadcast programmers tend to aim at the entire spectrum of ages, whereas children ideally need age-specific programming aimed at subgroups within the age two to age twelve range. Federal Communications Commission, "Children's Television Programs: Report and Policy Statement," 39 F.R. 39396, November 6, 1974, p. 39405.

completely inoffensive and universally understood but also utterly boring. As obvious as this danger may seem, television audiences nevertheless see television programmers falling into the trap season after season.

Another stratagem for taking advantage of audience heterogeneity is to appeal simultaneously to more than one level or type of audience interest. No program can be all things to all people, but it is possible to be several things to several different kinds of people. The most successful television entertainment program of all time, *Roots*, exemplified this quality of appealing to more than one audience stratum. It obviously held a fascination for blacks because they identified profoundly with Alex Haley's search for family origins. Had the appeal of the play stopped short at that level it would never have broken any ratings records. But ethnic consciousness is a worldwide movement, with minority groups everywhere seeking recognition of their distinctive heritages. The underlying appeal of the play therefore touched all minorities (and everyone belongs to a minority in the final analysis). Nonblacks saw in the black yearning for ancient roots a paradigm of their own yearnings. The tremendous odds against Haley's ever being able to reconstruct his family history heightened the drama of the search. Many other appeals helped increase the heterogeneity (and hence the size) of the audience: large dollops of sex and violence (legitimized by the serious nature of the play); the titillating sense of historic guilt; the very length of the play, representing a disruption of normal scheduling unprecedented in times other than national emergencies; and the extraordinary skill of the production staff and performers. *Roots* was, of course, a rare phenomenon, a timely program that tapped into a social movement at just the right stage and in just the right way. It is not too much to say, however, that all very successful national programs that attract truly massive audiences succeed because they have multifaceted appeal.

A well-known market researcher, Daniel Yankelovich, has made the point that a good marketer—and a program executive is after all a marketer of programs—combines the findings of research on social trends with a "reading of tea leaves."[6] Most of the social trends he enumerated in a 1971 article continue in evidence. He mentioned, as examples, contemporary emphasis on personal creativity, meaningful work, mysticism, return to nature, ethnicity, liberalized attitudes toward sex, use of stimulants and drugs, tolerance for disorder, challenge to authority, female careerism, reaction against the complexity of modern life. One can easily detect exploitation of these trends in broadcast programming at all levels, as the case of *Roots* demonstrates.

Yankelovich warned, however, that merely jumping on the bandwagon of perceived trends (as the unimaginative programmer does) is ill advised. The skillful marketer sorts out deep-seated trends from short-term fads generated by splinter groups. Similarly, a good programmer will anticipate what is likely to happen to a trend when it graduates from the status of an innovation among a few dedicated adherents to a genuine mass movement.

The five strategic principles we have listed—making programs compatible with audience patterns of living, capitalizing on habit formation, recognizing audience freedom of choice, using the utmost frugality in dispensing program material, and solving the riddle of mass appeal—are fundamental to all broadcast programming. These principles arise from the intrinsic attributes of the medium and so enable capitalizing on its unique features. They speak to the very nature of broadcasting and so can be used by decision-makers at every level and of every kind who are responsible for organized broadcast services.

RELEVANCE OF CABLE TELEVISION

Strictly speaking, cable television, as a nonbroadcast source of programming, falls outside this discussion. However, with the development of national satellite distribution systems for cable programming, the line dividing cable and broadcast operations grows less sharply defined.

Programmers of the cable systems—the local companies that hold franchises to serve individual local communities or parts of large cities—have so far played a role very different from that of broadcast programmers. Cable operators line up a smorgasbord of program sources, leaving it to their subscribers to pick and choose at will from a number of channels—anywhere from a half-dozen to thirty. On most of their channels, cable operators act merely as relayers of programming that arrives at the cable headend already structured. Thus, when cable operators pass on the output of television or radio stations to their subscribers, the programming function has already been performed by the originating stations. Cable's own originations thus far have consisted mostly of automated readout services such as news tickers. Local cable public **access** programming is typically a first-come, first-served proposition, with cable operators exerting minimal controls.

Major national **pay-television** distributors, however, use satellites to relay full-time program services to cable companies. If the cable companies are regarded as retailers of programming to individual subscriber homes, the national distributors can be regarded as wholesalers. Their immediate clients are their cable company affiliates, not the general public. They function, in fact, like broadcast television networks, supplying their affiliates (including even **subscription-television** broadcast stations) with structured program services, not merely strings of unconnected program items. For this reason, a chapter on national distributors of programming for cable companies seems to belong in a study of broadcast programming strategies, even though cable operators are not engaged in broadcasting as such. (See Chapter 12.)

To what extent does cable television share the attributes ascribed to over-the-air broadcasting? Cable can match broadcasting's attribute of continuousness. Moreover, its multichannel nature enables it to serve specific audience interests with far greater fidelity than can broadcast stations or networks. Cable can afford to devote entire channels to services aimed at limited audiences. A children's channel, for example, can offer uninterrupted programs designed exclusively for children throughout the day instead of just on Saturday mornings. Such *dedicated* channels offer novel challenges to program strategists. Certainly cable is also capable of realism. Live sportscasts form a major element in cable's repertoire.

However, by its nature, cable lacks broadcasting's distinctive attribute of wirelessness at the delivery point (although wireless microwave and satellite links interconnect some of the components of cable systems). Absent, too, is broadcasting's unique ability to reach every home in a service area at no more cost or trouble than it takes to reach one home. In contrast, each cable customer must be connected individually to the cable distribution network. Cable becomes prohibitively expensive in thinly populated rural areas that can be served easily at no added cost by broadcasting.

The differing natures of the media impose other cost differentials. The broadcast consumer makes what, in the short term at least, amounts to a one-time investment: the purchase of a receiver. The cable subscriber must not only make an initial investment but also pay monthly fees. If the subscriber chooses to receive pay-television services, still another fee must be paid. These add-on costs tend to make for high turnover among subscribers and to limit the ultimate size the national audience is likely to reach.

All five of the principal programming strategies of broadcasting can be applied, with little adjustment, to the national cable program suppliers. They have to think in much the same terms as broadcast network programmers. Indeed, pay-television programmers compete with broadcast programmers for both program materials and audiences.

SUMMARY

Broadcast programming can be defined in terms of strategy, in contrast to production—here defined as tactics. This book is about the strategies of broadcast programming, which involve not only program selection but also program scheduling, long-term planning, and anticipation of future social developments. Programming takes place in highly varied situations, ranging from the situation of primetime network television programming to that of the small local radio station.

Nevertheless, all broadcasting benefits from unique attributes of the medium—its wirelessness, its accessibility to all who have a receiver, its continuously unfolding nature, its ability to mediate real events, and its overall social influence.

The major universal programming principles that can be deduced from these attributes are the strategies for (1) making programs compatible with audiences members' daily round of activities; (2) using scheduling strategies to form listening and viewing habits; (3) taking the audience's freedom of choice into account; (4) using program materials frugally so as to get the maximum use out of limited resources; and (5) exploiting the medium's mass-appeal potentials.

In the field of cable television, the programming strategies of broadcasting are used primarily by major national distributors of pay-television programming, which act as wholesalers to the local cable companies.

NOTES

[1]Les Brown, "Strengths and Weaknesses, Private and Public Forces, in U.S. Broadcasting," *Intermedia* (October 1977): 27. Based on an address to the International Institute of Communication.

[2]National Association of Broadcasters, *The Television Code*, 20th ed. (Washington, D.C.: The Association, June 1978), p. 8.

[3]Les Brown, *New York Times Encyclopedia of Television* (New York: The *New York Times* Book Company, 1977), p. 516.

[4]Thomas Thompson, "The Crapshoot for Half a Billion: Fred Silverman Rolls the Dice for CBS," *Life*, December 10, 1971, p. 58.

[5]William S. Paley, *As It Happened: A Memoir* (New York: Doubleday, 1979), p. 260.

[6]Daniel Yankelovich, "What New Life Styles Mean to Market Planners," *Marketing/Communications* (June 1971): 38–45.

ADDITIONAL PERIODICAL READINGS

The selected readings following each chapter stress recent trade and research articles pertaining to the subject of the chapter. Generally the articles were published in the late 1970s, but a limited number of unusual-interest items are included from the early 1970s. Additional sources appear in the bibliography of books and reports at the end of the text.

Bowman, Gary W. "Consumer Choice and Television." *Applied Economics* 7 (1975): 175–84.

Research study employing a model of past viewing to predict future viewing.

Gutman, Jonathan, and **McConaughy, David.** "Ambivalence and Indifference in Preference for Television Programs." *Journal of Broadcasting* 22 (Summer 1978): 373–84.

Application of ambivalence/indifference analysis to adult tuning behavior.

Pearce, Alan. "The TV Networks: A Primer." *Journal of Communication* 26 (Autumn 1976): 54–59.

A review of the basic facts of their reasons for existence, economic structure, profitability, and power.

"Satellites: Tommorow Is Here." *Broadcasting* (March 27, 1978): 62–68.

Special report on the use of transmission through space by MBS, NPR, PBS, the commercial networks, and others.

Shelby, Maurice E., Jr. "Criticism and Longevity of Television Programs." *Journal of Broadcasting* 17 (Summer 1973): 277–86.

Investigation of the relationship between critical reviews of network programs and their long-term success rate.

2 Programming Practices and People

Sydney W. Head

*In this chapter the author analyzes the factors that pro-
grammers consider in arriving at decisions and the constraints
operating on those who make the decisions. First, however, he
examines two preliminary topics of major concern to programmers: where programs come from and how programmers get
information about their audiences.*

SOURCES OF PROGRAMS

A basic fact of life for programmers is that program material is
neither inexhaustible nor infinitely repeatable (even though the scarcity
factor mandates a great deal of repetition). Programmers therefore are
constantly on the prowl for fresh programming ideas and sources. New
programming trickles steadily into the pool, keeping it replenished, but
at any given moment there is never enough that is new, fresh, cap-
tivating—and reasonable in price. Nor can money alone solve the problem. Every season the industry invests millions of dollars in new programs that turn out to be expensive failures.

Television programs come from three fundamental sources: *networks, syndicated program distributors,* and *local production.* Most television
stations are affiliated with ABC, CBS, or NBC, and rely on their **networks** for about 60 percent of their programs, including those that draw
the largest audiences. A small amount of programming also comes from
regional and ad hoc (occasional or one-time) networks. Sources of this
kind are taking on more importance as stations acquire their own satellite relay receive-only **earth stations.** Such facilities make it easy for
distributors to deliver programs in the network manner (that is, by
simultaneous direct connection) without necessarily having to set up
full-service networks of the traditional type.

Network programming is the most important single source in
television, whether measured in terms of scheduled hours or in terms of
millions of viewers at any one time. This generalization on the network
programmer's role would be misleading, however, if it were not followed by the reminder that networks in fact do not create much of their
own programming. Aside from news and news-related public affairs
programming, networks buy most of their programming from a relatively small group of independent production firms located in southern
California. In other words, the creative work—the writing, producing,

performing—usually is done by outside specialists, not directly by network programmers.

Syndication refers to the method of distribution rather than to the programs themselves. In fact, network entertainment series, after their original network showings, "go into syndication" as **off-network** shows: the networks sell rights to the shows to distribution companies. (Networks themselves are forbidden to distribute their own programs in the domestic syndication market.)* When networks rerun their own shows, the line between networking and syndication gets tenuous. This is a symptom of the fact that the network itself is fundamentally a form of syndication, even though in the trade the term *syndication* is limited to programs distributed by non-network means, that is, without benefit of the relay interconnections that enable simultaneous delivery.

Syndicated programs are rented (called **buying**) by stations from firms that specialize in program distribution on a non-network basis. Their programming is therefore limited to material that is not critically dependent on time. Daily syndicated talk shows such as *Merv Griffin* and *Phil Donahue* are the most timely programs of this type, typically aired two or three weeks after being recorded. Both network **affiliates** and **independent** stations use syndicated programs, but the independents depend much more heavily on this source.

A score of major Hollywood firms produce most of the new syndicated material. At the 1979 National Association of Television Program Executives convention (a major occasion for distributors to showcase their products), 175 new program series were offered. Twelve of these were instances of **barter** syndication, programs in which some of the commercial spot availabilities have been **presold** to advertisers who then offered the programs and the remaining open spots to stations in exchange for time. (See Chapter 4 for details on this practice.) The ratings services list upward of 400 series currently available in syndication, some of them having been on the market as far back as the 1950s. Distributors of syndicated material also handle the rental of feature films, many thousands of which have accumulated over the years. (*TV Guide* carries 22,000 feature film plot summaries in its computer data bank.)

Local production of television programming centers on daily news

---

*A rare instance of reverse program flow, from syndication to network, occurred in 1978 when CBS bought some episodes of *Mary Hartman, Mary Hartman*—a satire on the tribulations of soap opera heroines—after it had already been seen on about a hundred stations as a syndicated show. Ironically, CBS had originally paid for a pilot program in the series but finally turned it down, as did ABC and NBC, fearing that the series' candid, though humorous, treatment of sex would cause a wave of affiliate refusals to clear time for the series. See Les Brown, "CBS Buys 'Mary Hartman' Reruns for 11:30 Niche," *New York Times*, August 6, 1979, p 17.

shows, which get the lion's share of the local program budget because they attract advertisers.* Some stations produce local sports **remotes**— live coverage from the scene of action—but most find frequent remotes too expensive in relation to the income they generate. Beyond news, local production is usually confined to nonprimetime public service programs in simple talk formats. Some television stations are justifiably proud of more ambitious local-production achievements, but the economics of the medium force the choice of syndicated material most of the time in preference to local production. Minimal local production can be inexpensive, but syndicated material is cost-effective because it is generally much more attractive to advertisers.†

It is not surprising, therefore, to find the Federal Communications Commission (FCC) reporting that at the average television station less than 10 percent of all programming from 6 A.M. to midnight is locally produced.[1] More than two-thirds of that small percentage is news and public affairs programming. Of course, even 10 percent of a full day's schedule amounts to a tremendous amount of programming when looked at cumulatively. Nevertheless, the statistics indicate that most nonnews station-level programming decisions concern the purchase of syndicated material, including feature films. The task of negotiating syndicated buys therefore looms as a major duty of television station programmers.[2]

Among radio program sources networks play only a minor role, furnishing short segments of news and feature material at intervals throughout the broadcast day. Several hundred firms supply syndicated radio program material (a list can be found in *Broadcasting Yearbook*). Syndicated programming items vary from featurettes of 1 or 2 minutes in length to complete **dayparts**, such as *American Top Forty*, a weekly 4-hour presentation of the current top tunes woven together with com-

---

*We exclude decision making about news and public affairs programming from this discussion. Responsibility for this area of programming is normally assigned to a news director who deals directly with management. This division of responsibility is essential because of the timeliness and special sensitivity of news-related programs. Program directors take news into consideration in their overall scheduling strategies, of course, but have little or no direct control over the programs themselves.

---

†A unique combination of syndicated and local production was initiated by Norman Lear, the independent writer and producer well known for such successes as *All in the Family*. Lear produced a situation-comedy series called *The Baxters* for first-run syndication in the 1979–80 season. About ten minutes into each episode, after a basic **sit-com** dilemma has been developed, the syndicated portion of the program comes to an end, and the station switches to its own studio for a localized discussion kicked off by the situation presented in the syndicated segment. The burden imposed by the need to go to the trouble of local production was said to have slowed down sales of the series.

mentary and interviews. By far the most influential form of syndicated radio programming, however, is made up not of individual items but of entire program **formats.** Format syndicators supply ready-made music for the entire broadcast day, carefully selected and sequenced according to specific formulas, along with a wide range of programming, production, and promotional services. Local radio production tends to be minimal at stations using music formats, but the "all-talk," "all-news," and "news/information" formats use a great deal of local reporting, interviewing, and discussion.

Information on available television and radio programming comes automatically to programmers through the diligent sales efforts of the syndication firms that deal in program distribution and through the trade press. **Station representatives** are supplemental sources of syndicated television programming information. These firms act as sales agents for their client stations in the national market. The major "reps," as they are called, have vice-presidents in charge of programming, despite the fact that they are in the business of selling time, not the program business. But because of their experience in markets all over the country, reps can assist programmers at their client stations by bringing a national perspective to bear on local decisions. *Broadcasting* commented in a special report on television reps, "It's not unusual today for a station to expect its rep to keep an eye out for new programming. Or, less frequently, even to negotiate a deal with a syndicator."[3]

SOURCES OF AUDIENCE INFORMATION

Another basic need of the broadcast programmer is information about audiences. Every programmer has to master the complex field of audience research, which furnishes information on audience behavior, audience characteristics, and the predicted outcome of programming decisions. The most basic data are the **ratings** that come from national audience-measurement firms. They issue regular reports estimating the size and composition of audiences for both stations and networks, both radio and television. With these tools, programmers can evaluate the size and basic **demographic** characteristics (sex, age) of their audiences and also the relative success of their programming strategies vis-à-vis those of their competitors. When considering purchase of syndicated materials, programmers have at their disposal special reports from the same national research companies, giving the track records for the major syndicated television shows: where they played, how they stood up against the competition, and what sorts of people they attracted in each market.

Before introducing new shows or formats or making major changes in existing programs, programmers who can afford the time and money try to pretest their decisions. Tests are usually made on small groups of presumably fairly representative audience members. Sometimes people give simple like/dislike responses at intervals while watching a program; sometimes they are given more objective physiological tests that measure responses by means of scientific instruments attached to their bodies. Researchers follow up these response measurements with discussion to probe reasons for audience members' reactions. Radio music-format programmers research audience reactions to new music releases as a guide in the selection of recordings for their **playlists**, using both the indirect measure of tabulating record shop sales and the direct method of telephone interviews with actual audience members.

It is safe to say that programmers rarely make a program decision of any consequence without first researching it. At a minimum they use the standardized data of the commercial research services but often supplement that with tailor-made research, either commissioned or conducted by the station itself.

THE PROGRAMMER AS JACK-OF-ALL-TRADES

Most programmers work in a small-station environment in which they are expected to wear many different hats. A National Association of Broadcasters' manual for small-station radio program directors points out that, as the individual charged with achieving the station's "overall sound," the program director

> gets involved in just about every aspect of broadcasting. He is as interested in the budgets for various program services as an accountant. He scrutinizes the *FCC Rules and Regulations* pertaining to programming as carefully as a lawyer. He spends as much time reading the trade press for the latest "sounds" and other trends as a teacher, while advising fellow employees as thoughtfully as a coach. Add to this list of duties the coordination of network programming, selection of jingles and liaison with other department heads and with the community at large, and you find that the Program Director is the resident jack-of-all-trades at the station.[4]

The many-faceted responsibilities of the small-station radio programmer leave little time for creativity. The Center for Public Resources studied the problems that stand in the way of obtaining more diversified programming in broadcasting. The center pointed out that, although the radio program director holds the key to program diversification, he or she "is often the person least able to focus attention on the subject." The report goes on to list the many duties of the programmer, including an on-the-air shift. It concludes that "it is impossible for a program director to be creative, or to think about diversity, unless station management actively encourages it."[5]

In television programmers are more likely to be able to specialize, especially as they move up the ladder in station size. At the network level, programmers specialize in just one type of program or one part of the broadcast day. Even in television the jack-of-all-trades nature of the job still holds, however, in the sense that the programmer who wears only one hat still has to keep a tremendous quantity and wide-ranging store of information under that hat.

The Programmer as Information Processor

One way of looking at the programmer's role is in terms of *information processing*. Programmers have to be able to understand, analyze, and base recommendations and decisions on quantities of data—external data about markets, competition, audiences, program sources, program histories, and advertiser preferences, as well as internal data on station policies, budget, personnel, and production resources. The sheer quantity of the research data on most of these topics is formidable. To answer a simple question, the conscientious programmer has to ask a host of supplementary questions. It is never as simple as "Looks like a good show—let's schedule it at 8:30." First the programmer must ask whether this or similar shows played in this market before. What was the prior experience? How did the audience break down as to sex in the five different adult age groups plus teens and two children's age groups? What is the competition doing at 8:30? Before 8:30? After 8:30? Will the proposed program attract an age group not attracted by the competing programs? What kind of audience will the station's own previous program feed to the new program? What kind of audience will it deliver to the next program in the schedule? Is the likely audience of the new program the type that the existing or prospective clients want? What kind of budget will it take to buy or produce the program? How does that fit into the station's overall program budget? Will spending that much on this program hinder or help other programs?

One example of a simple question that is difficult to answer is "Who listens to my station?" One of the major national research organizations, Arbitron, has issued a booklet, *Research Guidelines for [Radio] Programming Decision Makers.*[6] It is based on the information radio programmers can extract from the basic Arbitron audience-data reports, which are issued periodically for each market. The booklet explains how to calculate answers to the following questions:

1. How much time does the average person listen to my station?

2. Am I doing a good job of reaching my target audience?

3. How many different groups of people contribute to my station's average audience?

4. What percentage of the listeners in one of my time periods also listens to my station in another time period?

5. During which hours of the day does my station do the best job of reaching listeners?

6. How much of my audience listens only to me and to no other stations?

7. Is my station ahead of or behind the market average of away-from-home listening?

8. Which are the most available audiences during certain times of day?

9. How often do my listeners hear the same record?

With little adaptation, these questions could come from a television programmer. They not only tell us about kinds of information a programmer must seek out and process, but also they illustrate two generalizations about the programmer's work. First, note that Arbitron, like the other companies in the business of furnishing regular audience-measurement services, supplies only the raw data for the market as a whole. In order to put the raw data to work, the programmer must extract and process the information in terms of one individual station vis-à-vis all the competing stations in the market.*

Second, note that none of the Arbitron questions has anything to do with the quality of program content. None bears directly on such questions as how good the programs are, how useful, how beneficial, how original, how innovative. Most of the time programmers necessarily deal with programs like so many packages of "stuff"—as "product" or "commodity." We make this point not to denigrate the role of the programmer, but to emphasize how economic pressures affect the nature of the programmer's job.

The Decision-Making Environment

In describing the programmer's professional environment, most commentators refer to "factors that influence program decision mak-

---

*For a fee, the ratings companies will do some of this "customizing" to order for individual station clients. Arbitron, for example, offers a service it calls "Arbitron Information on Demand (AID)." It includes reprocessing data in the original viewer diaries to extract information on individual station **audience flow**, audience loyalty, competitive schedules, and so on.

ing." This is the approach of J. David Lewis, who attempted to identify the factors most widely recognized as important by programmers themselves.[7] On the basis of interviews with television programmers, Lewis drew up a list of forty-five different influences. He then sent a questionnaire about them to each of the 521 stations listed in the *Broadcasting Yearbook* of 1965. He received 301 usable replies, a high rate of return for an out-of-the-blue questionnaire. He asked programmers to rate each of the forty-five influences, using an eleven-point scale running from "unimportant" to "important." Lewis's analysis of the responses indicated that influences could be grouped into factor-clusters, which he described as follows:

> *Direct feedback*—various types of personal audience response, notably viewer phone calls and letters
>
> *Regulatory constraints*—including station policy, FCC rules, and industry self-regulation
>
> *Inferential feedback*—formal audience research plus input from syndicated program salespersons, which ranked high as an influence
>
> *Conditional feedback*—opinions of friends, family, critics, and the trade press
>
> *Staff feedback*—opinions of fellow professionals at the station, including the news director, whose influence ranked highest
>
> *Personal judgment*—including instinct, common sense, knowledge of the community, personal experience, and opinions of the general manager
>
> *Financial constraints*—opinion of the sales manager, cost, advertiser opinions
>
> *Tactical* considerations*—scheduling, viewing trends
>
> *Miscellaneous*—factors that did not correlate closely with others, including technical quality of station's signal

The order in which these clusters are presented should not be taken as their order of importance. Our main reason for quoting Lewis's study is to show the number and variety of factors that a national sample of programmers themselves said had an influence on their decisions. Nor should we assume that Lewis's forty-five influences necessarily exhaust all the possibilities. Doubtless some are unique to particular programming situations; others may be too subtle to pin down easily. For example, another researcher, Paul Virts, mentions an elusive but some-

---

*Lewis's term. Commentators on programming often use both terms (tactics and strategy) for scheduling decisions. As this book uses the term, all of Lewis's factors offer bases for *strategy*.

times important factor not in Lewis's list (unless, perhaps, by implication): a station's overall "style," the role it sees for itself in the market.[8]

In a more recent study, Michael Fisher surveyed television programmers nationally. In response to a question about the relative importance of factors that influenced their decisions, they listed, in order of
importance, (1) total potential audience; (2) management policies; (3)
specific audiences sought for particular programs, sales potential, and
FCC requirements (three-way tie); and (4) personal judgments of the
program manager.[9]

In the more specialized decision-making situation of formula
radio, the influences emerge in somewhat different form. A model
offered by the Arbitron Company as a guide for program directors of
formula music stations contains twenty-one factors (Figure 2–1). They
are divided about equally between "internal" and "external" items. The

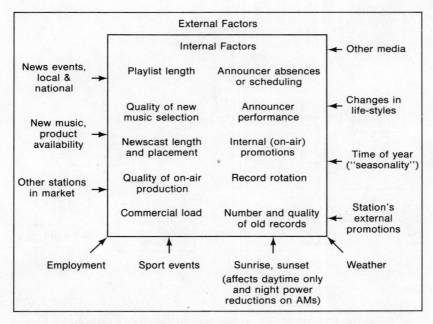

Source: Arbitron Radio, *Research Guidelines for Programming Decision Makers, 1977.* Beltsville, Md.: Arbitron
  Co., 1977. Used with permission.

Figure 2–1. Factors in Radio Programmer's
Environment

contrast between this list and the one gleaned by Lewis from television
programmers signifies the difference between the two programming
situations. Television programming comes in large ready-made units

(program series), whereas radio depends on a homemade product assembled from many separate fragments. This emphasis shows up in the Arbitron chart in the choice of such items as "playlist length," "quality of new music selection," "record rotation," and "number and quality of old records."

Factors of whatever kind can usually be categorized as information—or sources of information—that the programmer must process in the course of making decisions. They are things a programmer needs to know, or know about. In fact, a commercial programming executive writing briefly on principles of programming for a book on broadcast management boiled the subject down to eight injunctions in "know thyself" form.[10] It is essential, he said, for the programmer to "know" his or her *audience, product* (meaning programs), *competition, budget, staff, community, management,* and *self.*

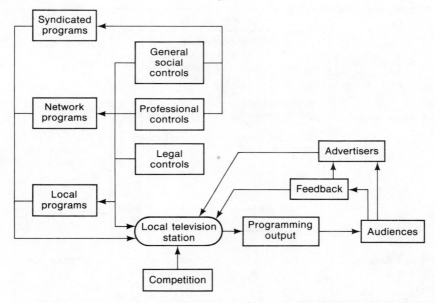

Source: Paul H. Virts, "Television Entertainment Gatekeeping: A Study of Local Television Program Directors' Decision-Making." Unpublished Ph.D. dissertation, University of Iowa, 1979, p. 7. Used with permission.

Figure 2–2. Model of Television
Decision-Making "Inputs"

In his study of local television decision making, Virts used, instead of "factors" or "knowledge," the word *input,* more explicitly suggesting the idea of a dynamic process. Virts diagrammed the television programmer's inputs, as they were reported to him in interviews, in the model shown in Figure 2–2.

CONCEPT OF CONSTRAINTS ON DECISION MAKING

It is noteworthy that Virts speaks of social, professional, and legal controls in his model of the programmer's inputs. Is there any reason why the other inputs he mentions—competition, advertiser influence, audience demands, and availability of program materials—could not also be regarded as controls, as forms of constraint? They, too, put constraints on the programmer's freedom of choice. We use the concept of *constraint* in these chapters. We believe this concept makes it easier to perceive a unifying principle behind the various "factors," "inputs," and kinds of "knowledge" that influence program decision making.

What if an audience member writes a letter of praise? Would positive feedback be properly regarded as also suggesting constraint? In practice, most direct feedback from audience members comes in the negative form of complaints rather than in the form of praise. They say, in effect, "Don't do that any more if you want us to tune to your station." Even when feedback is positive, however, the question is whether a programmer views the glass as half full or half empty.

Constraints can, of course, also be seen as opportunities. If management allocates $100,000 to the programmer's budget for a new program series, the programmer could regard the money as either an opportunity to spend that much or a constraint that prevents spending more. If a massive outpouring of abuse arrives from audience members who detest a program, this could be regarded as an opportunity either to serve the audience better (by changing the program) or to stand up to pressure (by defiantly continuing the program). Most programmers probably see the glass as half empty because their reach always exceeds their grasp. The programmer who tamely accepts constraints without resistance is not likely to go far. Rather, one pictures the successful programmer as eternally struggling like Laocoon against the stifling coils of fiscal conservatism, bureaucratic regulation, reactionary politics, managerial timidity, and sales staff cynicism.

As it works out, the programmer has leeway in coming to terms with some constraints, but not with others. We might call these two types of constraints *negotiable* and *nonnegotiable*. The programmer sees the latter as more or less fixed but the former as leaving room for the play of alternative strategies and the power of persuasion. A striking example of this distinction was afforded by a realistic decision-making simulation staged as an industry/faculty seminar by the International Radio and Television Society in 1978.

College professors assumed the roles of programmer/sales manager/general manager teams. Industry members played their own real-life roles as representatives of syndication firms and advertiser time-buyers. The professorial teams were responsible for making a decision on behalf of hypothetical stations, carefully modeled according to the facts of life in real television markets. Their task was to compete, as stations, in filling a specific early-evening time slot with a replacement series in which three advertisers would be willing to buy spots. They could opt to produce a local series or to buy a syndicated series selected from the actual catalogs of distribution firms. Most teams opted for a syndicated package, but one team chose to place its bets on a local news program. The following were the nonnegotiable constraints:

> A program series had to be produced within a pre-scribed budget or bought competitively from those offered in the syndicators' catalogs (program source constraint).
>
> The stations had their respective network affiliations, coverage areas, existing audiences, program schedules, production resources, and competitors (facilities and market constraints).
>
> The stations had to make a profit; that is, they could not pay an exorbitant price for a **loss leader** program series.

The negotiable variables consisted of the following strategies:

> Program selection from the available sources.
>
> Manipulation of the existing schedule, if the team so desired, to enhance the attractiveness of the new program with a strong **lead-in** and the like.
>
> Dickering with representatives of the syndication companies and competing with the other stations in the market to get the best possible programs for the best possible price (including the option of offering to buy other syndicated programs as part of a package so as to get a lower price).
>
> Persuasive presentation to convince the advertisers that the proposed program was their best buy in the market.

The teams used as their principal tools standard audience data for the market and the Nielsen Company *Report on Syndicated Program Audiences*, which they used to evaluate the probable success of the programs they chose. Of course, the exercise illustrated only one kind of program decision-making situation, and not all the constraints that would intervene in a real-life situation were present. Nevertheless, it did point up four significant aspects of commercial broadcasting programming practice: (1) how programming decisions are dominated by money questions; (2) how little the content or quality of programs enter into the equation; (3) how much reliance is placed on research data; and (4) how large a role persuasive personal relationships play.

Nonnegotiable Constraints

Among the fixed limitations over which the programmer has no latitude for negotiation, the three most important are those imposed by facilities, market, and government regulation.

The first of these, *facilities*, refers in part to a station's physical equipment (such as studios and transmitter). But more important in this category are station class, channel class, authorized power, and the extent to which environmental factors—natural and artificial—favor or impede propagation of its signal. An owner may improve facilities by petitioning the FCC for such changes as higher power or permission to move the antenna to a more favorable location, by increasing engineering efficiency, and so on, but these remedies take time and are beyond the control of programmers.

Physical coverage area translates into the second type of nonnegotiable constraint: the economic limitations of the *market* where the station is. A market has at any given time certain maximum potential for the broadcaster in terms of size, population density, demographic characteristics, economic character, and economic relationships with surrounding areas. These constraints are not, of course, immutable. Some markets change rapidly as economic fortunes rise and fall. Bankruptcy of a town's sole large manufacturing plant can wreak market changes that are both sudden and devastating. Some areas are locked into steady curves of economic and social growth or decline. Alert programmers must understand and react to these market changes, but rarely can the programmers influence the course of events. Although market constraints are beyond the programmer's control, they are neither static nor beyond the programmer's ability to predict.

A third set of relatively fixed constraints comes from *regulation* by the Federal Communications Commission. Of course, neither its enabling statute—the Communications Act of 1934—nor its own rules and regulations are immutable: The commission constantly tinkers with the regulations. Moreover, in some instances a licensee can negotiate waivers of rules. For example, the commission sometimes grants exceptions to the **primetime access rule**, which normally bars licensees from clearing more than three of the four prime evening hours for national television network programming. On the whole, however, government regulation imposes relatively permanent constraints on the ethical programmer's freedom of choice. The nature of regulatory constraints will be discussed in detail in Chapter 3.

Negotiable Constraints

The constraints classed here as negotiable are those that may be modified as a direct result of the ingenuity, knowledge, and persuasive resources of a program executive. Programmers can marshal their persuasive skills to breach or modify barriers set up by restrictive management policies, by union contracts, by the demands of the sales department, by the paucity of external program sources, by the limitations on local production resources, and even by competition from other stations.

It may seem paradoxical to classify competition from other stations within one's own market as a negotiable constraint. Of course, the programmer cannot persuade rival stations to surrender superior facilities or change the nature of the market shared with them. In this context, the term *negotiable* is stretched to include the art of **counterprogramming**, a major weapon in the programmer's strategic arsenal. In its simplest form, counterprogramming means scheduling an alternative type of programming head-to-head against the one or more types already available in the market. In practice, however, counterprogramming strategies are rarely that simple.

In the case of radio, counterprogramming usually means adopting an alternative music or talk format. In a large market in which twenty, thirty, and even forty or more radio stations compete, there are simply not enough unique formats to go around. No opportunity for simple counterprogramming with an entirely new format exists. Edd Routt, in Chapter 14, describes how a programmer might solve such a dilemma by choosing to duplicate an existing format while giving it unique new coloration. Here, the deeper skills and instincts of the programmer come into play.

The FCC has recognized the existence of such subtle programming strategies. From time to time the commission is faced with listener demands that it intervene to prevent an existing format from being abandoned (usually in connection with a proposed change of ownership of a station). The FCC has pointed out that programmers make fine distinctions that listeners recognize and appreciate but that defy easy explanation. "In most large markets," said the FCC, "there are a number of . . . formats which seem identical on any objective or quantifiable basis; yet they are far from interchangeable to their respective audiences."[11] The commission went on to quote a study sponsored by the National Association of Broadcasters analyzing the audiences for the radio formats available in the twenty-five largest metropolitan markets. The study found that only about 7 percent of the variations in audience size could be attributed to different format types. In fact, "the variation between different shares within given format types is nearly as large as the variation between different types."[12] In other words, greater differences in ability to attract audiences were found among stations with the same format than among stations with different formats.

Television, with its far more stringent limits on the number of stations per market, poses a different counterprogramming problem. Alternative program types can usually be found to oppose types already on the air in any given time period. The problem is, however, that some program types are so overwhelmingly popular that the programmer sometimes may do better countering with a second program of the same type as the competition than countering with a contrasting program type.

At the station level, programmers have limited scope for making decisions about the details of program form and content. As indicated earlier, relatively few opportunities arise for local program production. This means that television station programmers deal largely in entire series of programs, bought as packages. Obviously, one of the negotiable constraints is the availability of such program materials at prices a station can pay. And it is not unusual for availability to be restricted by **stockpiling** on the part of the competition—preemptive buying of programs just to keep them out of the local market for the time being. Moreover, well-informed counterprogrammers make it their business to know all about programs in the competing stations' inventories, including their rental contract expiration dates.[13]

As to costs, a programmer must calculate per-program rental fees in terms of two or more repeated "plays" of each series because rental contracts normally stipulate a fixed number of plays over a stipulated period of time. Virts points out that programmers must be aware of the implications of future on-air schedulings. Stations use two basic methods of program cost **amortization**: straight line or prorated. Stations using straight-line amortization divide the cost evenly among all the plays; those using the prorated method charge off the largest percentage of the cost against the first play, charging less and less against subsequent plays.[14]

Counterprogramming becomes virtually the main business of programmers at independent television stations in competitive markets. Because they are exempt from the constraints of clearing time for network schedules, independents can be freewheeling in their countermoves. Examples: Independents usually schedule strong off-network syndicated series daily, capitalizing on the habit-formation factor, against the network's weekly scheduling in **primetime**; independents can schedule many live sports events without having to **preempt** network programs.

Production resources become a constraining factor whenever local programming is involved. Program ideas have to be trimmed to fit local studio equipment and personnel capabilities. As previously indicated, most local production tends to focus on news and public affairs programming for which large, complex studio equipment is not needed. Such programs can usefully employ remote facilities, especially portable electronic newsgathering (ENG) gear that can be used not only for coverage of spot news but also in the production of inexpensive public affairs documentaries.

National television network programmers work under constraints basically similar to those that affect stations. That point is suggested by this summary of strategic considerations enumerated by Frederick S. Pierce, president of ABC Television:

> Programming decisions are made only after the "votes" are in. And the "votes" take many forms and come from many directions. Input comes from ratings and research, from thousands of letters from viewers and from countless phone calls. It comes from advertisers, who aren't shy, believe me, about communication of their views; and it comes from the creative community.
>
> We also measure reactions from our affiliates, who are important in measuring response in over 200 separate communities. And we pay attention to polls, surveys, and to special interest groups, who are very vocal and visible.[15]

At the television network level, all the familiar constraints on station programmers are magnified by the enhanced consequences of decisions. Network research is more varied and complete (for example, primetime ratings, based on sample markets, are received daily instead of only every few months); feedback comes from hundreds of different markets instead of just one; advertisers and their agencies have more sophisticated input and more investment in the outcome than local commercial interests. But networks have more strength to resist some types of constraints than do stations simply because of their size and their diversified national constituency.

Pierce mentions one constraint that networks do not share with stations: the influence affiliates exert on their own network organization. Each national television network owns only five of its approximately 200 affiliates; all the rest are tied to the network only by contract, and the law forbids contracts that prevent affiliates from refusing to accept network programs. The process of acceptance is called **clearance**, meaning that the affiliate holds network time in its schedule clear of other commitments. Refusal to carry a particular episode in a series for which time has already been cleared is called **preemption**.

Clearance can be refused for a variety of reasons, ranging from the affiliate's desire to make more money from a syndicated entertainment program than it can from network public affairs to the affiliate's judgment that a proffered program would be unacceptable to the local audience. A national network is large enough to withstand occasional defections of these sorts, but if a substantial number of affiliates refused clearance frequently and regularly, that network would soon be in serious difficulties. The owners, managers, and programmers of affiliates thus constitute a special constituency of the networks—an absolutely essential constituency, since networks could not exist without affiliates and their voluntary clearance of time. A notable example of a nonclearance revolt occurred in 1973 when CBS scheduled *Sticks and Bones*, a highly controversial play about a Vietnam war returnee. The network originally scheduled the play at the same time that real-life prisoners of war were being released and made much of in public by President Richard Nixon. Even though CBS delayed release of the play for six months, the clearance rate for *Sticks and Bones* dropped as low as 50 percent in the Midwest.*

Scheduling strategies assume extraordinary importance in network primetime television programming. As the writer of a *Life* profile of Fred Silverman put it, "Half a program director's job is coming up with new shows. The other half, some would say the other 90 percent, is in knowing how to design a weekly schedule, in knowing where to put shows to attract maximum audiences."[16] Another commentator wrote of network scheduling as an "arcane, crafty and indeed, crucial network business."[17]

The drama of primetime network program strategies is heightened by the element of suspense. When network programmers introduce new shows, they are placing multimillion-dollar bets on horses with no previous track records. It is little wonder that they try to hedge their bets by imitating past successes and **spinning off** variations of current successes. Because of the drama inherent in the situation, analyzing the networks' scheduling strategies has become a seasonal rite in the columns of newspaper and magazine television critics.

There are, of course, many more negotiable constraints and strategies for dealing with them at every programming level than are discussed here. Programming specialists in later chapters provide detailed analyses of decision making in their respective programming situations. The purpose of this chapter is to offer integrating concepts to help the reader fit specific instances of decision making into a larger framework.

PROGRAMMING AS TEAMWORK

In an ideal world, programmers, free of external constraints, would program according to their personal tastes and standards. In the

---

*Robert G. Pekurney and Leonard D. Bart made a study of this episode, finding that the chief reasons given by affiliates for not clearing *Sticks and Bones* were "not a good story," "offensive to local audience," station management "personally offended," "bad timing" (vis-à-vis the actual POW arrivals in the United States), "bad for station's image," and "unpatriotic." Among affiliates that carried the program, the chief reasons for doing so were listed as "pressure groups favored carriage," "major segment of audience would like the program." Neither the executives of stations that carried the play nor those of stations that refused it reported fear of FCC reprisal as an influence on their decisions. One of the least frequently cited reasons was fear of offending local advertisers. Robert G. Pekurney and Leonard D. Bart, " 'Sticks and Bones': A Survey of Network Affiliate Decision Making," *Journal of Broadcasting* 19 (Fall 1975): 427–37.

real world, one of the first things a programmer learns is that personal preferences must take a backseat. Broadcast programmers are not creative artists, able to wait for coming generations to appreciate their avant-garde insights. They have to deal with today's tastes and standards as they are defined by masses of people.

The boards of directors of commercial stations have a single, clear-cut, compelling goal—to make money. The programmers they hire have a correspondingly unambiguous mandate. Noncommercial programmers work in a somewhat more forgiving environment, except for the constraints imposed by a chronic shortage of funds. The boards of directors of noncommercial stations have a far more varied outlook than do those of commercial stations. They, too, often include business leaders but also educators, church officials, politicians, consumer advocates, labor leaders, and many other types of people. Some boards preside over university stations, some over public school stations, some over state networks, some over community-sponsored stations. The mandate of noncommercial program executives is correspondingly varied. Natan Katzman, in a study of program decision making in public television stations, concluded that—after money and program availability—"personal preferences and attitudes of station managers and program managers are the third key to understanding programming policy. . . . One tends to feel a surprisingly large impact of top-level personalities on the overall mood of a station."[18]

Nevertheless, it is probably safe to say that the best programmers, whether commercial or noncommercial, are people able to identify with mass tastes without being confined to them. One of the most imaginative and creative of the pioneer commercial television programmers, Sylvester "Pat" Weaver of NBC, is a certified intellectual—a Phi Beta Kappa, an Ivy League magna cum laude graduate with a degree in philosophy. Yet, he really seemed to enjoy mass-appeal television programs as well as philosophy, and he invented some of television's most successful and enduring program strategies.

It is in the nature of the mass media generally to submerge creative urges under layers of corporate bureaucracy. Commercial broadcasting tends to bury creativity even deeper because of its unique technology, its special legal status, its dependence on advertising, and the fact that so much of the creative work is actually done by independent production companies outside the networks and stations. This is why leading writers and producers such as Norman Lear complain so bitterly about the frustrations of creating television entertainment.[19] The innovative realism of *All in the Family* was at first regarded by network programmers as far too risky. It survived relatively intact only because Lear has far more clout with network executives than do less well known creative people. As Les Brown has put it, television is "an executive's medium."[20]

Symptomatically, when television programmers formed their own professional organization in 1962, they avoided calling themselves "program directors" or "managers." Instead, they became the National Association of Television Program *Executives*—a tacit acknowledgment that membership would have to be open to general managers and other executives who share the programming role with those designated specifically as programmers. The usual arrangement at the television station level is a troika of decision makers: the general manager, the sales manager, the program manager.

Within this hierarchy, the programmer ranks a distant third in salary. Television sales managers earned almost twice as much as program managers among personnel surveyed by a trade publication, *Facts, Figures and Film,* which makes the survey annually.[21] An earlier survey by a trade journal found that the more successful salespersons earned more than program directors.[22] The lower status implied by lower salary works to the disadvantage of the programmer's autonomy in program matters, especially if the general manager fails to redress the balance.* Paul Virts, after interviewing a group of programmers in the Midwest, concluded that one of their basic roles was that of briefing the other two members of the troika. The program manager assembles pertinent data on audience, scheduling, program availabilities, and program costs, then presents the findings to the sales manager and general manager.[23] In the terms we have been using, the programmer defines the constraints, from the programming point of view, within which the final decision has to be made.

How much attention the others pay to the program manager's specific proposals or recommendations varies with the makeup of the team. If the sales manager happens to be aggressive and the general manager is sales-minded, the programmer's point of view tends to get submerged. To cite a practical illustration at the most basic level, Bill Drake of Drake-Chenault Enterprises, one of the most influential figures in modern radio programming, recalled in an interview his start as a small-town **disc jockey** in Georgia:

> Stations would sell everything they could, because most General Managers were sales oriented. . . . A lot of commercials would be recorded by the owner and the Sales Manager who were in tight with the account (i.e., advertiser) and the account wanted them to do the com-

---

*Recent figures on radio salaries are not available, but the same pattern of relationships was indicated in a 1974 study by the National Association of Broadcasters. According to it, on the national average, radio program directors were paid only 62 percent as much as commercial managers. National Association of Broadcasters, *Employee Salary Report* (Washington, D.C.: The Association, 1974), p. 3.

mercials. As it turned out, you'd have what were supposed to be one minute commercials and by the time they got through ad-libbing and recording the damned things they were two minutes and fifteen seconds, which I guess was why the accounts loved them. [24]

Drake attributes much of his later success to his insistence on separating radio programming from sales. As he puts it, Cadillac dealers sell the product; they do not spend their time calling Detroit to tell General Motors how to design Caddies.

Of course, neither the extreme of complete programmer autonomy nor that of complete subservience is ideal. Probably the best results are achieved by management that has the skill to referee the warfare between sales and programming fairly, encouraging the best efforts of both, without giving too much firepower to either. In the final analysis, however, from the management point of view, programming is far too important to be left entirely to programmers.

CHARACTERISTICS OF PROGRAMMERS

The National Association of Television Program Executives cooperated in a study of television programmers, done as a master's thesis by Michael Fisher. He obtained a 40 percent response from the more than 400 members of the NATPE. Not all programmers belong to the NATPE, of course, and the nonresponding members may represent a group that differs significantly from the group that responded. But Fisher's sample represents the more successful members of the profession, in the sense that they are employed by the larger stations in the larger markets. In summarizing the personal characteristics of the program executives in his sample, Fisher noted that they tended to be:

> male, relatively young, likely to be college educated—especially those in the top markets and at the largest stations; have considerable experience in broadcasting—both in terms of longevity and in terms of variety of jobs held; believe that a person should start his or her career in a station where he or she can perform many different tasks, but also believe that it is not so much the possession of particular skills that will lead to success as it is the possession of an appropriate attitude. The program managers in this sample watch a lot of television as part of their job and at home, and they perceive themselves as having something less than complete freedom in decision-making, subject always to the scrutiny of the station manager. [25]

Among Fisher's more detailed findings about the NATPE respondents were the following:

> *Education:* Sixty-five percent of the program executives surveyed had a college degree, most of them from a department of broadcasting or a related field such as journalism.
>
> *Prior experience:* The great majority had experience in television production before becoming program managers.
>
> *Perceived qualities leading to success in field:* When asked about qualities that lead to success in the program executive's field, most mentioned such nonspecific attributes as diligence, willingness to learn, self-confidence, decisiveness, ability to work with all kinds of people, and ability to handle details.
>
> *Whom does the program manager consult?* In addition to the general manager and sales manager, program executives mentioned consulting their film buyers, news directors, corporate officers, network scheduling coordinators, treasurers, corporate attorneys, business managers, and comptrollers.

A more recent study focused on testing whether different types of programmers could be identified on the basis of their responses to identical sets of constraints. Paul Virts analyzed decisions made by twenty-eight television programmers at thirteen midwestern stations.[26] He asked the programmers to make decisions about a syndicated program series, given specific conditions as to the following types of constraints: (1) audience shares the series had earned in previous runs; (2) cost of the series; (3) scheduling considerations, both internal and competitive; (4) feedback from local audiences; and (5) the opinion of the programmer's general manager. Each of these constraints was manipulated by specifying three different levels. For example, the cost levels were set at $50, $75, and $100 per episode; management opinions were expressed as "less successful program," "moderately successful program," and "highly successful program."

The programmers were asked to make two types of decisions under the specified sets of conditions: whether to buy a hypothetical program series and whether to retain a hypothetical series already in their stations' schedules. Both parts of the experiment, the researcher concluded, indicated that the programmers in the group of twenty-eight (which included two women, incidentally) fell into two distinct types that he called "high risk" and "low risk":

> High Risk programmers wanted programs which offered high [audience] shares and were willing to overlook

high costs, negative feedback, and negative opinions from the general manager. . . . On the other hand, Low Risk programmers were more conservative. They wanted programs with high shares, but they were less willing to pay high costs and were more concerned about negative feedback and general managers' opinions.[27]

The weight allotted to each factor in the part of the experiment in which the programmers indicated the likelihood of their making a given program purchase is shown in Figure 2–3.

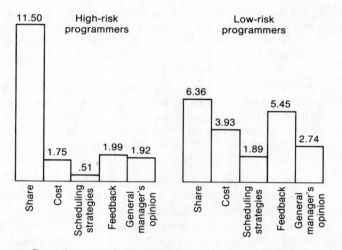

The numbers attached to the columns for share, cost, scheduling strategies, feedback, and general manager's opinion represent estimates for each item's contribution to the total decision-making process. Analysis of variance was the statistical procedure used; the lowest main-effect mean was subtracted from the highest main-effect mean to create an estimate of the size of the main effect for each column.

Source: Paul H. Virts, "Television Entertainment Gatekeeping: A Study of Local Television Program Directors' Decision-Making." Unpublished Ph.D. dissertation, University of Iowa, 1979, p. 165. Used with permission.

Figure 2–3. High-Risk vs. Low-Risk
Programmer Profiles

In the absence of studies such as those of Fisher and Virts of programmers at the network level, conclusions can be drawn from anecdotal evidence. Such evidence suggests that, despite a higher degree of specialization, network programmers also function as part of a troika of interests representing management and sales as well as programming. William S. Paley, CBS chairman of the board, started out in broadcasting in 1928 at the very top—as president of the network. But he has always been known to participate actively in programming. According to one observer, Paley "had a sixth sense about a program, whether or not it would work. At programming meetings he was always the most alert, genuinely listening, never underestimating (or overestimating) any ideas."[28] Paley himself describes in his autobiography how major seasonal programming decisions are made at CBS, starting with some 800 proposals "from professional sources." These are parceled out to three specialized West Coast programming units—comedy, drama, and variety—and to a general unit for the East Coast in New York; each unit is headed by a vice-president. Eventually they narrow the 800 proposals down to about 200 orders for sample scripts. These in turn are screened and only 40 emerge as pilot programs. Finally, in the spring, the moment for the most critical programming judgments arrives:

> In our full programming meeting, which decided our final lineup for the 1978–79 season, fourteen of us met in a conference room of the programming department on the thirty-fourth floor of our New York headquarters. Like all such meetings, this one was long, agonizing, painful, ego bruising, and extremely stimulating.[29]

When the ego bruising was over, fewer than ten programs survived as series for the fall schedule.

Fred Silverman, who is credited with engineering the programming decisions at ABC that enabled it to take the lead away from Paley and CBS, has served all three networks. He went from head of programs for CBS to president of ABC Entertainment to president and chief executive officer of NBC. It is unusual for a pure programmer to advance to the very top of the corporate hierarchy like this. Sylvester "Pat" Weaver went from programming to the NBC presidency in the 1950s, but his prior experience had been in advertising.

Commentators have analyzed Silverman's every word and every move, trying to ferret out the secret of his phenomenal success as a programmer. They have come up with such qualities as decisiveness, unrelenting attention to the fine details of programming, a capacity for extraordinarily hard work, creative use of on-air **promotion**, and a genuine liking for television entertainment. They all eventually return, however, to that undefinable quality: the ability to foresee mass appeal. As pointed out earlier, this ability is an element in all programming, but at the network level it becomes especially crucial because the network programmer has the unique task of appealing to over 200 markets at the same time.

In a appraisal written in 1971, relatively early in Silverman's primetime career, a *Life* profile quoted Les Brown as saying that if Silverman "got wind that Greek tragedy or Pinter or Shakespeare was what people wanted, he'd deliver them quickly."[30] Five years later a *New York Times* writer said his gift was that "he can size up what kind of personality will appeal to the mass audience better than any other programmer."[31] The next year *Time* magazine, in its cover story on Silverman, concluded that "he was born with perfect pitch to American popular TV taste."[32]

Beyond this elusive qualification, there seems to be no consistent pattern of characteristics that make individuals successful as programmers that is any different from the sets of characteristics that make people successful in other fields. Certainly they include the ability to absorb and process large amounts of detailed information and persuasiveness in interpersonal contacts.

SUMMARY

Programmers are information processors who have to master a vast amount of information about programs—their sources, their costs, and their track records—and about their own audiences and those of competitors. Most programming comes from three fundamental sources: networks, syndicators, and local production. Information on programming comes from sales agents, the trade press, station sales representatives, and personal monitoring. Information on audiences comes from both national research services and local research. Programmers study both the past performance of existing programs and the probable future performance of new programs in making purchasing and scheduling decisions.

Data on programs and audiences, on internal policies and budgets, and on the market serve to inform programmers about the limitations placed on their freedom of choice in making program decisions. The various "factors" or "inputs" can be seen as constraints with which the programmer must contend. Some constraints (such as facilities, market, and government regulation) are relatively stable. These constraints can be classed as nonnegotiable. Others (such as station policies, audience preferences, and competitive programming) can be considered negotiable constraints in the sense that the programmer can use strategy, including personal persuasive powers, to modify, evade, or overcome them.

Significant program decisions are made not by programmers acting alone but by a troika of decision makers that includes sales and management executives as well as programmers. The programmer's role is to gather all the relevant information concerning a program issue, to digest it, and to make a recommendation to the team. The role of the programmer within the troika varies with the character of the organization. In terms of status and pay, however, the programmer generally ranks third in the troika.

This description applies generally to both radio and television and to both stations and networks, with appropriate adaptations. Thus, for example, network programmers have the same problems as station programmers. However, network programmers also depend on a special constituency that stations do not have—the network's affiliates, whose loyalty the network dares not undermine by offering too many programs that the affiliates refuse to run. Network programming is also more specialized, with top-level executives taking charge of specific program types or dayparts. On the other hand, music-formula radio programmers must be jacks-of-all-trades, often with a good deal of responsibility for production tactics as well as programming strategy.

Success in the field, according to programmers' responses in one study, depends on the same qualities that make for success in other fields, not on any special talent for programming. A study of a smaller group of television programmers produced evidence that they fell into two distinct groups in terms of the relative weight they assigned to specific constraints in deciding whether to schedule a particular program. One group, characterized as high-risk programmers, placed more emphasis on the program's previous track record than on scheduling strategies, letters from the audience, costs, and management opinion. The low-risk group evaluated the five constraints more equally. Anecdotal evidence about the qualities of highly successful network programmers suggests that, along with the other more generalized qualities for success, they have unique ability to sense what will have great mass appeal.

NOTES

[1]Federal Communications Commission, *Annual Programming Report for Commercial Television Stations, 1978* (Washington, D.C.: FCC, July 20, 1979), p. 219.

[2]See Paul H. Virts, "Television Entertainment Gatekeeping: A Study of Local Television Program Directors' Decision-Making" (Ph.D. diss., University of Iowa, 1979) for a study of programmers' syndication buying strategies.

[3]"The TV Reps: The Competition Gets Keener As the Pie Gets Larger," *Broadcasting,* Special Report (June 4, 1979): 37–62.

[4]National Association of Broadcasters, *A Basic Guide for the Program Director of a Smaller Operation* (Washington, D.C.: The Association, n.d.), p. 3.

[5]Center for Public Resources, *Radio Report: An Inquiry into the Potential for Expanding Diversity in Commercial Programming* (New York: The Center, 1979), p. 15.

[6]Arbitron Company, *Research Guidelines for Programming Decision Makers* (Beltsville, Md.: Arbitron Company, 1977), pp. 17–27.

[7]J. David Lewis, "Programmer's Choice: Eight Factors in Program Decision-Making," *Journal of Broadcasting* 14 (Winter 1969–70): 71–82.

[8]Virts, *Television Entertainment Gatekeeping,* p. 103.

[9]Michael G. Fisher, "A Survey of Selected Television Station Program Managers: Their Backgrounds and Perceptions of Role" (M.A. thesis, Temple University, 1978), p. 110.

[10]Edward A. Warren, "Programming for a Commercial Station," in *Televi-*

sion Station Management, ed. Yale Roe (New York: Hastings House, 1964), pp. 108–110.

[11]Federal Communications Commission, *Development of Policy Re: Changes in the Entertainment Formats of Broadcast Stations,* Memorandum Opinion and Order, 60 FCC 2d 858, July 30, 1976, p. 863.

[12]Ibid., p. 874. The study was submitted as part of the NAB's comments in the FCC's reconsideration of the WEFM case. Bruce M. Owen conducted the research. He later published the gist of the study under his own name: "Regulating Diversity: The Case of Radio Formats," *Journal of Broadcasting* 21 (Summer 1977): 305–19.

[13]Virts, *Television Entertainment Gatekeeping,* p. 141.

[14]Ibid., p. 135.

[15]Frederick S. Pierce, remarks before the International Radio and Television Society, New York City, November 6, 1978.

[16]Thomas Thompson, "The Crapshoot for Half a Billion: Fred Silverman Rolls the Dice for CBS," *Life,* December 10, 1971, pp. 46–58.

[17]William H. Read, *America's Mass Media Merchants* (Baltimore: Johns Hopkins University Press, 1976), p. 72.

[18]Natan Katzman, *Program Decisions in Public Television* (Washington, D.C.: National Association of Educational Broadcasters, 1976), p. 34.

[19]"Hollywood Fights Back," *TV Guide,* August 27, 1977, pp. 4–18.

[20]Les Brown, "Is Silverman Worth It?" *New York Times,* January 1, 1978, p. 26.

[21]"Special Report Prepared for the 1979 NATPE Convention by Broadcast Information Bureau," *Facts, Figures and Film* (March 1979), p. 32.

[22]*Gallagher Report: A Confidential Letter to Marketing, Sales, Advertising and Media Executives,* September 8, 1975.

[23]Virts, *Television Entertainment Gatekeeping,* p. 104.

[24]Quoted in "The Top-40 Story: Bill Drake," *Radio & Records* (September 1977): 30.

[25]Fisher, *A Survey of Selected Television Station Program Managers,* pp. 171–72. Used with permission.

[26]Virts, *Television Entertainment Gatekeeping,* p. 86.

[27]Ibid., p. 225.

[28]David Halberstam, *The Powers That Be* (New York: Alfred A. Knopf, 1979), p. 131.

[29]William S. Paley, *As It Happened: A Memoir* (New York: Doubleday, 1979), p. 262.

[30]Thompson, "Crapshoot for Half a Billion," p. 58.

[31]Jeff Greenfield, "The Silverman Strategy," *New York Times Magazine,* March 7, 1976, p. 22.

[32]"The Man with the Golden Gut: Programmer Fred Silverman Has Made ABC No. 1," *Time* cover story, September 5, 1977, p. 47.

ADDITIONAL PERIODICAL READINGS

Jaffe, Alfred J. "The TV Program Chief: Getting What He's Worth?" *Television/Radio Age* (February 8, 1971): 27 ff.

Discussion of salary range for programmers compared with sales and other executives' salaries.

Monaghan, Robert R.; Plummer, Joseph T.; Rarick, David L., and **Williams, Dwight A.** "Predicting Viewer Preference for New TV Program Concepts." *Journal of Broadcasting* 18 (Spring 1974): 131–42.

A research study locating two distinct types of viewers, Mr. Happy World and Mr. Realistic Conflict, that describe television preference patterns.

"Syndicated-Product Prices Chief Concern Listed by Stations in *Television/Radio Age* Survey." *Television/Radio Age* (February 28, 1977): 32 ff.

Results of survey of television station executives on issues and responsibilities related to syndication of programs.

"Television: Where We Earn Our Living!" *Facts, Figures and Film: News for Television Executives* (March 1979).

Sixth annual personal finance survey by the Broadcast Information Bureau, Inc., on earnings and job-related conditions of station managers, sales managers, and program managers; nineteen graphs and tables.

von Ladau, Philip F. "Ratings: An Aid to Programming and Purchase of TV Properties." *Broadcast Financial Journal* (March 1976): 36–42.

An elementary guide to the use of ratings in programming a television station.

3 Regulatory Constraints

Sydney W. Head

> *Most regulatory constraints on programming apply across the board to all types of programming situations. The rules differ in some details between certain broad groupings, such as between radio and television, television network affiliates and independents, large markets and small markets, and UHF and VHF. But regulation is sufficiently uniform to justify treating the subject in one place, forestalling repetition of the same information in each separate chapter.*

REGULATION AND DEREGULATION

In recent years the notion of deregulation has been popular in Washington. Federal agencies such as the Federal Communications Commission (FCC) have been attempting to cut away some of the underbrush of red tape that has grown up over the years. The FCC's mandate comes from the Communications Act of 1934, but in fact the substance of the broadcasting portion of the act dates all the way back to the predecessor act of 1927. Over the years Congress has altered the Communications Act continually, amending it scores of times. Nevertheless, the act's fundamental philosophy has remained unchanged. In 1978 a congressional committee proposed sweeping changes in the act, a complete **rewrite** as it was called, but it failed to generate sufficient political support. Congress went back to its traditional system of modernizing the Communications Act section by section, solving specific problems when the need for action becomes urgent.

Proposals for extreme changes such as the 1978 attempted rewrite arose only partly as a response to the urge for deregulatory reform. A second reason is that new technology, particularly cable television and satellite relays, has raised problems not anticipated in communications law. Cable television does not fit into any of the established service categories addressed in the existing statute. Cable is much like broadcasting and actually involves broadcasting to a large extent; yet as a wired rather than a wireless system, cable cannot be classed with broadcasting under the act and regulated accordingly.

AMBIGUITY OF LEGAL CONSTRAINTS

In actual practice, broadcasters encounter the Communications Act of 1934 indirectly, through the rules and regulations of the Federal Communications Commission, all of which derive from the general mandate of the act. Rules that affect programming tend to be couched in somewhat ambiguous terms. Direct program regulation by the FCC would violate both the Communications Act and the freedom-of-press clause of the First Amendment to the Constitution.

In order to avoid the charge of censorship, the FCC words its directives about programs in ways that leave ample room for licensee discretion. For example, the FCC's **fairness doctrine** requires broadcasters to give access to competing views on issues of public importance; however, the FCC does not dictate what constitutes an issue, what makes an issue of public importance, who shall speak on a particular issue, what form and at what time and for how long the issue shall be discussed. All these decisions are left to the good-faith discretion of the licensee. Again, in appraising licensee program performance, the commission considers programming only after it has been broadcast, carefully avoiding the possibility of being accused of imposing prior restraint, which is censorship by definition.

Licensees tend to use their discretion in sensitive program areas, such as the treatment of controversial issues, with caution. The last thing they want to do is to call attention to themselves by raising issues at the FCC about their interpretations of licensee discretion. If nothing unusual occurs, license renewals and other paperwork tend to go through the FCC automatically. The main work of the FCC as a bureaucracy is to process forms, the most important (for **stations** already licensed) being the license renewal application form, due every three years. The work of processing these and other forms has been delegated by the commissioners, in accordance with authority granted in the Communications Act, to staff members. Very few actions taken in the name of the commission ever come to the personal attention of the commissioners themselves; they seldom rise to the level of a place on the commissioners' official meeting agendas. Licensees are happy not to be honored by a place on the agenda.[1]

This means that programmers must be sensitive to the attitudes of their managements on the question of FCC compliance with the rules. Most licensees retain members of the Communications Bar Association to advise them on how to keep out of trouble. Some licensees are more willing to take chances or to stand up for what they consider their rights than are others. Most are willing to bend over backward to avoid raising compliance issues. Generally speaking, the more there is at stake, the more sensitive the licensee is to regulatory nuances. Large, successful firms have a high profile that invites scrutiny. On the other hand, such a firm may also feel more secure because of its power and resources and therefore be willing, when an issue of vital importance to its interest is at stake, to risk a confrontation. An example was NBC's refusal to accept the FCC's finding that a documentary program called *Pensions: The Broken Promise* violated the fairness doctrine. Although it would have been easy to submit, NBC felt that the integrity of broadcasting as a news medium was at stake. The network appealed the FCC's decision to the courts. NBC won the case but only after great expense and trouble.[2]

In any event, when licensees do get into serious trouble with the FCC, the reasons rarely have anything to do with programs.[3] Most license losses have occurred because of fraudulent business practices, technical faults, and misrepresentations to the commission. However, in recent years licensees have had to face increasing challenges by consumer groups. These public interventions often include allegations of program failures, usually charges of inadequate service to minorities. Although consumer objections to renewals rarely actually cause loss of license, they do cost licensees time and money. Moreover, they often result in licensees making voluntary program changes in order to mollify opponents.

Thus, although the constraints arising from the licensed status of broadcasters often have a certain ambiguity, they affect program decisions. Programmers need to be aware of the areas in which licensee discretion can be exercised and their managements' attitude toward the use of discretionary latitude. They also need to be sensitive to potential sources of opposition within the community so that they can program defensively to defuse possible complaints in advance. Programmers understand that few attacks on their programming are likely to originate within the FCC bureaucracy. Much more likely sources of complaint are would-be licensees who attack existing licensees at renewal time and groups or individuals whose complaints to the FCC call its attention to alleged violations or abuses of discretionary powers by licensees.

Programmers also need to be aware that one of the most pervasive and fundamental principles underlying the present system of regulation is that licensees have a "nondelegable" responsibility for *all* programming. This means that the programmers must always check the content of programming obtained from outside sources. The licensee cannot evade responsibility by claiming that a violation occurred because a program was not screened before being put on the air or was in a foreign language.

DOCUMENTATION OF PROMISE AND PERFORMANCE

As a practical matter, most legal constraints arise in connection with the formal documents in which licensees make promises about their future programming and disclose their past program performance. Central to these are (1) the license application itself, in the form of either an original authorization or the renewal application that must be submitted every three years, and (2) the daily program **log** that details what was actually broadcast.*

Original Application

The application for a construction permit (CP) for a new commercial station—form 301—explains licensee program obligations, quoting liberally from the FCC's 1960 report on programming.[4] The Commission emphasizes in that report that "licensees must make positive, diligent and continuing efforts to provide a program schedule designed to serve the needs and interests of the public in the areas to which they transmit." This is a personal licensee duty that "may not be avoided by delegation of the responsibility to others." The FCC specifies the procedures that must be followed in carrying out this duty, collectively known as **ascertainment**.

With regard to specific types of programs, the FCC avoids prescribing the amount of time that must be devoted to each of the several types; in fact, it even avoids stating that any specific program type *must* be broadcast. It merely says that "certain recognized elements of a broadcast service *have frequently been found necessary or desirable* [italics added] to serve the broadcast needs and interests of many communities." The application form quotes the following passage from the 1960 programming report:

> The major elements usually necessary to meet the public interest, needs and desires of the community in which the station is located as developed by the industry, and recognized by the Commission, have included: (1) Opportunity for Local Self-Expression, (2) The Development and Use of Local Talent, (3) Programs for Children, (4) Religious Programs, (5) Educational Programs, (6) Public Affairs Programs, (7) Editorialization by Licensees, (8) Political Broadcasts, (9) Agricultural Programs, (10) News Programs, (11) Weather and Market Reports, (12) Sports Programs, (13) Service to Minority Groups, (14) Entertainment Programming.[5]

An attachment to the application form gives definitions of each program type and of other terms used in the form. For example, a **local** program is defined as one originated by the station or one for which the

---

*Copies of FCC forms can be obtained by writing: Consumer Assistance Office, Federal Communications Commission, Room 258, Washington, D.C. 20554.

station has substantial production responsibility, which uses "live talent more than 50 percent of the time." Such a program may still be classed as local if it is recorded for later broadcast.

Because renewal forms contain the operational programming commitments made by commercial stations, we will examine their programming provisions rather than those of the original construction permit. First, however, we should review four subsidiary documents.

The Program Log

Any follow-up to check on the promises made in the original station application is normally based on what is known as the **composite week**. This is seven different days of program logs arbitrarily chosen by the FCC from different weeks of the year so as to form a rough sample of overall program performance.

Stations design their own program log forms, but FCC rules specify the contents in detail. Logs consist essentially of a minute-by-minute record of the day's broadcasts, filled in by personnel on duty as the day unfolds. They categorize each program as to type, length, and source. Commercial and public service announcements are also logged as to time, length, and subject matter. The program log serves as the official evidence of fulfillment by the station of its commitments to commercial advertisers as well as to the FCC, as the surrogate of the public.

The very fact that the logging rules select and define program types has significance as an indication of FCC expectations. The list corresponds approximately to the one in the 1960 statement of program policy. (Its relevant passage was quoted in the previous section on original applications.) The logging rules single out eight program categories: agricultural, entertainment, news, public affairs, religious, instructional, sports, and other programs. In addition, editorials, political programs, and educational institution programs are mentioned as subclasses that can be combined with the main classes. The rules also define other items of program content such as commercials and public service announcements.

The Annual Program Report

FCC form 304–A requires television stations to make an annual program report, based on the composite week logs. The report shows only the amount of time devoted to news, public affairs, and local programming. At this point, for the first time, broadcasters encounter a specific programming requirement. The FCC commissioners have instructed their staff to call to their personal attention any instances of television stations failing to meet the following minimum levels: local programming, 5 percent of schedule; news plus public affairs programming, 5 percent; total nonentertainment programming, 10 percent. The rule does not apply to UHF **independent** stations. Indeed, it does not even have the status of a rule in the formal sense. It is merely an internal FCC directive, not a part of the officially published FCC rules and regulations. It normally creates no hardship, for most television stations routinely schedule higher percentages of the designated program types in any event (a fact that is used as an argument for deregulation on this point). Even if a station fell far short of the designated levels in these program categories, it is not clear what, if anything, the commission would do about it.

In radio's case, the report on news, public affairs, and local programming is rendered every three years in the renewal application instead of annually. The critical level of nonentertainment programming for AM radio is 6 percent and for FM, 8 percent. Here some hardship occurs, as Edd Routt indicates in Chapter 14 on music programming: radio music programmers tend to regard the need to insert nonentertainment material into their carefully crafted music **formats** as a gross intrusion from an alien world.

The Public File

Each commercial station must maintain, at a place readily accessible to the general public, a file of materials that explains the station's policies and documents its practices. This documentation aids consumer groups that may want to appraise the station's performance. Among the documents that must be placed in the public file are records of the licensee's ascertainment efforts, a checklist of community leaders who have been consulted in this connection (television only), and an annual list of the salient problems and needs identified in the course of the ascertainment process.

Renewal Applications

Most broadcast applications to the FCC are in the form of renewal applications that must be filed every three years, unless short-term renewal has been imposed because of past violations by the licensee. Three separate forms are used: form 303 for commercial television, 303–R for commercial radio, and 342 for all noncommercial stations. The two commercial forms are similar in requirements. The application for renewal is of critical importance to programming because it gives the FCC an opportunity (not necessarily always exercised) to compare what licensees have said they were going to do with what they have done in actual practice. This comparison, usually referred to as "promise vs. performance," is essential if the renewal process is to have any meaning.

In making promises, however, the broadcaster by no means

makes a hard-and-fast commitment. The television renewal form reassures the applicant that "it is not . . . expected that an applicant will or can adhere inflexibly in day-to-day operation to the representations made herein." It also provides for the licensee to notify the commission between renewals if substantial program changes have been made since the last set of promises.

The parts of the commercial renewal application that deal explicitly with programming can be summarized under four headings:

1. *Ascertainment.* A list of the community leaders consulted must be attached to the application along with the results of a survey of the general public's perception of community problems. If the description of the station's ascertainment efforts and the annual list of salient problems it has identified are not in its public inspection file, an explanation must be made.*

2. *Nonentertainment and local programs.* Nonentertainment refers to three classes of programs: news, public affairs, and all other programs not classified as either entertainment or sports. Television stations must show how much they propose to schedule of each type, divided according to the following breakdown: 6 A.M. to midnight, midnight to 6 A.M., and 6 P.M. to 11 P.M., and whether locally originated. Radio's form asks for the proposed program breakdown only, without the daypart and local distinctions; however, there is an additional radio question asking for descriptions of all programs in the composite week classed as public affairs or other nonentertainment, with titles, sources, types, times of broadcast, and lengths. Television **network affiliates** must also state whether they carried 50 percent or more of the news and public affairs programs offered by their networks.

3. *Promise vs. performance.* A copy of the logs for the composite week must be attached to the application. Television stations must explain if the nonentertainment and local proportions in this sample of programming differ from the

---

*The FCC uses the ascertainment procedure to force licensees to devote some of their programming to relevant local community affairs. First, the licensee must consult with community leaders and survey the general population to ascertain local needs and problems; second, the licensee decides which of the ascertained items should have priority; third, the licensee designs programs to deal specifically with the ascertained needs and problems. A relatively small number of programs satisfies the requirement, as indicated by the FCC's expectation that a minimum of only 5 percent of a television station's schedule need be devoted to local programming.

proposals made under item 2. They also must explain the circumstances if the annual programming reports differ from the program promises made in the previous renewal application.

4. *Special program aspects.* Radio stations must identify the format(s) they have used and propose to use. Television stations must describe for the previous license period the programs they scheduled for children up to age twelve, including in the description of each its source, time and day, frequency, and program type. A television station must also indicate any "procedures applicant has or proposes to have for the consideration and disposition of complaints or suggestions from the public."

These four items are only extracts, chosen for their bearing on programming. Forms 301 and 303 ask for a great deal of additional information on commercial policies, ownership, engineering plans, and so on. It can be seen from the extracts how the FCC avoids making explicit program demands. Would-be licensees are left with wide latitude in constructing program proposals. Nevertheless, the very existence of a list of "usually necessary" program types gives a strong hint of what the FCC ideally expects. Herein lies some of the deliberate ambiguity previously mentioned.

For noncommercial broadcasting, a single renewal document—form 342—serves for both radio and television. It simply asks for a self-selected week of program logs (not a composite week), an accounting of the sources from which programs are obtained (local, network, recorded), a breakdown of the schedule by a short list of six program types: instructional, general educational, performing arts, public affairs, light entertainment, and other (including news and sports).

Public Complaints

The FCC has a Complaints and Compliance Office that handles the tens of thousands of individual public complaints about broadcasting that reach the Commission each year. The great majority of these complaints simply seek to enlist the help of the FCC in imposing censorship on some program, topic, treatment, or performer.

There are formal avenues whereby certain public complaints get a hearing at the FCC: allegations of unequal treatment of political candidates, biased treatment of issues of public importance, and personal attacks. The Communications Act itself guarantees equal treatment of political candidates in the use of broadcasting facilities and mandates allocation of reasonable amounts of time for candidates for federal office. The main programming problems raised by these provisions are the disruption of schedules at election times and the possibility that news-related programming about elections may be inhibited. News programmers may think twice about covering the activities of a political candidate for fear an appearance by that candidate will require granting similar coverage to all other candidates for the office in question. However, the act itself contains exemptions for bona fide news-related programs, and the courts have upheld the FCC in relatively liberal interpretations of these exemptions. A little good judgment by programmers should avoid the triggering of unwelcome obligations under the political candidates rule.

Somewhat more complicated are public demands for time arising out of alleged **fairness doctrine** violations. Under this doctrine the licensee has an obligation to deal with controversial issues of public importance and see to it that opposing views get reasonably comparable coverage. The FCC gives the licensee latitude to make good-faith judgments about whether the fairness doctrine applies in a given situation. In addition, individuals or groups who are attacked over the air have the right to be informed of such attacks and to be offered a chance to reply. None of these requirements imposes especially troublesome burdens on broadcasters who exercise reasonable precautions, but awareness by programmers obviously is essential.

OTHER OFFICIAL CONSTRAINTS

Rather different from the regulatory constraints on programming is the **primetime access rule** (PTAR). This rule, aimed at the television networks through their affiliates, affects the economics of programming as well as its content. The FCC classifies as **primetime** the high-density viewing hours between 7 and 11 P.M. on the coasts and between 6 and 10 P.M. in the other time zones. The FCC designed PTAR to create a market for non-network primetime programs by limiting weekday network programming to a maximum of three of the four evening hours.*

PTAR deals with economics because the FCC recognized that only during primetime can commercial stations generate sufficient income to justify paying the price for high-cost programming. At all other times, minimum-cost formats—notably **soap operas**—must be used, even by the networks. As long as the networks controlled all of the primetime (other than the half hour traditionally reserved for local news shows), producers of primetime types of television programs had only three potential customers—ABC, CBS, and NBC. The goal of PTAR was to

---

*The FCC limited PTAR to stations in the top fifty markets, but since it would be uneconomical for networks to program differently for the rest of the markets, in practice PTAR affects network stations in all markets.

make the network-affiliated stations also customers, either singly or in commonly owned groups. PTAR has substantially increased the purchasing and scheduling role of programmers at network-affiliated television stations. Before 1970, they simply plugged into the network; now PTAR gives them the opportunity to program five half-hour periods a week during primetime.

Finally, programmers must also be aware of the possibility of violating libel, right-of-privacy, obscenity, indecency, lottery, fraud, and other laws outside the Communications Act. Violations of these laws usually concern the news and sales department heads more than they do programmers. In any case, they can usually be avoided by alert management, especially with the help of a readily accessible communications lawyer.

INDUSTRY PROGRAM CODES

Although not legally binding, the self-regulatory codes adopted by the broadcast industry have a bearing on government regulation. Such codes incorporate essentially two types of constraints: those imposed or implied by the FCC and other legal entities and those imposed by public opinion. In other words, the primary aim of self-regulation is to keep the industry out of trouble, whether from Washington or the public. Self-regulatory codes offer programmers useful guidance, especially about details of program content to which the public reacts with particular sensitivity.

Industrywide codes—one for radio, another for television—have been adopted by the National Association of Broadcasters (NAB), the leading trade association of commercial broadcasters. Although not all licensees subscribe to the NAB codes, they can be useful even to programmers at nonsubscribing stations. The codes have no official, government status, and the code authority is prevented by restraint-of-trade laws from using any effective means of enforcement.*

Under the heading "Special Program Standards," the television code gives recommendations on sixteen specific types of content. For example, the code advises on how to handle scenes depicting crime (avoid revealing specific techniques of crime), sex (shall not be treated exploitatively or irresponsibly), obscenity (shall not be broadcast),

---

*In fact, the NAB was forced by court action to withdraw rules setting up a "family hour" in the early primetime segment, during which material unsuitable for children was to be avoided. Complainants alleged that the rules had been adopted as a result of indirect pressure from the FCC. In 1979 the Justice Department belatedly brought suit against the NAB on the grounds that the codes as a whole violate laws against restraint of trade.

hypnosis (forbidden on camera). Other sections deal with rules for news, controversial issues, politics, and religion.[6]

In the same category of codified nonlegal constraints are the **standards and practices departments** of the networks. Their editing of new programs is much resented by writers and producers, who call it censorship. These departments interpret both the NAB code and the internal set of standards observed by each network in the screening of new material. Individual stations sometimes have their own formal statements of policy that include program-related prohibitions.

These industry constraints concern the relatively few programmers directly involved in the creation and acceptance of new program material. Programs previously used have, of course, already run the gamut of the various editorial screenings and need further checking only if local conditions impose unusual constraints.

RELATIVE IMPORTANCE OF LEGAL CONSTRAINTS

When asked to estimate the importance of the FCC as an influence on their program decisions, the respondents to Michael Fisher's survey of National Association of Television Program Executives' members replied as follows:[7] always important, 36 percent; often important, 28 percent; sometimes important, 27 percent; hardly ever important, 3 percent; never important, 1 percent.* J. David Lewis also used a five-point scale of importance in his study of programmers. On the average, the respondents ranked the FCC highest in importance relative to other influences that the respondents themselves mentioned. This finding was not affected by differences in market size or geographical location.[8]

That programmers perceive the FCC as one of the most important, if not the most important, constraint on their freedom of action may seem paradoxical in view of the seeming mildness of FCC programming constraints. The perception of government regulation of programming as a serious threat to the freedom of even ethical broadcasters is the product of fear of the unknown. The very ambiguity of FCC rules that places the burden of decision making on the licensee creates a climate of anxiety, despite the objective fact that a license has hardly ever been lost because of program violations. Since licensees cannot shift responsibility, they place great pressure on their subordinates to refrain from actions that could conceivably place their licenses in jeopardy.

In a unique view of the FCC from inside the regulatory bureaucracy, Barry Cole and Mal Oettinger point out that licensees, espe-

---

*An additional 5% made no response.

cially the smaller ones who cannot afford to keep high-powered Washington communications firms on retainer, are "terrorized at the thought of dealing directly with the government. They seem convinced that anything they said might be used against them."[9] The authors point out that early in the 1970s, the FCC chairman invited broadcasters to send their recommendations about deregulation directly to the commission. This seemed like a golden opportunity for licensees to participate in the reform of the very broadcast regulations they found inhibiting. They shunned the opportunity almost unanimously. Cole quotes one broadcaster as saying, "It's like writing to the draft board"—a step that might cause the broadcaster's name to be put into a computer and perhaps singled out later for unwelcome attention. Even *Broadcasting*, the trade magazine that represents the point of view of management, was disappointed in the reaction. It sternly editorialized, "Broadcasters have been ignoring the invitation on the theory that no comment is wise, that anything they say may be interpreted as a disposition to fight city hall. If that attitude does indeed prevail, it bespeaks a servility that deserves all the regulation it gets."[10]

As long as licensees *act* as if the FCC is breathing down their necks with constant threats of dire economic loss unless they knuckle under to a myriad of programming regulations, programmers have to deal with that as reality. The lesson is that programmers need to understand regulatory philosophy and to be familiar with the statutes, with the FCC's interpretation and implementation of the statutes, and with the leading court decisions. Thus armed, they are in a better position to resist the tendency to panic, to avoid accepting unnecessary and unreasonable constraints alleged to be due to FCC intervention in programming matters, and to defuse in advance harassing fairness doctrine complaints.

REGULATION OF CABLE

The FCC and the laws that affect broadcasting impose some of the same constraints on cablecasting. For example, both are subject to the requirements for equal opportunities for political candidates, fairness-doctrine obligations, and prohibitions against obscenity and lotteries. There is a fundamental difference between the two, however: only broadcasting must make program promises reflecting public service commitments and undergo verification of their fulfillment at renewal time. These are the aspects of regulation that most affect programming by broadcast stations and networks, not so much because they influence specific program decisions as because they raise broadcasters' consciousness of their role as trustees of the public. Broadcast programming would have evolved quite differently than it has if market forces had acted alone. Relatively light but nevertheless persistent pressure from the FCC toward localism in programming and a leavening of news, public affairs, and "all other" nonentertainment programming has its effect.

Early in the 1970s, the FCC imposed a series of special constraints on cable. Some were aimed at limiting its economic impact on broadcasting. For example, there were rules on the extent to which signals from distant markets could be imported and rules to prevent cable companies from bidding against broadcasters for programs already established as regular broadcast fare. Other special constraints aimed at obligating cable companies to make their own localized contributions to program diversity; the FCC required operators to provide **access** channels on which both private and public users could have the opportunity to present local programming. Nearly all such special cable regulations have been found by the courts to exceed the Commission's authority under the Communications Act of 1934 (which says nothing explicitly about cable). These court reversals allowed the cable industry to respond more freely to market forces.

Two major issues were still unresolved as this was written: **retransmission consent** and **exclusivity**. Both these issues involve programming. First, cable companies need not obtain consent from broadcasters whose signals they take off the air for delivery to their subscribers. The question of retransmission consent did not arise at first because cable distribution simply enlarged the immediate coverage areas of the stations whose programs they retransmitted. This happy symbiotic relationship was upset by the emergence of the **superstation** concept. By using satellites to relay broadcast programming to cable systems throughout the entire country, the superstation undermines one of the fundamental assumptions of broadcast programming economics: the delineation of each station's market area by the inherent limitations of its transmitter's coverage ability. This circumscribed market is taken for granted in negotiations for the sale of program rights, in the setting of advertising rates, and in the strategies of market competition. Satellite relays to distant cable television markets undermine these assumptions. A program distributor negotiates a fair-market price for a program to be released over WTBS-TV in the Atlanta market, for example. Then a **common carrier** feeds that same program by satellite and microwave to more than a thousand cable systems outside Atlanta, some as far as 3,000 miles away. Should this enormously expanded market warrant an expanded price for the rights to show the program?

A provision of the new Copyright Act of 1978 attempted to solve the problem of cable's redistribution of off-the-air programs by creating a new copyright concept—retransmission right. It calls for compulsory licensing of cable companies by copyright holders. In return, the holders get subsidiary fees, in addition to the fees paid by broadcasters in the initial transaction covering station use of the material. Retransmission fees, calculated according to the size of each cable company, are assessed and collected on behalf of the copyright owners by a government Copyright Tribunal. In practice, fees have amounted to chicken feed. Joel Chaseman, president of the Post-Newsweek stations, in an address to the National Association of Television Program Executives, said the cable companies pay more in postage mailing out bills to their subscribers than they pay for the right to retransmit broadcast program materials.[11] The broadcasters argue that cable companies should be required to negotiate with program distributors for the right to carry their programs, just as the broadcasters do, paying at the going market rate for retransmission consent.

The related issue of exclusivity refers to what happens when program distribution companies "sell" programs to a broadcast station. Stations actually rent the use of programs, paying the rental fee in exchange for an exclusive right to use the programs for a stipulated time period in the station's own market. Without the exclusivity provision, a competing station could buy the same series already sold in its market and undercut the first buyer. Originally the FCC supported exclusivity as a protective measure, but in 1979 it proposed to rescind the rule.[12]

It can be seen that both issues arise fundamentally because of the continuousness attribute discussed in Chapter 1 and the corresponding frugality principle. Each party to the dispute is trying to get maximum use out of the limited supply of programming while doing all it can to stave off inroads on the supply by other parties.

SUMMARY

Broadcast and cable regulation is in a state of ferment, partly because of a Washington move toward deregulation, partly because of the novel problems introduced by cable television and satellite relays. Prevented by the Communications Act of 1934 and the First Amendment from directly regulating broadcast programming, the FCC regulates indirectly by requiring licensees to meet certain public interest standards in their programming judgments. Programmers need to understand the basis for this arrangement in broadcast law and in FCC regulations. They also have to consider the reluctance of licensees to take any actions that might cause difficulties with license renewal. Most regulatory constraints are documented in terms of program promises made in an original station application and subsequent renewal applications. The FCC judges performance by examining a sample of the program logs that must be kept by stations.

Allegations of specific program violations usually come to FCC attention as a result of public complaints or challenges at license renewal time. Programmers may get useful hints from the formal codes of program standards set up by the industry itself, which seek to forestall both government interference and public protest. Legal constraints are relatively mild, but programmers must take into account the sensitivities of their managements.

Cable television is subject to some of the same constraints as broadcasting but differs fundamentally in not being subject to the public service obligations of broadcasting. Cable regulation is changing rapidly, with most of the earlier FCC constraints now removed as a result of deregulation policy. Current problems with implications for programming are the issues of retransmission consent and program exclusivity.

NOTES

[1]Cole and Oettinger afford an inside look at how the processing work is handled at the FCC: Barry Cole and Mal Oettinger, *Reluctant Regulators: The FCC and the Broadcast Audience*, rev. ed. (Reading, Mass.: Addison-Wesley, 1978).

[2]*NBC v. FCC*, 516 F 2d 1101 (1974). The Supreme Court refused to review the decision of the appeals court.

[3]A study of revocations and license denials over a thirty-six-year period revealed that program violations were cited as reasons only twice in seventy-eight cases of license loss. John D. Abel, Charles Clift III, and Frederic A. Weiss, "Station License Revocations and Denials of Renewal, 1934–1969." *Journal of Broadcasting* 14 (Fall 1970): 411–21.

[4]Federal Communications Commission, *Report and Statement of Policy Re Commission En Banc Programming Inquiry*, 44 FCC 2303 (29 July 1960), p. 2306.

[5]Ibid.

[6]Single copies of the codes can be obtained free from the NAB Code Authority, 1771 N Street N.W., Washington, D.C. 20036.

[7]Michael G. Fisher, "A Survey of Selected Television Station Program Managers: Their Backgrounds and Perceptions of Role" (M.A. thesis, Temple University, 1978), p. 111.

[8]J. David Lewis, "Programmer's Choice: Eight Factors in Program Decision-Making," *Journal of Broadcasting* 14 (Winter 1969–70): 72–82.

[9]Cole and Oettinger, *Reluctant Regulators*, p. 31.

[10]"Writer's Cramp," *Broadcasting* (August 7, 1972): 60.

[11]Joel Chaseman, address to the National Association of Television Program Executives, Las Vegas, Nev., March 1979.

[12]Federal Communications Commission, *Cable Television Syndicate Program Exclusivity Rules: Notice of Proposed Rule Making*, 44 F.R. 2834F (May 15, 1979). In mid-1980 the FCC eliminated the syndicated program exclusivity rules, but it is likely that this decision will be appealed.

ADDITIONAL PERIODICAL READINGS

Bagdikian, Ben H. "Pensions: The FCC's Dangerous Decision Against NBC." *Columbia Journalism Review* 12 (March/April 1974): 16–21.

Discussion of fairness-doctrine issues raised by the FCC's deci-sion against NBC's public affairs program, "Pensions: The Bro-ken Promises."

"The Broadcast Media and the Political Process: 1976." *Broadcasting* (January 3, 1977).

Special report on local and national campaign coverage with background material on "The Great Debates" of 1976.

Chamberlin, Bill F. "The Impact of Public Affairs Pro-gramming Regulation: A Study of the FCC's Effective-ness." *Journal of Broadcasting* 23 (Spring 1979): 197–212.

Evaluation of the effectiveness of seventy-five television stations in public affairs programming.

Pennybacker, John H. "The Format Change Issue: *FCC* vs. *U.S. Court of Appeals." Journal of Broadcasting* 22 (Fall 1978): 411–24.

History of the issue of radio format changes and the disagreement between the FCC and the United States Court of Appeals.

PART TWO
Television Station Programming Strategies

Part I contains principles of programming applicable to the spectrum of broadcasting situations. Part II looks at programming from station programmers' perspectives. Two of the authors are master programmers of a single type of station, one oversees a group of stations, and two recommend strategy to many stations. Of the five chapters, four examine programming of advertiser-supported stations and one deals with noncommercial stations, reflecting the historical dominance of broadcasting by commercial interests.

Chapter 4 introduces the current professional language of programming as used by commercial station management and programmers. The author writes from the viewpoint of an independent VHF station in a mid-to-large-sized market competing with three network affiliates. The three-affiliate/one-independent situation is typical of the top 150 markets; smaller markets may have fewer affiliates and no independent; very large markets (top fifty) frequently have more than one independent as well as affiliates of each of the three networks competing for key demographic groups and ratings. Only in the 1970s did independents in general advance from sleepers to full competitors—upsetting two decades of three-way market division by network affiliates. The strategies presented in Chapter 4 apply to markets with VHF or UHF independents. The author makes clear the limitations that cost constraints impose on the freedom of independents.

Chapter 5 counters with the programming strategy of network-affiliated stations. They are the most prominent type of station in the public's view because of their association with the networks and the fact that, until the 1970s, virtually all successful stations were affiliates. Affiliates still tend to have higher ratings, more public visibility, and make more money than do independents. The author of Chapter 5 programs a CBS affiliate in a top fifty market with three affiliates and a public station. He compares the strategy of the affiliate with that of other affiliates and independents within one market. He spells out the programming options for each daypart and emphasizes the specific decisions an affiliate programmer must make in each time period. The author then selects the treatment most likely to win ratings points for an affiliate that counterprograms two rival affiliates and a contending independent.

Group ownership refers to common ownership of two or more broadcasting stations. There are 165 group owners of television stations, averaging three television stations each; altogether they own half of the nation's television stations. The most conspicuous cases are the groups owned and operated by the national networks—O&O groups. The fifteen network-owned television stations (five owned by each of the three national networks—ABC, CBS, and NBC) are the flagships of the networks. Thus New York and Los Angeles stations represent peaks of financial success as well as programming visibility. Although network-owned stations have separate station managers and are not directly operated by the networks, obviously the ties between parent and offspring are close, and network management may participate in key station programming decisions.

Other group owners include some of the most prestigious broadcasting organizations in the business. Some examples, in addition to the national television network O&O groups, are Capital Cities Communications (six television, six AM, six FM), Cox Broadcasting (five, five, seven), General Electric (three, three, five), Metromedia (seven, six, seven), RKO General (four, six, six), Storer (seven, four, three), Taft (six, five, six), and Westinghouse Group W (five, seven, two). Group-owned stations vary from all network-affiliated (as in the case of Group W and Post-Newsweek) to all independent (Field Group) to a mix of affiliates and independents (Metromedia). Group-owned stations tend to be the most economically successful stations, in part because they can practice economics of scale and in part because they are usually in the largest and wealthiest markets. The author of Chapter 6 is executive vice-president of a television-only group of stations. He discusses the influences that group ownership can have on station programming and reports projections for the 1980s by other prominent group broadcasters.

Chapter 7 introduces another perspective—that of station representatives. Large full-service agencies consult on programming in addition to their advertising-sales functions. They are motivated to help their client stations with programming because stations in dominant market positions are easier to sell to advertisers. The job of "rep programmers" is to ensure that client stations' program schedules are salable. This in turn earns more money for the station representative firm. The author of this chapter was a television program consultant for a leading station representative firm, and he gives a clear picture of the contributions reps are making to station programming strategy.

Chapter 8 brings in the third type of television station that coexists in America with affiliates and independents—the public television station. Public stations themselves come in four major varieties, which are described by the author, an educational television consultant and expert who has professionally advised all four kinds of public stations. He delineates the complex territory of current noncommercial broadcasting and deals with many of the successes of public television broadcasting. His views on its future can be compared with those in Chapters 11 and 17 on national public television and public radio.

Each of the chapters in Part II focuses on one type of television station. Each differs from the others in philosophy, economics, and regulatory requirements that in turn create the need for diverse programming strategies. These chapters precede Part III on network programming in order to spell out the details of station daypart strategy. It is at the station that technical and legal responsibility for what is broadcast resides.

4 Independent Station Programming

Edward G. Aiken

Independent television stations lack clear definition in the eyes of the public. They are not associated with national newscasts or first-run entertainment programming, yet they do not share the cultural and service image of public broadcasters. They compete for commercial advertising dollars in the same market with network affiliates and generally must be satisfied with a smaller portion of the audience. Nevertheless, it is the independent station that has the full range of television programming options. Edward G. Aiken gained experience as producer/director and promotion manager at WBAY-TV in Green Bay, Wisconsin, before going to WNEM-TV in Saginaw, Michigan, as program director in 1970, and joining KPHO-TV in Phoenix, Arizona, in the same capacity in 1973. Having programmed both WNEM and KPHO, the author brings experience with midsized and large-market VHF stations to this chapter on independents. In 1980, Mr. Aiken became director of television programming for the Katz Agency, Inc. The options he describes apply to small-market stations and UHF independents as well as to larger-market UHFs. Mr. Aiken points out that from behind the smorgasbord of options available to the independent programmer, whatever the station size, beckons the unappetizing question of costs. As both purchase and production costs escalate, the research, teamwork, and vision of programmers, sales staffs, and management become the pivots of programming policy.

THE REALITIES OF INDEPENDENT TELEVISION

An **independent** television **station** provides a stimulating challenge to its program director since it has no automatic foundation for its **primetime** schedule in a **network** feed. However, an independent television station need not assume the posture of an economic stepchild. It may be next to impossible for an independent to achieve an overall number one rating against network **affiliates,** but an independent can reach number one ranking in key **dayparts**. A professionally programmed and managed independent with an equally professional, aggressive sales force can attain economic parity within a given market against network-affiliated stations. However, independent programmers must face two unhappy realities—high costs and negative buyer attitude—while learning to use the primary advantage that independents possess: scheduling flexibility.

For the most part, it is more costly to program an independent than a network-affiliated station. Virtually all the programs on an independent must be *purchased,* and their cost escalates at an ever-increasing rate. Stations now pay as much for an individual program series such as *Happy Days, Laverne & Shirley,* or *Maude* as they did for an entire week's schedule not many years ago.

National and local spot time-buyers look down their noses at most independents, making it hard for independents to earn their share of the advertisers' dollars. The buyers discount the **ratings**, arguing that there are "too many kids" or that "the women aren't watching" or that they "don't care what the books say," they "just don't believe people watch independents."

However, the important reality is that independents have scheduling flexibility because they are not tied to the program flow from a network. They can effectively (1) **counterprogram** the other stations in a market; (2) target specific audiences either not being served by the networks or not programmed for at times during the broadcast day convenient for the potential audience; and (3) create the perception among the audience that traditional programming which airs at nontraditional times is a viable alternative.

POSITIONING THE INDEPENDENT

Making the audience believe that the independent station is really different from its competitors is called **positioning** the station. When "in position," the audience holds the view that there really are only two choices for programs regardless of the number of stations—the independent and the others (network affiliates and other independents).

Experience teaches that independents establish their positions by creating "islands of success," using counterprogramming and **promotion**. To develop counterprogramming and promotional strategies, independent programmers must ask themselves what audiences are being served by the network affiliates or other independents in the market and what kinds of programs get sets turned on and tuned in.

For instance, research continually points to a substantial audience that does not watch news. They may not care about what goes on, may want their news in capsule form, or may prefer to be entertained. The independent programmer who selects the right kind of programming to counter the news on the network-affiliated stations can effectively establish an island of success of at least an hour's duration. It can extend up to 2 hours depending on how the competition programs. There are many other **dayparts** that present similar entrée for the independent programmer. Countering the late news and the plethora of weekend sports and public affairs on the networks with comedy/action/adventure programs or movies is good strategy.

An independent can counterprogram in an overall way by developing an image as a sports station featuring local, regional, professional, or amateur sports; as a movie station with films in virtually every daypart; or as a local news station, scheduling it in nontraditional time periods, concentrating on local news, and tying in local angles on national and international stories.

Borrowed and Bartered Programs

To build these islands of success, many strategies are used. But regardless of strategy, success requires money. Depending on the market and the competition, it may mean a lot of money—because an independent does not have a magic button labeled NET to supply up to 15 hours a day of programming. It also does not receive revenue from a network for carrying network programming. Depending on the relative performance of network programming within the market and the persuasive powers of the general manager, network revenues may go a long way towards paying affiliates' overhead and, in many instances, allow network-affiliated stations to operate with fewer personnel. The notable exceptions are those stations that choose to dive into the news game head and feet first to see who can outspend the other in people and equipment to gain a valuable rating point advantage. The independent, however, must pay cold, hard cash for almost everything it programs.

The exceptions to bought or independently produced programs are the relatively few "network" programs that the stations beg, borrow, or steal (1) from network-affiliated stations that from time to time **preempt** network programs, (2) from "independent networks" such as the one Mobil Oil set up for quality programs such as *Edward the King*, or (3) from special networks set up for sporting events like Hughes and Mizlou. The other exception consists of **bartered** programs, which are supposedly free but are in reality not free. Although there is no actual exchange of dollars from the station to the program supplier for bartered programs, something of equal and sometimes greater value is given to the supplier—inventory.

Television stations have two customers—viewers and advertisers. Without the first, it is difficult if not impossible to attract the second. Assuming the station attracts a reasonable number of viewers to its programming, it can sell time in or **adjacent** to its programs to advertisers. Time in this context is "inventory." The inventory of a television station (its salable time) acquires an arbitrary dollar value based on the rating each program achieves (or is expected to achieve if it is new programming or in a new time slot) by the station's sales management. The ability of the station to receive this dollar value is based on supply and demand for the program itself, the overall inventory position of the station, and the condition of the market as a whole. If a station pays cash for a program, it has the option of charging whatever it feels it can get from advertisers for the inventory within or adjacent to that program, and the station receives all the revenue generated by those sales efforts. But if the station barters for that program, it must give up part of that precious commodity—inventory—to the program supplier.

If the station, for example, pays a program supplier $1,000 per telecast for a program that has an inventory of 6 minutes within for sale and if the value of each of those 6 minutes, based on ratings and supply and demand, is $500, the total potential return to the station is $3,000 or a program cost-to-potential-return ratio of 33.33 percent. In the barter case, the program supplier says to the station, "I'll give you the program for no cash outlay. All I want is 2½ minutes for my clients, which you must incidentally protect against their competitors." Using the same value for those 6 minutes of $500 each, this program "costs" the station a total of $1,250 in inventory it cannot sell or a program cost-to-potential-return ratio of 41.7 percent. In addition, "protecting" the program distributor's clients against possible competitors restricts the station's sales effort. This places another roadblock in the path of the sales department.

The programmer must answer some rather critical questions concerning barter programming: is the cost-to-return ratio too high? Does the quality of the program in potential ratings and **lead-in** possibilities outweigh the cost ratio? Is this the only way to obtain the program? How many barter programs can the station afford at any given time?

A number of programs that formerly enjoyed successful runs on different networks have become available to independent stations via the barter route, some of the most notable being *Hee Haw, Lawrence Welk,* and *Wild Kingdom,* along with a list of game shows as long as an arm. The rationale for network cancellation of programs such as the three named are many and curious. They range from "It skews too young" to "It skews too old" or "That's not our image." All three did well in household rating points and **share** of audience and continue to do as well (and in some markets better) in syndication as they did on the networks. Such programs can form the islands of success that underpin an independent program schedule, whether obtained for cash or as barters. However obtained, there are three basic forms of program material that dominate independent programming: **syndicated** programs, **local** programs, and movies.

Syndicated Programs

Varying in length—15, 30, 60, 90 minutes—**syndicated** programs range in cost-effectiveness from the "bread and butter" to the "caviar" of an independent station. The bread-and-butter programs are those that have a relatively low cost in relation to potential return on a per-run basis. Virtually all **off-network syndicated** programs are bought on a multiple-run basis; the most cost-efficient ones are those that are **strip-**

pable (a series run Monday to Friday or Sunday to Saturday in the same time period). The most successful syndicated program type on independent stations is the **sit-com** that has a **kiddult** appeal. It appeals to both children and adults, especially women 18 to 34 or 18 to 49.

Children and women dominate the early **fringe** (4 to 7 P.M. or 5 to 8 P.M. audience, depending on the time zone) in which spot time-buyers look not only at household rating points but also at specific **demographics**, most often women 18 to 34 or 18 to 49. The kids in the audience provide the bulk of household rating points while the women in the audience give programs salability to advertisers. Programs such as *Brady Bunch, My Three Sons, I Dream of Jeannie,* and *Bewitched* and oldies but goodies such as *I Love Lucy, Dick Van Dyke,* and *Andy Griffith* fall into this category.

Syndicated programs with primary appeal to kids such as *Gilligan's Island* and *Little Rascals* and various cartoons such as *Bugs Bunny* and *Tom and Jerry* have proven to work well for independents in midafternoon (2:30 to 4:00 or 5:00 P.M.). Kids take control of television sets immediately after they come home from school; it is crucial for an independent station to entice as many children as possible into tuning its signal as early as possible, in order to hold them through the early fringe viewing time.

Deciding which off-network shows will work in a given market often is highly frustrating for programmers. Considerations include (1) the rating and share of a program while it was on the network—both nationally and in the market in which it will play when purchased; (2) the time period(s) in which the program has the best opportunity to prove itself cost-efficient; (3) whether the program will have enough staying power as a strip; and (4) whether the program will do better as a strip, a single, or a two-time-per-week entry. In the best of circumstances and given the maximum of research and historical data, programmers sometimes must rely on intuition and their best professional judgment. The historical data needed to document each program in each market is not available from Arbitron or Nielsen at affordable prices.

Adult-oriented game shows such as *Newlywed Game* and *Family Feud* have experienced ratings success in early fringe, in **access** time, against late news, and in late fringe (10:30 or 11:30 P.M., depending on time zone). These programs are especially attractive to a potential advertiser since they deliver an audience that is predominantly young adults (men/women 18 to 34 and 18 to 49). Action/adventure types such as *Gunsmoke, Rookies, Big Valley,* and *Star Trek* work well in early fringe, in primetime, in early afternoon (as strips), and on weekends as counterprogramming to network sports. They generally attract a woman-dominated audience, which counters the man-dominated audience of most sports programming.

Another bread-and-butter programming type for independent stations is the talk/variety program such as *Merv Griffin, Mike Douglas, Dinah Shore,* and *Phil Donahue.* All these programs except *Phil Donahue* have success stories in virtually every daypart. *Donahue* seems to work best in the morning between 9 A.M. and noon; however, some experimenting has been done in access time with success. A few dramatic programs also have an appeal to independent stations because they fall into the category of **soap operas**—the most successful of which has been *Marcus Welby, M.D.*

The caviar programs are a 1970s innovation due mainly to a superior marketing technique developed by Paramount Television Sales under Dick Lawrence and later, Rich Frank. The off-network syndication rights to both *Happy Days* and *Laverne & Shirley* were sold as **futures**, and the amount of revenue generated by Paramount put them in a class by themselves.

The buying of futures is a strategy filled with potholes of danger for both the syndicator and the station. In theory and practice it works as follows: the syndicator has or purchases the rights to sell a certain series for airing by individual stations either after the series's network run or by a certain date even though the series may continue on the network after going into syndication. This occurs after a program has had a successful run on the network for three or four years—in some instances, only two or three years. The syndicator assumes the series will continue for a minimum of five years on the network. With the current network schedule of about twenty-two original programs each year, the syndicator has a minimum of 110 episodes to sell for stripping, allowing for 2.36 runs per program per year based on 260 exposures (strip-slots) per year. The more episodes produced beyond 110, the much more valuable the series becomes to both the syndicator and the purchasing stations. The series brings a greater dollar return to the syndicator, and it requires fewer repeats in a year's time, which the station can **amortize** for a better return on dollar expended.

Until *Happy Days* was offered for syndication, pricing of series was determined for the most part by a formula for each market, as applied to the entire country, times the number of dollars the syndicator paid out for the rights to distribute and sales costs plus profits. Paramount changed all that with *Happy Days.* Seeing the potential for the program to generate not only large household rating points, but also key demographics (children, teens, women 18 to 34 and 18 to 49, men 18 to 49), they elected to market it on a what-the-market-will-bear or supply-and-demand basis. Since there was only one *Happy Days* series with unique potential for attracting the kind of audiences stations could sell at premium prices and since several individual stations in many markets competed for the opportunity to program it, Paramount let the marketplace determine the price after setting a minimum starting point. The strategy worked: *Happy Days* became the most successful syndicated program in broadcast history—sold at premium prices to be played two to three years from the time the commitment was made.

Many independent stations bid for the program to use it to establish a franchise for themselves in prime access time. Affiliated stations were prevented from playing off-network programs in access. The independent stations could charge more for spot advertising within *Happy Days* and/or demand that an advertiser take a less desirable program availability concurrent with advertising in *Happy Days*. Only time and the whims of the viewing audience will determine whether a station made the correct decision. Later, Paramount used the same marketing technique for *Laverne & Shirley*. The prices paid for *Laverne & Shirley* have far exceeded those for *Happy Days* and stand today as the hallmark for syndicated program pricing (as much as $65,000 per episode in 1979).

Movies

Considered to be the most cost-efficient form of programming available, movies allow the independent programmer considerable flexibility with a relatively low cost. They fill many hours of independent schedules and allow the programmer to go after target audiences, generally segmented on the basis of sex and age.

Movie watchers tend to be women, 18 to 34 or 18 to 49, especially if the title is familiar or the star value of the movie is strong enough. One successful strategy is to create "theme" weeks, generating a desire to watch through heavy promotion. These theme weeks can range from "monsters we all know and love" to "beautiful ladies week."

Movies also have the built-in flexibility for being either stripped or **stacked**. Stacking allows a programmer to air many hours of the same *kind* of program in one day while varying the *type* every few hours. KPHO-TV (Phoenix, Arizona), for instance, has aired a 7-hour **block** of movies on Saturdays for many years with great success by targeting for specific audiences:

9:00 A.M.	*Saturday Morning Movie*	The type of movies selected for this particular showcase appeal to kids (getting the set away from the traditional cartoon fare on competing network-affiliated stations). It also attracts young adults. Examples are Tarzan movies, *East Side Kids*, Lassie.
10:30 A.M.	*World Beyond*	Science fiction and monster films will attract kids, teens, men and women 18 to 34.
12:00 noon	*Action Theatre*	Western, war, and sword-and-

sandal films have been very
successful in attracting men and
women 18 to 49. Particular attention
is given to picking titles with big
name stars such as John Wayne or
James Stewart.

2:00 P.M.   *Adventure Theatre*   This is similar to Action Theatre
with the added dimension of
thrillers and long-form sci-fi. It has
greatest appeal to men and women
18 to 49.

Stacking is most successful when used as a thematic showcase
device and allows the programmer to select titles for specific showcases
when purchasing movies, thus further increasing the cost-efficiency of
movie programming.

Local Programs

Local programs may be as inexpensive or expensive as the station
chooses and may take as many forms as syndicated programs or movies.
These include (1) public affairs, (2) news, (3) sports of a local or regional
nature, (4) children's programs, (5) women's interest, (6) musical variety, or if the station is so inclined and well heeled enough, (7) drama.

1. *Public Affairs:* Of all the possible program types, this is the
one with which independent stations have the best opportunity to excel.
As someone once said, "Public affairs need not be dull affairs." An
inspired public affairs department in an independent television station
can show what television can do at its best, if management permits.
Costs are the main factor in the decision-making process as far as public
affairs programming is concerned. It is difficult to sell public affairs
programs to advertisers, and most stations refuse to invest time, personnel, and money in non-revenue-producing programs. The forms
that best demonstrate public affairs commitment are the documentary
and **magazine formats**. These require people and equipment costs that
will reflect the amount of commitment on the part of management. Very
few UHF independents do more than a bare minimum of public affairs.

2. *News:* News can be approached with a simple **rip-and-read**
formula or as a sophisticated, expensive, competitive information showcase. One practice is to program it in nontraditional hours. If the "late"
news traditionally airs on competing network affiliates at 10 (C/MST) or
11 (EST) P.M., successful independents program their news at 9 or 9:30
P.M. in the central/mountain time zones or 10 or 10:30 P.M. in the eastern
and western time zones. This allows viewers to see the news on the
independent and allows the independent to position itself in two different time periods, counterprogramming news against entertainment on

the affiliated stations and entertainment against newscasts on the affiliated stations. The following independents use this strategy by placing their news earlier than network-affiliated stations in their markets:

New York		
WNEW	10:00 P.M.	
WPIX	10:00 P.M.	
Los Angeles		
KTLA	10:00 P.M.	
KHJ	10:00 P.M.	
KTTV	10:00 P.M.	
KCOP	10:00 P.M.	
Indianapolis		
WTTV	9:30 P.M.	
Denver		
KWGN	9:30 P.M.	
Phoenix		
KPHO	9:30 P.M.	
Tucson		
KZAZ	9:30 P.M.	

News programs show wide cost variance depending on the approach the station chooses to take. If the rip-and-read approach is used, the cost factor is minimal. A 60-second update every three or four hours with a news reader giving details under a slide or series of slides creates no problems.

When an independent takes the expensive, sophisticated, and thus competitive approach, it involves hiring a full-time staff of at least a news director, an assignment editor/coordinator, and a producer plus weather/news/sports anchors and reporters, photographers, editors, and writers. The exact numbers of each will vary with the areas to be covered and the depth of news treatment desired.

Equipment looms as the next cost consideration. If the station opts to go the ENG (electronic newsgathering) route, thousands—even hundreds of thousands—of dollars will have to be expended, especially if the station chooses to have live capability by means of microwave. The national/international news service for independent stations, the Independent Television News Association (ITNA), requires an **earth station** to receive satellite signals, which also adds capital outlay. The cost for an earth receiver station varies according to the sophistication needed and wanted by the station. It can range from $75,000 (plus site) to $200,000. The station can have many options, such as mechanical movability from one satellite to another, an **uplink** to provide transmit capability, multiple **transponder** receivers (channels) on each satellite, and redundancy in both **uplinks** and **downlinks**. Additionally, if the station is located in an area with heavy microwave signals, shielding of the station will add costs.

Although some VHF independent television stations have been relatively successful with news, especially when programmed at non-traditional times,* few compete in household rating points with network-affiliated stations. This is due to the audience perception that independents cannot or do not do news as well as the affiliates. This perception persists although analysis of an independent newscast is likely to show no difference from a network-affiliated newscast in reporting style, content, or overall quality.

This audience myth has proven a stumbling block for many independents trying to program news head-to-head with affiliated stations; it has caused independents to abandon the head-to-head strategy in favor of the nontraditional time period. The notable exception is WGN-TV in Chicago, which continues to program news at 10 P.M. against the network-affiliated stations—although it still rates fourth in the market. In the May 1979 Arbitron at 10 P.M. (Monday–Friday average), the Chicago stations performed as follows:

Station	Rating
WLS (ABC)	20
WBBM (CBS)	18
WMAQ (NBC)	12
WGN (IND)	5

Of the fifty-five news rating points available, WGN-TV, one of the biggest and best independents in the United States, could garner only a 5 rating and a 9 share.

3. *Sports:*   Identification with sports in a market has been the hallmark of some of the most successful independent stations in the country: WGN, Chicago; WTCN, Minneapolis (now an NBC affiliate); WOR, New York; and KTTV, Los Angeles. Independents have the scheduling flexibility to accommodate sporting events, which occur during virtually every daypart. Sports attract a desirable demographic target (men 18 to 34 and 18 to 49) and a number of advertisers are willing to pay premium prices to be identified with a televised sport because it sells their products. This fact makes sports programming a hot strategy for a number of independent stations.

Sports programming can take one of three cost approaches: A wealthy station can purchase the rights to the telecasts from the team,

*These stations include WGN, Chicago; WPIX, New York; KPHO, Phoenix; KWGN, Denver; and WTTG, Washington.

add on the cost of producing each game including talent (play-by-play, color) and the cost of delivering the signal, both video and audio, back to the station (by AT&T Long Lines, satellite, or a combination of both). This is a very expensive route, but the potential return in revenue is the greatest. Risks come from (1) not selling all the availabilities, reducing the potential profit, and (2) the team's place in the won/lost column (in some markets, place determines ratings, which in turn determine advertiser support). In another option, the team itself assumes all costs for production and delivery and pays the station for the time. With this method all dollar risks are assumed by the team, but it also stands to reap the potential profits. However, the station airs the games, gets paid for the time, and in the minds of viewers gets the credit for bringing them the games. In the third possibility, an outside producer/syndicator pays the team for the rights to telecast, sells part of the available time within the games, and barters with the station for the time.

The ideal time for sports programming on independents is primetime (7 to 10 P.M. or 8 to 11 P.M.), since this is when the independent traditionally does not do well against network competition. An independent carrying a lot of sports programming takes risks because the audience composition for sports tends to skew to men both during the game and following. Since women are the primary target of most advertisers, the station may lose out on potential sales.

4. *Children's Programs:*   Children's programming of a local nature has been very successful for independents in both revenue and ratings. During certain dayparts (early morning and afternoon), a great deal of set control is exercised by children. Although the rising costs of live programs eat away at the profit margin, there are some workable formats for local live children's programs. What is crucial is identifying which segment of the children's audience the station wants to attract: preschool, grades one through four, grades five through eight, or high school. High schoolers are the most difficult to reach since they are the most fickle in their viewing habits. Preschoolers require sophisticated, well-researched material, obtainable at considerable cost. The age groups easiest to program for are grades one through four and five through eight. Costs vary depending on the complexity of the production, with the major cost being talent and studio time. Care must be given to proper continuity acceptance standards (vocabulary level, pacing, intensity and type of sales pitches, and so on) so as not to take advantage of the audience.

5. *Women's Interest:*   The daytime audience in most markets is made up primarily of women, and a number of them are looking to television to give them more than just entertainment. They want to be informed, enlightened, and challenged, and a stimulating local live (or taped) program can do all three if properly produced.

Local programs that appeal to women are fairly easy to produce and in most instances not overly costly. The foremost ingredient is the producer/host or hostess. This person must be in tune with what is happening in the community that will be of interest to and challenging for area women. The least expensive way of producing the shows is in the studio with brought-in guests. More expensive in time, equipment, and people is the **remote**, using ENG equipment to relay (or tape) some or all of the material from the places at which the activities occur.

6. *Musical Variety:*   These programs can be successful in varying degrees depending on the market. For every type of music there is an audience, although some types attract very small audiences. In certain parts of the Midwest, for example, polka music attracts a loyal and rather large audience on television; country music draws enthusiastic audiences in the South and Southwest. Musical variety programs are fairly inexpensive to produce because they can be done in the station's studio using local talent. The largest expense comes from the musicians' fees as determined by the local musicians' union. The rest of the costs (sets, props) can be spread out over the run of the show. This kind of programming has many places on the schedule as its audience tends to seek out the program rather than the station having to seek out the audience.

7. *Drama:*   On a local level, drama is a very ambitious undertaking and should be examined in detail before proceeding. The most expensive items involved are time and people. Rehearsals take up a large amount of time; some personnel from the station must be present, especially the director who must block the play for television and rehearse all the technical people. Although tackling drama can be professionally satisfying, it is very expensive, has a poor cost-to-return ratio, and is rarely done.

THE RISK

Independent programmers must be constantly alert to all the foregoing program possibilities if they expect to compete effectively within their marketplaces. Being aware of product is only the first step however; programmers must aggressively pursue and be willing to take a chance on programs their judgment says will "work" in their markets. The establishment of ongoing candid relationships with program suppliers and producers is of paramount importance. Without those pipelines, independent programmers will find themselves out in the cold. Keeping in touch with the business means making time to read about trends and tastes and to learn what is going on in the production centers of Los Angeles and New York.

The short-term effect of a lack of programs means programmers spend more for a program than they normally would, thus eroding the profit margin; an even worse option is scheduling programs that do not attract a large enough audience and have the effect of reducing advertising revenue, also eroding the profit margin. The long-term effect of not having access to programs is that the programmer cannot plan on a long-range basis.

PROGRAMMING AND SALES AT THE INDEPENDENT

It is imperative for the programmer at an independent station to become familiar with and involved in sales. Finding out about, aggressively seeking out, purchasing, and effectively scheduling a program that the sales department (for whatever reason) cannot sell is an exercise in futility—a waste of time, effort, and money. When making plans for the future, the programmer must know what budgets spot advertisers have, what target demographics are sought by each advertiser, and what effect the economic development of the country, region, or local area is likely to have on advertising budgets. All this depends on a firm knowledge of which programs appeal to national advertisers and which to local advertisers. Ideal programs, of course, do both.

An ongoing working dialogue between the programmer and the sales manager should cover subjects such as rating potentials or projections, pricing for spots within programs, budgets for both national and local advertisers, advertiser resistance to certain programs or time periods, recommendations on spot versus sponsored programs, and methods of selling programs other than the traditional **cost per thousand**, cost per point, and cost per person. With the high cost of programming today and higher forecasts for the future, it is crucial for programmers to know the revenue potential for a program before it is purchased. This requires an open relationship with sales management.

Obvious questions arise when certain programs cannot be sold by an effective sales team. One explanation is that a program may be scheduled in a time period not meshing with an advertiser's planned marketing campaign. For instance, if a series of advertisers devise a marketing plan to break during the middle part of the second quarter of a given year, but the television station schedules a program that would be an obvious "buy" for those advertisers in the first part of the second quarter, the advertisers are automatically eliminated because their marketing campaigns do not correspond with the planned airing of the program. Another problem comes from **buying** or creating a program with an initial high cost that demands a premium price from advertisers but which appeals to advertisers with marketing plans that exclude premium prices. Much time and effort, to say nothing of money, can be fruitlessly expended in seeking out, negotiating for, and eventually buying the license rights to programming that subsequently proves to be nonsalable.

RESEARCH AT THE INDEPENDENT

If effective communication with program suppliers is the lifeblood for the independent programmer, research is the nerve center. Independent programmers need every scrap of research material they can lay their hands on to leaven the mix at decision-making time. First and foremost of the information crucial to the independent programmer is how an off-network program performed in a given market, especially the market in which that programmer operates.

Tracking an off-network program in similar markets is essential to learning how that program might perform in a given market. The programmer can check the Arbitron and Nielsen ratings books for the essential information on how the program performed in rating, share, total women, women from 18 to 34 and from 18 to 49, total men, men from 18 to 34 and 18 to 49, teens, kids from 2 to 11, and kids from 6 to 11. Although a program may perform very well on the national level, it may not necessarily have appeal in a particular market. The opposite can hold as well: a program may perform very poorly on a nationwide basis, but a given region or market may have an affinity for it. The independent programmer needs to track that kind of information. National ratings are available through both Nielsen and Arbitron as well as from the research done by the syndicators. Although this information should be taken with a certain amount of salt, it is an additional input for the decision-making process.

Programmers cannot operate in a vacuum; it takes an effective team of program manager, sales manager, and general manager working in concert to bring dividends in both audience shares and revenue. Often the perspective of the general manager is 180 degrees from that of the programmer or the sales manager; then the effective programmer must communicate to the general manager and/or sales manager the rationale for programming decisions. Sometimes personal likes and dislikes enter into the picture, and raw research data and extracted data become the tools for determining whether a program should be actively sought and purchased and how it should be scheduled. Independent stations especially must face the reality that successful business managers faced many years ago: monies must be set aside for research and development; chances must be taken with fresh, innovative programming; and imagination must never go out of the programmer's approach to doing business.

OUTSIDE CONSTRAINTS

Most programmers are vividly aware of the numerous constraints imposed on them by various individuals, groups, and circumstances of the moment. Specifically, budget and equipment limitations may force the programmer not to buy and schedule a particular program simply because the station cannot afford it.

The independent programmer also should be aware of the constraints, rules, and regulations (of the Federal Communications Commission, the Federal Trade Commission, the National Association of Broadcasters, and others) imposed on independents and be prepared to work within these constraints. Chapter 3 details regulatory constraints, but independents have some special interests.

At license application time, independents, like other stations, make promises to the FCC about what percentage of each program type they will present. Independent programmers must keep an ongoing record of whether these promises are being kept. An excellent way of tracking this is to do a mini FCC license renewal within the station either quarterly or semiannually. Examining a typical week of logs will tell if the station is performing at or above the level promised to the FCC. Changes can be made either by notifying the FCC of altered promises, which may be politically disadvantageous, or by the more obvious method of changing the programming.

The Federal Trade Commission (FTC) is entering the world of the independent as well as of the network affiliate. Government bureaucracy is inserting itself in children's programming, children's advertising, and truth in lending. Government bureaucracy continues to be a deadweight around the necks of independent and affiliated stations. To keep apprised of events at all levels of government requires time, effort, and money, but they are time, effort, and money well invested. The Independent Television Station Association (INTV) and the National Association of Broadcasters (NAB) provide programming guidelines that should be followed.

Pressures from within the community are also an area of concern and importance to the independent programmer. Organizations such as ACT, NOW, NAACP, Urban League, LULAC, and Chicanos Por La Causa are all out to "have their day in court" with the media. They represent needs that independent programmers must be willing and able to address in their programming. Independent stations are no less responsible for addressing these needs than are affiliated stations. In some respects, independents are even preferred vehicles because of their flexibility in programming and concurrent ability to make time available in nontraditional time periods.

THE INDEPENDENT FUTURE

One of the most severe problems facing an independent programmer today is the growing dearth of **off-network syndicated** programming available for stripping. The high cost of production coupled with network cancellations of programs that do not perform at a given national rating and share level has diminished the supply of strippable programs. Although there is some relief available to independent stations from minimethods such as Operation Prime Time (*Testimony of Two Men, The Bastard, The Rebels,* and other such first-run products), it is not sufficient to meet the insatiable product appetite of independent stations. Not enough proven product becomes available. This could lead to a situation parallel to that of radio in the early 1960s; radio stations recognized that they could not be all things to all people all the time and consequently specialized in single **formats**. Independent stations may have to become specialty stations such as "the movie station" or "the sports station" to survive in the future.

ADDITIONAL PERIODICAL READINGS

"BM/E's Program Marketplace." *Broadcast Management/ Engineering,* monthly series, January 1977 to date.
Profiles of program syndicators.

Dengler, Ralph. "The Language of Film Titles." *Journal of Communication* (Summer 1975): 51–60.
A content analysis by title of nearly 8,000 American movies suggesting a shift in style from the "public and good" to the "personal and perverse."

"Facts of Life for Feature Buyers: More Made-for-TVs, More Runs Before Syndication." *Television/Radio Age* (March 12, 1979): 101–03 ff.
Discussion of the shortage of new theatrical films resulting in more made-for-television movies being produced for networks and offered for syndication.

"Independents." *Broadcasting* (January 30, 1978): 41–64.
Special report on the profits and programming of independent television stations.

Jones, Kenneth K., and **Kimmel, Joel K.** "How Cable (and Small UHFers) Can Compete in Programming." *Television/Radio Age* (March 13, 1978): 31 ff.
Analysis of the advertising dollars and audience shares potentially available to cable franchises and small UHF independents.

Korn, Alexander, and **Korn, Stanley D.** "A Look at the

Economics of a New Independent Television Station Entering the Market" and "Adding One More Independent TV Station to the Market: What's the Success Potential?" *Television/Radio Age* (June 6, 1977): 29 ff., (July 18, 1977): 32 ff.

Parts one and two based on a report to the Federal Communications Commission on the "Economics of New Entry of Independent Stations into Television Markets" (Docket No. 20418).

Rosenthal, Edmond M. "As List of Independents Grows, 'Fourth Market' for National Advertising Develops Gradually." *Television/Radio Age* (January 30, 1978): 66 ff.

Analysis of the economic stability of independent stations and prognosis for future growth.

Rosenthal, Edmond M. "More Indie Newscasts Get Solid Audiences, Thanks to Satellite, Time Period, 'Tight' News." *Television/Radio Age* (January 29, 1979): 59 ff.

Overview of news on independent television stations.

Sobel, Robert. "Prosperity for Indies Is Well in Evidence." *Television/Radio Age* (January 29, 1979): 55 ff.

A look at the economic position of independent television stations, briefly mentioning superstations.

"UHF: TV's Last Frontier." *Broadcasting* (February 26, 1979): 43–80.

Special report on all phases of UHF including competition in programming.

5 Network Affiliate Programming

John A. Haldi

> *The kind of station that typifies television to the general
> public is the network affiliate. Of more than 1,000 television
> stations in the United States, 212 are affiliated with ABC, 198
> with CBS, and 197 with NBC (as of 1979). Individual stations
> associate more closely in the minds of their viewers with the
> network names than with the station call letters. This occurs in
> part because affiliates air between 10 and 20 hours per day of
> network programming, leaving very few hours in which to de-
> velop unique local images. John A. Haldi, vice-president of pro-
> gramming for WBNS-TV, Columbus, Ohio, analyzes the prime
> tools of the affiliate—early-morning, late-afternoon, and late-
> night programming and noon-evening-night news—to suggest
> strategies for advancing an affiliate to top position in a market. He
> has served on the Board of Directors of the National Association
> of Television Program Executives (NATPE) and was elected presi-
> dent of the organization in 1966. His honors include receiving the
> 1966 Governors' Award by the Columbus, Ohio, chapter of the
> National Academy of Television Arts and Sciences and being a
> nominee for "Man of the Year" by the National Association of
> Television Program Executives in 1972. WBNS-TV has won nu-
> merous awards for broadcasting excellence under his leadership,
> demonstrating this author's status as a master of television pro-
> gramming strategy.*

AFFILIATE-NETWORK RELATIONS

In programming a **network-affiliated station**, the program director should regard the network schedule merely as another source,
much in the same manner as **independent** station programmers view a
major source of **syndicated** programming. A local station enters an
affiliation agreement with a network to carry the network's programs in
exchange for money that the network pays to the local station for
carrying its programming. It sounds simple, but an affiliation is more
like a marriage—until cancellation. Cancellation is like divorce without
alimony. Just ask some of those exaffiliates whose networks deserted
them for another station in the market, driving them into independent
station status.

The network connection means more than receiving money for
each show a station carries. By carrying the network programs, the

affiliated station automatically has commercial **availabilities** (unsold spot time) around and within these network programs. The more popular the network programs, the more the affiliate can charge for these spots. Networking and affiliating are big business and, again like marriage, it takes more than a paper agreement to make it work for both parties.

The television affiliation agreement differs for each network, but in general it contains the following elements:

1. The affiliate shall have first call on all network programs.

2. Acceptance or rejection of these programs must be made within two weeks or a minimum of 72 hours for certain programs by notifying the network accordingly. Upon receiving a rejection of a program, the network has the right to offer the rejected program to another television station in the same market.

3. The network obligation to deliver the programs is subject to the network's ability to make arrangements satisfactory to it for such delivery.

4. The network agrees to pay the affiliate on the basis of an established affiliated station's network rate. This rate is reached by analyzing the market size, audience reach of the station, and other elements that measure the effectiveness of the station in the local area.

5. Payment for each network commercial program broadcast over the affiliated station during "live time" is based on a percentage table similar to this:

Monday through Friday	Percent of Affiliate Station's Network Rate
7:00 A.M.–11:15 A.M.	7
11:15 A.M.– 5:00 P.M.	12
5:00 P.M.– 6:00 P.M.	15
6:00 P.M.–11:00 P.M.	32

Saturday	
8:00 A.M.– 9:00 A.M.	7
9:00 A.M.– 2:00 P.M.	12
5:00 P.M.– 6:00 P.M.	15
6:00 P.M.–11:00 P.M.	32

Sunday

4:00 P.M.– 5:00 P.M. 12
5:00 P.M.– 6:00 P.M. 15
6:00 P.M.–11:00 P.M. 32
11:00 P.M.–11:30 P.M. 15

In addition to this chart of payments, there are other variations of payment and deductions for BMI and ASCAP music license fees.

6. The agreement also has a paragraph that allows the network to reduce the affiliated station's network rates in general if market conditions change. The network will give the affiliate at least thirty days' notice, in which event the broadcaster may terminate the agreement within a predetermined time period.

7. The network agrees to make payments reasonably promptly within a monthly accounting period.

8. The broadcaster agrees to submit reports related to the broadcasting of network programs.

9. The term of this agreement is fixed by Federal Communications Commission (FCC) rules to a two-year term with prescribed periods during the agreement at which time either party can notify the other of termination. If everyone concurs, the agreement is automatically renewed for another two-year cycle.

10. In the case of a broadcaster desiring to transfer its license to another party, the network retains the right to examine the new owner before deciding whether to honor the change.

11. The agreement also lists conditions under which the affiliate will carry the network programs; **clipping**, reselling, or altering any of the contents of network shows is prohibited.

12. The rights of the broadcaster are also itemized:

a. The broadcaster can refuse or reject any network program that is reasonably unsatisfactory or unsuitable or contrary to the public interest.
b. The broadcaster has the right to substitute programs in lieu of the network's, if the substitution is considered, in the broadcaster's opinion, of greater local or national importance. The network, in turn, has the right to substitute or cancel programs as it feels necessary.

13. The network is obligated to disclose information to the broadcaster of any money, service, or consideration accepted by the network in the preparation of the network's programs. This is in response to Section 317 of the Communications Act of 1934.

14. The network also agrees to indemnify the broadcaster from and against all claims, damages, liabilities, costs, and expenses arising out of the broadcasting of network programs that result in alleged libel, slander, defamation, invasion of privacy, or violation or infringement of copyright, literary, or dramatic rights involved in programs furnished by the network.

While this condensation of a television affiliation agreement is brief, it reflects the basic considerations involved in the partnership between an affiliate and its network.

The network should be thought of as a supplementary programming source for the local station. It is the job of the program director to make up the local schedule according to the licensee's commitment to the FCC and to blend with it programs provided by the network, coming up with a schedule that (1) answers the needs of the community, (2) makes a profit for the local station owners, and (3) advances the station to the status of number one outlet in the market.

In a three-station market with a PBS affiliate as the fourth entity, a programmer is in a more permissive position than programmers in areas with more than four stations. Nevertheless, the principles of programming an affiliate are valid and workable in any size market.

WEEKDAY PROGRAMMING OPTIONS

The heartbeat of the local station starts around 6 A.M. and extends usually to about 2 A.M. the next morning. This means twenty hours per day of programming for seven days every week. The broadcast weekday is made up of the following time segments (EST):

1. 6:00 A.M.–9:00 A.M.: early morning

2. 9:00 A.M.–12:00 noon: morning

3. 12:00 noon–4:00 P.M.: afternoon

4. 4:00 P.M.–6:00 P.M.: late afternoon or early fringe

5. 6:00 P.M.–7:30 P.M.: early evening

6. 7:30 P.M.–8:00 P.M.: prime access time

7. 8:00 P.M.–11:00 P.M.: primetime

8. 11:00 P.M.–11:30 P.M.: late evening or late fringe

9. 11:30 P.M.–2:00 A.M.: late night

These time periods are accepted zones for Arbitron and Nielsen testing of viewership in the East and are used by sales departments for selling commercial time segments throughout each day. The choices that exist for all programming persons who are network affiliated differ according to which time segment is involved.

Early Morning (6 to 9 A.M.)

The programming strategies for 6 to 9 A.M. are very simple. The program director for the station in first place in the **ratings** will probably ignore it. The competing program directors have five options:

1. When news is leading the time period, the following can be tried: **local** or children's programming will attract a segment of the audience that is not being reached. A local live 30- or 60-minute program will find favor with the FCC and encourage sales during the fall and spring quarters of the sales year.

2. Paid religious programming will bring dollars and figure into the FCC's "other" category; however, it will account for only minor ratings in the 6 to 9 A.M. time period.

3. A successful ploy in several markets has been to invest in a women-oriented program that can start as a 1-hour entry and expand to 2 full hours (from 8 to 10 A.M.) when it is ripe for expansion. This local reflection is most successful when directed specifically toward the female audience remaining alone after families have left for school and work. The 8 A.M. start is advantageous because it **bridges** the 9 A.M. slot that *Phil Donahue* has managed to "own" throughout the United States. A women's show is also highly salable every week in the year. Women's programming can have frequent community-oriented segments that are applicable to FCC commitments. A good example is WEWS-TV's *Morning Exchange*, 8 to 10 A.M., Monday through Friday.

4. The most expensive and risky gamble is to challenge a network with a full-blown local news/talk program. This is recommended only if the market is rich with talent, visitors, and money to justify the expense. So far, no local station has been successful in this 6 to 8 A.M. time period.

5. If the program director is desperate, nonentertainment material such as public affairs, instructional, educational,

and agricultural programs can serve immediate needs and free the program director to walk away from the time to address the problem of grabbing a bigger audience after 9 A.M.

Morning (9 to Noon)

This is a frightful time period that has housed *Dinah Shore, Merv Griffin, Mike Douglas,* syndicated hours, **sit-coms**, network repeats and delays, syndicated half hours, and children's programming. The audience during this time is mainly preschoolers and homemakers, and the homemaker is the main advertising target. Stations having *Phil Donahue* during this time period have no problems. These are the alternative options:

> 1. Write off the station's investment in syndicated properties (after use elsewhere in the schedule) by placing them very carefully from 9 to 10 or 10:30; then join the network until noon.

> 2. Develop a strong local live show that can accordionize up into the morning as the audience grows. A women's service program with provocative overtones with the right talent and program segments could capture the audience that leans to magazines for information and emotional stimuli. This is expensive but worth a try because such a program can be very salable once it gets off the ground.

> 3. Many markets have tried a movie from 9 to 10:30, using the ABC afternoon movie editing formula (shortened to 90 minutes) which has been successful in the 4:30 to 6 P.M. period. This has been mildly successful depending on the competition, but it appears that the female audience of the late 1970s did not support the 90 minutes to make this a predictably winning formula.

In the 1970s the 9 A.M. to noon time period has been characterized by passive viewing, a condition in which viewers often leave the room to perform household tasks. The syndicators and local stations have not been able to find the ideal structure to capture the available audience well enough to separate themselves from their competitors. More research is needed, but it is likely that a locally produced program, reflecting the local community, would take the marbles once it establishes a structure that the female audience could not afford to miss viewing. The networks provide game shows, and only one network dominates in any part of the morning—ABC, with reruns of its **kiddult** nighttime programs (light sit-coms appealing to both children and adults) during the 11 to 11:30 A.M. period. Properties such as the reruns of *Happy Days* and *Laverne & Shirley* have hit the mark.

With the technical innovation of the **minicam**, morning programs using live cameras become an option; portable cameras could take the viewer to private or hidden parts of the local area to entrance the audience by showing areas that it had never been able to see. Soft features mixed with government and human interest elements (to direct the rest of their day's activities) could provide the daytime audience with insight into what goes on in their communities. The major-market stations (such as those in Boston, Los Angeles, and Cleveland) have attempted to do this, but because they favor specific local regions, there has been no universality in the subject matter.

Afternoon (Noon to 4 P.M.)

There are several programming possibilities for this time period:

1. Noon news is popular with the stay-at-home audience and expected because radio provides it. The group that goes home for lunch and the pause that occurs at noon in at-home activities create an ideal information slot. Noon coverage of world and local activities is a ritual, as much for stations as for the audience. Stations that aspire to leadership in news coverage cannot omit the noontime period. It makes good money in spot sales and justifies the large news expenditures that most stations experience because much of the material can be reused at 6 and 11 P.M. (or is drawn from preceding news shows).

2. An afternoon movie was always popular with audiences in the 1950s and 1960s. Most affiliates have abandoned this programming formula. The 1 to 3 P.M. period is most nearly ideal, but it is really impractical because of the continued popularity of **soap operas** that suds up that time period. It could be an option for a station from 12 to 2 P.M. if its news commitment does not take priority.

3. Most network affiliates would commit hara-kiri if they **preempted** the soaps during this period, but a few do manage with either local or regional talk shows or syndicated properties. It is not advisable for an affiliate to consider canceling soap operas, because once the cement of the drama hardens, there is no escape from the enduring life of the property in the eyes of the viewers (as much as ten or fifteen years for some). Even a presidential speech or a news special will bring an eruption of ire from soap opera addicts.

Late Afternoon (4 to 6 P.M.)

The half hour from 4 to 4:30 P.M. is no problem for affiliates, but by 4:30 the networks have concluded their afternoon schedules, and the ball is in the affiliates' court. The 90-minute span can house the following:

1. *Merv Griffin, Mike Douglas, Dinah Shore,* or some other hour-and-a-half talk show designed for this period. Such shows will do rather well, but the age bracket of the viewers will probably be fifty plus. Older viewers consider these shows as similar to *The Tonight Show,* without requiring that one stay up until 11:30 P.M.

2. The ABC-owned stations have designed a movie format that has been very successful. They purchased movies and shaved them down to fit a 90-minute time slot. It is common to take a 100-minute feature film and edit it down to 78 minutes so that 12 minutes of commercials can nestle within the film. There is an ironic story about Fred Silverman, now president of NBC, who (when he was a novice film editor at WGN-TV in Chicago) solved this problem when he had to edit an Elvis Presley movie called "Jailhouse Rock." He merely eliminated the musical numbers. Silverman, too, was almost eliminated. This format needs the support of experienced editors to do the surgery. It can be and is done every day to the delight of viewers in the 18 to 34 age bracket.

3. Another approach is to buy **made-for-television movies** that average about 75 minutes. No editing is needed; they can simply be **slotted** and filled with commercials and promotion spots. The problems with this solution are that the quality of these productions rarely matches theatrical standards, the name value of the stars is less, and the promotion is weaker. Station ratings reflect all this.

4. Another answer to the 4:30 to 6 P.M. problem is to split the time period into two parts—a 30-minute show followed by a 60-minute unit, or the converse. Half-hour programs for the 4:30 period are easily found: *Brady Bunch, Gilligan's Island, Bob Newhart, Sanford and Son,* or, if economy is necessary, *Little Rascals, Superman, Spiderman, Gomer Pyle,* or *Hogan's Heroes.* The big problem is to find the following hour show which will be a good **lead-in** to the 6 P.M. news. Historically, the best 60-minute property has been *Perry Mason,* but this series dates back to the 1960s. Since then, there have been *Bonanza, Mission Impossible, The FBI,* and *Emergency,* but these shows did not live up to expectations in the ratings. The only recent hour program that has done reasonably well is *Star Trek.*

5. Successful affiliates have solved the problem by preempting the network's 4 P.M. show. As much as 40

percent of affiliates do not **clear** the 4 to 4:30 period. This expands the 90-minute period into a 2-hour time slot. This combination has been used successfully by independent stations for many years. In 120 minutes, the 4 to 6 P.M. zone can be used as follows:

a. Movies can be divided into 96 minutes of feature and 24 minutes of commercials. This gives a film breathing room, and the viewer sees a reasonable amount of the motion picture. The station can also use the 2-hour edited version for other compatible time periods. This form is more economical for films than 90-minute edits since cost is based on the entire film. Using all the footage is financially sensible.

b. Instead of leaning solely on Hollywood for feature films, television has started to depend on **reruns** from the networks. Comedy series have been the most successful and the most expensive, which points up the problem of the lack of programming in the market. Research has shown that sit-coms have captured the audience and held them from 4 to 6 without any defection. The best strategy is to start with kiddult properties around 4 P.M. and phase into family-appeal programs, then finally into adult fare as a lead into the adult 6 o'clock news:

Ideal Example

4:00 P.M.: *Batman, Gilligan's Island, Beaver, Brady Bunch*
4:30 P.M.: *Bob Newhart, Sanford and Son, Good Times, Kotter*
5:00 P.M.: *Mary Tyler Moore, Alice, One Day at a Time, Rhoda*
5:30 P.M.: *M*A*S*H, Happy Days, Laverne & Shirley, Three's Company*

Future acquisitions for this comedy block are likely to be expensive. Reruns with built-in success have gone up from $600 an episode to $6,000 a unit in a three-year period in the Columbus market. Independent stations have paid high prices in order to program reruns against affiliates between 6 P.M. and 8 P.M. In four-or-more-station markets, the independent attacks the soft underbelly of the affiliate during local and network news by syphoning off the younger audience with *Odd Couple, Mary Tyler Moore,* and *Carol Burnett* reruns.

This condition has forced the affiliate station to compete with the independent and vie for the high-priced network reruns. The top fifty affiliate is compelled to program them in the 4 to 7 time zone because of the **primetime access rule**. Nevertheless, the sit-com will continue to be a staple appealing to the younger television viewers as well as adults in the late afternoon **fringe** time period.

Long-running series on the networks have been very scarce in recent years; properties with 120 to 160 episodes are rare. This number is needed to program on a Monday through Friday (**stripped**) basis. There are actually 260 time slots per year to fill if stripping is used; with 130 episodes of a show, each individual program will be repeated twice a year and have a six-month rest between exposures, which is ideal for cycling a good show.

Only about twenty-four new episodes of any series are produced each year. This means for a series to amass 130 episodes, the series has to run for about six years. Very few programs have had longevity like that. When a show does stay that long on the network, most stations want to buy it, and the marketplace jacks up the price to match the demand. Some shows that have made this golden circle in recent years have been *Mary Tyler Moore, The Waltons, M*A*S*H, Maude, Little House on the Prairie, All in the Family, Hawaii Five-O, Barnaby Jones, The Jeffersons, Good Times,* and *Carol Burnett.* Most of these shows came from the great days of CBS.

In the late 1970s, ABC acquired the magic formula for comedy, but most ABC series had only about seventy-two episodes in the can in 1979. Consequently, distributors sold **futures**. Series that were still on the air were coming to the marketplace for sale at exorbitant prices to be used at future dates, sometimes three years in advance. Will the series last? Will the main characters still be there? Will the property have a network strip run before the local station acquires the rights? Those are tough decisions, hard judgments, calculated risks—that are still being made every day by programmers everywhere. As of 1979, the collection of precious programs included *Laverne & Shirley, Kotter, Three's Company, Charlie's Angels, Fantasy Island, Love Boat,* and *Mork & Mindy.* The sales passed from CBS's syndicators to ABC's. Perhaps someday NBC's syndicators will have something besides *Little House on the Prairie* to sell off to the local stations.

Early Evening (6 to 7:30 P.M.)

The 6 to 7:30 time period is usually a news zone. The network provides 30 minutes of national coverage. Affiliates below the top five markets have followed one of two patterns: precede or follow the network news with 30 minutes or 1 hour of local material or sandwich the national news between two news programs, a 30-minute one preceding and a 30-minute one following.

1. Some stations in the top five markets have instituted news programs that start around 5 and stretch to 7, at which time they add the network news, making a total of 2½ hours of news. This amount of news, of course, must dominate the ratings or be subject to counterprogramming that usually wins in total audience preference.

2. For the average affiliate, 90 minutes of news between 6 and 7:30 P.M. is all the market can handle. The most successful structure has been the sandwich, which splits the local news into two sections: the 6 o'clock unit carries the fast-breaking items and the 7 o'clock segment handles the follow-ups and feature material. Of course, sports and weather can be sprinkled throughout both portions.

The affiliate with the strongest news team usually dominates the entire market. Evening local news is television's front page, and in recent years the competition has been so fierce that consulting firms have sprung up to advise stations concerning presenters, content, format structure, set design, pace of program, and even the type of clothing worn by the on-the-air personnel.

3. How does a station counterprogram against news? If one cannot win with better news, then one can split the viewing audience by scheduling entertainment programs against the news:

Station A	Station B	Station C
5:30 Local program	5:30 Local program	5:30 Local news
6:00 Local news	6:00 Local news	6:00 Network news
6:30 Network news	6:30 Local news	6:30 Rerun comedy
7:00 Local news	7:00 Network news	7:00 First-run quiz or game show

The counterprogramming unit (station C) will score very well since about a third of the audience does not want to watch the news to begin with; a station can depend on getting about a 30-plus share against news at any time. Programs in rerun that have done well against news are *Andy Griffith, Gomer Pyle, Hogan's Heroes, Six Million Dollar Man, Sanford and Son, Carol Burnett,* and game shows.

Access Time (7:30 to 8 P.M. Technically; 7 to 8 P.M. Practically)

Access time is that one hour moat dug by Don McGannon of Westinghouse to prevent the networks from invading further into af-

filiates' schedules and as a self-serving device to further Westinghouse's
syndicated arm which was producing first-run programs suitable for this
time period. The bubble that access time would stimulate quality programs has long burst, and what remains is largely a nightmare of
game shows, recycled quiz formats, and soft smut from Chuck Barris
confessionals.

1. The brightest flower in the access desert blooms in the
form of the *Muppets*, a family-oriented musical comedy.
The anemia is self-evident in the following list of the top
ten prime access shows from November 1978.

*Table 5–1. Top Ten Prime Access
Shows ADI Ratings–ADI TV Households*

Rank and Program	Type[a]	Dura-tion	No. Stations	Percent Coverage	Ratings % ADI	% US
1 *Family Feud*	QG	30	126	82.5	14.5	12.0
2 *Muppet Show*	CV	30	148	90.3	14.4	13.0
3 *Evening Magazine*	TI	30	5	10.7	13.8	1.5
4 *$100,000 Name That Tune*	QG	30	121	82.0	13.2	10.8
5 *PM Magazine*	TI	30	9	9.5	13.2	1.2
6 *Newlywed Game (New)*	QG	30	106	84.7	13.1	11.1
7 *Hollywood Squares*	QG	30	71	87.0	12.9	8.7
8 *Price Is Right*	QG	30	57	47.0	12.9	6.1
9 *Hee Haw*	CV	60	195	94.8	12.8	12.1
10 *Lawrence Welk*	MV	60	191	96.1	12.2	11.8

[a]These symbols refer to: QG = quiz/game; CV = children's variety; TI =
talk/information; and MV = musical variety.

Source: Arbitron Television Ratings, November 1978 Audience Estimates.
Used with permission.

2. As new properties falter and as old programs die from
fatigue, the new idea of stripping accelerates in popularity.
If one episode of a show works once a week, why not five
times a week? Consequently, television **logs** are loaded with
Monday through Friday gems such as *Jokers Wild, Liars Club,
Newlywed Game, Dating Game,* and *Three's a Crowd.*

3. Some stations are not waiting for the syndicators to
develop a long-lasting new program to fit the 6 to 7:30 or
8 P.M. time period; they are doing it themselves. Several
years ago the Group W station in San Francisco, KPIX, took
its budget for prime access and applied it to an innovative
local show entitled *Evening.* This program reflected the

life-style of San Francisco, its people, its oddities, and its beauty. The show was such a success that the remaining Group W stations in Pittsburgh, Boston, Philadelphia, and Baltimore adopted the pattern. The group stations started to exchange program segments, and it became apparent that other stations might be able to use this material if a show like *Evening* were begun in markets across the country. *Evening* went syndicated as *PM* in 1978 and has become the backbone in the access time period for more than eighty stations.

However, the problem with this concept is finding the proper balance between syndicated material and local stories. If the local is subservient, the entire show loses its local flavor and is dependent on the universality of the syndicated pieces. The Group W *Evening/PM* concept is worthy and should lead other broadcasters to develop new formats that can be produced right in their own markets rather than continue dependence on established programs from national syndicators.

Primetime (8 to 11 P.M.)

Primetime for the affiliate is the highest viewing period of the daily schedule. From 8 to 11, the network pours in expensive and highly competitive programs, supported by arresting promotional campaigns on the air and in newspaper and magazine ads. Independent stations have not been able to bite into this time zone consistently. This is the payground of the three networks. Clearances by affiliates are a necessity to maintain parity.

1. From time to time, an affiliate may spot a section of the network schedule that is in need of repair but that cannot be fixed until later in the season. Under these conditions, an affiliate might "pick off" a weak night for a local movie special, a musical-hour special, or a local program that has some significance to the community.* The networks are tolerant of these variations, and the station need only convince its viewers that the preemption is justified. When the public is not convinced, phone calls, letters, and the press scold the affiliate for its actions.

2. It is best to preempt on different days rather than take the same time slot week after week. Local basketball

---

*Preemptions also allow the local station to charge national rates rather than local rates for its primetime creating a strong incentive to preempt if program options are available.

schedules tend to recur on the same days of the week, and preemptions irritate viewers who are robbed of certain shows until the basketball schedule is completed. This can be painful for all concerned, especially if some network specials are eliminated for a losing local team. Judgment must be exercised when bumping a new network show that appears to be doomed in New York or Los Angeles. Many a programmer has been burned by preempting a big-city loser only to find it is a hit in the local market, with only time needed to make it a hit in the big city. This happened with *The Waltons, Little House on the Prairie,* and *60 Minutes.*

Late Evening and Late Night (11 P.M. to 2 A.M.)

1. The 11 P.M. time slot for affiliates is traditionally for newscasts. A carry-over from radio, the eleven o'clock news is part of the fabric of affiliates. Independent stations have tried to break this hold for years, and only one show—*Mary Hartman, Mary Hartman*—was able to dent the public's news loyalty; this happened for only a quick twenty-six weeks, then the news returned to its former dominance.

2. The last time segment for the programmer is the 11:30 P.M. to 2 A.M. period. NBC's *The Tonight Show* was untouchable in the ratings until Johnny Carson's 1979 contract allowed him to be nonlive two days a week in addition to seventeen weeks' vacation during the year. Both ABC and CBS made gains against this irregularity on NBC.

3. A local affiliate can double its inventory over that the network provides if enough property can be purchased to fill the 260 occasions needed for a year's programming. Motion pictures provide a good vehicle if one can buy enough new product and mix it with golden oldies from the rerun files.

4. The networks have bought large numbers of cop and detective shows to fill this period in rerun; *Hawaii Five-O, Streets of San Francisco,* and *Kojak* are obvious examples.

5. Of course, one can try *Mike Douglas* or *Merv Griffin* at 11:30 P.M. and fight talk with talk. Griffin was on CBS during the heyday of Paar and early Carson and was unable to make inroads, but today he might work.

6. Many affiliates have tried 30-minute shows at 11:30 P.M. and then begun their movies at midnight. This gambit usually got numbers in the ratings for the half hour, but the nonmovie people defected at midnight, so the early

gains were wiped out when the averages were examined. It appears the **long-form** and an 11:30 P.M. start is the wisest structure, especially since feature films can be used in other earlier time slots to complete the contractual runs necessary to pay for the product and make it profitable.

WEEKEND REALITIES

Saturday and Sunday provide different programming problems than Monday through Friday. Football, basketball, bowling, baseball, tennis, auto racing, horse racing, and boxing all take their turns at capturing the viewer.

Saturdays

On Saturdays, if a station can capture a morning time for a 2-hour movie, perhaps from 10:30 A.M. to 12:30 P.M., family viewing can be encouraged in a time period that has been historically restricted to children. A movie can also yield 52-week advertising sales and not be dependent on kid-oriented commercials, which are usually viable only during the second and fourth quarters (because of Christmas and back-to-school sales patterns). The trick is to lure the parents to watch, in addition to the children, by careful selection of the movie stars and titles. Elvis Presley, Jerry Lewis, John Wayne, Francis the Talking Mule, Ma and Pa Kettle, and science fiction titles are all sure-fire audience getters.

Country-western and Nashville music can also be used for counterprogramming. Saturdays from 2 to 4 P.M. or 4 to 6 P.M. are ideal time blocks for such programming. These shows are usually low in cost and easy to promote if the community appreciates this type of music.

The toughest hour on Saturday night for the affiliate is the 7 to 8 P.M. time slot. This is especially true if the competition owns *Lawrence Welk* and *Hee Haw*. The best attack is to program a *Bugs Bunny* or *Tom and Jerry* "house show" against these giants. The cartoon half hour will garner young **demographics** (18 to 34 years) and set up whatever is planned at 7:30 to complete the hour. Use the rabbit, mouse, or cat to lead the way, and almost anything will work at 7:30 P.M.

Late Saturday night has been used to telecast feature films. With the arrival of NBC's *Saturday Night Live*, a large new audience has been developed: the college-age group. Their taste for sophisticated comedy has relegated the theatrical film to second place in most markets. A programmer must choose from contemporary box office hits to stay even within competitive reach of *Saturday Night Live*. If this doesn't work, one can try vintage films that are considered "classics" ("Citizen Kane," "Rebecca," "Casablanca"). A form that should be tried is a comedy block from 11:30 P.M. to 1:30 A.M. made up of half hours back-to-back in the genre of *M*A*S*H, All in the Family, Maude, Three's Company,* and *Mary Hartman, Mary Hartman.*

Sundays

The affiliate has very little room to move on Sundays. The afternoons contain season-to-season sports, news from 6 to 7 P.M., and network entertainment from 7 to 11 P.M. The only period for development is the morning. This ghetto has usually contained public affairs, religious, cultural, and panel shows; some kids' shows; low ratings; and low income.

Consider those "service people" who work in the evenings all week and never see primetime programming. The night people are out there; they just need something with mass appeal. How about all those people who go to church early and all those people who do not go to church?

The most successful property one can schedule on Sunday mornings is a primetime-type feature film. Name the 10 A.M. to noon period something other than "Atheist Theater" and watch the numbers roll in. With limited competition, the HUT level will explode, and the money will follow shortly. If success comes quickly, consider backing up to eight o'clock for the fifth and sixth runs of sit-coms that are always tough to play off. A wasteland can be turned into a highly watched and lucrative programming period.

The late Sunday night period following the 11 P.M. news is still a difficult time to program. If the community is large enough, a 60-minute adventure or a short movie is the best a programmer can do because of the low number of homes watching television. This is the Siberia of the weekly schedule.

SUMMARY

Programming is war. You are a general. The object is to win—win in all time periods. Winning means high ratings. High ratings bring top dollars from the advertiser, and top dollars allow you to continue the cycle of controlling the market for another season of programming strategy. If you can do this and still keep a balanced schedule that reflects the community needs, cultural roots, and entertainment demands of your audience, then, indeed, you are a programmer.

A program schedule must be analyzed hour by hour to take account of the options available, the competition, and the economic benefits of reuse of already-purchased programs. The network affiliate is bound by contract and by economic advantage to its network; it is more highly restricted by FCC regulation than an independent is. If its options are fewer, its visibility is generally greater than an independent's (or a public station's), and one of the network affiliates holds top place in nearly every market.

ADDITIONAL PERIODICAL READINGS

"ABC TV Stations' Studies Arouse Independents." *Television/Radio Age* (November 20, 1978): 38 ff.
Report on and criticism of an ABC study of programming, audiences, and advertising revenue at affiliates compared with independents.

Austin, Bruce A. "People's Time in a Medium-Sized Market: A Content Analysis." *Journalism Quarterly,* 57 (Spring 1980): 67–70.
An analysis of commercial network affiliate programming during the 4:00 to 8:00 P.M. time period.

Austin, Bruce A. "Prime Time Television in a Medium-Sized Market: A Content Analysis." *Communication Quarterly,* 27 (Summer 1979): 37–40.
An analysis of commercial network affiliate programming during the 8:00 to 11:00 P.M. time period.

Austin, Bruce A. "Public Interest Programming by Commercial Network Affiliates." *Journalism Quarterly* 56 (Spring 1979): 87 ff.
A quantitative analysis of the primetime programming of three commercial network affiliates.

Pekurny, Robert G., and **Bart, Leonard D.** " 'Sticks and Bones': A Survey of Network Affiliate Decision Making." *Journal of Broadcasting* 19 (Fall 1975): 427–37.
An attempt to determine factors used by television station executives and program directors to arrive at decisions.

Rosenthal, Edmond M. "Local Children's Television Programming Has More to Do with Public Service than Profit." *Television/Radio Age* (August 15, 1977): 26 ff.
A discussion of the effects of the FCC's 1974 policy statement on children's programming.

Sobel, Robert. "Syndicated Kidvid Lively; Top Dollar for

Cartoons." *Television/Radio Age* (August 15, 1977): 23 ff.
A look at the children's programming syndication business.

Sobel, Robert. "Syndicated Program Buyers See Even More Access Stripping." *Television/Radio Age* (March 12, 1979): 98 ff.
Discusses what is currently being syndicated for prime access time and what is planned by individual syndicators.

"Television Programming & Production for Profit." *Broadcast Management/Engineering,* monthly series, March 1977 to date.
Discussion of programming strategies and techniques, including reports on syndicated programs and features.

Wirth, Michael O., and **Wollert, James A.** "Public Interest Programming: FCC Standards and Station Performance." *Journalism Quarterly* 55 (Autumn 1978): 554–61.
Analysis of 1975 programming data to determine the effect on network affiliates of the FCC's 5–5–10 rule (5 percent local, 5 percent informational, 10 percent nonentertainment).

6 The Group-Owned Station

Lewis Klein

Lewis Klein is executive vice-president of Gateway Communications, Inc., a group owner of four television stations: WBNG, Binghamton, New York: WTAJ, Altoona-Johnstown, Pennsylvania; WLYH, Lancaster-Lebanon, Pennsylvania; and WOWK, Huntington-Charleston, West Virginia. Gateway Communications is a wholly owned subsidiary of the Bergen Evening Record Corporation. *Mr. Klein was the director of television programming for Triangle Publications from 1967 to 1972, supervising the program activities of Triangle's six stations. He served WFIL-TV in Philadelphia from 1950 to 1972 in various program department functions and was executive producer of the award-winning* Frontiers of Knowledge *series as well as* American Bandstand *and* College News Conference. *He has served on the faculty of the University of Pennsylvania and is an adjunct professor of Radio-Television-Film at Temple University in Philadelphia, having taught there for twenty-eight years. Mr. Klein is past president of the National Association of Television Program Executives, the Television and Radio Advertising Club of Philadelphia, and the Delaware Valley Chapter of the Broadcast Pioneers, and he became president of the NATPE Educational Foundation in 1979. In this chapter he discusses the varied patterns of controls among group stations, their operating methods, and the economic advantages and disadvantages of shared research, resources, and recruiting among group-owned stations. In the final section of the chapter, Joel Chaseman, president of Post-Newsweek Stations, Inc., shares a survey he conducted for this book of fellow group presidents on group programming stategy in the 1980s.*

TYPES OF GROUP OWNERSHIP

Group stations are a broad class of stations. They can be owned by a **network** or by a nonmedia corporation; they can be network-**affiliated** or **independent**, UHF or VHF, and located in the nation's largest markets (New York, Los Angeles, Chicago) or smallest markets (Tuscaloosa, Alabama; Binghamton, New York; Austin, Minnesota; Waterloo, Iowa). More than 70 percent of television stations in the top 100 markets and more than half of all television stations are group owned. Corporations buy stations because of their tremendous profitability. The average pretax profit for VHF television stations in the top 10 markets was about 40 percent of gross revenues in 1979.

The most prominent group-owned stations are the network-owned WNBC, WABC, and WCBS in New York. The nine network O&Os in the top three markets—the New York stations plus the Los Angeles stations (KABC, KNXT, KNBC) and the Chicago stations (WLS, WBBM, WMAQ)—garner the greatest gross dollars of all groups of stations. Most of the fifteen network-owned stations are located in top ten markets, are highly profitable, and quite frequently lead their markets in ratings.

The remainder of group-owned stations are controlled largely by giant corporations, many also owning radio stations, newspapers, and cable systems. The number of stations a group owner can own is limited by the FCC's 7–7–7 rule restricting a single licensee to no more than five VHF stations or up to seven UHF stations.* In addition to the ABC, CBS, and NBC groups, about 135 of the 165 television group owners can be considered major multiple-station owners, controlling valuable stations in many midsized and large markets. Table 6–1 shows the top ten groups (excluding the network groups), the number of television stations they own, and the percentage of total U.S. households having sets (HHs) reached by the combined signals of each group's stations, namely, the total potential audience.

Table 6–1. Top Ten Group Owners
(Excepting ABC, CBS, and NBC)

Group Owner	Number of Stations Owned	Percent of HHs Reached
Metromedia	7	20.27
RKO General	4	17.22
Field	5	14.09
Group W	5	10.58
Storer	7	9.80
Gaylord	7	8.55
Capital Cities	6	7.27
Taft	6	7.14
Cox	5	6.37
Chris Craft	2	6.08

Source: FCC Network Inquiry Special Staff, "An Analysis of the Network-Affiliate Relationship in Television: Preliminary Draft Report," *1978 Broadcast Yearbook* (October 1979): 1–10.

*The FCC imposes rules aimed at preventing undue concentration of control over broadcasting as a result of multiple ownership of stations. Chief among these is the "rule of seven," which limits a single owner to control of seven stations in each class (AM, FM, and television, with no more than five of the television stations in the VHF band).

Each group of network-owned stations covers about 22 percent of U.S. homes. The reach of Metromedia's stations is closest to that of a network group because Metromedia owns stations (largely independents) in the top three markets.

Although the issue of cross-media ownership remains thorny in many markets, overall group ownership is one of the more positive trends in American broadcasting of the last twenty years.[1] An enormous gap separates the individual station and the national network. Groups have the appropriate size and strength to form an intermediate force between these extremes.

PATTERNS OF CONTROL

Most group broadcasters employ an executive (headquarters programmer) and staff to oversee and coordinate the programming functions of commonly owned stations. Some headquarters closely supervise station program budgets and programming-related decisions at their stations. Cox Broadcasting, Storer Broadcasting, Corinthian, and Group W are examples of this type of group owner. They require approval by the headquarters office before an individual station may proceed with a major program purchase. The headquarters staff typically does not instigate purchases but does retain final approval. However, the Combined Communications group often purchases programs for all of its stations together and thereby centers program strategy at the headquarters.

Other groups restrict themselves to veto power over their owned-station plans. Still others serve in an unstructured, advisory role. Capital Cities Communications allows its stations the most autonomy of all television group owners in the area of program determinations. The three sets of network-owned and operated stations and Group W stations are among those that operate with close program ties to their headquarters. In groups in which considerable program autonomy is encouraged, such as in Capital Cities, the headquarters uses very detailed financial reports to track the profit picture of individual programs. Most group owners rely on their local program directors to assume day-to-day program responsibility including scheduling, but the headquarters staffs play vital roles in major program-purchase decisions, key personnel hiring, program **syndication**, and program department budgeting.

ADVANTAGES OF GROUP OWNERSHIP

The overriding advantage of group ownership is that group buying cuts programming costs. It costs distributors less to sell to groups, and they often pass on part of the savings to the group-owned stations. Group stations also often share in the use of film prints and videotapes of program series, thus further reducing their program costs.

Group broadcasters have the financial strength to buy desirable new programs that might otherwise be snapped up by competitors. Producers and distributors of a syndicated series call on headquarters programmers first because group program sales are safer than making market-by-market offerings. Sometimes programs are sold to group-owned stations even before competing stations become aware that they are available. Often producers of a proposed new series delay initiating actual production until at least one of the major station groups has contracted for the series. Many **primetime access** program proposals languish on the drawing boards because no group of stations has made an advance commitment to purchase.

Group program staffs provide guidance to their stations on commercial copy, contests, staffing, government affairs, budgets, and set design. The temporary exchange of program personnel often occurs when illnesses or special productions create problems for members of the group. Most contacts between a local program director and the group program director are channeled through the headquarters office, but occasionally exchanges occur directly between one program director and another within the group. Some groups hold periodic instructional sessions or idea-exchange meetings for their program directors and production managers. Some routinely exchange video cassettes, program activity reports, and station visits. An attractive feature of group-owned stations for program directors is that they have the incentive to strive for promotion to more challenging and rewarding stations within the group without giving up the tenure already established in their companies.

DISADVANTAGES OF GROUP OWNERSHIP

The nongroup program director is generally a more independent, more aggressive, and faster-moving executive than the group programmer. Groups usually employ experienced programmers along with extensive staffs. Nevertheless, group-owned stations are hampered by the committee-type decisions that group management imposes. They tend to be slow to arrive at programming decisions and often breed several layers of inert program management. Nongroup programmers must make program decisions more quickly.

Group-owned or not, a station's programming strategies should be geared to specific *local* market factors. A small-market station's program director may find that a group-acquired program selected to suit the large-market stations of the group is not of particular interest to the smaller market. Joining forces to purchase a syndicated program series in order to have first crack and perhaps a lower cost per episode has advantages for stations. But groups that force purchases on unenthusiastic stations potentially reduce their profitability. When **formats** are regimented for local origination and certain numbers of entertainers and personnel required, individual stations suffer from the strictures of such inflexibility. Group W has required some regimentation at its stations. Group advantages are most alluring when tempered to allow accommodation of specific market needs and tastes.

THE SPECIAL CASE OF NETWORK O&O GROUPS

Network-owned stations in the top three markets have extraordinary collective power as members of groups. Since each group reaches about 22 percent of the total U.S. households with television sets, their purchase of a syndicated program property often makes the crucial difference between the success and failure of the property. Their powerful impact enables these few group-owned stations to set programming trends for the entire syndicated-program market.

Although network O&Os are not directly controlled by their networks, they naturally share many common goals and interests with their networks. For example, an ordinary network affiliate does not necessarily give consideration to its primetime access programs' **lead-in** effect on the 8 P.M. network programs. A network O&O, however, is extremely conscious of lead-in effects, since the parent company's success depends in part on the audience delivered by its owned stations and affiliates.

Another consideration carrying increased weight at owned stations is that of image. Especially in New York, where they live next door to company headquarters, **rep** firms, and advertising agencies, the O&Os worry more about their image than in markets with less visibility. In the seven-station New York market, image determines certain viewing habits. For instance, on weekend afternoons when the NBC network programs sports, WNBC generally programs sports in its local time. This imitative practice may seem like overkill, but it maintains a consistent image with viewers and advertisers.

Network-owned stations use their networks' logos on the air and in their overall **promotion**; many nonowned affiliates do the same. WNBC begins local news with the NBC chimes; WCBS opens local public affairs programs with the CBS-eye design. This practice makes it difficult for viewers to distinguish between network programming and the owned station's **local** programming. Often, in consequence, owned stations spend large amounts of time conveying station identity in the market—generally by more and better community programs, extensive on-air support of community projects and activities, and occasional station-image campaigns like "your community-minded station." Despite these efforts, the average viewer does not differentiate between the television network and the local network-owned station.

The fifteen network-owned and operated stations produce tremendous profits for their corporate owners. At times the O&Os have made even more money than their networks. O&Os are also valuable to their networks because they assure **clearance** of all network programs in the top markets, setting a precedent for the rest of the country. Inability to clear programs in major markets can be very damaging to a network's program schedule. Capital Cities, for example, owns stations affiliated with ABC that contribute almost 10 percent of ABC's national coverage. If Capital Cities decided not to carry a given program on its group of stations, the effect on the viability of that program on ABC would be considerable. It is understandable, therefore, that the network O&O groups play an important role in ensuring clearance in major markets.

Some syndicators offer special inducements to get exposure for their wares in the prestigious access time slots in the top O&O markets. These inducements may take the form of cash discounts for outright program buys or extra commercial spot **availabilities** for the station in **syndication barter** buys.* The latter, known as "compensation incentive," is a common practice in New York because, as the premiere market in the country, New York coverage has critical importance to advertisers. Beyond the very top markets, however, barter with compensation is rarely used.

LOCAL PRODUCTION BY GROUP-OWNED STATIONS

The sources of television programming are the same for every station in the country. Sixty-five percent of the network-affiliated or network-owned station's schedule is network originated. These programs are seldom preempted by affiliates and rarely rescheduled from their original-feed time period. The remaining 35 percent of the affiliate's schedule is programmed locally. About 15 percent actually originates locally; the remaining 20 percent comes from syndicators who distribute programs produced by a variety of sources on a national basis.

Syndication barter refers to a practice by which advertisers (rather than stations) purchase the rights to use syndicated programs. After incorporating its own advertising into some of the commercial breaks in the program, the advertiser then offers the program to stations at no cost other than the presence of the advertiser's own spots. The station makes its profit by selling the unfilled commercial breaks in the program. The advertiser and the station usually split the commercial spots fifty–fifty in barter deals, but the advertiser may offer the station more than half as a special incentive to accept the deal.

Group owners have been assuming the syndicator's role, producing programs not only for use by other stations within their groups but also for regional and even national syndication. This trend resulted from the success of several pioneering group-produced programs introduced in the 1970s. Another factor encouraging syndication by groups is the escalating cost for **off-network syndicated** programs. Of course, when a program is produced for use by more than one station, additional expenses, such as increased talent fees, union scales, and music **royalty** payments, accrue. Nevertheless, multiple use of good program ideas can be a money-saving programming strategy in the long run.

Group W's *PM Magazine* is one such program series. This **magazine-format** series originated at Group W's San Francisco station, KPIX, as *Evening Magazine* in the early 1970s. Later it was shared by all five Group W stations, and ultimately distributed to over a hundred stations as well. Other group-owned syndications are Multimedia's *Phil Donahue* and Metromedia's *Golden Circle*.[2] As a result of this trend, some group program directors are becoming increasingly active in local programming.

COMMUNITY RESPONSIVENESS

Programmers of group-owned stations have to be more sensitive than non-group-owned station programmers to the pressures of community groups and government regulation. The high visibility of broadcast groups and the factor of absentee ownership make them an easy target for some consumer groups. The feeling of vulnerability induces a corresponding sense of local responsibility among group-owned station managements. The result is that group-owned stations make strenuous efforts to demonstrate sensitivity to consumer interests in their communities and to serve local needs with extensive local programming efforts. Many single-owner stations also do considerable public affairs programming, but, of necessity, group-owned stations tend to be even more public-affairs oriented. The stations licensed to the large corporations that own the national networks also have to be particularly sensitive to such programming needs.

THE 1976 WATERSHED IN PROGRAMMING

A turning point for television came in 1976 when television revenues took a significant upward surge. One of the reasons was the quadrennial combination of national elections and Olympic games. Their effect was to limit program inventory and thereby raise prices of programs. In addition, the number of UHF receivers increased, and the independent UHF stations took advantage of their new prosperity by buying off-network programs at prices they could not have afforded in previous years. The consequent shortage of syndicated programs led to higher price levels throughout the industry.

With this historical fact in mind, Joel Chaseman, president of Post-Newsweek Stations, Inc., asked representatives of ten group-broadcasting firms about their views on their post-1976 programming strategies. He asked three questions: (1) Has your group programming strategy changed since 1976? If so, in what way? (2) Do you believe that the new technologies will affect your fundamental programming strategies? If so, can you outline what the effects will be? (3) Do you anticipate less dependence on existing networks? If so, how will you fill the programming gap?

Program Strategy

Most of the correspondents agreed that 1976 was a watershed year in their programming strategies, initiating increased emphasis on local news and information programs:

> Our program strategy has changed since 1976 with greater emphasis now placed upon local program productions which include magazines, documentary, children's shows, public affairs programs and weeks devoted to special interests and projects within each of our communities. . . . Our local news programs have been enhanced through the utilization of research, expansion of program time periods, additional news shows, larger staffs and upgraded technical equipment. —*Richard B. Belkin,* Vice-President—Broadcasting, Lee Enterprises, Inc.[3]

> Our program strategy has always been to generate the largest audiences possible, consistent with the other objectives of diversity of programming, station image, and, of course, operating in the public interest. Since 1976, I feel we have had a general increase in news and informational programming—and, certainly an upgrading. In the early evening hours, we have gotten away from totally adult, hour-long action/adventure and dramatic shows, toward more family-oriented programming. —*William A. Schwartz,* President, Broadcast Division, Cox Broadcasting Corporation.[4]

> About the only group dicta for our affiliated stations are that they should become and remain preeminent in news and informational programming and should strive for quality as well as ratings in their other non-network programming areas. —*Crawford P. Rice,* Executive Vice-President, Gaylord Broadcasting Company.[5]

> We are developing systems and methods to provide for

greater independence of the network services. Our objectives include greater local origination (i.e., entertainment, news, and public service) through ENG and remote equipment.   —*Ancil H. Payne,* President, King Broadcasting Company.[6]

Influences of New Technology

There is no question among group broadcasters that the emphasis on news and informational programming ties in directly with the advent of new technology. It has increased local mobility, reduced costs of transmission and production, created opportunities to produce local programs, and stimulated the creative imagination of program strategists. Here are some evidences of the impact of technology:

Smaller, high quality electronic cameras permit us to do a better job of news coverage, and, for the first time, permit us to seek out local programming that is not confined to in-the-studio, talking-heads programs. Satellite earth stations will permit greater diversity of program choices to stations, particularly for the independents, by reducing the cost of transmission of sports, entertainment, and news programming.   —*Crawford P. Rice* (Gaylord group).

We foresee less dependence upon film as a medium in all local and syndicated production, greater mobility, reduction of studio production, greater emphasis upon post production, and the prominance of video disc/video tape cassette programs developed for retail sale to local market consumers.   —*Richard B. Belkin* (Lee group).

We will not only originate more, but will turn more frequently to creative sources other than the network. We will continue to develop local programming, increase news, emphasize local over national sales.   —*Ancil H. Payne* (King group).

Our philosophy has always been one of a desire to create and produce programming within our organization. We are entering one of the most exciting periods for programming that has yet existed. The market for original programming will grow in quantum leaps in the next few years. The new technologies will open up new program marketplaces.   —*John T. Reynolds,* President, Golden West Broadcasters.[7]

New technology will have an effect on our programming strategy. Satellite transmission, video cassettes, cable, etc., offer ways of cutting costs and/or increasing revenue potential for program producers. This will result in more programming, especially live and locally produced programs.   —*William A. Schwartz* (Cox group).

Network Dependence

The effect of all of this will be less dependence on network programming (and the syndicated rerun derivatives from network programming) along with a tendency toward specialized programming focused on the segmented life-styles increasingly evident in society. The economic underpinning of this strategic thinking was described by George Koehler:

> Our group programming strategy has not changed since 1976 in any really apparent way, except that we are more interested now than we were then in local specials and some of the off-network series like *Roots*. What *has* changed is the way local stations now are forced to buy successful network series substantially in advance of their network termination periods of use, eight to ten years from the date of the original commitment. No longer is it possible to assess one's program needs accurately and to fill those needs through purchases in the marketplace. The game has become a gamble of frightening proportions.
>
> It seems to me that this is rather the reverse of the networks' gamble. The networks put a lot of money into development, winnow the development product, come up with new programs for insertion into their schedules and hope to get two or three hits every season. When those hits start to miss—in three months or three years or ten years—the networks simply terminate their commitment.
>
> Stations now are being asked to risk millions of dollars on the prospect that a *Happy Days* is not just faddish, that it will not have worn out its acceptance in six or eight network showings, that it will appeal to viewers in 1986 as it has appealed to viewers in 1976. The number of runs dictates that the series will last three or four years in stripping; the price committed dictates that the station must use most of the runs to make the series pay out.
>
> Our small group of four stations has committed over $6.5 million on a long-range bet that says *Happy Days*, *Laverne & Shirley, Little House on the Prairie*, and *Eight Is Enough* will retain their popularity for six to eight years. That amount of money programs just three hours a day, five days a week. And just now there is no way of telling how many stations will be feeding these same programs into our medium and small markets via cable. At present that conduit of culture, *The Odd Couple*, may be seen *six times each day* in Altoona.
>
> While reruns are not original programming, it is true, they are a vital part of programming a station, and in this respect programming has changed mightily in the last sev-

eral years. The risks have become enormous.   —*George A. Koehler*, President, Gateway Communications, Inc.[8]

With this candid picture of the economics as background, these additional comments from Messrs. Belkin, Glaser, and Reynolds become pertinent:

Although we do not foresee less dependence upon existing networks for the current and future hours of programming, we do recognize that entrepreneurship will become a greater factor in the development of local programming and the acquisition of available programs from national syndicators. Sports features and specials will be available from a variety of sources. We feel alert programmers who maximize each opportunity will be the major winners in the years to come in the quest for fresh programming. We also recognize that costs will increase significantly. Therefore, greater attention must be paid to the return on investment. —*Richard B. Belkin* (Lee group).

With price escalation of off-network reruns, we have gravitated to first-run game shows, supplemented by British product. So far as our stations that have network affiliations are concerned, our dependence upon conventional network programming will remain. In the late 1980s, there is a real possibility the major networks as we now know them, will be fragmented. If this occurs, expanded sources of "software" will have to evolve. It is from these sources that I believe we will find the means to flesh out our program schedules. It will be incumbent upon group operators that have limited resources to form consortiums.   —*Robert L. Glaser*, President, RKO General Television.[9]

Certainly 1976 will come to be regarded as the benchmark when syndication prices went crazy. By 1979, it became virtually impossible to buy feature motion picture product, off-network programming, and original syndication programming at prices that can be justified and amortized. We anticipate less dependence on off-network programming. This is because of the exorbitant prices charged by syndicators and moreover, the lack of programming of a type that fits our programming needs.   —*John T. Reynolds* (Golden West group).

The Challenge to Network Hegemony

In organizations like Operation Prime Time (OPT) and Program Development Group (PDG), separately competitive broadcast groups such as Golden West, Cox, Gaylord, and Field put aside their rivalry to contribute prorated financial support to major programming ventures. These ventures, ranging from dramatizations of full-length novels to game shows, were much too big for individual groups to finance. Since they compete with network-financed programs and with the best feature films, these efforts must be mounted stylishly.

Al Masini of Cox's television sales representation firm (Telerep) conceived the idea of Operation Prime Time and sold it simultaneously to several group broadcasters, a producing organization (MCA/Universal), and certain national advertisers. In the words of Joel Chaseman, "His foresightedness and perseverance—and the courage of the independents and groups and stations involved—were rewarded with acceptable production quality and ratings." In the process, of course, network primetime was preempted on seventy-three network-affiliated stations in addition to twenty-two independent stations, and a precedent was created for other ventures similar to Masini's pioneering success, *Testimony of Two Men.* [10]

> Where group operators have a limited resource base it may be possible for them to form consortiums. The next ten years will be really exciting, and program developments will take their place in the forefront of the business even more than today. —*Robert L. Glaser* (RKO General group).

On the other hand, some respondents remind us of the enduring mutuality of network and affiliate:

> As we get into the changing technologies of the 1980s, I believe the two billion dollars per year that the three networks in combination spend on programming will be critical to the continuation of broadcasting as we know it. I certainly believe the broadcaster's localism, his commitment to his local community, is what sets us apart from a national programming service and gives us the right to expect continued development of our business in the future. In other words, it is the broadcaster's localism plus the cooperation between affiliated stations and their networks that has and will continue to provide the outstanding entertainment and information service that the public will continue to demand. —*Wilson Wearn*, President, Multimedia, Inc. [11]

> We do not see less dependence on existing networks, but recognize the emergence of excellent alternatives to network programming. Whether this results in less dependence on the networks depends a great deal on the ways the networks move in their strategy of maximizing the ability of broadcasting not only to entertain but also to meet the mounting crucial needs of the public to be

better informed about the significant issues of our day.
—*Arch L. Madsen*, President, Bonneville International
Corporation.[12]

The primary and untested question is how many
people will be willing to pay to see the movies and sports
events they now receive at no charge? The pay-cable subscription television operators are now offering their wares
without commercials and at nominal monthly fees. Business history and common sense tell me that these monthly
charges will begin to increase and that commercials will
find their way into these schedules; just as they have
found their way to the screens of neighborhood theaters.
—*Dick Woollen*, Vice-President—Programming, Metromedia Television.[13]

PROGRAMMING CHANGES IN THE 1980s

In Joel Chaseman's view, an examination of ratings and of qualitative research findings indicates that "there is a new hunger among the
American public for more serious attention to the fundamental concerns
we share as human beings, as world citizens in parlous times, and as
Americans."[14] The success of *60 Minutes*, some special-events programming, and even some extraordinary documentaries seems to support the position taken by, among others, Arch Madsen and Bill
Schwartz.

Joel Chaseman's own experience (based in part on the *Urban
America* series with Dick Hubert produced for Group W in the late 1960s
and early 1970s and in part on the remarkable success of Post-
Newsweek's *Agronsky & Company*) convinces him that the industry can
do more to satisfy a hunger for knowledge among people for whom
television is the primary medium of enlightenment and intellectual
stimulation. He believes that this means a new generation of doc-
umentarians, if indeed that is still a valid term. It also means, however,
that the new technology and the best writing skills must be focused on
bringing to factual programming the same desire for bigger audiences
and greater understanding that the new techniques and equipment have
lent to primetime entertainment vehicles. In Chaseman's words, "It is
not enough that we *do* the fact programs, we must commit ourselves to
producing them so that middle-class America will wish to watch them."

What emerges from this informal survey is a picture of the industry already radically changed during the late 1970s. Aided by technology
and by new awareness among the consuming public, group-owned
stations have moved toward more local production, more factual production, more mobile production. The economics have at one and the
same time lessened station dependence on off-network production and

created a marketplace for new programs in competition with network and off-network programming.

SUMMARY

Group-owned stations divide into those owned by networks and those owned by others. They tend to be affiliates rather than independents. Group owners frequently own other media such as newspapers, which can create potential conflicts of interest but also introduce advanced management practices benefiting many group-owned stations. Particular economic advantage comes from group program purchases and experienced management and often is accompanied by pronounced community responsiveness. The 1980s should be a period of slowly increasing local and non-network production, reflecting this responsiveness in part but also strongly influenced by technological advances and new economic freedom from traditional program sources.

NOTES

[1]See extensive discussion of cross-media ownership in Benjamin M. Compaine, ed., *Who Owns the Media? Concentration of Ownership in the Mass Communications Industry* (New York: Crown/Harmony, 1979), especially chap. 3 by Christopher H. Sterling, "Television and Radio Broadcast," pp. 92–96.

[2]*Golden Circle* is a first-run syndication vehicle of Metromedia's Entertainment Division, producing and distributing four major multipart dramas per year. *Golden Circle* is licensed to individual stations for cash; barter and time-banking arrangements are not used. Peter Warner, "Metromedia Productions Broadening Base with 'Wild Times,' " *The Hollywood Reporter* (September 19, 1979).

[3]Lee Enterprises consists of one AM, one FM, and five television stations, including KHQA, Hannibal, Mo.; WSAZ, Huntington, W.V.; and KOIN, Portland, Oreg. Lee Enterprises also owns 49.75 percent of the *Lincoln* (Nebraska) *Journal*.

[4]Cox Broadcasting controls five VHF television stations in major markets (including WSB, Atlanta; WIIC, Pittsburgh; WHIO, Dayton; and KTVU, Oakland–San Francisco), five AM and seven FM radio stations, and two national sales representative firms. In addition, Cox owns more than half-interest in Cox Cable Communications, which operates thirty-six cable systems.

[5]Gaylord Broadcasting owns two AM stations, one FM, and seven television stations. The latter are WTVT, Tampa; KTVT, Fort Worth; KHTV, Houston; KSTW, Tacoma; WVTV, Milwaukee; WUAB, Cleveland; and WVUE, New Orleans. Gaylord is also heavily involved in newspaper publishing through its parent company, Oklahoma Publishing Company.

[6]King Broadcasting, Inc., owns five AMs, four FMs, and three television stations. The stations are KGW-AM-TV and KINK-FM in Portland, Oreg.; KING-AM-FM-TV in Seattle; KREW-AM-FM-TV in Spokane, Wash.; and KYA-AM-FM in San Francisco.

[7]Golden West Broadcasters is owned 50.1 percent by the famous western

movie star Gene Autry and his wife Ina Mae Autry. The company headquarters is in Hollywood, Calif., and the stations owned include KMPC-AM and KTLA-TV in Los Angeles; KSFO-AM, San Francisco; KEX-AM, Portland, Oreg.; KVI-AM, KPLZ-FM, Seattle; and WCXI-AM and WTWR-FM, Detroit.

[8]See chapter introduction for a description of Gateway Communications.

[9]RKO General, Inc., owns and operates six AM, six FM, and four television stations. This broadcasting company is wholly owned by General Tire and Rubber Company. Stations include WOR-AM-TV and WXLO-FM, New York; WGMS-AM-FM, Bethesda, Md.–Washington, D.C.; WHBQ-AM-TV, Memphis; KHJ-AM-TV and KRTH-FM, Los Angeles; and WFYR-FM, Chicago.

[10]*Testimony of Two Men* carried 6 minutes of advertising in each of its 6 hours. OPT's second vehicle, *The Bastards*, was telecast by sixty-eight affiliates and twenty-five independents, including forty-nine of the top fifty stations, and carried no advertising.

[11]Multimedia Broadcasting Company, a division of Multimedia, Inc., is one of the fastest growing broadcast companies of the nation. Ownership includes six AM, six FM, and six television stations, including WMAZ-AM-FM-TV, Macon, Ga; WXII-TV, Winston-Salem, N.C.; WLWT-TV, Cincinnati; and WFBC-AM-FM-TV, Greensville, S.C. Multimedia is also a very successful publisher of newspapers including *The Montgomery* (Alabama) *Advertiser,* and the *Asheville* (North Carolina) *Citizen Times.* Ten percent of the parent company's earnings come from Multimedia program productions such as *Phil Donahue,* and *Young Peoples' Specials.*

[12]Bonneville International Corporation is owned by the Corporation of the President of the Church of Jesus Christ of Latter-day Saints and operates five AM stations, seven FM, and two television properties. The television stations are KIRO in Seattle and KSL in Salt Lake City; radio stations include KIRO-AM-FM, Seattle; KOIT-FM, San Francisco; WCLR-FM, Chicago; KMBZ-AM and KMBR-FM, Kansas City, Mo.; WRFM-FM, New York; KAFM-FM, Dallas; and KSL-AM, Salt Lake City.

[13]Metromedia, Inc., is the largest non-network group, owning primarily independent stations in major markets. It boasts a total of six AM, seven FM, and seven television stations and is one of the most active broadcast companies in the industry. Some of the most outstanding broadcast properties are operated by this aggressive and forward-looking company. Stations owned by Metromedia include WIP-AM and WMMR-FM, Philadelphia; KTTV-TV, KLAC-AM, and KMET-FM, Los Angeles; WTTG-TV, Washington, D.C.; WXIX-TV, Newport, Ky.; WTCN-TV, Minneapolis; KMBC-TV, Kansas City, Mo.; WCBM-AM, Baltimore; WOMC-FM, Detroit; KRLD-AM, Dallas; and WNEW-AM-FM-TV, New York. The company is involved in program syndication and production and various sports and entertainment activities.

[14]Joel Chaseman is president of Post-Newsweek Stations, Inc., which consists of WFSB-TV, Hartford; WPLG-TV, Miami; WJXT-TV, Jacksonville; and WDIV-TV, Detroit. The broadcasting company is a subsidiary of the Washington Post Company, publisher of the *Washington Post, Newsweek,* and the *Everett Herald* (Washington State) and part owner of the *International Herald Tribune.*

ADDITIONAL PERIODICAL READINGS

Howard, Herbert H. "Cox Broadcasting Corporation: A Group-Ownership Case Study." *Journal of Broadcasting* 20 (Spring 1976): 209–31.

A case study of one of the oldest and largest group owners, based on a Ph.D. dissertation at Ohio University.

Patrick, W. Lawrence, and **Howard, Herbert H.** "Decision Making by Group Broadcasters." *Journal of Broadcasting* 18 (Fall 1974): 465–71.

Results of a survey of thirty-six group owners on the level of policy and management decision, including programming—whether at local or headquarters level.

Prisuta, Robert H. "The Impact of Media Concentration and Economic Factors on Broadcast Public Interest Programming." *Journal of Broadcasting* 21 (Summer 1977): 321–32.

A study examining the relationship between economic success, public interest programming, and media concentration.

"Public Affairs: Magazine Shows Proliferate; Investigative, Ascertainment Efforts Sharpen." *Television/Radio Age* (October 24, 1977): 36 ff.

Report on changes in public affairs programming between 1976 and 1977; discusses several group productions.

Sobel, Robert. "The 'Fourth TV Network': What are the Prospects?" *Television/Radio Age* (July 3, 1978): 21 ff.

Analysis of several attempts to create a fourth commercial network.

"Stations Continue Strong in Local Kid Shows Despite Typically Low Ratings and Unprofitability." *Television/Radio Age* (August 13, 1979): 41 ff.

Analysis of locally produced children's programming efforts, emphasizing role of group-owned stations.

"Syndicated-Product Prices Chief Concern Listed by Stations in *Television/Radio Age* Survey." *Television/Radio Age* (February 28, 1977): 32 ff.

Highlights of responses to survey on programming from general managers, program directors, and general sales managers.

"TV Programming & Production for Profit," *Broadcast Management/Engineering* (July 1977): 28 ff.

Report on local production at Post-Newsweek stations.

"TV Programming & Production for Profit." *Broadcast Management/Engineering* (October 1978): 32–34.

Report on Post-Newsweek group programming.

"TV Programming & Production for Profit." *Broadcast Management/Engineering* (February 1979): 33–36.

Report on Capital Cities group programming.

Wirth, Michael O., and **Wollert, James A.** "Public Interest Program Performance of Multimedia-Owned TV Stations." *Journalism Quarterly* 63 (Summer 1976): 223–30.

Analysis of 1973 FCC programming data, demonstrating better-than-average performance in news and public affairs of group-owned and multimedia-owned stations.

7 Station Representatives' Role in Programming

Richard A. Bompane

When he was vice-president of research and programming at Avery-Knodel Television, Richard A. Bompane oversaw the collection and analysis of programming research and its application to station strategy at one of the largest New York representative firms. Avery-Knodel, among others, advises client stations on entertainment programming purchases, newscasts, and on-air scheduling, as part of a package of research, promotion, and marketing services. Such services are offered by major, full-service station representative firms. Generally firms specialize in network-affiliated stations or independent stations in similar-sized markets. Avery-Knodel Television represents clients primarily in midsized markets. Before joining Avery-Knodel Television in 1974, Mr. Bompane was a research manager for Harrington, Righter & Parsons. His background since 1961 includes the positions of director of research and sales promotion for WCBS-TV in New York, director of research for WTOP-TV in Washington, D.C., research manager for H-R Television in New York, assistant director of research and sales promotion for Storer Television Sales, Inc. in New York, and research analyst for RKO General Broadcasting in the National Sales Division. In this chapter, Mr. Bompane examines the sensitive role of the station representative programmer in the television industry.

THE EMERGENCE OF THE REPRESENTATIVE IN PROGRAMMING

One of the significant changes in the television industry since 1970 has been the increased influence of national sales representatives in programming at the local station level. Changes in key sources of revenue, in regulation, in program supply, and in technology created a need for improved program strategy, which in turn created a new role for **station representatives**.

As **network-affiliated station** revenues shifted from dependence on network compensation to local and national spot advertising, competition among the stations in a market increased in vigor. Many managers felt unprepared to program their stations without reliable information and sought professional advice. Several segments of the industry responded to this need, among them television news and radio program consultants and sales representatives.

Another change since 1972 resulted from the Federal Communications Commission (FCC) **primetime access rule** (PTAR) that opened up six half hours of **primetime** each week for **local** station programming. More and more **off-network situation comedies**, westerns, drama series, and cartoons became available to stations through **syndicators** to fill the half-hour access slots for markets smaller than the top fifty. Affiliates in the major markets were prohibited from using off-network programs and had to rely on new sources of **first-run** programming. This increased the need for accurate information on which to base program purchase decisions.

Although some first-run programs were available, feature films—the mainstay of television in the 1950s and early 1960s—became increasingly scarce. As all three networks expanded the number of movie nights in their schedules and CBS began to televise late-night movies five days per week, stations faced higher costs for the movie packages remaining after networks' purchases. Since the networks purchased the best titles, the local stations could choose only among movies of less **promotional** value. By the mid-1970s, another problem arose: the "increasing supply" of off-network reruns had dwindled as fewer series survived the five-year primetime run necessary to generate enough episodes for effective **stripping**.

In addition, increasing competition from **independent** stations in the major markets, the growth of cable in the small markets, and growing sophistication in the use of **demographics**, computers, and coverage data by national (and some local) advertising agencies altered the local competitive television program arena. A combination of all of these factors created a growing interest in local station programming on the part of national sales representatives and a growing need for professionalism in program purchases, newscasts, and program scheduling.

The mutual interests of both station representatives and stations are served by the existence and expansion of the programming support provided by reps, and station managers now rely on reps for a great deal of advice and specific recommendations in the program area. In local programming, however, representatives remain in an advisory capacity. The rep does not have, and should not have, decision-making responsibility or actual control over a station's programming policy. The station, as a licensed trustee of the public airwaves, has ultimate responsibility for everything it broadcasts. Advice from reps is just one of several factors that experienced station managers consider before committing funds to a particular program or deciding on a specific schedule. Other important sources of information are local station program and promotion departments, local and network sales management advisers, and local community representatives in some cases.

REP PROGRAMMERS VS. STATION
PROGRAM DEPARTMENTS

One might ask why, since stations have their own program departments, they need advice from a rep's national program department?
The answer lies in the difference in backgrounds and areas of expertise
of local program managers and their counterparts at the station representative firms, in the information available to each, and in their differing approaches to the same problems, particularly in the smaller
markets.

The Local Program Director

Local program directors, with some exceptions in the largest
markets, are generally products of stations' production staffs. Their
major responsibilities lie in producing and directing local programs,
commercials, newscasts, sports, and other special-event telecasts. Seldom do they have any experience with national sales representatives,
agencies, or national advertisers. However, they are knowledgeable
about station budgets and facilities, the local market, the nature of the
competition, and the socioeconomic, religious, ethnic, and cultural
backgrounds of their viewing audience. They also are well aware of their
stations' obligations and commitments to locally produced programming and public service.

In medium and small markets, the primary responsibilities of
program directors remain in production. They handle other program-
related functions such as issuing the station's program schedules, maintaining liaison with network program sources, and coordinating the
arrival, telecasting, and **bicycling** of program tapes. In larger markets,
the station program director may have acquired considerable experience
in programming strategies, but medium- and small-market program
directors rarely have background in this area. Consequently, rep program departments deal infrequently with local station program directors; their main point of contact is the station manager at midsized and
small-market stations.

The Rep Program Director

Program directors in national representative firms typically have
some local station experience, generally in programming, probably
combined with experience in research. They also frequently have experience in sales and promotion. Rep program directors are knowledgeable
about analytical tools such as local and national **ratings** service data,
flow of audience, duplication of viewing, **demographics**, and **psychographics**. Rep program directors deal with several different television

markets and are attuned to a greater variety of programming situations than are local program directors or station managers.

Rep program departments also have sources of information that are unavailable to their local counterparts because of the expense of major research reports, the specialized interpretation some require, and the inability of program syndicators to disseminate their information effectively to all stations in a reasonable time. National sales representative firms, in addition to their daily contact with stations in several markets that yields program trends and new techniques, often purchase the full spectrum of audience-research information available from the Arbitron and Nielsen ratings services. This information includes all ratings reports published in every television market in the country, performance reports on all programs on network television and in syndication on a market-by-market basis, cable penetration information, and special analyses such as TvQ data and the like.

Rep programmers also maintain constant lines of communication with all three networks, independent groups, syndicators and producers, news and program consultants outside the firm, and all of the various trade organizations, including the Television Bureau of Advertising (TvB), the National Association of Television Program Executives (NATPE), the Television Programmers' Conference (TVPC), and the Independent Television Station Association (INTV). The everyday contacts among national sales representatives, advertising agencies, and major advertisers also add to the myriad information sources available to rep program directors.

The Rep/Station Program Team

Because of varying degrees of experience, diversification, and sources of information, rep program directors complement local station program directors and station managers. Their relationship involves a two-way flow of information—from the station manager (who in turn is informed by the local program department) to the national representative firm and from the rep programmers back to local management. More extensive and higher quality data for all parties result from this kind of teamwork. For the station, the outcome is a more competitive position in its market; for the representative firm, the goal is a station with higher ratings that has more valuable time to sell, resulting in an across-the-board gain in profits.

REP PROGRAMMERS' RELATIONSHIPS WITH SYNDICATORS

Rep programmers offer syndicators the opportunity to screen programs at a central location for a single person or group of people who inform and influence a large number of prospective buyers. If a syndicator can convince the rep programmers that a series will produce high ratings for some or all of their stations, the syndicator gains their support for the series in several different markets throughout the country without the added expense of travel to each market to make a presentation. This is especially important in medium- and small-market sales in which expenses greatly reduce potential return to the syndicator.

By presenting programs to rep programming departments and supplying them with relevant information on the program, a syndicator covers dozens of potential clients at one time. Syndicators know reps inform their clients of all presentations and recommend programs to individual stations as warranted. Even when the rep programmers do not believe in a program's appeal for a mass audience, they inform client stations of the existence of all shows, giving syndicators free publicity, if not open support.

Although syndicators maintain as close contact as possible directly with stations, most apprise rep programmers of their activities. Syndicators arrange periodic screenings of new and old program availabilities, discuss plans for producing new series, and keep reps aware of contacts with their client stations. Syndicators with faith in the viability of their programs frequently suggest that local program directors or station managers contact their rep program department for its evaluation. Syndicators sometimes contact reps to get their opinions on the possibility of placing the show in the market and to discuss pricing before they approach specific stations.

Restrictions on Rep/Syndicator Relationships

Because the rep programmers are indirect agents of the stations their company represents, they must constantly be aware of their responsibilities to the client stations and must exercise caution in dealing with syndicators. Certain unwritten rules of ethics apply to the relationship between rep programmers and syndicators:

First, rep program departments almost never give blanket recommendations for any program or series. No program will have equal appeal in every market, and each must be considered on a market-by-market basis. Second, rep programmers do not supply information to syndicators to aid them in negotiations with stations. This precludes any indication of prices paid by a given station for other programs, contract expiration dates, recent program purchases, future plans, and speculation on which other programs are being considered by a station.

The Reps and Program Pricing

National sales representatives have no control over the prices charged for programming or those paid by clients or other stations in a market. Rep program directors are occasionally involved in negotiating with syndicators, but instances in which the rep has the authority not only to negotiate but also to purchase programming on the station's behalf are rare. However, pricing is an important factor in programming, and the rep programmers keep track of prices of major syndicated properties throughout the country, particularly in light of escalating program costs in the late 1970s. This information helps the rep programmers inform a station on the relationship between a program's asking price in its market and other markets.

SERVICES PROVIDED BY REP PROGRAMMERS TO STATIONS

A national representative's program department offers its clients extremely diversified programming services. Much of the information disseminated by the rep program department is of a general nature covering networks, syndication, **barter**, **specials**, program performance, movies, trends, and **pilots** in production or still in planning stages. Local station sales staffs as well as sales departments in the rep firm receive reports apprising them of program developments relative to the overall rating performances of new series and specials.

Network Program Information

The rep program director, being located in New York, has access to key programming sources at each of the three networks, in independent groups, and from trade press publications. Until the end of the 1970s, an adversary relationship existed between reps and the networks. Obtaining any information from a network regarding program changes, specials, or sports was like pulling eyeteeth for a rep program department. Consequently, reps turned to other sources of information and frequently uncovered data not yet sent to one or more network affiliates. Occasionally the reps' lists of the networks' upcoming specials, for instance, included twice as many programs as lists sent by the networks to some of their affiliates. This pointed to a serious problem: some network affiliates received program information sooner than others. Although the networks denied that this was true, reps encountered instances in which one client station had been told of thirty upcoming specials and another client affiliate was aware of fewer than a dozen.

NBC was the first of the three networks to take a step toward conciliation with national sales representatives by inviting all firms to a preview presentation of the 1978–79 NBC network schedule. NBC also appointed a staff member in its Affiliate Relations Department as the contact for reps seeking information on NBC programming. The timing of this decision may have been related to the fact that the network was in third place nationally and had lost several key affiliates to ABC. Although this gesture may have been to gain rep support in an effort to prevent further desertions, it solved one-third of the reps' problems in gathering network program information. In 1979 both ABC and CBS followed NBC's lead and held similar presentations of their 1979–80 schedules, announcing an end to the adversary atmosphere between networks and reps.

As a consequence of these changes, rep program departments are able to issue information on all three networks' program schedules with much more ease than in the past. Rep program departments generally provide network information as follows:

Primetime network schedules (monthly)
Daytime network schedules (quarterly)
Sports schedules (quarterly)
Specials (quarterly)
Movies (monthly)

Changes announced by the networks in any of these areas are sent out to the rep's client stations as addendums to monthly or quarterly reports. Because of the frequency of program changes and specials telecast by the networks, rep program departments usually issue night-by-night primetime schedules covering a one-month period.

Syndicated Program Information

Keeping clients informed of new developments in syndicated programming includes notices on (1) off-network programs that have been released for syndicated rerun—as well as keeping track of those yet to be offered, (2) new programs produced especially for syndication, (3) barter programs, (4) specials, (5) sports series, and (6) mininetwork ventures such as Operation Prime Time (OPT).

When rep programmers screen a pilot or an episode of a new series, they issue program bulletins to client stations indicating their reaction to the show's content, production values, possible demographic appeals, and proposed time periods. These reactions are typically stated in very general terms. Although rep programmers usually do not give blanket recommendations to new series, even more rarely do they suggest that none of their client stations consider a particular series. *The Muppet Show* was one of the positive exceptions; few reps could resist high praise for it after seeing only a **demo-tape**—not even a full pilot.

Similar program bulletins are issued to stations when the rep program department learns of a network television series to be offered to stations in syndicated rerun. Traditionally, these series had become available after network cancellation. However, in the late 1970s, currently scheduled network series began being offered several years prior to their release dates, generally with a guaranteed availability date (**futures**). This sometimes led to stations airing a series of reruns while new first-run episodes of the same program were aired by the network in primetime. In these circumstances, syndicators usually are required by network contracts to change the on-air title of the reruns until the first-run show is canceled by the network. For example, *Bonanza* reruns were called *Ponderosa* in syndication; *Marcus Welby, M.D.* became *Family Doctor; Emergency* became *Emergency One;* and *Happy Days* was *Happy Days Again.* CBS's *M*A*S*H* is an exception: It carries the same title in syndication as on the network.

Unlike bulletins about totally new programs, bulletins about off-network series or specials usually include some audience information relative to network performance in primetime plus daytime or late-night rerun track records. The syndicator generally supplies this information, but rep program departments have the resources to gather such data on their own.

Program and Research Trends

Rep programmers provide client stations with detailed information on the ratings of syndicated programs and feature films, along with data on developments in audience research. To perform this function, rep program departments invest several hundred thousand dollars each year in a variety of audience-research data from Arbitron, Nielsen, and other sources.

1. *National and overnight ratings.* Nielsen reports national Nielsen Television Index (NTI) data from a sample of about 1,500 metered households throughout the country. These data give rapid information about the ratings levels achieved by network programs. NTI is extremely expensive and is purchased solely by the networks for their exclusive use. However, much of this information is supplied to trade publications by the networks, and weekly reports thus are available to rep programmers.

In New York, Chicago, and Los Angeles, both Arbitron and Nielsen use meters for audience measurement, and Nielsen also uses meters in San Francisco. The **overnight** reports for these markets are extremely expensive, but a few major-market sales representatives do purchase them. The ratings services print weekly reports based on these overnight samplings, which are part of the package of materials purchased by the other representative organizations. These reports are valuable because they give information about the performance of new network programs—particularly important at the start of a new television season. These weekly reports also include data on audiences for syndicated programs carried on stations in those markets.

2. *Sweep reports.* Most reps subscribe to either the Arbitron or Nielsen "rep package." It includes a copy of every ratings report published for every television market. Rep program departments use these reports to keep track of program performance under all possible circumstances: how particular programs perform on weak stations (or small-market UHFs), on strong stations, in various **dayparts**, in particular regions of the country, in small markets and large markets, and against every conceivable type of competition. These reports are used to measure the potential of a program in an untried market. If a client station is considering scheduling a new show in access, rep programmers can report on how the program did in any number of similar circumstances including daypart, competition, cable influence, and other relevant factors.

3. *Syndicated-program reports.* Following each major **sweep** period (November, February, May of each year), the ratings services publish a compendium of the performance of all major syndicated programs. To qualify for inclusion, a program must be carried on at least five stations during the survey period. Arbitron's report is entitled *Syndicated Program Analysis*; Nielsen calls it *Report on Syndicated Programs*. These reports are among the most valuable tools of the rep programmer. Although they are published at least a full month after the usual ratings reports for the sweep, the syndicated-program reports list all the markets in which a program ran in a simple easy-to-use format that includes information such as

   a. Average **share** and demographics by daypart
   b. Average share and demographics by number of stations in market
   c. Program audience in individual markets including comparative data on **lead-in** audience and competitive programs
   d. Rankings of each program by average demographic rating delivery and by program type

   When rep programmers look for a group of the best programs to recommend to a particular client, these syndicated-program reports are generally the first source they refer to after ascertaining what the client station requires and what programs are available in its market. Rep programmers use the information in syndicated-program reports to back up their estimates of anticipated audience levels for a recommended program.

4. *Network-program reports.* Both ratings services issue an analysis of network programming three times a year. These reports (which Arbitron calls *The Network Program*

Analysis and Nielsen calls *Network Programs by DMA*) list ratings levels achieved in every market in the country by every network program telecast during a ratings period. These reports lack the detail of their syndicated programming counterparts because they show only ratings in each market, not shares. They include an index indicating the relationship of each rating to each program's national average. These reports have little value for program decision making at stations. Occasionally some local affiliates do not **clear** a network program, and the network offers it to other stations in the market. In this case, the network-program reports can be used as guides to the audience levels likely for the network program if picked up by client stations.

5. *Syndicator-supplied material.* Syndicators often have their own research and promotion departments that issue information on the performance of the programs they distribute. This material is sent to all prospective purchasers and to national sales representatives. Rep program departments check the accuracy of these data and inform the syndicator and their client stations if the material is erroneous. Although rep programmers sometimes use research information supplied by syndicators, they do so with full knowledge that it is promotional, generally including only positive aspects and ignoring negative data. Occasionally, the syndicator of a new program retains a nationally known audience-testing firm for special research similar to network pilot testing. The results of such tests are made available to reps and stations. However, this is done rarely because audience-reaction testing is expensive for any series produced especially for syndication.

6. *Computerized research.* Arbitron's Information on Demand (AID) and Nielsen's NSI-Plus are computerized research programs that allow subscribers to solicit more specific viewing information from the diary samples than is available in standard printed research reports. The types of special studies obtained from these services include the following:

a. *Flow of audience.* This analysis shows what the audience does between programs. It shows the effectiveness of a program in holding onto the audience that viewed the preceding program. It shows how good a lead-in a program provides to a more important show. For instance, if a stripped syndicated series leads into the local news at six o'clock, the series may generate a high share of audience and therefore appear to be a success. However, if, at the end of the series' episodes, a large percentage of its audience turns to nonnews programming on the competition or turns the set off, this series

harms the station's local news because it is not supplying a strong flow of viewers to that newscast. If a large
portion of the lead-in program's audience stays tuned
for the news, then the show is a success in that it not
only performs well but also helps build the audience of
the succeeding program. In another scenario, the lead-
in series' viewers watch local news at six o'clock but on
the competition, leading to the conclusion that the station's local news is weak.

b. *Duplication of audience.* These studies are audience-
flow studies, but the programs being compared do not
run adjacent to one another. A study of this type is used
to determine the extent to which a station's news viewers tend to watch both the early and late local newscasts
or which of several programs in one genre (such as
sit-coms or adult adventure dramas) should be placed in
a station's schedule and in what order.

c. *County-by-county studies.* Using computerized research or the county coverage studies published annually by the two ratings services, a programmer or news
consultant can determine if there are any weak areas in a
station's coverage or in the performance of local news in
any particular county or group of counties. If some
counties appear not to be viewing a newscast to the
same extent as "the average county," rep programmers
may recommend additional promotable news features
of interest to the residents of that area.

7. *Research trends.* Programming is a chess game in which
the station strives to achieve the highest ADI and DMA
share (CHECK) combined with a dominance in key demographics (MATE). All national advertisers and a growing
number of local advertisers concentrate their advertising
pressure on particular demographic categories. The most
requested demographic in the 1970s was women viewers
between 18 and 49 years of age. The station that achieved
and maintained a strong 18 to 49 women's audience in the
1970s had a strong advantage when soliciting revenue from
most advertisers. However, because of changes in population growth, buying power shifts, and myriad other factors, some major television advertisers changed their key
target audience to women aged 25 to 54 as they entered the
1980s. Such trends are monitored by rep programmers,
and information of this nature is passed on to the stations.

News Consulting

The Katz Agency formed the first formal rep news department in
1974. In 1975 Avery-Knodel Television entered into an exclusive agreement with an outside news consulting firm to conduct news analyses for

its client stations and by 1977 had organized its own news consulting department. As of 1979 these were the only two national sales representatives with formal news departments, but other rep firms are expected to become involved in this important aspect of station programming in the 1980s.

Both the Katz Agency and Avery-Knodel Television charge about $10,000 a year plus travel expenses for this extra service. Although station representative firms generally do not charge their clients more than the sales commission rate for programming services, news consulting is an exception. The added fees for news consulting do not nearly cover the full costs of operations, but the rep firms benefit by the stations' ability to deliver higher news ratings because they can sell their client stations' news at higher rates.

The first step in news consulting is to review videotapes of the local news in the market from the client station and its competitors. An initial evaluation of the qualities of the client's news—including set design, camera work, performance of talent, content, and use of ENG and **Chromakey** techniques—is based on these tapes. A follow-up visit to the station involves meetings with station management, news directors, producers, and on-air personalities, with detailed discussions of the news consultant's preliminary evaluation to gain added insight. Attitudinal research is used sometimes but requires an independent research study, which is usually quite expensive.

During initial and subsequent station visits, the news consultant studies the station's on-air news broadcasts in depth, as well as the behind-the-scenes operations that are so important to a newscast. The production and assignment desks are given a critical inspection, as is the role played by the news director. Among the most important factors in a successful news operation are the capabilities of the people in these departments and the systems by which they conduct their functions. The news consultant also trains on-air news talent during these station visits to aid them in improving their camera presence, voice, and delivery styles.

All of these station visits and meetings aid progress toward short- and long-term goals and focus on precise plans for their implementation. Priorities, deadlines, training, and personnel responsibilities are clearly assigned in a written evaluation, which covers every possible area of news broadcasting, including the following:

News set design
On-air talent (performance and training)
Format (newsroom, eyewitness, magazine, action)
Graphics
News administration (structure and control)
News director (evaluation of role)

Assignment desk (library, news sources, story assignment)

Production desk (strategy, techniques, control)

Special projects

Staff training

Special series and features (**mini-doc** series)

Electronic newsgathering (ENG)

Reporting (roles, story coverage, investigative)

Writing

Photography and editing

Promotion

When a member of a station's own representative firm evaluates and makes recommendations on news programs, these comments often are seen as less threatening to the station's talent and staff than those originating with an "outside" consultant firm. A sales representative has a long-term relationship with its stations and affects many aspects of the ongoing activities of the stations. Maximized news performance is generally acknowledged by station staffs to be in the best interests of both the rep firm and its client stations.

THE PRIME REP SERVICE: PROGRAM RECOMMENDATIONS

The most important service provided to client stations and the one demonstrating the real effectiveness and expertise of rep programmers is the individual program recommendation. The station program department or station manager assumes responsibility for successfully programming one station, but rep programmers must successfully recommend programming to all the stations their companies represent. Rep programmers cannot improve every station's audience in every time period, but their recommendations are expected to bring improvement in an inordinate number of cases. Consequently, rep programmers rely heavily on quantitative audience-research data. Rep programmers also scrutinize all client stations to locate pending problems—inroads made by competitors, downtrends in shares or demographics, and unusual program availabilities in any market—to initiate recommendations for changes without waiting for client stations to ask for them.

Station/Market History

The most recent ratings book tells programmers only that a problem exists; it ignores the extent and source of the problem. To become familiar with long-term trends in a market, rep programmers study the programming posture of each client station over a period of as much as five years. This embraces (1) tracking the programs aired successfully in the past in those markets, (2) determining whether problems are with the individual programs, related to overall station problems, or due to an increase in the competitiveness of other stations in the markets, and (3) locating other program areas that need improvement. If a problem extends beyond a single half hour of programming, it will not be visible in one ratings period; a long-term analysis is needed to bring it into perspective.

Counterprogramming

Once a program problem is located and a clear understanding of the program preferences of the market is determined, the next step is to study the weaknesses and strengths of the client station's competitors. One key question is always whether the client station should try to draw audiences away from competitors with similar-appeal programs or should build its own image with a different viewer group.

The station that offers viewers a strong alternative to the types of shows available on other stations in the market will maximize its audience potential and draw some viewers from its competitors. This is particularly effective when all competing stations are vying for similar demographics. For example, in a market in which two of the three stations are scheduling talk shows in early **fringe** (*Merv Griffin* against *John Davidson*), the third station will maximize its potential by programming a very different type of fare (for example, a series of half-hour situation comedies). This assures the station higher shares and younger demographics than either of its competitors because talk shows appeal to older adults and sit-coms generate 18 to 34 audiences. Children and teens also tend to favor situation comedies over talk shows.

In most markets, however, finding the right **counterprogramming** formula is not quite so easy. Consider a hypothetical three-station market in which all stations seek the same demographics, women 18 to 49. If one station carries strong sit-coms and another schedules a popular western series, the best alternative for the third station may be a talk show, although it would not do well among the 18 to 49 demographic group. A movie is a better choice, but stations must purchase the broadcast rights to several hundred features in order to develop a strong library of films for stripping. Some stations have tried stripping a block of first-run syndicated game shows in early fringe—a practice that has met with limited success, except in a few markets. The answer to this particular problem is not counterprogramming with specific programs but developing a stronger overall lineup of programs than either competitor.

Access time is the period in which the Federal Communications

Commission (FCC) has decreed that the networks cannot schedule other than the regularly scheduled newscasts (with a few exceptions). In consequence, other counterprogramming factors often enter the picture. In the fifty largest television markets, network affiliated stations are forbidden by FCC regulation to air reruns of off-network programs previously telecast in the market. Therefore, only first-run syndicated series are available for broadcast between 7 P.M. and 8 P.M. (EST). This restriction has led many producers to develop new products specifically for access, mostly in the game show genre. Although most of the access shows were produced originally as once-a-week half hours, the trend has been in the direction of strip programming, that is, five episodes per week.

Stripped programs are considerably more effective in generating viewer loyalty and are much easier to promote than a series of five different shows each week (**checkerboarding**). Since 1976 the success of such stripped game shows as *Newlywed Game, Tic Tac Dough, Jokers Wild, Crosswits,* and *Liars Club* has caused several stations to abandon any attempts at diversification in access-time programming. It is not unusual to see three or four stations in major markets vying for viewers with game shows in access. The independents in these markets, however, are not subject to the same restrictions and have been able to compete very effectively against the network affiliates in access with strong situation comedies that had previously run on network television in primetime (*Happy Days, All in the Family, M*A*S*H, Mary Tyler Moore,* to name a few).

In the smaller television markets, affiliated stations can schedule off-network series in access time and have a greater opportunity to counterprogram than in the top fifty markets. A small-market station facing two game shows in the 7:30 to 8 P.M. time period, Monday through Friday, should look for a popular sit-com and, conversely, should consider a game show strip if its competitors have sit-coms. Faced with a game show on one station and a sit-com on another, some stations have opted for the *PM Magazine* series produced by Group W in conjunction with local stations. Each station is required to produce some features for inclusion in *PM Magazine*; most of the program airs features submitted by other stations carrying the series. The main problems with this program lie in the expense of the ENG (electronic newsgathering) equipment and the on-air talent and production staff required by the program contract.

Creating an Audience Flow

To develop a strong schedule for a station, the rep programmer and local program staff must look beyond individual half hours. Each program in turn must feed viewers to the next show, creating **audience flow**. Special computerized research studies spell out the most effective order for a group of on-air programs to create the strongest flow of audience. If, for instance, a station wants to build a large young adult following, the most effective way is to begin its early fringe schedule with a strong kid-oriented cartoon series. This show, at about 4 P.M. (EST), will shift control of the television set from adults and effectively counterprogram the rest of the competition. To build up a totally adult audience, the next half hour should contain a sit-com with strong nonadult appeal (to hold the kids and teens from the lead-in) but with additional appeal to the 18 to 34 adults (**kiddult** programming). The third half hour should contain an even more adult oriented sit-com to continue building up to the news block at 5:30 or 6 P.M.

Some programs do not need the benefit of a strong, or even compatible, lead-in to generate high viewing levels. At certain times of the day the available audience changes to such a degree that it is not wise to rely on a lead-in strategy. Although these factors vary by market, general rules of thumb operate in early fringe and following the evening news. The time local schools let out—taking into account travel time—suggests the most appropriate time to begin scheduling for a nonadult audience. Generally 4 P.M. in eastern time zone markets offers the best opportunity for switching from an adult-oriented network daytime schedule to a kid's show. Following the local or network newscasts, which lean toward older adult demographics, many stations attempt to draw more young adults using a highly popular comedy or a stripped game show.

Choosing the Right Program

To determine the best program choice for a client station, rep programmers list all available programs fitting the desired category. The next step is ranking them based on the average share performance of each show according to the ratings service syndicated reports. The programs that fall below par in share value or have undesirable demographic appeals are eliminated from further consideration. The remaining programs are then examined for performance on similar stations, in markets in the same geographic area, and versus competitive programs of the type facing the client station. Potential lead-in strength is also considered.

The program director then presents the client with recommendations on first, second, and third choices plus raw research data, projected audience levels for each show, and the rationale behind the recommendations. Occasionally a list of eliminated programs is prepared with brief statements on the reasons for dropping each one.

The Sales Factor

Each rep organization approaches the relationship between its sales and programming departments differently. Some firms allow the sales department to override the decisions of the program director. Others have group meetings, allowing programming, sales, promotion, and other personnel to voice their opinions. A few firms give total program responsibility to their program departments.

Most program directors do not report to sales departments, but rather to corporate management. The rep programmer's function is to aid stations in developing the strongest and most salable schedule possible, while remaining aware of other important factors: FCC commitments, pricing, local pressures, station image, long-term planning, and something that should never enter into decisions but often does—the personal viewing tastes of the prime decision-maker, usually the local station manager. Although obviously important, sales value should not be the overriding factor in program recommendations because of the host of other considerations that play a part in programming strategy.

THE FUTURE ROLE OF THE REP

The role of the national sales representative in local station programming increased dramatically during the 1970s, but this growth will appear slow compared to the accelerated pace of the 1980s. The programming arena of the 1980s will be one of greater competitive pressure on all fronts. More television stations on the air, cable penetration exceeding the "magic" 30 percent level nationally, **pay-television** telecasting in virtually every major market, and more superstations— combined with home video recording, video discs, and two-way cable operations—will vie for more and more of the viewers' leisure time. Some foresee the day when an affiliated station will not be tied to a single choice for its primetime schedule but will be able to pick and choose from a variety of sources via satellite transmission.

Television stations will need increasing input for local program decision making and added sources for programs. As of 1980, several rep firms were considering entry into the field of production for syndication.

There is little doubt that the role of the rep in programming will be magnified by increasing competition in all markets. The question exists, however: is the television industry ready to face the challenges ahead? In 1971, Les Brown, then television editor for *Variety*, wrote:[1]

> The system seems to change but never really does;
> there are only modifications and changes in style. The
> president of a network can buy shows and set operating
> policies, but he is powerless to alter the machinery of his
> industry. Whatever their capabilities, however forceful
> they may be as leaders, the men in television are lashed to
> the system.

But the public is not lashed to it, and hope for the medium survives in that implicit freedom. The freedom of the public, in fact, is the time bomb in television.

NOTE

[1]Les Brown. *Television: The Business Behind the Box* (New York: Harcourt Brace Jovanovich, Inc., 1971), p. 365.

ADDITIONAL PERIODICAL READINGS

"Local TV Journalism in 1978." *Broadcasting* (August 22, 1977): 35–79.

1977 annual report assessing effects of consultants, new technology, competition, and the correlation between news and overall station ratings.

"The Radio Reps: Down in Number but Up in Ambition." *Broadcasting* (July 2, 1979): 39–63.

Special report on the role of station representatives in radio, dealing briefly with their influence on radio programming.

"Rep Segmentation Makes Buying Easier and Harder." *Television/Radio Age* (September 12, 1977): 29 ff.

Analysis of the effects of the proliferation of rep sales teams.

"The Skyrocketing World of TV Reps." *Broadcasting* (June 4, 1979): 37–62.

Special report on the job of the television station representatives including a new role as programmers for stations.

8 Public Television Station Programming

James Robertson

James Robertson is president of his own independent consulting firm in the public broadcasting field, Robertson Associates, Inc. He gained experience with the major aspects of public broadcasting while serving as director of programming for WTTW-TV, Chicago; vice-president of network affairs for National Educational Television (NET, the predecessor of PBS); vice-president and general manager of KCET-TV, Los Angeles; director of broadcasting for the University of Wisconsin; and executive director of National Educational Radio for the National Association of Educational Broadcasters (NAEB). His current role as president of Robertson Associates involves evaluation of the effectiveness of existing stations, plans for new ones, and research and community surveys preparatory to the development of statewide public broadcasting plans. From his work in evaluation, planning, and research for public radio in Ohio, Nebraska, and Virginia and for public television in Indiana and Illinois, he brings an authoritative view of the programming needs and concerns of public broadcasting stations.

PROGRAM PHILOSOPHY

Public television is a confusing term. All broadcasting is, by definition, public. The Communications Act of 1934 and the Federal Communications Commission (FCC) call the public television service "noncommercial educational broadcasting." That terminology reflects the fact that the service came into existence in 1952 because of the concerted efforts of educational interests. They lobbied the FCC into creating a special class of reserved channels within the television allocations exclusively **dedicated** to "educational television."

Ever since, an argument has been going on as to what the term should mean. One extreme in the argument thinks of "educational" in the narrow sense of "instructional." From that viewpoint, public television should devote most of its attention to teaching—directed not only to school and college classrooms but also to those outside classrooms. The last thing it should do is to compete for the mass audience of commercial television. At the other extreme are those who think of "educational" in the broadest sense. They want to reach out to viewers of all kinds and to generate mass support for the service. They perceive instructional television, if used at all, as a duty that must be performed, but their hearts are devoted to the wide range of programs that most people have come to think of as "public television."

That term was introduced in 1967 by the Carnegie Commission on Educational Television. The commission was convinced that the growing but struggling new service had to generate wider support than it had in its fledgling years. One of the impediments to such support, the commission felt, was the name "educational," which gave the service an unpopular image. They suggested "public television" as a more neutral term. Thus, a distinction has grown up between ITV (instructional television) and PTV (public television)—a distinction that is not altogether desirable or valid.

The first task of any public television programmer is to come to terms with the particular philosophy of a particular station. Philosophies vary from one extreme to the other, but there is at least one common theme that runs throughout: the fact of being noncommercial. The term implies that public television must directly serve "the people"; it must be, at the very least, different from—if not better than—commercial television. And one of the implications of this fundamental difference is that public television programming need not pursue the biggest possible audience at whatever cost to programming. Public broadcasting has a special mission to serve audiences that would be neglected otherwise because they are too small to interest commercial broadcasting. This difference in outlook has great significance for programming. It means that the public station programmer is relieved of one of the most relentless constraints that limit the commercial programmer's freedom of choice.

It does not mean, however, that public television can afford the indulgence of catering only to the smallest groups with the most esoteric tastes in the community. Broadcasting is still a mass medium, whether commercial or noncommercial, and can justify its occupancy of a broadcast channel and the considerable expense of broadcast facilities only if it reaches relatively large numbers of people. Public broadcasting achieves the goal cumulatively rather than instantaneously. It can afford to serve comparatively small groups as long as they add up to a respectably large cumulative total in the course of a week.

In recent years, public television has overcome its alleged tendency to attract only the so-called cultural elite. A January 1979 study revealed that in the two preceding years public television viewing increased among two of the population segments in which it had been relatively low: persons sixty years of age or older and blacks and other minority racial/ethnic groups.* The same study showed that although 53

---

*This study was undertaken by Statistical Research Inc. for the Corporation for Public Broadcasting in January 1979. The same study also showed that among those describing themselves as viewers of public television, 87% were white and 13% were nonwhite. This is remarkably parallel to the proportion of whites and nonwhites in the total U.S. population then within reach of a public TV station: 86.7% white and 13.3% nonwhite.

percent of those who described themselves as viewers of their public television channel were white-collar workers, *31 percent were blue-collar workers.* And although 21 percent were college graduates and another 22 percent had some college, *33 percent had finished only high school, and 18 percent had less than a high school education.*

Another consequence of the noncommercial approach to programming is its special obligation to produce programs locally, since **local** production is needed to serve distinctively local needs. Local programs are, almost by definition, small-audience programs. Largely for this reason, commercial television neglects local production (except news). It can gather larger audiences using relatively cheap syndicated material than it can with relatively expensive local production. Local production is no less expensive for noncommercial stations, and they must contend with the combined disadvantages of low budgets and higher demand.

TYPES OF STATIONS

One of the difficulties of describing programming strategies for public television is that the **stations** are so diverse. The 160 licensees, operating more than 275 stations, represent a wide spectrum of management viewpoints.* Much of this diversity is explained by the varying auspices under which they operate. Licensees can be grouped into four categories:

1. *Community stations.* In the larger cities of the country— particularly those with many educational and cultural institutions but without a dominant single institution or school system—the usual pattern of licensing is the nonprofit community corporation created for the sole purpose of constructing and operating a public television station. Because the governing board of such a station exists for the sole purpose of governing the station (as compared with university trustees who have many other concerns), there are those who feel community stations are the most responsive type of licensee. There are seventy stations of this type.

---

*There are more stations than licensees because in twenty states there is a legislatively created agency for public broadcasting that is the licensee for as many as eleven separate stations serving its state. Also, in several communities, one noncommercial educational licensee operates two television channels. In these latter cases (Boston, Pittsburgh, and Milwaukee, among others), one channel usually offers a relatively broad program service while the second channel is used for more specialized programming, particularly instructional materials.

Compared with other types of licensees, community stations derive a higher proportion of their operating support from their public: about 50 percent, compared with 29 percent for licensees as a whole. As a result, much of their programming reflects the urgent need to generate funds from those who are served by the station's programs. Programmers at these stations, therefore, are more likely than those at other types of stations to be sensitive to the general appeal of programs under consideration for airing. They will lean toward high-quality production values to attract and hold a general audience. These stations cannot grow or improve without a rapidly ascending curve of community support.

Within the community category, eight stations stand somewhat apart because of their metropolitan origins, their large size, and their national impact on the entire noncommercial service as producers of network-distributed programs. These flagship stations of the public broadcasting service are located in New York, Boston, Los Angeles, Washington, Chicago, Pittsburgh, San Francisco, and Philadelphia. The first four are particularly notable as production centers for the nation.

2. *University stations.* In many cases colleges and universities activated **public television stations** as a natural outgrowth of their traditional role of providing extension services to their states. As they see it, "The boundaries of the campus are the boundaries of the state,"* and both radio and television can do some of the tasks formerly done in person by extension agents. There are nearly eighty stations in this group.

Here, too, programmers attempt a fairly broad spectrum of program services, sometimes with an emphasis on adult continuing education and culture. And, as operating costs mount while academic appropriations remain limited, university stations also turn to their communities to supplement the budgetary support from their licensee institutions. This often is accompanied by broadened program appeals.

3. *Public school stations.* Local school systems initially became licensees of stations in order to provide new kinds of learning experiences for students in elementary school classrooms. From the outset, some augmented instruc-

---

*This particular expression is that coined by President Charles Van Hise of the University of Wisconsin in the early 1900s, but all land-grant colleges espouse similar traditions.

tional broadcasts with other kinds of programming consistent with the school system's view of its educational mission in its community. By the mid-1970s there remained fewer than twenty of these school stations. Most of them have organized a broadly based community support group whose activities help to generate wider interest and voluntary contributions from the community at large. Programmers at these stations naturally are heavily involved with in-school programming (instructional television on ITV), but because of the desire for supplementary community support, they are also concerned with programming for children out of school and for adults of all ages.

4. *State television agencies.* More than a hundred of the nation's public television stations are part of state networks operated by legislatively created public broadcasting agencies. Networks of this type exist in twenty states. Most of them were authorized initially to provide new classroom experiences for the state's schoolchildren. Most have succeeded admirably in this task and have augmented their ITV service with a variety of public affairs and cultural programs furnished to citizens throughout their states.

Although in recent years these state network stations have generated increasing support from foundations, underwriters, and even viewers, 70 percent of their dollar support still comes by way of legislative appropriation. This fact, plus the need to perceive their "community of service" as an entire state rather than a single city, gives programmers at these stations a different perspective than programmers at the other three types of stations. Most state network programming decisions are made at a central office, although there is a growing desire for mobile equipment to enable production to originate from anywhere in the state.

It should be evident from these brief descriptions that each category of public television stations poses special problems and special opportunities for programming strategies. Each type of station is ruled by a different type of board of directors—community leader boards, university trustees, local school boards, state-appointed central boards. Each type is likely to have its own kind of impact on program personnel. University boards, preoccupied with higher education's problems, tend to leave station professionals free to carry out their job within broad guidelines. School boards likewise are preoccupied with their major mission and in some cases pay too little attention to their responsibilities as licensees. State boards must protect their stations from undue political influences. All groups struggle to function with what they regard as inadequate budgets, but there are wide discrepancies in funding between the extremes of a large metropolitan community station and a small local public school station.

It is significant that in all types of stations the initial financial base has been broadened in recent years in order to keep up with rising costs and to improve both the quality and quantity of programs. Licensees who have had the greatest success in securing new funding have, in general, made the strongest impact on public television programming. This is partly because the firms or agencies that underwrite programs want to get maximum favorable impact from their investments. In turn, successful public television producer/entrepreneurs are motivated to create attractive new public television programs with broad audience appeal in the hope of securing still more underwriting. These kinds of programs increase viewership and hence draw more support in the form of memberships and subscriptions. While this trend has its salutary aspects, it has also tended to divert noncommercial television from some of its original goals. For example, controversial public affairs programs and programs of interest only to specialized smaller audiences tend to be neglected.

THE PROGRAMMER'S AUDIENCE-INFORMATION SOURCES

Before attempting to build a public television station's program schedule, a programmer must know the people who live in the area the station serves—not as objects for commercial exploitation but as constituencies entitled to special program services. An in-depth study undertaken in 1977 under the auspices of the television station managers themselves shows much about how programming decisions are actually made. It revealed the kinds of information on audience needs that programmers have available and the kinds of programming sources to which they can turn to fill those needs.

The study was conducted by Robertson Associates, Inc., to gather information on how local stations developed their own program service and the role that PBS and other nonlocal program sources played in total local offerings. Personal on-site visits were made to twenty PBS member stations, carefully selected to make the sample group proportional to the total PBS membership in several respects: UHF vs. VHF facilities, geographic location, licensee type, and size of market. The results of those interviews were measured against questionnaire responses from program managers of a different sample of twenty stations, equally representative of the total PBS membership. Thus, the findings of the study (many of which are reported in this chapter) were based on a double sample that included more than 25 percent of all public television station programmers in the country.

This study showed that public television programmers secure information on the public's needs and interests in at least seven ways:

1. *Mail and phone calls from viewers.* Public television stations generally keep fairly detailed records of viewer mail and phone calls. Of stations visited during the 1977 study, 20 percent keep very specific records and furnish reports to program decision-makers on numbers of letters and calls, topics mentioned, and attitudes expressed—both positive and negative.

2. *Viewers' evaluations through questionnaires and screenings.* Nearly half of U.S. public television stations use questionnaires (often published in their program guides) to solicit viewer responses to programs already aired and suggestions as to types of programs desired in the future. Some stations hold screening sessions for program advisory groups to tap a more representative sampling of opinion than can be acquired from the staff alone.

3. *Commercial ratings services.* Commercial ratings services are used by between 50 percent and 75 percent of U.S. public television stations. These services are not designed to rate public television but rather furnish profiles of viewing of the commercial channels within a given market. Public television programmers can use this information about the other stations in planning their schedules.

4. *Local studies commissioned by stations.* Since many public television stations are licensed to educational institutions with research capabilities, they are in a position to coopt faculty members and students to measure the impact of programs and to ascertain community needs. Several stations in metropolitan areas retain professional polling organizations to conduct periodic studies for them. Of stations visited, 70 percent used especially commissioned research, as did 50 percent of those polled.

5. *Information supplied by PBS.* Partly in response to urgings from television managers, the PBS administration decided in 1977 to increase its efforts to acquire audience information from both stations and national ratings services and to supply it to stations.

6. *Exchange of information with other programmers.* Program executives of public television stations have ample opportunities to exchange information on programming strategies when they meet at the frequent conferences of executives and during the annual PBS **station program cooperative**. This is a four-month process by which the

affiliates determine the **network** programs they are willing to help finance during the coming season.

7. *Formal ascertainment.* Since 1977 the FCC has required noncommercial as well as commercial stations to determine—through interviews of key community leaders and random sampling of the general public—the needs, interests, and problems of the station's local community. When obvious lacks are identified (needs or interests that are not being served), most public stations take this as a cue and endeavor to develop programming in response. Of stations polled in 1977, 70 percent said the results of their local ascertainment efforts had made a difference in their local programming decisions.

PROGRAM SOURCES

After gaining an understanding of the needs of their service areas, program managers face a second task: evaluating the full range of program sources at their disposal. Public broadcasting set out to be different from commercial broadcasting, and the development of unique

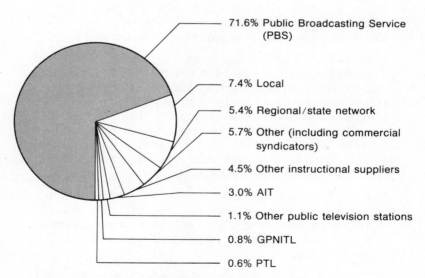

71.6% Public Broadcasting Service (PBS)

7.4% Local

5.4% Regional/state network

5.7% Other (including commercial syndicators)

4.5% Other instructional suppliers

3.0% AIT

1.1% Other public television stations

0.8% GPNITL

0.6% PTL

Totals more than 100 percent because of rounding

Source: Corporation for Public Broadcasting, 1977–78. Used with permission.

Figure 8–1. Percentage of Total
Public Television Program Hours,
by Sources, 1977–78.

program sources has been one of its most difficult problems. It had to have a national program service but not a network organization that dominates programming as do commercial networks. It needed **syndicated** material but could not depend on competing with commercial broadcasters for existing syndicated programs such as **off-network** series. It needed the means for syndicating instructional programming; there was no backlog of it as there was of syndicated entertainment material. And finally, it needed to stress local production, both because commercial programming neglects local production and because public television has a special obligation to serve local needs and interests.

The Public Broadcasting Service provides by far the largest amount of programming aired by public television stations across the country. Stations in major cities produce many of the series offered by PBS, but programming produced locally for local audiences accounts for less than 7.4 percent of all air hours. Since instructional programming is generally no longer produced locally, less than 1 percent of the 7.4 percent local programming is instructional. Total hours devoted to instructional programming *not* produced locally (from PTL, GPNITL, AIT, and other instructional suppliers) amount to 8.9 percent of all air hours. Regional and state networks and commercial syndicators supply the remainder of the programs (11.1 percent). (See Figure 8–1.)

The National Program Service

By all odds the most significant program source for most public television stations is the national program service, delivered by satellite to member stations by PBS, the Public Broadcasting Service. PBS is not a network organization in the customary commercial sense. It does not have "affiliates"; it undertakes no program production itself; it does not own or operate any stations. It is a membership organization to which every public television licensee belongs and for whom it administers and distributes the national program service according to policies and patterns set by the stations themselves.

PBS was the first national program distributor to adopt the satellite method of interconnection. This development came in 1978, and its consequences will continue to reverberate for years. PBS and the stations—with financial assistance from the Corporation for Public Broadcasting (CPB)—devised a system initially able to deliver two programs simultaneously. Eventually each member station may equip itself to "access" four channels. This novel aspect of satellite interconnection opens up possibilities whose ultimate significance cannot yet be calculated. One thing already is clear, however: many different program sources will use the network distribution facility, not just PBS itself. These sources include state and regional network sources, ad hoc groups of stations with common interests, and others that are yet to be thought of.

Most of the network offerings are determined each season not by the network headquarters but by the member stations themselves. The mechanism is far from simple. As early as February, PBS begins the process of offering to the network members programs for the season starting the following fall. Each station bids for the programs it wishes to schedule and can afford. The more takers for a program, the lower its price per station. Programs that receive too few bids to defray costs are cut from the offering. It takes several rounds of bidding over four to six months to evolve a list of accepted programs for the coming fall. The process—called the **station program cooperative** (SPC)—was adopted because the stations rejected the idea of centralized control of public broadcast programming such as that of the commercial networks.

Since station programmers do not have enough dollars for all SPC products they would like to buy, they tend to use the funds they have to assure continuation of already-proven series. This breeds a tendency to neglect the unfamiliar, the untried, the innovative—a widely recognized weakness in the SPC system.

At their 1979 annual meeting, PBS member stations endorsed a multiservice network plan: one service includes prime offerings for evening broadcast plus the children's daytime block led by *Sesame Street*. A second service features programs furnished by regional consortiums of independent producers and groups not yet formed as of 1979. A third service is made up mainly of in-school instructional and adult educational programming.

Although these multiple services promise new riches in the future, they also create two new factors that complicate local choice of PBS programs: one is the amount of lead time local program managers need to provide a place in their schedules for a desired PBS offering (and the consequent need for abundant advance information about the offering if it is a new one, so that a local decision can be made about whether and when to carry it). The other factor is operational. PBS feeds most programs more than once to accommodate stations located in six different time zones (including Alaska and Hawaii). Stations may carry a PBS program either at one of the times it is fed over the network or may tape-record it and play it at a time more convenient or appropriate for the station's schedule. (The local programmer must keep in mind that taping costs money and ties up personnel and equipment.)

Subnational Networks

Programmers are not limited to PBS for network programs. There are four regional telecommunications associations: the Eastern Educational Television Network (EEN) with members from Maine to Virginia; the Southern Educational Telecommunications Association (SECA) including stations from Maryland to Texas; the Central Educational Network (CEN) in the upper Midwest from Ohio to the Dakotas; and the Pacific Mountain Network (PMN) serving stations from the Rockies to the West Coast. These associations serve not only as forums for discussion of policies and operating practices of stations but also as agents for production and acquisition of programs. Set up to make group buys of instructional series, the regionals' role in providing nonlocal programming for general audiences as well as for ITV use was on the rise by the late 1970s. This trend was accelerated by the availability of the public television satellite distribution system, which enables any of these organizations or any combination of them to deliver a program at will to any public television station in the country.

The state networks in more than twenty states, as mentioned earlier, provide both instructional and general-audience programming, including legislative coverage and special events of statewide interest. In some states (such as Kentucky, Georgia, and Nebraska), programming decisions are made by a central programming office for the entire state. In other states (such as New York, Ohio, and Florida), programs scheduled on the state interconnection are the result of joint planning by the program managers of the stations within the state. Thus, although state networks are another source of programs for local stations within a state, most materials they produce do not serve stations beyond the state's boundaries.

Noncommercial Syndication

Because of its role in formal education, public television has had to develop its own unique body of **syndicated** material. The only precedent for this type of program stockpiling is the audiovisual film distribution center, an educational adjunct that came into being long before television. Public television gradually created a new appetite for instructional material, introduced technological resources for its production, and stimulated the founding of new centers for program distribution that perform the same functions as commercial syndication firms except on a noncommercial or cooperative basis.

The Agency for Instructional Television (AIT) in Bloomington, Indiana, produced ten new series during 1978–79. Altogether its catalog lists thirty series for primary grades and twenty for high school use. Among the best known are *Ripples, Inside Out, Bread and Butterflies,* and the Essential Learning Skills series, *Thinkabout.*

The Great Plains National Instructional Television Library (GPNITL) of Lincoln, Nebraska, offers dozens of series for elementary school use along with a great many materials for college and adult learning. Titles in their 124-page catalog for 1980 ranged from *The Art Consumer* and *I Can Read* for first graders to *Anyone for Tennyson* and *The Media Machine* for high schoolers and adults.

The International ITV Co-op, Inc., Falls Church, Virginia (known to most programmers for *Cover to Cover, Write On!,* and other widely used instructional series) has won international awards for its earth-space science series, *L–4.* Western Instructional Television, Los Angeles, offers more than 500 series in science, language arts, social studies, English, art, and history. The abundance of such cooperatively planned and produced ITV materials means that most instructional programming is no longer produced locally, except in cases in which the subject matter is unique to a local area or community.

Instructional materials for in-school use are usually selected by local school authorities, although providing liaison between sources for this material and users is an important function of the public television station's staff. Stations that serve schools usually employ an "instructional television coordinator" or "learning resources coordinator" to work full time with present and potential users: assisting teachers in proper use of the television materials, identifying classroom needs, and selecting or developing materials to meet the specific goals of local educators.

Programming for adult learners is available now to public stations at a level of quality not known in the earlier decades of public broadcasting. By the late 1970s, consortium efforts in higher education were turning out television courses designed to be integrated into the curriculums of most postsecondary institutions, yet produced in a way that made them attractive to the casual viewer as well. Budgets for such series range from $100,000 to $1 million for a single course. These efforts center particularly in community colleges, led by Miami-Dade (Florida), Dallas (Texas), and Coastline Community College (Huntington Beach, California).

Concurrently, the University of Mid-America (UMA), an "institution without walls" created to reach distant learners through off-campus television and other media, enlisted eleven major midwestern state universities as partners.* By the fall of 1979, under the leadership of the University of Nebraska and with both academic and media experts imported from elsewhere, UMA had developed a dozen courses with prominent television components on such varied topics as accounting, pesticides, and the history and culture of Japan.

Meanwhile, faculty members at other leading postsecondary institutions began developing curriculum materials to accompany several outstanding public television program series distributed nationally through PBS for general viewing. Of these, the first was *The Ascent of*

---

*As of mid-1979, UMA members included Iowa State, Iowa, Kansas State, Kansas, Minnesota, Missouri, Nebraska, North Dakota, North Dakota State, South Dakota, and South Dakota State universities.

Man, with the late Dr. Jacob Bronowski, a renowned scholar as well as a skillful and effective communicator on camera. More than 200 colleges and universities across the land elected to offer college credit for that course. Quickly others followed (*The Adams Chronicles, Classic Theater,* etc.) as programmers discovered such series furnished the casual viewer with attractive public television entertainment and simultaneously served more serious viewers desiring to register for college course credits.

This experience led many public television programmers to the realization that in the past too much had been made of the supposed demarcation between ITV and PTV. Too often during earlier years, those who saw themselves as producers of programs for a broader audience than "students" avoided even considering so-called instructional television. The first Carnegie Commission in 1965 strengthened this presumed gap by not concerning itself with television's educational assistance to schools and colleges and by adopting the term *public television* to mean programming for general viewing.

Recent experience has demonstrated that, although some programs are not designed for use in systematic learning and some programs are designed for this special purpose, both kinds can be appealing and useful to viewers other than those for which they were especially intended. The Bronowski series, *The Ascent of Man,* is only one example. Another is *Sesame Street,* initially intended for disadvantaged preschool children to watch at home so that they would be better prepared when they went to school. The target was youngsters in ghetto households, prior to their school years. Yet one of the most significant occurrences in kindergarten and lower elementary classrooms throughout America in the decade of the 1970s was the in-school use of *Sesame Street.*

An additional source of noncommercial syndicated programs available to the public television programmer is the Public Television Library (PTL), a repository for many programs that were initially distributed through the PBS interconnection or by NET (PBS's predecessor). PTL also handles the nonbroadcast distribution of these materials. Few stations use this source to any great extent (used in less than 1 percent of the total time on all stations in 1978).

Commercial Syndication

More extensively tapped sources, however, are such commercial syndicators as Time-Life, David Susskind's Talent Associates, Wolper Productions, Granada TV in Great Britain, and several major motion picture companies such as Universal Pictures. Public television stations sometimes negotiate individually for program packages directly with such syndicators; at other times they join with other public stations through regional associations to make group buys for their local schedules. Programs obtained in this way include historical and contemporary documentaries, British-produced drama series, and packages of highly popular or artistic motion pictures originally released to theaters.

The proportion of programming secured from commercial syndicators in specific public television station schedules may range from none at all to as much as 25 percent. The variation appears to derive from two factors: first, commercially syndicated programs that public television stations find appropriate are relatively expensive. Unless outside underwriting can be secured to cover rental fees, many stations simply cannot afford them. The second factor has to do with philosophy. Although much commercially syndicated material has strong audience appeal, its educational or cultural value is arguable. Thus, the extent to which commercially syndicated programs are used on a public television station's schedule depends on the station's programming philosophy and the availability of funds.

Local Production

The percentage of total on-air hours produced locally at public television stations has been decreasing gradually over the years, as both network and syndicated programming have increased in quantity and quality. The percentage of total on-air hours produced locally by public television stations declined from 16 percent in 1972 to 7 percent in 1978. Moreover, expectations in terms of production quality have edged upward. More time, facilities, and dollars must be used to produce effective **local** programs than before. A medium-sized station intending to produce 200 to 320 hours of local programs per year (or up to 1 hour per day, six days per week) should possess at least the following equipment:[1]

> One studio of 3,000 square feet
>
> Three studio color camera chains ($100,000 quality range each)
>
> Six videotape machines (a mix of one-inch and quad-ruplex)
>
> Two limited programmable videotape editing units
>
> Two film islands
>
> One graphic font character generator
>
> For film production: two 16-mm cameras and one 35-mm slide camera
>
> For remote production: one electronic newsgathering (ENG) unit and one **minimote**

The total cost for this equipment can range from $2.5 million to $3 million. With such equipment and a reasonably proficient engineering and production staff, a station should be able to turn out an hour a day of creditable local programming and handle up to 6,000 total hours of broadcasting per year, or 110 to 120 hours per week (a seven-day, 17-hour schedule).

Increasingly these days programmers opt to spend their limited local budgets on regular nightly broadcasts devoted to activities, events, and issues of local interest and significance. These are somewhat different from local "news" programs. Since commercial television stations concentrate on spot news and devote only a minute or less to each story, the public television stations see their role as giving more comprehensive treatment to local affairs.

Live and recorded news coverage outside the studios is becoming easier to handle as public television stations gradually acquire lightweight portable television equipment. ENG units and minimotes (small remote units) enable public stations to involve themselves more closely in their communities and surrounding service areas by capitalizing on television's unique ability to take viewers to places and introduce them to people they otherwise would never see or experience.

THE SEQUENCE OF SCHEDULE BUILDING

The programmer faced with the ideal opportunity of building an entire schedule from scratch must think in terms of sequencing. Types of programs must be phased in, one by one, with the most essential types having first choice of the most appropriate schedule positions. Program types of lesser importance must be fitted into the nooks and crannies left over after the more essential programming has been locked into place.

Instructional Programs

More than the general audience realizes perhaps, public television remains committed to its original primary mission of providing in-school instruction. Broadcasting still is the least expensive way to reach thousands of students in hundreds of elementary schools scattered over a wide area. In 1977, 95 percent of respondent stations told the Robertson Associates researchers they were committing the major share of their daytime hours to the broadcasting of instructional programs for in-school use. Moreover, about 80 percent indicated that in-school programming ranked "very high" or "rather high" among their own local program priorities. A few stations reported that use by schools of their daytime instructional service was steadily increasing— as much as 15 percent each year. However, other programmers expressed a desire to recapture some of those daytime hours for programs to serve viewers other than those in school. Evidently most public television programmers block into their schedule chart first of all the hours for classroom television for their area schools.

Network Programs

Another major element established early in the schedule building of most stations is network programming from PBS.* There are two reasons for this. One is that about two-thirds of the stations depend on PBS programs to generate their largest audiences. The second is that a number of PBS series have become staples in the local audience program diet, and viewers expect them to remain in the same time periods from season to season. For these reasons as well as to capitalize on national **promotion**, local programmers are increasingly inclined to carry major PBS features in the **primetime** spot proposed by the PBS programmers, so that a given telecast can be seen more or less simultaneously on all PBS stations across the country.

But unlike commercial networks, which expect their affiliates to carry national programs at their originally scheduled times, PBS cannot be sure that this will occur. Member stations control PBS. Consequently they are free, without fear of reprisal from their national organization, to rearrange PBS programs in any way they wish. This is part of the stress on local autonomy, a very strong principle of operation that is almost universal among public television stations. Programs coming from PBS via the satellite interconnection system can be recorded by the station for later insertion in its schedule. Indeed, when the satellite is feeding two programs simultaneously, the station has three scheduling choices: to air program A without delay, recording program B; to air program B without delay, recording program A; or to record both for later use. Programmers are not always completely free to take advantage of these options, however, because videotape recording machines are expensive to operate and maintain and may be tied up with other functions when needed to record off the network.

More than 155 earth terminals feed 90 percent of public television stations in the United States and associated territories. Access to national programs has become more readily controlled by individual stations. Figure 8–2—a map of originating and receiving terminals (**earth stations**)—shows their wide distribution. Virtually every public television station had its own earth station or access through a network to satellite signals as of 1980.

Commercially Syndicated Programs

Programs acquired from commercial syndicators usually form the next priority in schedule building. These features possess the same

---

*In the 1977 study, 35% of stations visited and 30% of those polled said they placed PBS programs into their schedules first. Another 35% of stations visited and an additional 45% of those polled said they placed PBS programs into their schedules second, after either ITV or key local programming.

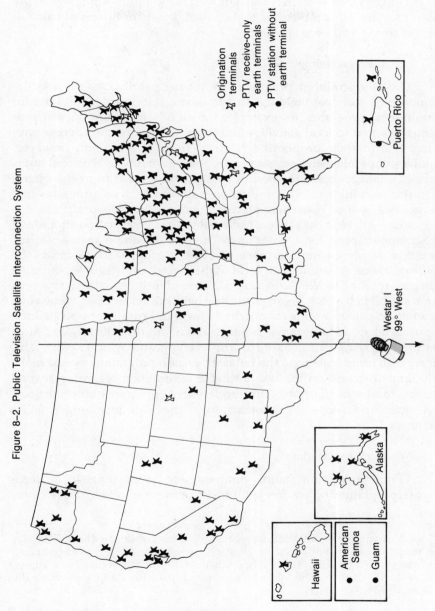

Figure 8–2. Public Television Satellite Interconnection System

Origination terminals

PTV receive-only earth terminals

PTV station without earth terminal

Puerto Rico

Westar I 99° West

Alaska

Hawaii

American Samoa

Guam

Source: Public Broadcasting Service, January 1979. Used with permission.

high quality and broad appeal as the best offerings from PBS but are acquired from other sources in order to add variety to a station's schedule (as long as they remain consistent with station philosophy). In many cases they are motion pictures that contain artistic or historical value as well as strong audience appeal.*

Local Programming

Locally produced programs do not necessarily come last in the sequence of schedule building. In fact, some stations block in time for certain **local** programs (for example, the nightly **magazine-format** programs devoted to local activities and interests) before considering anything else in their proposed schedule. There is a maxim, however, among public television programmers, that is not often verbalized but is usually implied: secure the best of whatever is needed from elsewhere, then use your limited local production resources to make programs that cannot be obtained elsewhere precisely because they are local.†

Just where in the schedule of a public television station should the programmer insert local programs? There is no single answer to this question, judging from the practices of the various stations across the country. Some schedule their local nightly news-and-feature magazine adjacent to *The MacNeil-Lehrer Report,* an in-depth news interview program supplied by PBS. Because viewing habits differ from one time zone to another, some stations cannot do this without running opposite local commercial news programs. Some stations air their local news-and-feature programs twice, once in early evening and again late at night. Here, as in other instances, the public television programmer must make a judgment, based on the best available information regarding several factors: local viewing habits and preferences, programs on other local channels, and programs available from the PBS incoming satellite channels.

Counterprogramming

Public television station programmers do not engage in fierce **counterprogramming** warfare with their commercial colleagues. Rather,

---

*Among the twenty PBS member stations visited during the 1977 study, ten reported use of syndicated programs as "negligible." Eight more indicated they constituted less than 10% of their schedule. Of the two remaining stations, one said 25% of their schedule was syndicated materials (largely movies); the other said 20%.

---

†Percentage of total on-air hours produced by public television stations locally, as reported by the Corporation for Public Broadcasting, in 1972 was 16.1%; in 1974 was 11. 4%; in 1976 was 10.1%, and in 1978 was 7.4%.

counterprogramming in public broadcasting takes a somewhat different form. Although practices differ from station to station, most public television programmers avoid putting their strongest drama opposite another station's strongest drama, preferring to play theirs at an hour when other stations are not appealing to the drama devotee. Instead, they may play their strongest public affairs feature or their strongest programming of some type other than drama. In areas in which viewers have a choice of more than one public television channel as well as the usual array of commercial channels, public television programmers usually confer with one another to develop a mutual pattern designed to give viewers the greatest possible choice of viewing times. Most PBS member stations play most PBS programs at least twice, and some also repeat selected local features a second time since there is always a large potential audience available to see repeats.

Audience Carry-Over

The 1977 Robertson Associates study discovered an interesting difference of opinion among public television programmers about viewers' tuning inertia. Do public television viewers watch a program merely because it follows one already tuned in? Or are they so selective that they make a conscious choice of which station to switch to next? The prevailing notion is that it is sometimes possible, with due regard for related interests and tastes, to schedule a sequence of programs that will hold viewers from one time period into the next. However, public programmers consider devoting a whole evening to one type of programming unwise because it excludes all potential viewers who happen not to be interested in that particular type of program.

FUTURE DEVELOPMENTS

Many people in the noncommercial field believe that the public television station of today will become the "public telecommunications center" of tomorrow—a place where the production, acquisition, reception, duplication, and distribution of all types of noncommercial educational-cultural-informational materials will be handled by telecommunications professionals who will stand ready to advise and counsel people in the community. Existing public television stations will contrive to transmit programs of broad interest and value to relatively large audiences of viewers scattered throughout their respective coverage areas. But they will also feed these and other programs to local cable channels and transfer programs of more specialized interest to video cassettes or video discs for use by schools, colleges, libraries, hospitals, and industry or for use on home video equipment.

Newly designed antennas capable of picking up superb quality video and audio signals directly from satellites without going through any ground-based broadcasting station ("direct broadcasting") may become available in the relatively near future at an estimated cost of $200. When the problem of scheduling multichannel satellite traffic is solved, this could mean distribution of public television programming directly from satellites to schools, colleges, libraries, industrial locations—and even homes—within the 1980s.

Companies with billions of dollars in assets are investing heavily to bring these new systems of communications into daily use. Thus they are elements that program decision-makers at every public television station must be aware of. For today's programming challenges—complex, difficult and rewarding as they may be—may turn out to be simple compared with those of the future.

NOTE

[1]Based on "Facilities Guidelines for Public Television Stations," prepared by the PBS Engineering Committee, coordinated by Kenneth S. Dewire, June 1978. Similar guidelines are furnished for smaller and larger stations.

ADDITIONAL PERIODICAL READINGS

Avery, Robert K., and **Pepper, Robert.** "Politics in Space: The Struggle over PTV Satellite Governance." *Public Telecommunications Review* 7 (January/February 1979): 19–28.

A historical perspective on the struggle over public television's use of the satellite interconnection. Last part of an extensive series.

Gunn, Hartford. "Inside the Program Cooperative." *Public Telecommunications Review* 2 (August 1974): 16–27.

Interview on the workings of the public television program cooperative.

Lindsay, Carl A., LeRoy, David J., and **Novak, Theresa A.** "Public Television: Whose Alternative?" *Public Telecommunications Review* 6 (March/April 1978): 18–23.

A study of the audience of public television by viewing habits and age, based on reinterviewing of 208 households from an Arbitron sweep sample.

PART THREE

Television Network Programming Strategies

Part II examines the programming strategies of individual stations. The authors of the five chapters in part III are concerned with programming that serves many different broadcasting stations or cable systems. They look at programming strategy from the perspective of network programmers, professionals who must consider more than a single configuration of stations in more than one size of market. Part III includes the national commercial and noncommercial networks as well as pay-television services and superstations.

As the programming strategies of the three commercial networks—ABC, CBS, and NBC—differ more by time of day than they do from network to network, part III subdivides national commercial programming by daypart rather than by network. Two chapters examine primetime and nonprimetime strategies. They cover the types of network entertainment programs but maintain the operational separations characteristic of the industry. The industry divisions reflect the pivotal importance of primetime ratings and revenue and the operational separation of news and public affairs from entertainment programming.

Primetime programs generate a network's image in the public's eyes; primetime ratings define a network's commercial importance in the minds of advertisers; affiliate images and revenues tie directly to network programming successes and largely revolve around the primetime period. Consequently, Chapter 9 on primetime programming has special importance. It covers the competitive strategies used by the three national networks. The author separates the elements of programming strategy and shows how each of the three networks has used these elements when introducing new programs and counterprogramming the other networks. Written by a former ABC, CBS, and NBC programmer, the chapter uses examples from the recent schedules of the three networks to isolate the typical programming characteristics of each network. However, the movement of figures such as Fred Silverman from one network to another and ultimately to the third has a long-term leveling effect on the potential differences between the networks' strategies.

Chapter 10 deals with nonprimetime programming, the prolific revenue geyser of the networks. It examines talk shows, soap operas, game shows, children's programs, and late-night programs. The author is a vice-president and programmer at ABC, which has rocketed from third position in the ratings to leadership in nearly all kinds of programming. The author expertly analyzes the key elements of the major types of nonprimetime programs for all three networks and describes the role of program development for each type. The chapter is divided into sections covering the problems of network weekday morning, afternoon, and late-night strategies, and the special problems of weekend and children's programming.

Chapter 11 introduces a perspective on national noncommercial television, which many industry observers would like to see competing head-to-head with the commercial networks. The author examines the national public television network service and its current philosophical contradictions and incapacities. As a former PBS programmer, the author is familiar with the constraints operating on the national service, and he focuses particularly on the conflict between the need for a truly national program schedule that can be supported by national promotion and the desire of individual stations for programming control. The fragmentation of philosophies and needs described in this chapter and in Chapter 8 provide a strong counterpoint to the apparent monoliths of the commercial networks.

This part also examines two "alternate" services—pay-television and an economic inspiration, the television superstation. These two forms of programming constitute, in some measure, threats to present commercial network dominance. Pay-television services on cable are themselves a type of networking, in that centralized services provide schedules of programming for many cable "affiliates." For a monthly fee, house-to-house cable hookups improve picture quality and expand channel choices; a pay-television service, for an additional fee, fills another channel with programs not available to nonsubscribers. Pay-television services provide formatted packages of movies, entertainment specials, and sports. The author of Chapter 12, as president of a pay-television service, is able to describe the practices of the pay-television industry from the point of view of a programmer inside the industry. The strategies for selecting and scheduling programs to attract cable audiences are explained in terms of the options available to the pay-television programmer. Unlike the national commercial network programmers, pay-television programmers do not have advertisers operating as additional constraints at this time. Whether this will remain the case is open to question. The recent swelling of pay-television revenues and total cable subscriber numbers suggests that alternate services may be making a dent in advertiser-supported network viewing. In the broadcasting industry, pay-television services and superstations have been referred to as "HUT stealers"; from the point of view of pay-television programmers, this epithet is a sign of their financial success.

Chapter 13 deals with the phenomenon of the television superstation. Fewer than a half-dozen superstations exist in the United States, and the total is not likely to swell substantially. The importance of these few stations lies in the challenge they represent to traditional networking. A superstation is an independent television station; its signal is redistributed by satellite to far-distant cable companies and delivered in competition with "local" television signals. To compete effectively, superstation programmers incorporate the needs of various-sized markets and more than one time zone into their scheduling strategy. This makes superstation programmers more like national network programmers than like those at independent VHF or UHF television stations that operate within the constraints of a single market. The dilemma of the superstation programmer is that under present law, all stations must program for their broadcast markets, despite the fact that cable homes represent by far the largest audiences for some superstations. Under current interpretation of the Communications Act, superstations are restricted from programming solely as networks. A juggling act results when a superstation programmer tries to meet all a station's audiences' needs.

The author of this chapter is vice-president for programming of the most controversial of the superstations. The owner of the station, Ted Turner, is credited with inventing this potentially revolutionary idea and aggressively markets it. Until his station became a superstation, it was an obscure UHF independent; in contrast, the other stations that have been picked up for redistribution by satellite are well established and economically strong independents. However, if other ailing UHFs were to adopt the superstation strategy, the competitive market situation could be severely dislocated and current affiliate counterprogramming strategies vitiated. Were superstations to begin drawing large revenues from advertisers seeking regional markets, sales practices at the national networks would be affected; fragmenting of national advertising revenues in turn would be likely to affect programming through reduced budgets and through altered network philosophies. However, for superstations, the key to success lies in convincing advertisers to pay more than the usual independent station rates. Whether they will do so remains a question. Two related unknowns are the costs of copyright royalties and program acquisition.

The chapters in Part III deal with programming strategy for complexes of stations or cable systems. They take account of national audiences in widely diverse markets and networks' competitive struggles to command the scarce resource of unduplicated programs.

9 Primetime Programming

Robert F. Lewine

Robert F. Lewine is president of the Academy of Television Arts and Sciences Foundation, an office he assumed in 1964. He has the distinction of having served as a vice-president of programming at all three networks—ABC and NBC in New York and CBS in Hollywood. His background includes commercial production, program research, advertising, and program production, and he was vice-president of television at Warner Brothers. He was first elected president of the New York chapter of the National Academy of Television Arts and Sciences in 1959 and then president again in 1961, serving two consecutive terms for the first time in its history. He returned to the presidency of the National Academy in a long-term role beginning in 1970. In addition to founding Television Quarterly, *Mr. Lewine has been actively involved in the development of the Emmy awards since their inception and the establishment of the ATAS/UCLA television archival library in Los Angeles. He teaches at the University of California in Los Angeles, Columbia College, and California State University at Northridge while serving as trustee of Columbia College and of the American Women in Radio and Television Foundation. Drawing from this wide background, he writes authoritatively on the current programming practices of the networks in primetime. Mr. Lewine analyzes the networks' options in selecting programs and counterprogramming with them to delineate the strategies commonly used by ABC, CBS, and NBC.*

THE NETWORKS' AUDIENCES

Network television visibility makes it an inviting target. Its national popularity focuses public attention on its strengths and weaknesses. Out of the almost 15,000 hours the three commercial networks program each year, a little more than one-fifth is singled out for special critical attention—the weekly 22 hours of **primetime** programming. That figure multiplied by 52 weeks and again multiplied by three networks equals 3,432 hours of primetime programs a year.

Audience **ratings** are important to the networks throughout the day, but the ratings in the 22 primetime hours are vital. A failure in primetime programming may take years to remedy. It affects loyalty, strength, and public image as well as advertising revenue. The primetime hours—from 8 P.M. to 11 P.M. (EST) six days each week and from 7 P.M. to 11 P.M. on Sundays—constitute the center ring, the arena in which each network's ranking is put to the test. Primetime programs are the most vulnerable because they are the most viewed and the most rewarding to advertisers. Both advertisers and networks expect the highest return from primetime hours.

Some advertisers are interested mainly in "tonnage"—the sheer, raw-total size of an audience. This shotgun approach best suits advertisers of soaps, foods, and over-the-counter drug products. Other sponsors prefer a rifled approach, aiming at particular audiences most likely to buy their services or products. Consequently, the **demographics** of each network's primetime audience influence advertising sales. Broadcasters generally agree with advertisers that the major consumer purchasing power rests in the hands of young marrieds in their twenties and early thirties. The primetime hours are programmed to attract an even younger audience, ranging from 18 to 34, and in certain time periods, reaching down as low as 16 or 17 years of age. The lower end of this group finds programs like *Mork & Mindy, Charlie's Angels,* and *M*A*S*H* most satisfactory.

A close look at ABC's overall schedule in 1979 shows that its goal was a very youthful viewer. But, as a *Los Angeles Times* television critic wrote recently, "You can't sell bubble gum to ballet fans or Xerox copiers to teenagers."[1] The effort to appeal to a very young audience throughout the primetime schedule may run contrary to advertisers' interests. ABC stoutly defends its strategy by arguing that it is in the business of providing entertainment; nobody can deny that ABC shows proved entertaining in the late 1970s.

Over the two decades in which CBS commanded the highest primetime ratings (the 1950s and 1960s), its overall audience demographics slowly aged.[2] NBC found itself in a similar position as it entered the 1980s. CBS and NBC have charted courses similar to ABC's since the late 1970s, at the same time trying to hang on to some of the older people as well. But the demographics for a particular program or night may be more crucial than a network's overall age demographics. For example, in 1979 CBS's Thursday night was "very old" because of *The Waltons, Hawaii Five-O,* and *Barnaby Jones.* On Sundays, *Paris* appealed to an older audience, while *Quincy* and *Eischeid* on NBC shared a generally older appeal. These programs provided an older audience (25 to 54) for advertisers who look more to demographics than to the level of programming.

Unfortunately, the issue of quality programming rarely has concerned networks or most advertisers seriously—at least not enough to affect their practices. Of course, there are exceptions. A select circle of sponsors (including Firestone, Hallmark, IBM, Xerox, and AT&T) insist on quality programs as vehicles for their advertisements and therefore tend to sponsor special programs only. In contrast, the majority of advertisers look only for programs that reach appropriate markets for their products.

What the networks look for is flow—**audience flow** from program to program. Each network hopes to capture and hold the largest possible (young) audience from 8 P.M. until midnight or later. The choice of programs for the seasonal schedules and the arrangement of those programs are directed primarily by considerations of flow. The networks seek to control the movement of audience members in and out of their audiences over time. Flow typically takes place at the junctions where programs end and others begin. It assumes five forms: (1 and 2) additions and losses of audience due to the turning of sets on and off, (3) inflow from other networks and stations, (4) outflow to other networks and stations, and (5) flow-through—the continued viewing of one network's programs. The strategies of the networks are centrally directed to achieving flow-through in primetime programs.

FALL SCHEDULES

To attract and hold young viewers in large numbers, the networks introduce new primetime schedules of programs each fall. Discounting movies and specials, the 1979–80 season had twenty-two new programs, added to the forty-two established ones returning to the air. Which new entries will survive each year's critical sweepstakes is never known in advance. On the average, somewhat more than 60 percent bite the dust along the line. Some retire within a few months; others last only a half-dozen episodes. The total number of failures for all three networks is sometimes higher than 60 percent, but is rarely lower. The network with the highest ratings naturally cuts the fewest programs; the network in lowest place scissors its schedule most drastically. What the network in the center does varies from year to year. Consider the following patterns in numbers of programs canceled after the seasons had begun:

	ABC	CBS	NBC	Total
1970–71	10	4	5	19
1971–72	6	5	7	18
1972–73	5	4	5	14
1973–74	5	3	9	17
1974–75	7	6	4	17
1975–76	9	7	7	23
1976–77	7	6	7	20
1977–78	4	8	5	17
1978–79	2	7	8	17

In the fall of 1974 the ABC network scheduled twelve new programs. Seven were 1-hour dramas or adventure shows, one was a 1-hour musical variety, and the balance were half-hour comedies. Of these, seven failed to finish the season or be renewed for another year. CBS fared much better, having scheduled only seven new programs. But six of these failed to return: Four were 1-hour and two were half-hour comedies. Only one half-hour comedy, *Rhoda*, survived. Nevertheless, considering the normal rate of failure, in the aggregate CBS enjoyed a good new season. NBC presented ten new shows in 1974–75, and their record was the best by far. Of their seven new 1-hours, only three failed, and only one of their two half-hour comedies was canceled. Out of the ten new programs on NBC (one a movie), six survived—an exceptional percentage. It should be remembered, however, that on four nights NBC offered movies, which reduced the number of new programs needed as well as lessened the number of potential failures.

From January 1974 to December 1978, the three networks suffered more than a hundred cancellations. Seventy of them—more than a two-to-one ratio—were 1-hour programs. These figures suggest either that a 1-hour drama is more difficult to fashion successfully or that comedies are accepted more readily by television audiences. (The number of cancellations does not include temporary substitutes used during the year nor does it disclose how many series struggled for only a few months and how many made it through the year.)

The selection of ideas to be developed and entered into program lineups may appear as speculative as betting on a roulette wheel, but nothing could be further from the truth. What may appear to be a relatively simple operation is, in fact, an involved complex of strategies as competitive as games of chess played by experts. Recent estimates of the costs of program development for the three networks in a given year range from $250 million to $300 million. Not included in this staggering sum are the overhead costs of maintaining the departments and individuals who make these decisions. The salaries of top programmers reflect the substantial rewards for picking winners. The entire process of program selection breaks down into three major phases: deciding to keep or cancel series that have been scheduled previously, developing and choosing new programs from those available for the coming season, and scheduling the entire group.

Existing Program Evaluation

Evaluation of on-air shows goes on all year. The final decisions for the following fall are usually made by April or May because the networks present their **affiliates** with the fall lineups at their annual meetings in May.* However, last-minute changes occur right up to the

---

*Program decisions at ABC, CBS, and NBC are not made by the vice-presidents of programming. Vice-presidents recommend, they contribute, they

opening guns in the fall. The critical times for new programs are the four or five weeks at the beginning of the fall season (September/October) and the November **sweeps**. Programs that survive the waves of cancellations at these times and last into January or February are safe until June—although a network may, as a result of the February sweeps, decide not to renew programs for the next season.

One change that took place in the 1970s was the speedup in the obsolescence of popular primetime series. In the 1950s and 1960s, popular programs enjoyed long lifespans. Shows like the *Ed Sullivan Show, Gunsmoke, What's My Line,* and *The Wonderful World of Disney* endured for more than twenty years. It is improbable that their records for longevity will be matched again. By 1979 a program life expectancy of ten years was regarded as a phenomenon. **Futures** were being purchased on such ratings wonders as *Happy Days* and *Laverne & Shirley* up to five years ahead of actual production, but betting on longer life, even for these programs, seemed chancy.

This shortened lifespan is accounted for by several factors: the increased sophistication of the viewing audience, the emergence of action/suspense series, the huge per-viewing network audience sizes, and the scarcity of outstanding program forms and fresh, top-rated talent. Another contributing factor is actor boredom with stereotyped roles. Many stars tire of repetitive characterizations and fail to renew their contracts although their ratings are still high. Redd Foxx left *Sanford and Son* and Rob Reiner and Sally Struthers left *All in the Family* while both programs were still thriving in the ratings; Jim Arness's leaving killed off the long-running *Gunsmoke*.

Deciding which programs to continue and which to pull out of the next fall's schedule is perhaps the easiest of the three phases of evaluation, selection, and scheduling. The decisions are based squarely on the ratings. A weekday rating below 20 (or a **share** less than 30) almost always results in cancellation on any network. It accounted for the end of an outstanding program in 1979, *Paper Chase*.*

The only difficult decisions involve the borderline cases, programs that show signs of fatigue but are still holding their own or just beginning to slide in the ratings. The personal preferences of William

assert themselves. But at NBC Fred Silverman makes the final decision; at ABC and at CBS these decisions are jointly made by Fred Pierce and Elton Rule at ABC; Gene Jankowski, Bob Daly, and even William S. Paley at CBS. The familiar bromide that network programs are chosen by three men is flagrantly false. The company presidents, the entertainment division presidents (Anthony Thomopoulos, Robert Daley, and Brandon Tartikoff), and others who kibitz and have the clout to do so, enter the decision-making process.

---

*Paper Chase was the first canceled commercial network program to be rerun on PBS, with the possibility that another eight new episodes may be made at PBS expense, a tacit confirmation of the program's quality.

Paley at CBS and advertiser politics may influence some of these decisions, but the prevailing view is that cancellation had far better come too
soon than too late. The three networks differ little in their attitudes
toward cancellation of long-running programs on the decline and in
their hesitant commitment to slow builders (programs that acquire a
loyal audience only after months of patient nurturing). Strategy is basically the same at ABC, CBS, and NBC. Like a duel, a boxing match, or a
football game, the maneuvers are alike, the countermoves alike, and the
goals the same.

The Second Season

Until the mid-1970s, television programs were scheduled in
thirteen-week cycles, usually for a minimum of thirty-nine weeks each
year. The new "season" traditionally started in September. However,
the competitiveness of the three networks has greatly altered the concept of the television season. The high cost of programs and their
extreme vulnerability put an end to the pattern of thirteen-week cycles
and thirty-nine-week minimums. Although most new programs and
new episodes of returning programs still start in September each year,
many new network programs first start their runs in January or February, thus creating a **second season**. By late fall the fate of most
programs is clear, and holiday seasonal specials preempt the weakest
programs—those usually destined for cancellation. In the early months
of the new calendar year, the networks launch their second season with
almost the same amount of **promotion** and ballyhoo as was accorded the
new season in September.

New Program Selection

Phase two in planning a new fall season—the selection and
development of new program ideas—is more difficult than on-air program evaluation. As many as 5,000 or 6,000 new submissions are considered over a year by all three networks. These come in forms ranging
from a single-page outline to a completed script. Decision-makers favor
those that resemble previous successes and quietly agree that *all*
so-called original successes are in fact patterned after long-forgotten
programs.

1. *Submissions.*   The three networks invite submissions from the
established producers, such as Tandem, Lear, MTM, and Lorimar, that
enjoy substantial track records. Studios, independent production companies, and individuals are sought after if some of their prior output
ranks high in the ratings. In addition to previous successes, these companies or individuals need to possess financial stability and the know-

how required for dealing with network pressures and red tape. Further, established organizations have the most accepted writers under contract or have the muscle to hire exceptional talents. All this makes their submissions more persuasive than those from less well known or experienced sources.

The job of reading and reviewing all of the ideas that find their way into a network's program pool is tedious and time consuming. Many ideas are dismissed out-of-hand; others are read and reread, only to be shelved temporarily. A few get a favorable nod with dispatch. Many times the choices are extremely difficult because the major value sought is staying power—that elusive combination of elements suggesting that a series will remain fascinating to viewers over years of new episodes using the same characters and same situation idea. It is then that the established creators with known companies behind them are favored over the lesser known.

Once the network program executives make preliminary selections, the idea suppliers receive what is commonly known as a **step deal**—television parlance for allocation of development funds. Of the many thousands of submissions that land on the networks' desks, roughly 500 are chosen for further development at network expense. As a rule, step deals are no more than authorization to progress to scripting, in some cases to expanded treatments. The concepts take the form of **special** programs, **made-for-television-movies**, and **miniseries**. If a script was initially submitted, a rewrite may be ordered with specific recommendations for changes in concept, plot, or cast (or even writers). ABC has traditionally supported many more program ideas at this stage than CBS or NBC. However, recent shifts in the balance of the ratings have led CBS and NBC to allocate development funds to an expanded number of comedy program ideas. The bulk of new program ideas are for half-hour comedies; those for 1-hour dramas are far fewer in number.

2. *Scripts.* Before authorizing a pilot, the program executive will first order one or more scripts. Although in the early days of television, certain program ideas received immediate guarantees of **pilot** funding and even guaranteed places on schedules, such decisions usually were contingent on the promise of a first-magnitude performer as the star or big name participation in a comedy-variety format. This practice has been abandoned because of the unusual risk it entails. As of 1980, average expenditures ranged from $20,000 for a half-hour comedy script to $40,000 for a 1-hour drama script at all three networks. Exceptional creators attract even higher prices. Then, as often as not, a second script for the proposed series may be called for or even a third. Multiple scripts and extensive revision protect network programmers against the risk of expending development funds for an unwelcome pilot.

3. *Pilots.*   A **pilot** is a sample or prototype of a series under consideration. Pilots afford programmers an opportunity to get a preview of audience reaction to the property. In total, the networks order between forty-five and fifty pilots in anticipation of filling about two dozen gaps in their new season lineups. Once initial decisions have been made to commit an idea to a pilot on tape or film, a budget must be drawn and the dollars advanced to the producer. This may be regarded as the third major step of the program development process. Depending on whether videotape or film is used, half-hour pilots cost from $300,000 to $400,000 in 1979, with 1-hour dramas running to more than twice that amount. If the pilot passes final muster and gets into a network's primetime lineup, each subsequent episode of a half-hour series will cost between $200,000 and $250,000 (about $450,000 to $500,000 for an hour). These are average costs since each property differs as to number of sets, size of cast, and cost of talent. Movies made expressly for television cost from $1.3 million to $1.6 million, depending on ingredients. A multipart miniseries such as *Roots* or *Holocaust* will run into many millions of dollars but, unlike made-for-television movies, will provide a potential motion picture for theatrical distribution.

The very practice of "piloting" creates an atypical situation. A pilot's quality usually exceeds the quality of subsequent programs in the series. More money, more time, more writing effort are put into a pilot. All the people involved put their best feet forward. Everyone focuses intently on making the pilot irresistible to the network decision-makers. It is in a producer's best interests to pull out all the stops and spend even more money than the network agrees to pay.

About 150 pilots are produced to fill the two dozen newly opened time periods on the three networks. Those that fail to make the final selection list for the fall season will probably be held in reserve until later in the season in anticipation of the inevitable cancellations. The networks "short order" some backup series, authorizing the production of from two to six episodes and an additional handful of scripts instead of the usual thirteen episodes. An investment of nearly $1 million in a backup series creates the likelihood that the pilot and other episodes will be broadcast sometime during the year.

Most contracts require delivery of pilots in early spring. When received, they are tested on special audiences. Although such research is admittedly inconclusive, it exerts considerable influence. The pilots are also repeatedly screened by committees of programming experts. Factors entering into the decision to select a pilot for a series include (1) the current preferences of viewers as indicated by ratings, (2) costs, (3) resemblance between this program and ideas that worked well in the past, (4) ability of the series to appeal to the targeted demographics for that network and its advertisers, and (5) the types of programs aired by the competing networks. Of secondary weight but also relevant to a judgment are (6) the reputation of the producer and writers, (7) the appeal of the talent, (8) the availability of an appropriate time period, and (9) the compatibility of the idea with other returning shows. These and other considerations are blended by the experience of the chief programmer. Silverman, for example, is said to make the appeal of the talent his number one consideration; Paley has traditionally supported updated forms of older ideas; others weigh **counterprogramming** more heavily.[3]

Ratings

There are few aspects of television that precipitate as much controversy as cancellation of programs. Since television is first of all a business with tens of thousands of stockholders and hundreds of millions of dollars committed for advertising, the networks' overriding aim is the attraction of the largest possible audience at all times. Primetime is the **daypart** in which **ratings** most influence programming strategy, creating in their wake program decisions that are unpopular with some but that always aim at the number one position.

The networks have to make many quarrelsome decisions each year: (1) canceling programs that have become the favorites of millions of viewers, (2) countering strong shows by scheduling competing strong shows, (3) preempting a popular series to insert a special program, and (4) inserting **reruns** of episodes of a series during the year. ABC tends to keep its schedule intact for as long as possible when it has ratings leadership. CBS has a commendable record for giving new programs every chance to be sampled. However, when program weaknesses are recognized at CBS, instead of shifting time periods to shore up inherent problems, CBS pulls the slow starters off the air and replaces them with specials during salvage operations. NBC, lacking the luxury of patience, yanks its unproductive entries before they endanger the overall ratings of a night.

Perhaps most irritating to the public is the industry's dependence on ratings. All three networks rely equally on ratings services as a measure of their programming success. To be on the top of the ratings means millions in revenue. It is estimated that a single rating point translates into 763,000 viewers, which in turn translates, over the course of a year, into about $30 million in pretax profits. The Nielsen Television Index (NTI) measures audience size for national network television; the Nielsen Station Index (NSI) is limited to measurement of the 727 commercial station audiences in slightly more than 200 local markets. The combination of the NTI and the NSI provides information that the networks, stations, and advertisers use in making their decisions about

Figure 9–1. Sample Nielsen Pocketpiece Page

EVE. SUN. JULY. 16, 1978   A-15

U.S. TV Households: 72,900,000

(margin label: W E E K 2)

ABC TV

Program	Total Aud (000)	TA %	Avg Aud (000)	AA %	Share %	½-hr ratings (*)	¼-hr ratings %
Hardy Boys/Nancy Drew Mysteries (R)	9,910	13.6	7,220	9.9	24 (23*, 25*)	9.1*, 10.8*	8.7, 9.5, 10.5, 11.0
How the West Was Won (OP) (1)	10,940	15.0	7,510	10.3	23 (22*, 23*)	9.7*, 10.9*	9.5, 9.8, 10.8, 11.1
ABC Sunday Night Movie "THE TAKE" (9:00-10:53PM) (2)	18,370	25.2	12,250	16.8	33 (31*, 33*, 34*, 35*)	15.0*, 17.1*, 17.6*, 17.8*	14.8, 15.2, 16.8, 17.3, 17.4, 17.8, 18.3, 16.7

CBS TV

Program	Total Aud (000)	TA %	Avg Aud (000)	AA %	Share %	½-hr ratings (*)	¼-hr ratings %
60 Minutes (R)	13,920	19.1	10,720	14.7	35 (35*, 36*)	13.9*, 15.5*	12.9, 14.8, 15.4, 15.7
Rhoda (R)	11,590	15.9	10,130	13.9	36		13.5, 14.3
On Our Own (OP) (R)	11,740	16.1	10,420	14.3	31		13.8, 14.9
All in The Family (R)	16,620	22.8	14,870	20.4	42		19.6, 21.2
Alice (R)	16,690	22.9	15,160	20.8	40		19.9, 21.7
Switch	18,950	26.0	13,920	19.1	38 (37*, 37*)		19.5, 18.9, 18.6, 19.4

NBC TV

Program	Total Aud (000)	TA %	Avg Aud (000)	AA %	Share %	½-hr ratings (*)	¼-hr ratings %
Wonderful World of Disney "THE WHIZ KID AND THE CARNIVAL CAPER" Pt. 1 (R)	11,080	15.2	7,950	10.9	26 (25*, 27*)	10.0*, 11.8*	9.7, 10.3, 11.6, 12.0
Project U.F.O. (OP) (R)	14,140	19.4	10,720	14.7	33 (32*, 33*)	14.0*, 15.5*	13.6, 14.4, 15.4, 15.5
Big Event "SEVENTH AVENUE" Pt. 1 (9:00-11:00PM) (R)	13,850	19.0	7,070	9.7	19 (18*, 18*, 20*, 21*)	8.7*, 9.1*, 10.2*, 10.8*	9.2, 8.1, 9.0, 9.1, 10.2, 10.2, 10.4, 11.2

TV HOUSEHOLDS USING TV

	¼-hr values (%)
WK 1 (See Def. 1)	38.2, 39.9, 41.6, 42.4, 42.5, 43.7, 44.9, 46.6, 49.3, 53.3, 55.1, 57.0, 57.3, 57.5, 57.7, 56.9
WK 2	39.0, 40.8, 42.9, 43.7, 42.8, 44.5, 45.8, 47.3, 48.3, 49.3, 50.8, 52.3, 51.9, 51.7, 51.2, 49.8

* Half-hour ratings (for immediately preceding and subject quarter-hours).   (R) Repeat, see page B.   (OP) See Other Programs Section Page A-36

(1) "ABC MINUTE MAGAZINE": ABC. (7:58-7:59PM) (SUS).
(2) PROMO FILL: ABC. (10:53-11:00 PM) (SUS.).

Source: Nielsen National TV Ratings. July 16. 1978. Report A-15. Used with permission.

Figure 9–1. Sample Nielsen Pocketpiece Page

programming and time buying.* Except for four of the largest markets in the country—New York, Los Angeles, Chicago, and San Francisco—which use both the meter and the diary, NSI measurements come solely from diaries. NTI measurements come from a national sample of 1,200 homes equipped with **audimeters**.

The report of greatest interest to the creative community is published in a pocket-sized booklet commonly known as "The Nielsen Pocketpiece." This report includes not only audience size but also audience composition, program type averages, number of sets in use on given days and at given times, a comparison of television usage between the current season and the one preceding, plus other details important to the industry. (See Figure 9–1 for a sample Pocketpiece page.) The two ingredients of interest to programmers are *ratings* and *shares*.†

It is generally estimated that the three networks account for 90 percent of the viewing universe. A 20 rating and a 30 share are safe numbers for a primetime program; anything lower is probably headed for cancellation.

National Nielsen ratings take several different forms. One is the **overnights** available only in Los Angeles, Chicago, and New York. These ratings provide only total quantities of viewers, without demo-

---

*Whereas the A. C. Nielsen Company is the best-known service without serious competitors on the national scene, it shares prominence on a local level with the American Research Bureau (ARB), which controls Arbitron. The principal differences between Nielsen and Arbitron are size and method. Basically, however, Arbitron relies on diaries as opposed to the Nielsen **audimeters**. Diaries are sent to a million homes, from which the expected return is half that number. As opposed to a two-week record required by Nielsen, the Arbitron service asks for a one-week entry only. It also has a meter panel that covers only the three largest markets in the country: New York, Chicago, and Los Angeles. But, like Nielsen, Arbitron delivers **overnights** and makes telephone calls to supplement metered information to find out which channels are tuned in. Interestingly, the Nielsen and Arbitron services come up with similar findings, yet charges of bias continue to reverberate. Despite claims to the contrary, the Nielsen and ARB ratings reflect quantitative rather than qualitative results.

---

†A rating is a percentage of the total number of television-equipped households in the nation; for example, a 20.0% rating is 20% of roughly 75 million homes (the total of the United States) equaling about 15 million households. A share shows how well a program competes against other programs being shown at the same time. *Share* stands for "share of audience" and is a percentage of the *homes using television* at any given time. If, for example, at 8:30 P.M. on a weekday night only 60% of the total audience (the 75 million households) is watching television, the available audience is only 45 million homes. If a particular program polls a 30.0% share of those 45 million sets in use at 8:30 P.M., its share translates into 13.5 million homes. The balance of 31.5 million must be divided among the other two commercial networks, local stations, and public television.

graphic breakouts such as age, sex, ethnic background, education, size of family, and income. Another is the *Multi-Network Area Report* (MNA). The statistics in the MNA cover the seventy leading population centers in the country—cities with at least three television stations—which permits competitive national measurement of the three networks. Since the seventy markets represent about two-thirds of the total television homes nationally, only two-thirds of the national Nielsen sample is involved.

Three times per year a highly controversial rating event occurs— the **sweeps**.* At those times the ratings data for all time periods for every television station in the country are gathered. The 1,200 audi-meters are not used since the panel is not large enough to reflect every individual station's audience.

The sweeps make use of diaries returned by almost 400,000 households. Diary keepers indicate which programs were watched, at which times, on which channels, and by which members of the family. Because the findings of a sweeps rating period have a direct effect on the rates affiliates and the networks' owned-and-operated stations charge for their advertising time, the stations demand that their networks' highest quality merchandise be on display.† The networks therefore schedule their best programs and their **blockbusters** during the sweeps to attract the largest possible audiences. **Stunting** makes the three periods of sweeps ratings the most competitive and, at the same time, the least revealing of a network's or station's real strength.

Scheduling

At the end of the opening week of the 1979 fall television season, Les Brown, the *New York Times'* television columnist said, "For the opening week of the new season, Mr. Silverman [Fred Silverman, president of NBC] mounted a potent schedule of programs that trounced both rival networks and broke a long losing streak for NBC-TV."[4] He went on to say, "Mr. Silverman scored his coup essentially by putting NBC's best movies forward—'Coming Home' and 'Semi-Tough'— which had been originally scheduled for the crucial November sweep ratings." This maneuver put the National Broadcasting Company in the top ratings spot for that week, although this lineup is not representative of NBC's regular programming schedule. It was a move to lift NBC from its last place position even if only for a brief time. Mr. Brown quotes a

---

*An additional **small sweep** occurs in July to measure summer program audiences.

---

†Sweeps determine the network rate cards as well as those of their affiliates. Fewer than half the million diaries mailed out prove usable for ratings.

rival network's spokesperson: "Silverman bought himself some time and a winning week by 'stacking' the schedule. Now let's see what he does for an encore." In this example, Brown singles out a typical instance of the kind of scheduling strategy network schedulers employ.

1. *Hammocking.*   Although scheduling strategies can help bolster weak programs, it is obviously easier to build a strong schedule from a strong foundation than from a weak one. Scheduling is a matter of taking advantage of the mistakes committed by rival networks as well as of making the right moves with one's own programming. It is comparatively simple to add new programs to an already successful evening of highly rated situation comedies.

Moving an established **sit-com** to the next half-hour and inserting a promising new program in its slot can take advantage of audience flow from the **lead-in** program to the rescheduled familiar sit-com, which will automatically provide viewers for the new program. This strategy is commonly known as creating a **hammock** for the new program—a possible audience sag in the middle will be offset by the solid support fore and aft. It may also partake of **block programming**—hammocking of a new program within a block of similar dramas or sit-coms filling an entire evening, a venerable and respected practice. In employing this strategy, the programmer accepts the risk that the new comedy may lack the staying power of its "protectors" and so damage the program that follows. In effect, however, surrounding a newcomer with strong, established programs ensures the best possible opportunity for it to rate as high as the established hits.

ABC's 1979–80 schedule revealed examples of the astuteness of providing hammocks for the network's newest entries. On Tuesdays, a new program on ABC, *Angie,* rested comfortably between *Happy Days* and *Three's Company. Benson,* a new half hour, safely nestled between *Laverne & Shirley* and *Barney Miller. Detective School* had a comfortable hammock between *The Ropers* and *Love Boat,* and the highly touted newcomer *The Associates* followed the hit *Mork & Mindy.* To create these hammocks, it was necessary to break up certain **adjacencies** that had demonstrated success in the 1978–79 season. Moving proven hits runs the risk of affecting their ratings appreciably.

2. *Tent-poling.*   Instead of splitting up successful half-hour adjacencies to insert an unproven half-hour show, in the 1979–80 season ABC and NBC turned to **tent-poling**—an alternative to the hammock. Each network focused on a central, strong 8 or 9 P.M. show on weak evenings, hoping to use that show to anchor the shows before and after it. Anthony D. Thomopoulos, president of ABC Entertainment, used the term *linchpin* to describe the tent-pole function: "Hopefully, the comedy at 8 o'clock, *Mork & Mindy,* will be the linchpin on which those other programs [two half-hour comedies at 7 and the two from 8 to 9 on

Sundays] will hold."⁵ This strategy is particularly useful when a network has a shortage of successful programs and consequently cannot employ hammocking.

3. *Stunting.*   The art of scheduling also includes maneuvers called **stunting**—a term from the defensive ploys used in professional football. Stunting refers to a variety of program moves intended to blunt the effects of competitors' programs. Generally these are one-time-only maneuvers because their high cost cannot be sustained over a long period. Scheduling blockbuster films, using big-name stars, and creating unusual program **crossovers** are stunts.

Another form of stunting adopted by all three networks in the late 1970s was deliberately making last-minute changes in a schedule to catch rival networks unaware. These were calculated moves, planned well ahead of time but kept secret until the last possible moment. Their purpose was to strengthen a particular time period or night while keeping the opposition off balance. NBC's surprise movement of its blockbuster movies from the November sweeps into the opening week of the fall season illustrates this kind of stunting.*

4. *Lead-in Placement.*   Another strategy employed by all schedulers is to begin an evening with an especially strong program. Known as the **lead-in**, the first primetime network show sets the tone for the entire evening. This maneuver can win or lose a whole night and thus appreciably affect the ratings performance of a full week. The three 1979 fall network schedules showed evidence of this strategem. ABC placed established hit shows in the 8 P.M. slot Monday through Saturday. Except for *Monday Night Football,* the 8 P.M. lead-in spots were *Happy Days* on Tuesday, *Eight Is Enough* on Wednesday, *Laverne & Shirley* on

---

*With the 1979–80 season a scant three weeks old, NBC (to everyone's surprise) found itself in first place after the first week, and within three-tenths of a rating point (19.1 compared with leader ABC's 19.4) after the second week. CBS, a close second to ABC for the past five or more years, had slipped badly to a 16.4. Applying the accepted figure of 763,000 homes for each rating point, ABC was delivering more than 2.25 million more households than CBS, but only somewhat less than 250,000 homes more than NBC. What brought about this sudden, spectacular turnaround? The record shows that NBC stacked three major feature motion pictures during its premiere week—"Coming Home," starring Jane Fonda, Jon Voight, and Bruce Dern; "Semi-Tough" with Bert Reynolds, Chris Kristofferson, and Jill Clayburgh; and Clint Eastwood in "The Outlaw Josey Wales"—which stole the audience away from the new program premieres of ABC and CBS. Strategically, this was a shrewd move on the part of NBC; it revitalized the image of the network which had been in third place and losing ground. But stunting of this sort is stopgap programming; it relies on the products of a different medium (film) and demonstrates NBC's failure to develop the comedies and dramas that traditionally have served as a network's basic program forms.

Thursday, *Fantasy Island* on Friday, and *The Ropers* on Saturday. On Sunday, ABC's program was *Mork & Mindy* at 8:00 P.M.*

On the other hand, CBS and NBC, lacking the muscle of ABC's array of ratings hits in 1979, chose to place their new entries in the lead-off time periods three nights out of the week: CBS used *California Fever, The Last Resort,* and *Working Stiffs;* NBC used *The Misadventures of Sheriff Lobo, Buck Rogers in the 25th Century,* and *Shirley*—all slotted at 8 P.M.. Ironically, in the 1979 fall season's first week, only ABC's *Benson* managed to rate within the top twenty shows.† Of the new arrivals in the 1979–80 season, one CBS show rated in twenty-fifth place, two NBC shows in thirty-first and thirty-third, and two ABC premiers in forty-first and forty-seventh places—early reminders of the high mortality rate for new programs.

CHANGING FORMAT EMPHASES

The late 1970s saw several major changes in the kinds of formats dominating primetime. One was the increased use of **specials**—a term encompassing one-time entertainment programs, sports, one-time interview shows, **docudramas**, and documentaries. Other changes were the increasing use of **miniseries**, **adaptations**, and **spinoffs** from existing series.

Specials

Although the situation comedy and dramatic series are the mainstays of nighttime schedules, other popular formats have found their way into the networks' affections. Television history was made in 1953 when Mary Martin and Ethel Merman, luminaries of the Broadway stage, joined in a song festival to enchant their audience on *Ford's 50th Anniversary Show.* Their setting was no more than two bookkeeper stools; there were no dancers, no gingerbread. It was straight and delightful entertainment for 90 minutes, and it remains one of the medium's highlights—a breakthrough of significant proportions. This program was the first of the **special** shows that become plentiful inserts in regular primetime schedules.

Mork & Mindy on ABC was preceded in 1979 by *Out of the Blue* and *New Kind of Family,* both new attempts designed to blunt the success of *60 Minutes* on CBS and *The Wonderful World of Disney* on NBC.

---

†All three of CBS's 1979 entries and one of NBC's had been canceled within two months of the beginning of the season.

In 1954 NBC introduced the **spectacular** in color with an original musical comedy called *Satins and Spurs,* starring the spirited motion picture star Betty Hutton. Introduced to television by NBC's legendary Sylvester "Pat" Weaver, the *spectacular*—a term later scaled down to the more modest *special*—became a fixture on all three networks. Since the mid-1950s thousands of specials have been presented on network television using as sources Broadway musical comedies, adaptations of Broadway plays, novels, historical events, original dramas, classics, and real-life stories, as well as comedy-variety especially designed for the medium. Once limited to 90 minutes, entertainment specials since the mid-1960s have run for 2 and even 3 hours.

In the 1978–79 season, the three networks aired 809 primetime specials. Of these, 574 were entertainment specials for adults (live, film, or tape) or children (Charlie Brown Christmas specials, for example); 14 were unusual interview shows such as those with Barbara Walters and her guests; 49 were sports specials, including World Series games; and the remaining 172 were divided among docudramas (79) and 30-minute and long-form documentaries (93).

Because of their popularity, the number of special programs has steadily increased each year. Some are motion pictures made expressly for television; others have established box office records in theaters. But the preponderance are taped performances using a variety format. The advantage of entertainment specials is that they usually attract first-magnitude stars whose regular motion picture work prevents them from participating in series programs. Specials also invigorate a schedule, encourage major advertiser participation, provide unusual promotion opportunities, and receive high ratings.

Docudramas and Documentaries

The outstanding ratings success of the **magazine-format** series *60 Minutes* in the late 1970s induced ABC and NBC to imitate it with *20/20* and *Prime Time Saturday,* starting in 1979. (In 1978 and 1979, *60 Minutes* was in the top ten programs, number one for part of 1979.) The success of all three of the programs encouraged the development of other non-fiction forms for primetime.

A type of special that reached new levels of popularity in the 1970s was the **docudrama**, a dramatized version of historical fact. *Behind Closed Doors* (based on Watergate events), *Missiles of October,* and *Roots* are perhaps the best known of the docudramas from the 1970s.

Less visible to the critics but steadily rising in popularity in the same decade were the standard, **long-form** documentaries. Out of 809 specials broadcast in the 1978–79 season, 93 were documentaries, and most did remarkably well in primetime. "Strangers: The Story of a Mother and Daughter" on CBS on May 13, 1979, earned a 40 share nationally. On ABC on March 4, 1979, "The Ordeal of Patty Hearst" gained a 34 share. NBC received a 30 share for "The Sea Gypsies" on January 7, 1979.* The success of these programs in primetime signaled the demise of the myth that public affairs programs are necessarily ratings losers.

Miniseries

The success of specials led to the creation of **miniseries**, multipart series presented in two to six episodes on successive nights or in successive weeks, adding up to as many as ten or more hours of programming. The best known of recent miniseries are *Roots* and *Holocaust*, both produced at enormous cost and both gaining unusually large audiences. Aside from the benefit of high ratings, the networks derived considerable prestige and critical acclaim from these programs that amply repaid the dollars invested.

Adaptations

Another format developed by the major motion picture studios is the **adaptation** of successful theatrical motion pictures in either dramatic or comedy form. Perhaps the foremost example is *M*A*S*H*, first made as a feature picture by Twentieth Century-Fox. In many adaptations only the title is transferred to the series, in the hope that it will attract audiences. Frequently the adaptation preserves a watered-down version of the original film's story line. From theatrical hits came series like *Mr. Deeds Goes to Town, Blondie, Peyton Place, It Takes a Thief, Hondo, Tarzan, Daktari, Twelve O'Clock High, Shane, Mr. Roberts,* and *Dr. Kildare,* but few of these mutations ever enjoyed real success. A recent attempt to overcome the built-in resistance to movie adaptations was CBS's *Paper Chase,* professionally and critically appraised as a worthy candidate in their lineup but canceled after only one season due to low audience response.

Spinoffs

The popularity of outstanding supporting players has led to the frequent scheduling of **spinoffs.** This practice is designed to elevate to stardom supporting players who demonstrate the potential of carrying their own shows. TvQs are ratings measuring an actor's familiarity (recognition by viewers) and popularity with viewers. A secondary actor receiving a high TvQ is likely to be considered to star in a spinoff. Such comedies as *Maude, Rhoda, The Jeffersons, The Ropers, Mork & Mindy, Sanford Arms, Fish,* and *Benson* were born out of successful series with strong actors in lesser roles. Networks welcome the spinoff in view of

---

*The Superbowl telecast January 21, 1979, got the highest of all 1978–79 ratings for NBC, a 70 share.

the track records compiled by the program creators, and audience familiarity with the characters that are used in an extension of the situation in which they first performed.

As much as 10 percent of primetime entertainment in 1979 consisted of spinoffs of characters from other situation comedies or adventure/dramas. This technique for creating new programs with an edge characterized Fred Silverman's strategy at ABC. Spinoffs bring an experienced production staff from the parent program to support the new series; they are familiar with the star's personality and with the characters as vehicles for the series idea. The original writers and directors generally move to a spinoff series, whereas fresh program ideas typically involve new combinations of producers, directors, writers, technical staff, and actors. Programs such as *Lou Grant* (a spinoff from *Mary Tyler Moore*) and *Maude* (a spinoff from *All in the Family*) benefited from their production teams' joint experience.

But the overriding advantage of spinoffs is that they bring a ready-made audience from the viewers of the parent program. Known characters such as Shirley and Laverne brought personal followings to their spinoff series from *Happy Days*. Spinoffs have the advantages of built-in promotion from the parent program and continuity of audience; they are most successful when the spinoff begins its run while the parent program is still in the schedule. Delay in realizing a spinoff can ruin its chances for success.

THE CENSORS

A behind-the-scenes group that exercises total authority over all network programming is the broadcast **standards and practices department**. Cynically and angrily called "censors," this department enjoys the right of absolute approval over every program—whether a single episode of a half-hour series or a 2-hour special. Language, mode of dress, idea, concept, and questions of taste are reviewed carefully by this department at the script stage and occasionally in the finished product. If, in its judgment, a program fails to conform to the code of the National Association of Broadcasters (NAB) or to the network's own regulations, the broadcast standards department can insist on changes and can be overturned only on appeal to the chairman or president of the company. Members of this department attend every rehearsal, filming, or taping and read every script beforehand. The broadcast standards department is the Supreme Court, the police officer on the beat. Its policy is to seek and agree to compromises if possible but, in the final analysis, their word is law in areas of program acceptability.

THE ROLE OF PROMOTION

All three networks use on-air **promotion** to introduce new programs. Beginning as early as mid-July and continuing through November (after especially heavy season-opening salvos), the networks intensify advertising promoting their programs and their overall image. Promotional spots push every form of program on the schedule from series to miniseries, from made-for-television movies to high-powered theatrical features, from special programs to sports. In addition, networks use newspaper and television guide announcements to list offerings for a particular evening. *TV Guide* magazine is so important to network television that programmers delay schedule changes until the changes can appear in individual station listings. The promotional value of *TV Guide* is essential both locally and nationally.

Promotional announcements play a significant role in the ratings success of a program. Not until a program is safely past the rocks and shoals of its first several airings (or until it becomes clear that nothing can help to get it past these early trials) are **promos** lessened or stopped. On-the-air promotions are apportioned to every program that is scheduled to appear in a lineup; those needing extra stimulus are generally allotted some extra exposure. New slogans and symbols created for each broadcast year, extolling the virtues of overall network offerings, accompany all promotional announcements for programs. The three symbols in Figure 9–2 illustrate network image promotion from the fall of 1979:

©1979 American Broad-   CBS Inc.   NBC 1979
casting Companies, Inc.

Figure 9–2. Network Image-Promotion
Graphics, Fall 1979

A PERSPECTIVE

Television programs in the 1970s narrowed down to comedy and drama for a combination of reasons—the passing of radio, stage, and motion picture stars; the indefatigable appetite of the medium; the

emerging influence of the motion picture industry; the growing sophistication of audiences; the efficiency of film and tape. Gone are the
westerns, the comedy-variety series, the dramatic anthologies, the
high-powered quiz shows, the unique panel programs. Indeed, gone is
the versatility that held viewers so enthralled in the beginnings of
television. A sameness pervaded programs in the 1970s unlike that of
any other program lineup of the past.

However, television—like show business in general—is cyclical
by nature, and once-popular formats are likely to be seen again. No logic
is apparent in the disappearance of western formats and primetime quiz
and audience-participation shows or the lack of musical-variety series in
the 1979–80 season for the first time in television's history.

The fact is that success in primetime cannot now be predicted.
Too many factors in the content of a program and its scheduling, promotion, and competition cannot be quantitatively weighed. Television programming remains a high-risk undertaking with large amounts of
money, prestige, and public interest at stake. For all of their dollars,
their care, their studies, their testing, their research, their meetings,
their professionalism, and their strategies, the networks' high hopes
for new programs are repeatedly dashed in a matter of weeks each
new season.

A program failure can be the result of the wrong time period, the
wrong concept, the wrong writing, the wrong casting, poor execution of
a good idea, poor execution of a bad idea, too strong competition, the
wrong night of the week, or any of a dozen other factors. Many shows
that were canceled out-of-hand because of low shares might have
turned into major hits had they been left long enough in the schedule.
The program graveyard is littered with shows that were buried alive, but
the price tag for even temporary failure is so high that cancellation is
safer than delay.

All three networks prowl for the breakthrough idea—the program that will be different but acceptable to audiences. *Mork & Mindy*
was one such show in the 1978–79 season; *All in the Family* was its
predecessor. Network programmers can only guess what and why the
next hit will be.

NOTES

[1]Jerry Krupnick, (syndicated columnist for Newhouse News Service),
Los Angeles Times, spring 1979.
[2]Interview with E. Donald Grant, vice-president of programs in the CBS
Entertainment Division, September 1979.
[3]Fred Silverman, president of NBC, former head of programming at CBS
and ABC. William S. Paley, chairman of the board at CBS, and CBS's most
influential programmer since the 1940s.

[4]Les Brown, "'Stacking' the Schedule Put NBC-TV in Top Spot," *New York Times* (September 27, 1979): C19.
[5]"Leading from Strength," *Broadcasting* (September 10, 1979): 68.

ADDITIONAL PERIODICAL READINGS

"Chaos in Television: . . . and What It Takes to Be No. 1." *Time*, March 12, 1979, pp. 60–69.
Network primetime programming strategies analyzed, including interviews with heads of the three networks.

Dominick, Joseph R., and **Pearce, Millard C.** "Trends in Network Prime-Time Programming, 1953–74." *Journal of Communication* 26 (Winter 1976): 70–80.
A historical study of the economic factors affecting primetime television programming.

Fast, Howard. "Why Endure the Humiliation?" *TV Guide*, November 18, 1978, pp. 39–43.
Claims that the huge size of the audience and potential for influence explain why writers write for television.

Kasindorf, Martin. "Archie and Maude and Fred and Alan: A TV Dynasty." *New York Times Magazine*, June 24, 1973, pp. 12–22.
Analysis of the major programs and characters created by Norman Lear.

Klein, Paul. "The Men Who Run TV Aren't That Stupid . . . They Know Us Better Than You Think." *New York*, January 25, 1971, pp. 20–29.
Statement of Klein's programming strategy at NBC including the concept of the least objectional program.

"The Man with the Golden Gut." *Time*, September 5, 1977, pp. 46–52.
Cover story on ABC's Fred Silverman.

"Paley on Programming: How He Views the Present, Future." *Television/Radio Age* (September 12, 1977): 51–54.
Responses from CBS Chairman William S. Paley to questions from Television/Radio Age *editors dealing with his long-range views on programming.*

Persky, Joel. "Twenty Years of Prime Time." *Television Quarterly* 14 (Summer/Fall 1977): 50–52.

Results of a quantitative study of primetime television program logs for the three commercial networks in 1955–56, 1965–66, and 1975–76.

Sobel, Robert. "The 'Fourth TV Network': What Are the Prospects?" *Television/Radio Age* (July 3, 1978): 21 ff.

Analysis of the advertising support for current and future additional networks.

Zoglin, Richard. "Program Testing—Support or Scapegoat?" *New York Times*, July 23, 1978, p. D25.

Overview of the current industry program testing methods used by the networks, research firms, and program consultants.

10 Nonprimetime Programming

Squire D. Rushnell

As vice-president of children's and early-morning programs for ABC Entertainment, Squire D. Rushnell has been responsible for all of ABC's children's programming since 1974 and for Good Morning America *since 1978. He is widely recognized for his achievements with the multi-award-winning* ABC Afterschool Specials *series and* Schoolhouse Rock, *the nation's most viewed educational series. Mr. Rushnell served in various management and program producer positions with Group W Broadcasting after attending Syracuse University. In 1969, he joined WLS-TV, the ABC-owned station in Chicago, as an executive producer and assistant program manager, later becoming program manager. He subsequently became vice-president, programming, for the ABC-owned television stations. In this chapter he covers the four kinds of programming that make up the network broadcast day aside from primetime: early morning, daytime, children's, and late night. He explains the development of ratings winners in each daypart and explores the options available to daytime programmers. The author delineates the constraints operating on children's programming at the network level and the strategies that result at the three commercial networks.*

NONPRIMETIME DAYPARTS

In the vernacular of the television **networks**, nonprimetime generally describes every programming **daypart** other than **primetime**. Specifically, those dayparts include early-morning programming—7 A.M. to 9 A.M., daytime programming—from about 10 A.M. to 4:30 P.M., children's programming—Saturday and Sunday mornings, and late-night programming—11:30 P.M. to 1 A.M.. Although the audience level in any of these dayparts is considerably lower than in primetime, each contributes competitively, economically, and in prestige to a healthy network performance. Moreover, the network program executives in charge of these areas are just as dedicated to competing for available viewers as are their primetime counterparts. Everything is relative: 4 **rating** points may spell victory for an early-morning program, but in daytime or on Saturday morning, 8 rating points represent success. Compare that to primetime: A program executive feels secure only with 25 rating points.

Another difference between primetime and nonprimetime programming is the considerable variance in **clearances**. Local **stations** have the option of clearing or not clearing any network program. If a show is not aired in three or four of the top twenty markets, its average in the national Nielsen ratings will be considerably lower than if it were. *Today* and *Good Morning America* are good examples: comparing the last hour of each in February 1979, *Today* had clearances on 214 stations or 99 percent of NBC's affiliates, whereas *Good Morning America* at the same time was cleared on only 184 stations or 93 percent of ABC's affiliates. In addition, the total number of affiliates of each network varies; as of 1980, ABC had a slightly greater number of affiliates.

Notwithstanding the effects of clearances and numbers of affiliates, programming strategy for different segments of the day do not vary greatly from network to network. For each daypart, the networks give primary consideration to the **demographics** of available audience, competitive counterprogramming, and economic viability. That is to say, the network determines which segment of the available audience they will target for, mindful of their competitors' programming and influenced in some degree by their ability to support that programming by attracting advertisers.

Although advertising cannot be dismissed as an unimportant aspect of television programming, it also should not be construed as the primary concern of television programmers. There actually is very little direct association between what happens in any given network program and the advertiser. Rarely if ever does a direct line of influence exist between an advertiser and people or policy in network programming. Networks are similar to newspapers in this regard. Editorial departments and advertising departments tend to operate independently of each other.

One network program executive, when asked about advertising influence, said, "My job as a programmer is to spend as much money as I can get away with in attracting the largest possible audiences, doing programs which make us proud. Whether my company makes a million more or a million less is the responsibility of another department entirely." Of course, if the executive failed to attract the largest possible audience, the sales department would find the programs less attractive to advertisers, and his employment would, in consequence, be jeopardized.

EARLY-MORNING PROGRAMMING

Early-morning programming by the three commercial television networks has followed consistent patterns over the years. Generally, network service has been provided between 7 and 9 A.M., with a return of an hour or two of time to the local stations until network daytime programming commences in midmorning.

The earliest of early-morning programming, NBC's *Today Show*, went on the air in 1952 with an information **magazine format**. It went on to become one of television's longest running programs. Not far behind in longevity was CBS's *Captain Kangaroo Show*, a program tailored for preschool children, which began in 1955. The great age of these two programs, relative to the rest of television, has given them the status of classics of the medium. It was twenty years before ABC's *AM America* (now *Good Morning America*) came on the scene in 1975.

The structure of *Today* came to be called the magazine format because of its resemblance to print publications with a series of articles or segments bound together within a common cover or framework. In television, the sense of continuity is provided by one or more central personalities in a common setting. One of the salient reasons for the success of *Today* is that during the first twenty years of its reign, it had only three full-time hosts. First was the bespectacled, bright, and articulate Dave Garroway, whose memorable sidekick was a mischievous monkey named J. Fred Muggs. He would make faces at the passers-by in the street who peered into the ground-floor studio window (the New York studio had been an RCA product display showroom). Newsman John Chancellor was the second host for *Today* (1961 to 1962), followed by Hugh Downs who prevailed as NBC's pleasant and intelligent early-morning greeter until 1971.

There was also little turnover in backup personalities: Barbara Walters launched her on-camera career as one of America's best-known women reporters through nine years on *Today*, and newsman Frank Blair spanned a longer tenure than anyone else—twenty-two years. Consistency of personalities on a program that offered more national exposure each week than performers could expect in other programs entrenched *Today* as a solid American habit.

Today has been equally consistent in format. News and weather are reported on the hour and half hour, with opportunities for stations to cut away to local news and weather. The bulk of the content of *Today* has remained interviews with entertainers, authors, and newsmakers.

CBS tried going head-to-head with *Today* with a magazine format hosted by Will Rogers, Jr., in 1956. Failing, they returned to a news block from 7 to 8, the *CBS Morning News*, followed by *Captain Kangaroo*. In 1973 CBS made another attempt at a live morning magazine with Hughes Rudd and Washington reporter Sally Quinn. Six months later, they returned to *CBS Morning News* and *Captain Kangaroo*.*

In 1975 ABC was beginning to become a competitor in other

---

*Captain Kangaroo has been on the air uninterrupted since 1955.

dayparts, including primetime, but its station lineup amounted to only 183 primary affiliates, compared with 218 for NBC and 212 for CBS. For ABC to woo away primary affiliates from its competitors, it needed to provide a full network service including early-morning programming. At that time, ABC was not offering network service until 11 A.M.

In many small and medium markets with only one or two television stations, affiliations usually went to the older and stronger networks. Station managers who might be impressed by ABC's gains in primetime and daytime would have to think twice about switching affiliation because they would have to fill the 7 to 9 A.M. period with additional local programming at added cost: NBC or CBS was both compensating them and filling the time period.

The evaluation of early-morning viewing patterns in Table 10–1 reveals the pattern of ratings performance prior to ABC's entering the competition.

Table 10–1. Fourth Quarter Ratings, 1974

	Rating	Share	Women 18–49 (000)	Men 18–49 (000)	Women 50+ (000)	Men 50+ (000)
7:00–8:00 A.M.						
NBC *Today*	5.5	37	1390	500	1690	930
CBS *Morning News*	1.7	16	480	260	410	260
ABC local programs						
8:00–9:00 A.M.						
NBC *Today*	5.5	36	1330	640	1940	830
CBS *Captain Kangaroo*	3.7	23	640	110	280	90
ABC local programs						

Source: NTI, December 1974. Used with permission.

NBC's *Today* was clearly ABC's main target as it launched a competitive news and information program. And with a twenty-three-year head start, *Today* was an institution for early-morning viewers. Most of their viewers had watched for years and found *Today* as comfortable as an old friend; research has shown that the older the viewers the more entrenched their viewing habits.

However, as in other dayparts, ABC aimed for a primary target audience of younger viewers, particularly women 18 to 49. Not only are women in this age group more fickle than over-50 viewers and thus more easily introduced to a new morning television alternative, they also are the audience segment most desired by advertisers.

Even more attractive to advertisers are women 18 to 35. In these early married years, they are apt to try out all kinds of new products and make many major purchasing decisions on home furnishings and appliances. As *Newsweek* magazine reported, "Anyone who has had lunch with an adman knows that the toddlers who love *Lassie* and the hayseeds who howl at *Hee Haw,* and the geriatric types who snap fingers with *Welk,* buy almost nothing compared with those voracious consumers in the magic 18 to 35 age group."[1]

ABC attempted, when launching *AM America* in January 1975, to present a clear alternative to NBC's *Today*, targeting for young women. Bill Beutel was chosen as host, and the program was indeed unique in style. However, nine months after *AM America* began, *Today* remained the unqualified leader, leading ABC executives to reevaluate. (See Table 10–2.)

Table 10–2. Third Quarter Ratings, 1975

	Rating	Share	Women 18–49 (000)	Men 18–49 (000)	Women 50+ (000)	Men 50+ (000)
7:00–8:00 A.M.						
NBC *Today*	4.2	39	920	530	1420	640
CBS *Morning News*	1.5	21	290	200	520	260
ABC *AM America*	0.9	8	200	160	190	110
8:00–9:00 A.M.						
NBC *Today*	4.1	34	970	450	1390	690
CBS *Captain Kangaroo*	2.8	22	460	120	280	110
ABC *AM America*	1.2	10	420	120	240	240

Source: NTI, September 1975. Used with permission.

Basing its decision on the ratings, ABC recast *AM America* as *Good Morning America*, debuting in November of 1975. Actor David Hartman was selected as host for his warm, caring style and his ability to ask the questions that the viewer at home might ask. A family of well-known contributors was added: Erma Bombeck with humorous reports; John Coleman, the friendly weatherman; Jack Anderson with "Inside Washington"; Howard Cossell on sports; attorney F. Lee Bailey on law; and Rona Barrett with reports from Hollywood.

Good Morning America adopted a framework similar to that of *Today:* news on the hour and half-hour, time and weather services, and interviews with interesting people. By early 1980, some four and one half years after ABC's quest began, *Good Morning America* slipped past *Today* in overall ratings, with impressive gains among its primary target audience of young women, as well as with other demographics.

Table 10-3. February Ratings, 1980

	Rating	Share	Women 18–49 (000)	Men 18–49 (000)	Women 50+ (000)	Men 50+ (000)
7:00–9:00 A.M.						
NBC *Today*[a]	5.2	27	1360	630	1770	1120
CBS *Morning News*[b]	3.0	18	630	530	790	590
ABC *GM America*[a]	5.5	28	1720	750	1610	1020

[a]7:30–8 and 8:30–9 A.M. average
[b]7:15–8 A.M. only
Source: NTI, February 1980. Used with permission.

Good Morning America had definitely carved out a place for itself at the breakfast table.

DAYTIME PROGRAMMING

The magazine formats of *Today* and *Good Morning America* have rarely been successful in network daytime programming—the period between 10 A.M. and 4:30 P.M. Two syndicated programs—*The Mike Douglas Show*, a talk/variety format, and *The Phil Donahue Show*, an audience participation/talk format—have provided stations with daytime **counterprogramming** to conventional network offerings. However, talk/variety efforts in daytime by the three commercial networks have repeatedly died.

In October of 1962 NBC tried *The Merv Griffin Show* during the early-afternoon hours. It was canceled in March 1963, although when shortly reintroduced in **syndication** by Westinghouse, it reached impressive audience levels. In April of 1968 ABC scheduled the *Dick Cavett Show* during late morning. It was canceled in January 1969, only to be rescheduled in late night. In July of 1978 NBC made another attempt with *America Alive* during the noon hour. It was canceled six months later. With this record of failure at alternative programming, it is little wonder that network programmers have stuck to the more successful formulas for daytime programming: **soap operas**, game shows, and **reruns** of popular primetime series.

Soap Operas

Successful **soap operas** have the advantage of being able to build loyal constituencies that last for years. Few television series have lasted as long as *Search for Tomorrow*, which went on CBS in 1951; *The Guiding*

Light, in 1952; and *As the World Turns,* in 1956. ABC started *General Hospital* in 1963, *One Life to Live* in 1968, and *All My Children* in 1970. NBC's *Another World* began in 1964 and *Days of Our Lives* in 1965. The subjects of these programs are very mature, but they operate within strict guidelines imposed by network **program practices departments**.

In daytime, audience composition is 55 to 60 percent women, and soap operas tend to provide vicarious exieriences for adults at home. As society's prevailing attitudes have altered, the themes of soaps have become more and more mature, with the familiar characters on the television screen becoming entangled in conflicts beyond the remotest expectations of the average homemaker. It is as if viewers peer into someone else's life-style and feel thankful that the conflicts of their own environments are not nearly as bad. The characters on the television screen become so assimilated that it is not unusual to hear viewers discussing soap opera characters by first name as if they were real people.

The task of establishing a new soap opera is one that the networks accept as a long-range commitment. It takes considerable time to achieve audience involvement with new characters. The development begins with an independent producer providing the network programmer with a basic premise for a new series. If it is promising, the network will advance development dollars, or "seed money," to commission a **treatment**, sometimes called a "bible." The treatment outlines each of the characters and their interrelationships and describes the setting in which the drama will unfold. The final step is to commission one or more scripts, advancing the necessary funds to pay the writers. The entire development process can take one to two years, with an investment of $10,000 to $50,000. Usually, several development projects are abandoned each season, with only a few finally achieving the chance to get on the air.

Once a soap opera is picked up or approved by the network, casting begins. Casting the appropriate, charismatic character for each role is highly important to its potential success. Some networks maintain their own casting directors to work with producers in locating the best possible actors.

Much network television is videotaped on the West Coast, where producers contend they can produce programs for less money than in New York, partly because of more favorable weather conditions for exterior shooting. Many soap operas, however, continue to be shot in New York where nearly all of the shooting is interior and where the Broadway theater provides a large pool of actors.

When a soap opera actually goes on the air, the program executives plan its scheduling with care in order to maximize opportunity for the audience to sample it, frequently slotting the new program opposite the competition's weaker programs. Promotion of the new entry is also vitally important. The day-to-day task of the program executive is to maintain a careful scrutiny of scripts to retain the highest levels of dramatic conflict and suspense.

Game Shows

Game shows are another mainstay of daytime programming. They give at-home viewers the vicarious thrill of seeing people just like them, winning thousands of dollars on *Family Feud* or exotic trips and home furnishings on *The Price Is Right*. These series can be produced fairly inexpensively for five exposures per week.

In daytime programming, the networks seldom invest in **pilot** programs because they involve large financial outlays without the opportunity to recoup by playing off pilots on the air, as in primetime. Game shows are developed somewhat differently from soap operas. Usually, a game show producer presents a premise, and if the network likes the idea, it advances development dollars for a **run-through**. The producer then rehearses the actors and participants required by the game, and network executives are invited to see the run-through. If a network is interested, it may commission a **semipilot**, allowing the producer to videotape various versions of the game show with a studio audience and appropriate production devices such as music but without going to the expense of an elaborate set.

Reruns

Beyond game shows and soap operas, networks rely on the **reruns** of their own successful nighttime programs to fill out their daytime schedules. Usually, **situation comedies** such as *Happy Days, All in the Family, M*A*S*H,* and *Sanford & Son* have had the best chance for success in daytime. In order to have enough inventory to **strip** the programs five times a week for at least twenty-six weeks before repeating, upwards of 130 sit-com episodes must have been accumulated.

The reason situation comedies have not been developed for original play in daytime is simple: The best comedy writers are already working in primetime where they can demand higher incomes. And a primetime series needs only twenty-two new episodes per year. For stripping in daytime, twenty-two programs scheduled five times a week would cover only a little more than a month of the needed programming.

Daytime has become one of the most lucrative dayparts for television networks. The investment to produce the average game show or soap opera is lower than for the average primetime show. However, there is a tradition of allowing more commercials in daytime. The television code of the National Association of Broadcasters (NAB) allows 9½ nonprogram minutes in a primetime hour and 16 minutes during daytime. In actuality, the networks generally allow only 12 minutes per hour in Monday through Friday daytime and 7½–8 in primetime. In every daypart, 1 to 2 minutes per hour are allowed for local station breaks.

A successful schedule in daytime programming is vital to a financially sound network. There are many program investments in other dayparts, such as ambitious primetime-quality specials, children's dramas, or Olympic coverage, which tend to cost as much or more than the advertising revenue they can generate. Traditionally, news programming and documentaries at the networks have been **loss leaders**, providing the viewers with important services, yet produced at a financial loss.* Daytime programming helps support these efforts.

CHILDREN'S PROGRAMMING

Network children's programming has become one of the battlegrounds of television in recent years, not only because of network competitiveness but also because of increased public concern about the quality of programming designed for children.

Historically, Saturday morning has been the time period reserved for children's programs. Children tend to be the most fickle of all viewers. Their attention span is shorter, they have fewer loyalties, and they tend to sample more new programs. As one programmer put it, holding his hands a foot apart, "It's more convenient for them to change the dial—they only sit this far away from the TV."

Until the early 1970s, children's programs tended to look alike on all three commercial networks. There were wall-to-wall cartoons, each striving to present more visual action than the other, which usually translated into violence. Storylines were thin, with writers depending on action rather than plots. As one writer put it, "In the old days the premise for a Saturday morning cartoon was, 'They're coming over the hill' . . . and it was biff-bam, zoom-zoom from there on."

ACT Influences

A group of mothers in Newtonville, Massachusetts, raised the consciousness of the networks about children's programs by forming Action for Children's Television (ACT) in 1968. Although they were short on the know-how of television production, they were certain that networks and stations could do a better job than they had been doing.

---

*Programs such as *60 Minutes, 20/20,* and *Prime Time Saturday* that once may have been considered loss leaders now sometimes do better in the ratings than the programs they replaced. In 1979 such magazine-documentary programs were used as a form of **stunting**, like specials, and drew more than satisfactory ratings.

Among the first acts of ACT were complaints to the CBS affiliate in Boston when *Captain Kangaroo* was about to be reduced in time by the local station. Armed with the knowledge that a loud voice from a small group of indignant mothers could find widespread coverage in the local papers and with a new sense of awareness about broadcasters' obligation to serve the "public interest, convenience and necessity," ACT took its campaign to Washington. There the Federal Communications Commission (FCC) lent a sympathetic ear and decided to do some investigating of its own.

The Public Broadcasting Service (PBS) introduced an ambitious new series, *Sesame Street*, about this time (in 1969). It featured a regular cast of likable characters who taught youngsters how to count up to ten and then twenty, with what appeared to be commercials, a form that was familiar to all children—the 60-second message.

At an FCC hearing in 1972, several difficult questions were posed: Why was violence necessary in children's programs? Why was it necessary for there to be more commercials—nearly twice as many—in children's programs than in adult programs in primetime? Questions like these were difficult questions for network executives (many of whom were parents) to respond to adequately.

From the combined pressure from the mothers in ACT, the FCC's echoing of their concerns, and *Sesame Street* (whose success embarrassed the networks), a new level of awareness began to take shape on New York's Sixth Avenue, the home of the three television networks. New standards were ordered at the networks. ABC president Elton Rule, at the Washington hearing in 1972, pledged that no children's program would be allowed by his network that employed "action devoid of comedy." This immediately provided the programmers at ABC with a challenge: to create violent programs that were also funny. It proved easier to simply present funny programs.

Within three years, all three of the commercial networks named vice-presidents in charge of children's programs, thus establishing individual departments. Before that, children's programming had been the last thing on the priority list for daytime vice-presidents, whose attention was largely on the more competitive talk shows, soap operas, and game shows.

Commercials

Responding to ACT's complaint that commercials in children's viewing hours were as culpable as the programs, along with pressures from parent-teacher associations and other groups, NAB issued new guidelines in 1976. The stipulations included a cutback of commercials from the allowable 16 minutes of nonprogram material per hour to 9½ minutes; a prohibition against hosts or program characters presenting commercial messages; and the elimination of vitamin commercials aimed at young people. NAB also developed guidelines for the presentation of toys, cereals, and other products to children.

Although ACT had contended from the very beginning that commercials should be eliminated from children's programming altogether, they tended to soften that position through the first decade of their existence. Perhaps they recognized that the total elimination of commercials might result in the cancellation of such quality efforts as the *ABC Afterschool Specials,* CBS's *30 Minutes,* or NBC's *Special Treats* as well as other programs desirable to ACT.

Content Changes

During the early 1970s, a new term crept into the jargon of broadcasters: *prosocial*. While violence in children's programs was considered largely antisocial, the antithesis was to approach programming for young people with the aim of integrating prosocial elements: (1) portraying constructive role models in storylines, (2) communicating respect for the feelings of others, and (3) providing youngsters with positive messages.

CBS recruited a panel of experts, mostly educators and psychologists, to assist them in reviewing scripts. One of the first programs to be aided by the CBS panel was *Fat Albert and the Cosby Kids,* an animated program starring Bill Cosby, which wove prosocial themes into an entertaining half hour.

ABC engaged Bankstreet College, noted for its experimental teaching programs, to review all its children's scripts. The Bankstreet advisers, in concert with ABC's Program Department and Broadcast Standards and Practices Department, issued guidelines on sex roles, role models, and age appropriateness for all scripts. They include general concepts and policies similar to those advocated at CBS and NBC. An extract from the 1975 ABC script guidelines on children's programming follows:

> The best way to sum up our approach is a list of qualities that we should strive for in our programs. It is keyed to the word "respect," and it includes: "respect for the individual; respect for differences; respect for religious beliefs and ethnic qualities; respect for all animal life and for the environment; respect for private and public property; respect for moral values; respect for the feelings and sensitivities of others; and, not least, respect for oneself."
>
> In short, a program designed for the 2–12 age group must be one in which members of that age group can directly relate or identify with (not passively) but in a positive or pro-social manner. In this regard, having children and/or animals in *featured* roles is *strongly encouraged*.
>
> The portrayal of reprehensible or dangerous acts by

children's heroes is particularly risky. Boyhood heroes and teenage idols fall hard, and sometimes carry a number of youngsters with them like toppling dominoes. Accordingly, the portrayal of untoward, imitatable behavior by such recent teenage favorites as rock-and-roll stars (including the far too celebrated predilection of a few of them for hard drugs) carries far greater temptation for imitation by youngsters than would the portrayal of similar behaviors by actors with whom they identify in a less hysterical fashion.

Bankstreet College was also commissioned to review all scripts for the *ABC Afterschool Specials,* a series of high-quality dramas for young viewers which commenced twice-monthly broadcasts in 1972. The *ABC Afterschool Specials* were an outgrowth of an ABC-sponsored children's workshop, held a few months earlier, at which critics complained of an absence of good children's programming in the postschool hours.

During the same season, ABC began telecast of *Schoolhouse Rock,* a series of 3½-minute programs, scheduled each hour during weekend children's programs. The first ten programs taught youngsters the multiplication tables through animation and music. These were augmented with *Grammar Rock,* the subheading for ten programs on the parts of speech, and *America Rock,* which described, for example, the story behind the Declaration of Independence and how a bill goes through Congress. Finally, *Science Rock* and *Body Rock* (nutrition) further expanded the ABC *Schoolhouse Rock* series, brightening the intervals between Saturday and Sunday morning children's shows.

Meanwhile, CBS augmented their weekend programming with *In the News* every half hour. These were 2-minute explanations of significant news stories, so as to make them comprehensible to young viewers. CBS also created the *Festival of Lively Arts for Young People,* periodic specials introducing viewers to various aspects of the arts.

NBC, although slower to react to the critics, won praise with a Saturday morning half hour called *GO.* Later NBC began its series of *Special Treats,* dramas designed for telecast in the afterschool hours.

The outcries of a group of angry parents through Action for Children's Television started a positive evolution in programming for children. The momentum continued with CBS adding *30 Minutes* (a miniversion of the network's primetime show, *60 Minutes*) to its Saturday schedule in 1978. ABC started a weekly series of quality dramas for Saturday morning, *ABC Weekend Specials,* and invested in original programming for Sunday mornings with a variety program (*Kids Are People Too*) and an advice column of the air for preadolescents (*Dear Alex and Annie*). NBC experimented with the unusual *Hot Hero Sandwich.* Whether these efforts for better children's programs by each network are a sufficient response to ACT and other critics remains to be seen.

However, it is clear that grass roots organizations such as Action for Children's Television have prodded the networks with a positive impetus.

Cartoons

In devising a program that will appeal to children, network programmers employ criteria similar to those in other dayparts. In the final analysis, people of all ages enjoy watching likable characters. This is as true with cartoon characters such as Scooby Doo and Bugs Bunny as it is with Lucille Ball, Jack Benny, Henry Winkler (The Fonz), and Penny Marshall and Cindy Williams as *Laverne & Shirley*. A program that puts its emphasis on story rather than characters is less likely to be attractive to any viewing audience.

Cartoons are likely to continue to represent the bulwark of Saturday morning programming, as opposed to *live action* shows, the term used to describe film and tape programs that portray real people. Cartoons withstand rerunning better than live action, and—due to higher residual costs for on-camera actors than for off-camera voices—animation is less expensive.

The development of an animated children's series begins about twelve months before telecast, with pickups of new series exercised in February or March to allow producers six to seven months to complete the order for September telecast. A producer—or in some cases a network itself—generates an idea. The first step is an outline and artwork. The outline describes the characters and the setting; the artwork provides sketches of the characters in several poses and dress. If a project passes these stages, the final step is to order one or more scripts, which usually go through many drafts before the final script is accepted.

Pilot programs are almost never commissioned for cartoons because of the long production time and the high costs. Therefore, decisions to pick up a cartoon series costing a million and a half or more dollars are based solely on artwork and scripts.

Live Action

Children's live action programs follow development similar to that of animation programs, often substituting for artwork a casting tape showing suggested actors for the major roles. The script development for children's live action programs must follow a "writer's guideline" provided by the network. For example, the ABC guidelines explain that the *ABC Afterschool Specials* always deal with problems that many youngsters can identify with; that the main character should be of the age of the target audience, 10 to 14; and that the main character should bring about the resolution to the story by his or her own actions, rather than those of an adult. Moreover, says ABC's guideline, there should be a happy ending that exemplifies to young people that they, too, can resolve their own problems. This type of guideline is typical of those used at all three networks. The *ABC Afterschool Specials* have won acclaim for dealing with such subjects as parental divorce, death of a sibling, appreciation for the handicapped, and the problem of having an alcoholic parent.

As with most other segments in the broadcast day, networks produce few children's programs in-house. Instead, independent producers own the rights to the programs, which are licensed to the networks for a certain number of telecasts. This is partly due to a Justice Department decision in the late 1960s that prevented the networks from entering into the syndication of network-aired programs and from sharing in profits from U.S. syndication. It is therefore more reasonable for the networks to license one or more runs, relinquishing the profitability of subsequent syndication to the producers.

In-house shows can be more costly for the networks to produce also because of their being signators to more restrictive union contracts than are many independent producers. However, in cases in which the network intends to air more than one or two runs of a program or series, it may make fiscal sense to produce them in-house. Such was the case with ABC that wanted to build a library of quality half-hour children's dramas that could be repeated, like classics, for several years. The ABC *Weekend Specials* resulted.

The conflicts over children's television programming can be expected to continue for many years to come. The networks will try to walk a fine line between providing programs that please youngsters, programs that please the growing number of activist groups demanding better quality, and programs with adequate space for the advertisers who want to expose their toy and food messages to young consumers.

LATE-NIGHT PROGRAMMING

The period following the local stations' eleven o'clock news is the domain of late-night programming. Most of the success in developing new audience viewing trends in that time period is attributed to NBC. After launching *The Tonight Show* in 1954, NBC held the leadership in that time period among the three networks for the next quarter of a century. NBC program executive Pat Weaver* gets the credit for the talk/variety format of *The Tonight Show* as well as for instigating *The Today Show* two years earlier.

Steve Allen was the first late-night host of *Tonight*, followed by

---

*Sylvester ''Pat'' Weaver, president of NBC in 1954 and 1955.

Jack Paar and then Johnny Carson. Each employed comedy, occasional singers, and light conversation with show business personalities. The basic concept is that at that hour viewers are not interested in more serious topics. It was a premise that seemed to be right for NBC, but CBS and ABC were never very successful in executing competitive late-night talk/variety formats of their own.

ABC tried the hardest. Over three-quarters of a decade, the network came up with four different approaches. After the short-lived *Les Crane Show, The Joey Bishop Show* (1967 to 1969) gave *Tonight* a run for its money in the Midwest but lagged far behind in the national ratings.

Table 10–4. *Ratings and Shares for Network Programs in 1960, 1965, and 1970*

| Network | | | | | Year | | | | |
| | 1960 | | | | 1965 | | | 1970 | |
	(Star)	Rating	Share	(Star)	Rating	Share	(Star)	Rating	Share
ABC		(local)		(Crane)	1	8	(Cavett)	3	12
CBS		(local)			(local)		(Griffin)[a]	4.6	20
NBC	(Paar)	5.9	35	(Carson)	7	36	(Carson)	7.4	31

[a]Ratings and shares for Merv Griffin averaged with the CBS *Late Movie* that filled the time slot during part of 1970.

Next the network gave the nod to Dick Cavett, who seemed to have enormous popularity among the critics despite his poor showing in the ratings with a daytime show. In late night, Cavett remained a favorite among critics, particularly because of the rare appearance of actress Katharine Hepburn and the interviews with Alabama Governor George Wallace. However, the mass audience judged him too erudite, finding his topics too heavy for that time of the day. Cavett was cut back to once a week in 1973. Although Cavett claimed the network failed to support him with promotion, ABC had given him a three-year chance in the time period.

Admiring ABC's determination to offer *Tonight* some competition, many industry observers thought the network had scored a sure-fire coup when they announced that Jack Paar would return to late-night television, alternating with Cavett and specials one week a month starting in 1973. Many thought Johnny Carson was in trouble. Who could better take on the current Goliath of late night than the king of talk himself?

It had been some ten years since Jack Paar had stormed off NBC's *Tonight Show* set. And when he returned, he looked almost exactly the same: the same style sports jacket, same hair length, and the same tone of curious astonishment in his interviews. During the opening week, Jack Paar boosted ABC's late-night ratings. Then they began to slide— back to Cavett's level.

American viewers were disappointed. Jack was the same, but the audience was not. In ten years, the viewers had become far more sophisticated, discriminating, and critical. Paar was canceled in November of 1973.

During most of the seven-year period in which ABC tried to go talk show against talk show, CBS was quietly garnering a respectable share of the audience by counterprogramming movies. With the exception of one crack at late-night talk/variety with *The Merv Griffin Show* for six months in 1972, CBS followed the strategy of scheduling movies 11:30 P.M. to 1 A.M., maintaining a comfortable number two position in the ratings.

In late 1973, ABC unveiled an ambitious and very expensive plan to program something different every night of the week. On Mondays and Tuesdays there would be dramas, on Wednesdays specials, on Thursdays personalities, and Fridays would garner a younger audience with rock concerts.

Although the rock concerts had some ratings success, the enormity of the task of coming up with enough consistently good drama in the early part of the week was staggering, as were the costs. Moreover, it became apparent that the audience was confused by ABC's scheduling, not being sure what they might see when they tuned in on any given night.

By September 1977, several factors had emerged. The complexity and expense of ABC's effort still was not offering any serious competition to NBC's *Tonight Show* or CBS's movies. Meanwhile, on another front, the industry was under renewed pressure to eliminate violence from their primetime programming, particularly prior to 9 P.M. This created a backlash problem for producers who had long counted on subsequent syndication of off-network programming to recoup initial production losses, otherwise known as deficit financing. The movement to eliminate violent programs from time periods when children might be viewing began to dry up the marketplace among television stations that normally would buy such action-packed series as *Starsky & Hutch* and *SWAT.* Capitalizing on this situation, ABC began to approach late-night television from another direction: rerunning successful primetime series. Shows like *Baretta, Starsky & Hutch, Police Woman,* and *Streets of San Francisco* provided counterprogramming to both NBC's *Tonight* and CBS's movie, while helping to resolve the financing problem for producers.

In the first quarter of 1979, ABC began reaching respectable ratings levels in the late-night time period. Johnny Carson and his NBC *Tonight Show* no longer remained the undisputed leader; CBS's movies had gone out in front, and ABC had carved off a larger slice of the available audience.

Table 10–5. *First Quarter Ratings, 1979*

	Rating	Share
CBS	7.9	28
NBC	7.3	27
ABC	6.8	23

Source: NSI, January–March 1979. Used with permission.

It took two decades for the "invisible network" to become a successful contender in the late-night time period.

In March 1980, ABC premiered the first regularly scheduled late-night network newscast from 11:30 to 11:50 P.M. The ABC program adopted an innovative in-depth treatment of a limited number of stories, rather than 11:00-type **hard news** or a magazine format. Audience response to expanded late-night news was surprisingly successful. This signals a new strategy on the part of the networks for the programming of this time period.

THE FUTURE OF NONPRIMETIME

It is clear that creating dramatic changes in viewing patterns is very difficult to achieve in nonprimetime. No early-morning effort, no daytime soap opera, and no late-night strategy has ever been greeted with instant success. Only in rare cases with daytime game shows or children's programs has a network been able to dramatically turn around an audience viewing trend. Instead, a steady commitment to long-range achievement is normally required for success.

With cable systems, home cassette recorders, video discs, super-stations, direct-to-home-satellite telecasts, and any other number of competitors to network television programming on the horizon, it is difficult to imagine that the number of available viewers during any time period will do anything but shrink, while the tasks of network programming become more and more arduous. It will be an escalating but exciting challenge to the network programmer of tomorrow.

NOTE

[1]"What's Ahead for Television," *Newsweek*, May 31, 1971, p. 73.

ADDITIONAL PERIODICAL READINGS

"The Biggest Game in Town for the Networks." *Broadcasting* (September 22, 1975): 37–50.

Discussion of network television coverage of sporting events with details on key personnel and approaches at each network.

"Network Kidvid Programs and Advertisers Much the Same, with Subtle 'Prosocial' Growth," and **"Networks' Efforts to Increase Educational Values of Kidvid Include Inserts, Specials, School Role."** *Television/Radio Age* (May 21, 1979): 40 ff., (June 4, 1979): 44 ff.

Two-part series on the upgrading of the content of network children's programs, expansion of educational and prosocial values, effects of hearings, and addition of informational spots.

Rosenthal, Edmond M. "TV Networks Change the Shape of Children's Programming as Competition Heightens." *Television/Radio Age* (June 20, 1977): 28 ff.

Overview of children's programming on the networks.

"The $201-Million Game Plan." *Broadcasting* (August 13, 1979): 29–38.

Special report on professional and college sports on television.

Wakshlag, Jacob J., and **Greenberg, Bradley S.** "Programming Strategies and the Popularity of Television Programs for Children." *Human Communication Research* 6 (Fall 1979): 58–68.

A quantitative study investigating the effects of various programming strategies commonly employed by the networks on program popularity for children.

11 *National Public Television*

S. Anders Yocom, Jr.

Local station programming options and regional network offerings for public broadcasters were explored in Chapter 8. Chapter 11 deals with national *public television strategies from the perspective of a former director of scheduling and program operations for the Public Broadcasting Service (PBS). In this capacity, the author directed the Station Program Cooperative and placed all programs and series in the national broadcast schedule. Prior to joining PBS, the author was vice-president of programming and program manager for the Connecticut Educational Television Corporation. He produced and directed hundreds of public affairs and instructional programs for the Connecticut corporation before becoming production manager, program manager, and then vice-president. He is presently director of program production for WTTW, the VHF public television station in Chicago. In this chapter, Mr. Yocom analyzes the programming strategies he employed during his tenure at PBS, delineates the constraints operating on all programmers at the national level, and offers personal observations on the 1979 restructuring of public broadcasting.*

THE PROGRAMMING ENVIRONMENT

Programming the national public broadcasting service is a little like trying to prepare a universally acclaimed gourmet meal. The trouble is that the menu is planned by a committee of 160, and the people who pay the grocery bills want to be sure that the meal is served with due regard for their images. Some of those coming to the dinner table want the meal to be enjoyable and fun; others want the experience to be uplifting and enlightening; still others insist that the eating be instructive; and the seafood and chicken cooks want to be sure the audience comes away with a better understanding of the problems of life underwater and in the coop.

The analogies are not farfetched. PBS is governed by a large board, reduced in number in 1979 from fifty-two to thirty-five. The board represents the needs of some 160 public television licensees who operate more than 260 public television (PTV) stations all over the country and in such remote areas as Guam, American Samoa, and Bethel, Alaska. Since PBS produces no programming, it must serve a host of program suppliers and try to give their programs proper treatment in scheduling and **promotion**. In addition, constituencies ranging from independent producers to minority groups are constantly applying pressure to make sure that public television programming meets their special needs. And, of course, the funders of programs have their own special agendas as well.

The Network Model

A national commercial American television **network**, as generally understood, acts as a centralized programming as well as sales and distributing agent for its **affiliates**, program suppliers, and clients. A commercial network supplies about 60 percent of an affiliate's entire program service, and the affiliate gets paid for the time it makes available. Commercial affiliates have little voice in the choice of network programs or the way they are scheduled. The network's great strength lies in its ability to program some 200 television stations simultaneously with a lineup of popular programs, which the network itself either produces or commissions for production, usually under its close supervision. Equally as important as the choice of individual programs by network programmers is their expertise in melding them together into a sequence capable of exerting a powerful hold over audience attention.

How closely does the national public television system or network, the Public Broadcasting Service (PBS), conform to this model? The real differences are vast and are probably best illustrated by one simple comparison: in 1978 the commercial networks and their affiliated **stations** grossed about $7 billion; in 1978 the entire public television industry was funded by about $430 million. This disparity is pervasive and underlies many of public television's problems. Money is power, and the amount available to public vs. commercial television is not the only significant difference between the two. Other differences arise from the way programming power flows and the parallel flow of money. In commercial television, programming and money flow from network headquarters to the affiliates. Production is centrally controlled and is distributed on a one-way line to affiliates, who are paid to push the network button and transmit what the network feeds. All of the economic incentives favor affiliate cooperation with the network. This places tremendous programming power in the hands of the networks.

In public television, money and programs flow the opposite way. Instead of being paid as affiliates, PBS members are stations that pay dues to PBS and pay as well for many, if not most, of their PBS programs. Instead of being corporate entities or subsidiaries whose directors are responsible to stockholders, PBS's directors are all members of station boards or station management. Although PBS has the authority to accept and reject programming, most of the programs distributed by PBS are produced or acquired by member stations without any supervision from PBS's staff. They are delivered to PBS, Washington, where they are reviewed for compliance with legal and technical standards and then are sent out over a multichannel satellite system. Programming agencies other than PBS also have access to the satellites so that every station has at least three programming choices from the satellite at most times of the day.

In the early years, PBS operated only five days per week with a limited schedule of evening programs plus an hour each weekday afternoon for *Sesame Street*. In ten years, it grew to a full seven-day service with an array of programs suitable for broadcast in **primetime**; a schedule of children's programs in the late afternoon and early evening; a 2- or 3-hour weekday-morning schedule suitable for use in school classrooms; daily **strip** programming for both the early and late weekday evenings (such as *Over Easy, The Dick Cavett Show, The Captioned ABC Evening News, The MacNeil/Lehrer Report*); and a variety of Saturday and Sunday morning and afternoon programs.

These schedules were developed when PBS, like the commercial networks, sent programs out over a one-way, single-line AT&T hookup. Despite some similarity to the networks, the PBS schedule was unique in one way: PBS fed programs at times stations could conveniently broadcast them, but there was no obligation for the stations to carry the programs at the time of feed. Only in the rarest circumstances did PBS pressure its members to do so.

As a **multitransponder** satellite system was phased in during 1978 and as low-cost recording equipment became available to the stations, the PBS schedule was carried less and less frequently as programmed. The programming flexibility introduced by the satellite interconnection signaled some fundamental changes in the system, some of which took place in 1979.

First to arrive was a concept called the **core schedule**. PBS's high-visibility primetime programs faced the loss of national promotional potential and underwriter appeal without the impact inherent in simultaneous distribution. Throughout its development, PBS had hoped that its seven-night-per-week schedule would be of sufficiently high quality to encourage simultaneous release of the entire schedule. Resistance by member stations, however, forced PBS to accept the reality that it lacked sufficient high-quality programs to justify being carried simultaneously over a seven-day primetime schedule. Moreover, many stations opposed simultaneous carriage on philosophical grounds.

In response, PBS identified 8 hours per week (over four nights) for simultaneous release as its core schedule. A majority of the members agreed to air these programs in 2-hour sequences on the night of feed. The core schedule was first put in place Sunday through Wednesday nights in the fall of 1979. Station managements and funders benefited from increased simultaneous national promotion and from greater program impact.*

Also in 1979 came the beginning of even more basic changes. For the first time, the PBS program service was divided into three services that were color coded blue, green, and red. Although not clearly delineated as of this writing, the services had rough parameters: PTV-1 would consist of general-audience, high-visibility programs within and outside the core schedule, generally thought of as evening programs. PTV-3 would consist of children's programs and programs designed for or adapted for instructional purposes. PTV-2 would incorporate everything else. In its preliminary development stage, PTV-2 was expected to carry special-audience programming or programming generated by consortiums of stations through their regional networks or other groupings.

The three-faceted PBS has yet to be put to the test, but the very concept speaks to the fundamental difference between noncommercial and commercial television network traditions. At PBS, all power is derived from the consensus of the stations, where it exists and can be aggregated. Instead of flowing from national to local, public television power—limited as it is—flows from local to national. Since one monolithic agency did not satisfy the stations, perhaps a three-faceted one will.

Role of CPB

The power of the stations, however, is tempered by the power of the purse, which resides in a number of places. The largest single funder of public television programs (other than the stations) is the Corporation for Public Broadcasting (CPB). As the agency established by act of Congress as the steward of certain federal appropriations for public broadcasting, CPB each year budgets a certain amount for national public television programming.† CPB has maintained its own program staff, which reviews program proposals and makes production grants.

---

*All indications are that the core concept is working. Average ratings for core programs were up 157 percent over those of fall 1978 for similar programs and programs from the same series during the first week that the core went into effect. While factors other than core may have contributed to the increase, 78 percent of the program managers in a PBS survey were positive about the core initiative and its earliest results. Dale Rhodes and Kenneth Wirt, "PBS Program Managers' Common Carriage Survey" (Washington, D.C.: PBS Office of Communications Research, 1980), presented at the PBS Annual Programming Meeting in San Francisco, January 14, 1980.

---

†Public television also receives federal grants from other agencies, including program grants from the National Endowments for the Arts and the Humanities and grants from other agencies for various other purposes.

Usually CPB consulted with PBS as the representative of the stations; sometimes it did not, and that failure was the greatest cause of the friction traditionally marking the relationship between the two Washington-based national public television agencies, PBS and CPB.

CPB also underwent reform in 1979 and is operating under a new president, Robbin W. Fleming. One of his initiatives is to separate CPB's program-funding decisions from the rest of the CPB management structure. Under its own director, the program fund will operate with advice of the advisory panels mandated by the Public Broadcasting Act of 1978.

No funder, be it CPB or other (such as agencies of the federal government, foundations, or corporations) grants funds without retaining some say-so as to how the money is spent. Each funder takes into account its own interests in making production grants. As a result, much of what PBS programs, worthwhile as it may be, is programmed not by PBS's considered choice but simply because it is available. PBS's lack of a program budget means that it cannot plan, develop, or implement programming except in certain limited areas such as fund-raising programs.

PBS Politics

As of this writing, it is difficult to foresee how the new initiatives will play out. The core schedule is in place but cannot yet be fairly evaluated. The development of the three distinct program services, although approved by the board and membership of PBS in June 1979, is still being worked out at two levels. A transition committee of the board is working out the policy issues, while the PBS staff is looking into the logistical questions. No one is certain whether there will actually be three program services. Plans may be cut back to two. CPB's new program fund is not yet in place. Meanwhile, program suppliers outside of PBS are showing new aggressiveness, particularly the Eastern Educational Network (EEN), which has increased its staff and plans to move into new programming initiatives.

The various reforms of 1979 are the result of a decade of operation under the constraints of at least four levels of politics. At the top of the list is the federal level, involving at times the Congress and the White House. Public television inevitably faces scrutiny by the Congress because Congress appropriates CPB's funding each year. During the Nixon years, the CPB/PBS system faced possible extinction when the Nixon administration reacted negatively to some public affairs programs it considered too critical of administration policies. The system survived, but even today when President Carter invites outstanding artists to perform at the White House, eyebrows are raised by some members of the Congress if public television wishes to cover the event. Some legislators charge that these events are staged to improve the image of the president. It is under such adverse conditions that public television tries to provide fair and thorough treatment of critical national issues. It does so with courage and integrity, but with the federal lifeline in the hands of the very subjects of public affairs programs, the road has gigantic potholes.

At another political level, some of the nation's zealous single-issue constituencies constantly criticize the performance of public television. The country is fragmented into groups organized to focus narrowly on change in their own behalf, sometimes without regard for the effects such changes would have on the nation as a whole. Like all public institutions, public television must try to meet a wide spectrum of public demands. At the very least, the service must expend limited resources in explaining why it cannot provide more programming for certain racial minorities, for the hearing impaired, for advocates of specific causes, and for many other claimants desiring public television's attention.

It has been alleged that a commercial television industry strategy for keeping public television from becoming a competitive threat was to support appropriation of just enough public money to keep public television alive, while keeping the money flow so meager that the individual institutions would, like hungry chickens, claw and scratch one another to get at the chicken feed thrown down to them. Whether or not this was ever a conscious strategy, it does describe practical effects of the current situation.

Especially vulnerable to "chicken-scratching" behavior are some of the individual stations themselves. The larger stations that specialize in production for national distribution compete with one another for the minuscule production funds that are available. They also compete against one another for national recognition and program underwriting dollars and against PBS itself. Stations interested in college credit courses and other forms of instructional television compete for their shares of the pie, resenting what they perceive as a disproportionate flow of the resources to the producers of general-audience programming.

In the middle of this bewildering complex of politics and disparate programming objectives sits PBS. It has operated with no clear instructions from its board of directors. It was governed by a committee system through which the political and programming pressures played themselves out to no purpose. These are some of the reasons PBS has been in trouble and reform movements have been rampant.

PBS Responsibilities

Since its founding, PBS had had two undisputed responsibilities: the acceptance or rejection of programming offered for national distribution and the scheduling of available programming. The acceptance/rejection responsibility is grounded partially in both technical and legal standards that were fully discussed and voted by the membership over the course of the 1970s. The technical standards are designed to protect the stations from Federal Communications Commission (FCC) violations and to maintain high levels of video and audio quality. By their very nature, they can be applied with reasonable objectivity. The legal standards were set up to protect the stations from libel and rights infringements and to alert them to **equal-time** and **fairness-doctrine** obligations that may result from PBS-distributed programs. As the steward for underwriting guidelines, PBS's legal department established the form for on-air crediting of funders. PBS's underwriting rules are more restrictive than FCC rules governing noncommercial television and stringently limit the acceptability of funders. They are designed to protect (some say overprotect) the integrity of public television vis-à-vis would-be exploiters and guard against possible station vulnerability in the public's eyes.

Two other member-approved documents touch on the PBS acceptance/rejection responsibility. The "Statement of Policy on Program Standards" and the "Document of Journalism Standards and Guidelines," adopted by the membership in 1971 and 1972, respectively, provide general guidance to the PBS staff and to producers on issues such as obscenity and newsworthiness. Both documents allow wide latitude for interpretation in judgments about program content.

PBS assumes responsibility for several activities indirectly related to programming. Advertising of programs and public information are an important PBS responsibility, carried out to the limited extent that funds permit. PBS also maintains a development office that assists producers in seeking funds for programs and explores long-range funding possibilities. The stations, in the 1979 reform initiatives, trimmed off three other PBS activities that were only tangentially related to programming. The Station Relations office, set up for liaison between the stations and PBS, was dropped; System Research, which provided information on programs and program funding, was eliminated; and a very controversial activity—direct PBS participation in national affairs (mostly representation before Congress)—was removed from the PBS portfolio. National affairs is now the responsibility of a new national agency, the Association for Public Broadcasting, which will also undertake system planning, heretofore under the direction of former PBS Vice-Chairman Hartford Gunn.

The PBS power to accept and reject programs and the power to schedule has in the minds of some members smacked of "networkism." The addition of some other activities has been seen as excess baggage designed to increase the power potential of the PBS, Washington, bureaucrats. These factors, along with aspects of PBS managerial style (which at times tended to promote PBS as an autonomous national institution rather than as an association of stations) contributed, along with the "chicken-scratching" syndrome, to the pressure for reform.

PBS Fund-raising Assistance

Through it all, one activity of PBS that has been enormously successful is the one over which PBS has the most discretionary latitude. The Station Independence Program (SIP), a division in PBS's Development Department, helps stations conduct on-air fund-raising appeals in which they solicit dollar pledges. The stations pay PBS special dues for this assistance with local fund-raising efforts. One of the SIP services is funding and consulting on the acquisition and commissioning of special programs by the PBS Program Department for use during local station fund-raising campaigns. Mass-appeal programming that has emotional payoff—such as heavy dramatic impact, warmly received performances, emotionally charged documentary subjects—seems to work best. The PBS programming staff has commissioned such programming in recent years with astonishing success, as shown in the growth of the systemwide on-air pledge yield of the annual March festival:*

Festival '75	$ 4,965,591
Festival '76	$ 7,814,724
Festival '77	$ 8,550,112
Festival '78	$12,421,008
Festival '79	$15,804,260

Commissioning activity was stepped up for the 1978 and 1979 festivals, resulting in such successes as *Live from the Grand Ol' Opry* (bringing in more than $1 million in 1978 and nearly $1.5 million in 1979), *That Great American Gospel Sound,* and *American Pop: The Great Singers,* both of which raised more than $1 million in their initial releases in 1979.

In the world of public television, SIP-funded programming is unique, for it meets the one universally accepted criterion for success: It raises money. Success can be documented in objective terms that everyone understands. It is also the one area in which the PBS staff has been given some real discretion to bypass the "programming by availability" mode of the rest of the national schedule.

Except for SIP, there are no universally accepted criteria for measuring the success of public television programming. This is another facet of the PBS dilemma. Despite the inevitable subjectivity of evaluating PBS performance, despite the various levels of political constraints, and despite funding problems, public television stations must pool their resources to accomplish in the aggregate what they cannot do independently. The PBS schedule of programs is one of the means for achieving joint action.

---

*It should be added that some of this yield is attributable to non-PBS programs acquired or produced independently by stations.

NATIONAL SCHEDULE STRATEGIES

In theory, it should be possible to develop a national program schedule by aggregating the needs of the licensees. The programming needs common to the greatest number of stations would determine what programs were proposed, funded, and produced. They would be delivered at times when the maximum number of stations could take them **off-line** (or off the satellite) to best serve their local audiences. Many outstanding programs could have educational components built in and ancillary print material produced for distribution when the programs are released. The national schedule could be balanced to ensure that no major areas of programming such as news and current affairs were neglected and to assure no surfeit of specific-content forms, such as televised performances by symphony orchestras.

Unfortunately, it does not work that way. PBS, and in fact most of the individual public television stations, are subject to the rules of programming by availability. PBS cannot schedule what the producers do not produce. The producers are not bound by any set of national public television programming priorities derived from a sense of balance among program types. They produce whatever their individual analyses and instincts dictate. They tend to produce what the various funders are willing to fund.

British programs such as *Masterpiece Theater* and *The Shakespeare Plays* appear on American public television because they are available, high-quality programs at one-tenth the cost of producing comparable fare in the United States. Very few government or commercial institutions have the financial resources and willingness to see program ideas through from conception to broadcast. That power does exist in limited amounts in a handful of places, all of which compete with one another for people and production resources and, within PBS, for national attention. But PBS lacks the unified national authority necessary for coordinated planning.

The major producers have portfolios of program ideas that they constantly "shop around" to all of the potential funders. The few ideas that do get funded become the programs presented to PBS for the national schedule. They have no particular part in any national plan that addresses any particular philosophy or set of objectives. By haphazard means and some aggressiveness on the part of the producers, they get produced.

Scheduling of programs is on an annual cycle. In the spring, PBS lists all of the programs that are potentially available for the fall and arranges them into the best possible schedule. This schedule attempts to meet two criteria: due regard for all of the strategies for maximizing audiences and consideration of the convenience of all the public stations.

Given the minute average audiences for public television programs compared to their commercial counterparts, it would be presump-
tuous to suggest that PBS engages in **counterprogramming** in any significant way, but it does have some options relative to the commercial
schedules. For example, one is to avoid scheduling anything important
on Sunday nights at 7 P.M. (EST). That is the hour that *60 Minutes* is on
CBS and *The Wonderful World of Disney* on NBC—series that appeal
heavily to just those audience members who ordinarily can be counted
on as public television viewers: the adult public affairs audience and
children. When both of those audiences watch the commercial networks
simultaneously, any competing PBS programming faces the stiffest possible competition.

Otherwise, PBS counters the commercial networks simply by
trying to conform its scheduling to their general scheduling patterns. If
two of the commercial networks have **long-form** nights [nights with
2-hour movies or specials running 9 to 11 P.M. (EST)], PBS may schedule
its own long-form programming opposite. The theory holds that when
two of the networks tie up audiences from 9 to 11, no viewers are
released to come to public television for a program starting at 9:30 or 10.
Since all of the commercial networks break every night at 9, the PBS
schedule does too, in the hope that if any dial twisting occurs at 9, some
of the viewers might come to public television.

PBS tries to avoid placing a valued program against the top raters
in the commercial schedules. Pressure to avoid these situations frequently comes from individual program producers. PBS also has traditionally avoided the placement of important programs during the three
all-market audience-measurement periods (**sweeps**) in November, February, and May. These are the times when commercial television throws
its **blockbusters** at the audience. Recently, however, PBS has revised
this strategy, acknowledging the value of **ratings**. Since the sweeps are
the times when the public television stations are also measured for all
time periods and for the all-important cumulative audiences reached
over a week (**cumes**), the major public stations demand priority programming. As one PBS programmer recently put it, "When they
announce the start of the contest, that is hardly the time to head for the
sidelines."

PBS's fresh approach has paid off. Recent audience figures show
growth in public television viewing, due in large part to programs such
as *The National Geographic Specials* and some of the *Masterpiece Theater*
serials and other specials fed by PBS during the sweeps.

Another PBS strategy is to schedule the most appealing programming on nights on which the greatest number of viewers are
available for viewing. HUTs (households using television) are highest on
Sunday nights, and *Masterpiece Theater* (which has traditionally done
well in audience size by public television standards) has played on

Sunday nights since its premiere. PBS takes the double advantage of exposing such programs to the largest available audiences and promoting programs scheduled later in the week to those expanded audiences.

Potential **audience flow** is always considered when placing programs in the national schedule. On ABC the flow from *Happy Days* to *Laverne & Shirley* virtually gushed (1978–79); PBS hopes that at least some of the crowd assembled for *Evening at Pops* on Sunday night will trickle into *Masterpiece Theater* in the following hour. Great care is taken to try to maximize this flow. But by their very nature, public television programs and their audiences seem unlikely to benefit from the passivity that characterizes commercial television series viewing. Individual public television programs differ so markedly from one another, requiring active rather than passive viewing, that its viewers rarely become immobilized. Nevertheless, compatible programs are placed **adjacent** to each other whenever possible in the PBS schedule with some positive results. One long-term example occurs on Friday evenings when *Washington Week in Review* is followed by *Wall Street Week*.

PBS gains another advantage on nights or in periods in which commercial television is not at its competitive best. One such night occurs every two years in November during national elections. While ABC, CBS, and NBC are busy seeking every last ratings point from their simultaneous election coverage, public television and **independent** stations have a rare opportunity to score with counterprogramming. There are also some times of the year when the ratings services are not measuring audiences anywhere, except in a few metered markets. The commercial networks use these **black weeks** for their low-audience-yield public affairs programs to minimize ratings damage. PBS has taken advantage of these times to introduce some of its high-quality programming. However, the advantage is diminished somewhat by the specific appeal of the public affairs programs tossed out by the networks. Sometimes they are of especial interest to the public television audience and provide even more competition than the regular commercial **sit-coms** and action-adventures.

NATIONAL RATINGS

PBS staff researchers interpret ratings data from the A. C. Nielsen Company and report them to the members. They derive not only overall reach and **demographic** profiles for each PBS program but also general scheduling indicators such as the best time of day or night for a particular program. But ratings data have limitations as tools both for day-to-day scheduling decisions and for long-term scheduling strategies. The main reason is that so much of the public broadcast schedule is made up of **specials** and short series. Some of the programs that carry series titles (such as *Great Performances*) are in fact collections of specials that appeal to widely differing audiences. Even *Nova*, the weekly science series, varies in audience response depending on the subject matter of the individual programs. For many programs in the PBS schedule, ratings data do not become available before the programs have completed their runs and are off the air. On commercial television, a formula sit-com can be adjusted over a twenty-four-week span, based on what the ratings reveal about its relationship to the **lead-in** program or the nature of the appeal of the show itself. There is little opportunity for corrective action on PBS programs, so many of which are on the air one day and gone the next.

One veteran public television programmer, now retired, likes to tell of the response he gave whenever he was asked how he did his job: "I don't know. I just did it." If pressed, even he would admit that his experience taught him many things about program quality, balance, and good scheduling. But his point is that most of the program decision making in public television is intuitive. In commercial broadcasting the criteria for success are objectively measured in amounts of advertising revenue generated by each particular program. Even if public broadcasting could set up clear-cut programming goals, it might still be impossible to measure success in objective terms. That being the case, one person's judgment about the importance, quality, and potential success of one program over another is as good as another person's judgment. In the absence of any better indicators, programs are placed in the schedule where they seem to "feel" best to experienced programmers.

The public television programs that are best at attracting viewers are usually those that are most heavily promoted. *The National Geographic Specials* are prime examples. Unless the schedulers make gross errors, the size of their audiences does not depend on when they are scheduled, because many individual public television viewers turn on their television sets solely to watch a single program. '

THE PUBLIC TELEVISION FUTURE

Public television has always been in a state of disorder. The national agencies that have been set up to serve the stations have been subjected to intense criticism by the stations they attempt to serve. Some stations distrust each other as well as the national agencies. The novel experience with satellite program distribution has touched off a new sense of station individuality. Some stations feel that the national programming agency should be limited in the amount of **transponder** time it schedules, leaving the remainder open for the stations themselves to use. Some have suggested that two or three separate, competing program services would best serve the interests of the different stations.

However, it still appears that the stations remain reluctant to entrust much power to any single national programming agency. At the same time, they recognize the need to aggregate resources in order to do collectively what they cannot do individually. Moreover, most can see the promotional benefit of at least some uniform scheduling of outstanding national programs.

As subjective as television program decision making is, committeelike decision making will not improve it. The best television programs—even the best program schedules—are usually the work of a single, intelligent, enlightened, responsive visionary. Public television must find within its own ranks such a person and give him or her more resources than ever accorded any institution in the history of public broadcasting. This benevolent administrator, democratically appointed, should have the power and resources to do the job. If the job is not done right, the administrator should be removed and replaced. Someone should be given the chance to succeed and the right to fail. A small, efficient board of directors (some appointed and the balance elected by station vote) should be put in place to name the top programmer and give the person clear instructions on what is expected.

Some of the rhetoric that was thrown about during the time of the reform movements in May 1979 envisioned the evils that could befall the public television system if it were put in the hands of a programming "czar." Such paranoid imaginings not only miss the point but also suggest a course guaranteed to prolong mediocrity in public television. Gourmet meals are not prepared by committees of cooks engaged in fratricidal bickering and equipped with inadequate resources. Public television needs the same chance to succeed as a gourmet chef.

ADDITIONAL PERIODICAL READINGS

Breitenfeld, Frederick, Jr. "Public Broadcasting: A Two Party System." *Public Telecommunications Review* 4 (March/April 1976): 19–23.

Delineation of the centralist and localist political approaches to the Corporation for Public Broadcasting and the Public Broadcasting Service.

Gingras, Richard. "The PTV Satellite System: Turning Point or High Anxiety." *Public Telecommunications Review* 6 (May/June 1978): 5–13.

A discussion of the possibilities and likelihoods resulting from public broadcasting's acquisition of satellite channels.

Gunn, Hartford N., Jr. "Window on the Future: Planning for Public Television in the Telecommunications Era." *Public Telecommunications Review* 6 (July/August 1978): 4–54.

Overview and recommendations for long-range planning for public television.

Hallstead, William F. "Is Corporate Underwriting Effective PR?" *Public Telecommunications Review* 7 (January/February 1979): 48–52.

A study of how the viewer perceives corporate funding and what motivates corporations to fund public television.

Hickey, Neil. "Public Television: There'll Be Some Changes Made." *TV Guide*, November 4, 1978, pp. 6–9.

Interview with Newton Minow in his role as chairman of PBS on his philosophy of public broadcasting.

Wald, Richard C. "Possible Courses for News and Public Affairs." *Public Telecommunications Review* 6 (May/June 1978): 50–57.

An abridgement of the author's report to the Programming Committee of the PBS Board.

12 *Pay-Television Networks*

Jeffrey C. Reiss

As president of Showtime Entertainment, the national pay-television network, Jeffrey C. Reiss was responsible for the overall direction of the Showtime organization. He was instrumental in the creation of the programming and marketing concepts that were introduced as Showtime in July 1976. Since that time, Showtime has developed its program service from a regional cassette operation to a national pay-television network distributed to local cable companies by satellite. At the beginning of 1980, Showtime—a joint venture of Viacom International Inc., and the Teleprompter Corporation—reached one million subscribers nationwide. Mr. Reiss began his career in television and show business with General Artists Corporation, now International Creative Management; worked as assistant to Norman Lear in program development for Tandem Productions; and in 1968 cofounded Kleiman-Reiss Productions, which produced five off-Broadway plays. He was director of programming for Cartridge Television, Inc., and director of feature films for ABC Entertainment. In 1980 he became executive vice-president of Viacom Entertainment Group. In this chapter, Mr. Reiss describes pay-television as a mushrooming national medium that complements commercial television services by providing alternatives to viewers. He details the programming philosophies, formats, and strategies used by monthly pay-television services and the program sources available to pay-television programmers. He highlights the differences between pay-television and commercial broadcast television, illustrating a rapidly changing aspect of television programming.

THE PAY-TELEVISION SYSTEM

Since the late 1940s, the word *television* has been used interchangeably to describe the electronic appliance found in most homes, the programs it brings into those homes, and the broadcast industry that creates and distributes those programs. The term *television* has been associated automatically with commercial broadcast television. At the beginning of the 1980s, however, the commercial television networks began to identify themselves in their advertisements as "free TV." Encroachment from a new form of program distribution—**pay-television** (sometimes called **pay-cable**)—precipitated this development. The growing phenomenon of pay-television has changed the meaning of the word *television*.

The businesses that provide programs for "pay" services no longer use the term *pay-cable* because it associates them with a single method of distribution. The term *pay-television* is an umbrella for "premium" programs distributed by cable systems, **subscription television** using over-the-air scrambled signals, and satellite-distributed direct-to-home programs requiring special receivers. The services described in this chapter can be made available in any of those ways but are most commonly distributed by cable operators. The content of the pay-channel (or channels) on a cable system comes from programming services that deliver a schedule of programs to the cable system, generally by satellite. The subscriber pays a fee for a pay-channel in addition to the charge for the basic cable service.

Between 1975 and 1980, pay-television became the outstanding moneymaker of the cable television business with total revenues of more than $30 million a month. Pay-television services significantly increased the cable industry's subscriber base, as well as operators' average revenue from each subscriber. Pay-television also spurred dramatic expansion of the cable industry into major urban and suburban markets where cable is not usually needed for adequate reception of broadcast television signals.

The large national program networks that have evolved as the dominant suppliers for pay-television on cable are Home Box Office (HBO), owned and operated by Time, Inc., and Showtime, a joint venture of Viacom International Inc. and the Teleprompter Corporation. Home Box Office was founded in 1972 and Showtime in 1976. Although there are other similar services operating throughout the United States, none of them approaches the size and stature of these two industry leaders. Together these rapidly growing program networks had five million subscribers nationwide in 1980. Their growth realizes Sylvester "Pat" Weaver's radical vision of the 1950s. The master programmer of NBC foresaw millions of viewers forsaking free television programming, eager to pay an additional fee for some form of "premium" entertainment.*

THE PAY-TELEVISION ALTERNATIVE

Since pay-television coexists with commercial over-the-air television, the key questions are: What constitutes premium entertainment? Why are people willing to pay for these optional programs? What does

---

*Sylvester L. Weaver was president of NBC during 1954 and 1955 and went on to head Subscription Television Inc., which attempted to establish over-the-air pay-television using scrambled signals in California in the early 1960s.

pay-television offer viewers in return for approximately $15 to $20 per month that they do not get for free on a regular channel?*

Pay-Programs

Pay-television provides several program alternatives to commercial television. The most significant of these are current major motion pictures, aired on pay-television soon after theatrical release, well in advance of their commercial television premiere. Films are shown in their full theatrical form, unedited and uninterrupted. All movies, including those rated PG and R that contain language and behavior normally censored on commercial television, appear in their entirety on pay-television schedules. And pay-television carries no commercials.†

In addition to movies, the pay-television networks offer original productions created expressly for their subscribing audiences—programs whose content and format are substantially different from those of commercial broadcast television. These **specials** feature entertainment such as Broadway shows and popular Las Vegas nightclub acts that command high ticket prices when seen live. Such videotaped performances are not available in their original, uncensored form on broadcast television. Other programming formats have been explored, including made-for-pay-television movies, sports, **magazine-format** series, and blends of entertainment and documentary styles. As pay-television grows, suppliers will attempt series formats targeted for specialized audiences. They are likely to be radically different from series on commercial television that appeal to mass audiences.

The third major element of pay-television programming is sports. Home Box Office schedules national sports events during the week in **primetime**. Austin Furst, vice-president of programming at HBO, argues that two-thirds of HBO subscribers watch sports and that that two-thirds is 30 percent more pleased by HBO than are nonsports subscribers.[1] Showtime programmers think that the evidence is less clear-cut and that the commercial networks and **independent** stations provide ample sports programming; in Showtime's view, the purpose of pay-television is to offer alternatives, not more of the same kinds of programs available from other sources.

Pay-Scheduling

Scheduling is a major area of difference between pay-television and broadcast television. Pay-television services offer a range of twenty

---

*These figures are the average monthly cost for cable service with one premium channel or for over-the-air subscription television.

†A new pay-television service, Warner Amex Cable Communication's Star Channel, carries some advertising between features.

to forty programs per month, scheduled from three to eight times on different days and at various hours during the daily schedule. The daily schedule runs from about 5 P.M. to 2 A.M. on weekdays and 2 P.M. to 2 A.M. on weekends.* HBO and Showtime offer different numbers of monthly attractions, but both services schedule the majority of their programs more than once. The viewer therefore has several opportunities to watch each program. These repeat showings serve to maximize the potential audience for each program offering. The programmer's scheduling goal is to find the various complementary time slots that will deliver the greatest possible audience for each attraction during the course of a month, not necessarily in one showing.

In contrast, broadcast television has standard scheduling practices for programs resulting in the weekly series, the daily **soap opera**, the nightly newscast. In each case the program or episode is shown only once.†

In addition, commercial network television follows established time frames for evening programs: 6 to 7 P.M. for news, 7 to 9 P.M. for family entertainment, 9 to 11 P.M. for general and adult entertainment, and late night for talk shows and classic movies. By programming major feature films and specials at "unconventional" times such as 6 P.M. and 11 P.M., pay-television has won large audiences among cable subscribers.

Pay-Appeal and Viewer Evaluation

Pay-television also offers an alternative to the mass-audience orientation of commercial television. The commercial networks and broadcast stations, to maximize advertising revenues, program to attract the largest possible audiences every minute of the programming day. Pay-television, on the other hand, attempts to attract cumulatively the largest possible audience over the period of a month. Consequently, pay-television's success is not determined by ratings of individual programs, but by the general appeal of its overall schedule. Since both schedules and subscriber billings are arranged by the month, viewers evaluate one-month blocks of programming. If viewers use their pay-television program service two or three times a week and benefit from its

---

*Showtime expanded its daily schedule to twelve hours per day beginning in April 1980; on weekdays it programs from 3:30 P.M. to 3:30 A.M.; on weekends it programs from 1:30 P.M. to 3:30 A.M.

---

†PBS is an obvious exception. It offers multiple showings of programs, but PBS is, in one broad sense, also a "pay-television" service—supported in part by viewers through their contributions to local community-supported stations.

varied viewing times, unique programs, and lack of commercials, they tend to continue the service for another month.

Subscribers who were not pleased with pay-television's overall program selection may opt to discontinue service at the end of that month. This seldom reflects dissatisfaction with one or two individual shows. When viewers disconnect, they feel that the service as a whole lacks essential ingredients. Customers who are repelled by violence, for example, may disconnect if a large number of one month's films contain high levels of screen violence. A family may determine that its desire for nothing but wholesome, G-rated fare is not being fulfilled by the programming mix of the local pay-cable service and cancel after a trial month or two. This process also works in reverse. Favorable word of mouth is the most potent method of attracting new customers, particularly in nonurban communities.

A handful of individual programs each month makes the difference between success or failure when a pay-cable service is new in a community and the local operator lacks a large and stable subscriber base. Having one or two **blockbuster** films on the order of "The Exorcist," "Annie Hall," or "Rocky" undoubtedly attracts new subscribers to the service and holds current subscribers even if their reaction to the balance of that month's schedule is negative.

PAY-TELEVISION FILM STRATEGY

The two major pay-television services use generally the same overall strategy of a standard but flexible prescription for balanced programming. An average month's content on Showtime demonstrates this prescription. It includes at least three major box office successes in premiere; at least one major G-rated film with family appeal; a variety of other films with varied audience appeals, including at least one foreign film; two or three "encore presentations" of major box office hits; and at least three entertainment specials exclusive to pay-television. These programs include a balance of PG- and R-rated films, a variety of film genres (comedy, drama, action, western), and specials targeted at different **demographic** audience groups. Sports are the controversial elements of pay-television programming and do not appear regularly on Showtime.

Decisions on which films and specials to purchase and which performers or events to feature in original specials are based on several criteria. The overriding consideration is that each program be "value-justified" to the consumer. This means that the films either have proven popularity at the box office or have a strong appeal for a particular segment of the audience. Specials considered worth paying for are distinctive, either capturing the top talent in the entertainment industry or exploring formats unique to television. Specific monthly choices are based on the availability of theatrical feature films and which specific entertainers and program forms best complement these features so as to reach a variety of demographic targets each month.

Selecting programs that will reach different target audiences through the course of the month becomes the challenge of the programmer. For example, if a particular month's feature films have strong appeal to teenagers and men 18 to 49, the obvious choice for an entertainment special would be a show that appeals to women, such as "Engelbert at the MGM Grand," rather than "Playboy's Playmate Reunion." In addition to urban/rural considerations, pay-television programmers break down their audiences into age groups of 18 to 24, 24 to 49, and 50+, and then further subdivide them by sex.* By scheduling programs each month that will appeal to all these groups, the programmer creates a balanced schedule.

Types of Films

Films constitute the dominant type of programming on pay-television. They subdivide into five groups with overlapping appeals, reflecting promotability, audience interest, and frequency of scheduling. The major audience attractions are the premieres for that month, that is, films played for the first time on pay-television. In the month of July 1979, for example, three films were headlined as *premiere audience attractions*:

> "The Goodbye Girl"—Neil Simon's highly acclaimed box office film hit, a romantic comedy starring Marsha Mason and Academy Award winner Richard Dreyfuss. Rated PG. Two showings during calendar month. Distributor: Warner Brothers (general audience appeal).

> "Eyes of Laura Mars"—Romantic thriller starring Faye Dunaway as a high-fashion photographer who can foresee murders and Tommy Lee Jones as the cop she falls in love with. Rated R. Six showings during calendar month. Distributor: Columbia Pictures (adult).

> "Damien: Omen II"—Successful sequel to "The Omen," one of the big box office hits of the 1970s, starring William Holden and Lee Grant as foster parents of a young boy who is the Devil incarnate. Rated R. Seven showings during calendar month. Distributor: 20th Century-Fox (general).

---

*Pay-television typically uses the age categories of 18 to 24 and 25 to 49 because these groups best separate people with the most similar entertainment tastes. Broadcasters tend to focus on consumer buying habits. (The 18 to 24 age group watches more films, for example, because the bulk of films are directed toward that age group.)

The second group of films placed in the schedule are the *major G-rated* movies. Films such as the following appeared during July 1979, establishing a strong pattern of family appeal in the schedule:

"Summerdog"—A charming family film about a vacationing family that adopts a stray dog on its summer outing. Rated G. Nine showings during calendar month. Distributor: G. G. Communications (family).

"Starbird and Sweet William"—One of the currently popular wilderness films, focusing on an Indian boy and an orphaned bear cub who try to survive together in the North woods. Rated G. Five showings during calendar month. Distributor: Gold Key Entertainment (children).

The third group of films are those with *varied audience appeals.* Films without notable box office success usually fall in this category. They are repeated as frequently as premieres and G-rated hits. July 1979 had these five films:

"Thank God It's Friday"—Topical musical story about life at a Los Angeles disco, starring the popular recording artist Donna Summer. Rated PG. Eight showings during calendar month. Distributor: Columbia Pictures (young adults).

"A Different Story"—A sleeper hit about a gay man and a gay woman who meet, fall in love, and change their life-styles. Meg Foster and Perry King star. Rated R. Six showings during calendar month. Distributor: Avco Embassy Pictures (adult).

"Secrets"—Provocative adult drama about relationships, starring Jacqueline Bisset. Rated R. Six showings during calendar month. Distributor: Simcom International (adult).

"Sasquatch"—An exciting docudrama about seven men who embark on an expedition in search of the manmonster Indians call Sasquatch—better known as Bigfoot. Rated PG. Eight showings during calendar month. Distributor: Gold Key Entertainment (family).

"Somebody Killed Her Husband"—The first feature film to star Farrah Fawcett-Majors, the former "Charlie's Angel" and worldwide sex-symbol phenomenon. Jeff Bridges costars in this romantic whodunit. Rated PG. Five showings during calendar month. Distributor: Columbia Pictures (general).

"Somebody Killed Her Husband" was not a big box office success, but as part of a monthly lineup in which twenty films cost the subscriber about what it costs two people to go out to see one movie, a film like this can be readily enjoyed by the pay-television viewer. Although only moderately successful by big screen standards, the film has Farrah Fawcett-Majors in her first role in a theatrical film.

In addition to the month's feature lineup, several attractions premiered in the latter part of the previous month may be aired once or twice the following month on Showtime, to assure an adequate number of plays.

Other films that were not major theatrical hits may still rate as important acquisitions for pay-television services. Viewers may value seeing a film on television that they might not be willing to pay three or four dollars to see in a movie theater. *Foreign films* fall in this group; one shown in July 1979 was

> "A Dream of Passion"—Highly charged drama about two women whose identities merge, starring two top screen actresses, Ellen Burstyn and Melina Mercouri. Directed by Jules Dassin. Rated R. Three showings during calendar month. Distributor: Cinema 5 (adult).

Encore films are separated from the other four groups in the Showtime schedule because they represent repeat showings of films that premiered in preceding months. July 1979 included the following *encore presentations*:

> "Coming Home"—Fresh from its sweep of three Academy Awards (best picture, best actress, best actor), an encore of this hit movie about the aftershocks of the Vietnam war, starring Jane Fonda, Jon Voight, and Bruce Dern. Rated R. Eight showings during calendar month. Distributor: United Artists (general).
>
> "Coma"—From Robin Cook's best-selling thriller. Genevieve Bujold stars in this story of a hospital's shady operations. Michael Douglas, Elizabeth Ashley, and Richard Widmark costar. Rated PG. Five showings during calendar month. Distributor: MGM (general).
>
> "The World's Greatest Lover"—Gene Wilder stars in this slapstick comedy about a man who auditions for Rudolph Valentino's successor in 1920s Hollywood. Carol Kane and Dom DeLuise costar. Rated PG. Eight showings during calendar month. Distributor: 20th Century-Fox (general).
>
> "The Turning Point"—Highly acclaimed story of two women's lives and their involvement with ballet, starring Academy Award nominees Anne Bancroft, Shirley MacLaine, and Mikhail Baryshnikov. Rated PG. Six showings during calendar month. Distributor: 20th Century-Fox (general).

Balancing the number of major films and lesser known but promotable titles every month, then adding a handful of encore presentations, is one of the key challenges a pay-television programmer must face. A crucial factor in preparing the lineup is the current availability of titles. Clearly, many of the films being exhibited on Showtime have enjoyed previous successful theatrical engagements with all the attendant advertising and promotion. Although many of the films with good track records at the box office are obtained from the major film distributors, an increasing number are purchased from a wide variety of independent distributors and producers. Independent production companies came to play a large role in theatrical distribution in the 1970s.

Film Availability

Theatrical films distributed by major studios are typically available to pay-television services nine to eighteen months after their initial theatrical release. This time period varies depending on the box office success of the film. "Star Wars" was a huge box office success; Twentieth Century–Fox kept it in theatrical release for almost two years and held off its theatrical rerelease for at least another year, substantially delaying its availability to pay-television services. In a similar situation, Universal rereleased its enormously successful film "Jaws" after the introduction of a sequel, "Jaws II," postponing the pay-television exhibition of "Jaws" for more than four years. Conversely, Irwin Allen's disaster epic "The Swarm" fell short of box office expectations, had a limited theatrical run, and was not rereleased. Hence, "The Swarm" was available for pay-television shortly after its initial theatrical release.

Sophisticated distributors have been extremely successful with several rounds of alternate theatrical rereleases and pay-television exhibitions. Showtime defines a pay-television "run" as a playing period of about thirty days in which an attraction is telecast three to eight times.

Another factor affects the flow of product: special time constraints are placed on distributors' sales of films by commercial television buyers who seek early telecast of key films to bolster their ratings in pivotal measurement periods (**sweeps**). This shortens the period of time in which the films are available to pay-television. (Some fine films are unsuitable for broadcast sale altogether, which increases their pay-television availability. Films such as "Carnal Knowledge" and "Lenny" would require such massive editing to become suitable for commercial television that their content would be virtually destroyed. Therefore, no limit is placed by their distributors on the number of times these films can play on pay-television.)

A limited number of older films are available to pay-television. The bulk of Hollywood's film classics is licensed to commercial television stations on an exclusive basis. Exceptions to this pattern include independent productions and major studio films that are removed from **syndication** or network release from time to time. Unfortunately, the rule prevails and not the exception; such classic favorites as "Casa-blanca," "Citizen Kane," and "Adam's Rib," which would be enhanced by being shown on pay-television without editing, extensive commercial interruption, or inconvenient scheduling, are not available to pay-television.

Recent theatrical films such as "Jeremiah Johnson" and "A Man Called Horse" played on HBO after they aired on the broadcast networks. In the view of Showtime, the risk of inducing viewer resentment by requiring payment for films that have appeared recently on free television overshadows the potential benefit of airing these films again. However, HBO finds that there is a pay-television following for these programs when they are shown without commercials, and evidence exists of viewer support for the reshowing of films that have been badly cut for commercial television presentation or have exceptionally strong appeal for repeat viewing. Ultimately, the marketplace will determine the desirability of playing **off-network** films on pay-television.

Film Licenses

Feature films are licensed to pay-television networks in one of two ways: per subscriber or by flat fee. *Per subscriber* means that a fee per customer for a specific number of runs within a fixed period is negotiated by the theatrical film's producer and distributor. With this type of payment, the film's distributor receives a fee based on the actual number of subscribers who had access to the film. In a *flat-fee* arrangement, a cash payment is negotiated regardless of the number of subscribers.

The per-subscriber method of payment suits the rapid growth of the pay-television subscriber base in the 1970s and 1980s. When growth begins to level off, per-subscriber license fees for programs will probably remain constant and translate into flat fees. Even in the late 1970s, some independent producers and distributors negotiated licenses on a flat-fee basis. Producing one's own special has a fixed cost, or flat fee.

Film Scheduling

Distributors create a distribution "window" for a film's release when it is offered to pay-television. Pay-television programmers negotiate for a certain number of first-run and second-run plays during a specific time period, generally ranging from four to twelve months. For example, a given film may be made available to pay-television from April to November. Programmers must project ahead to see that the scheduled play periods for similar films from different distributors do not expire at exactly the same time. Otherwise, viewers could be treated to five blockbusters or four westerns or three Paul Newman films in the same month, an inefficient use of scarce resources. Encores of popular films are assets to monthly schedules, and rescheduling these effectively is as important as placing them appropriately the first time they appear on the lineup. The programmer's goal is not to alienate viewers by repeatedly scheduling the same film in similar time slots.

General rules of thumb for film scheduling include beginning weeknight programming anywhere between 5 P.M. and 7 P.M., and starting final showings as late as 11:30 P.M. to 12:30 A.M. An evening may consist of three to five programs, depending on their individual running times; entertaining short subjects and promotional spots for other attractions fill the time between shows. Saturday, Sunday, and holiday schedules generally begin at 2, 2:30, or 3 P.M. and may include as many as six programs up to the final show that begins at 11:30 P.M. or as late as 12:30 A.M.

The following illustrates three typical days on Showtime:[2]

Saturday P.M.

3:00 "Sasquatch"
4:30 "The World's Greatest Lover"
6:30 "The Juliet Prowse/Foster Brooks Special"
8:00 "Eyes of Laura Mars"
10:00 "Damien/Omen II"
12:00 "Secrets"

Monday P.M.

6:30 "Coming Home"
9:00 "The Turning Point"
11:00 "Eyes of Laura Mars"

Tuesday P.M.

6:00 "Summer Dog"
7:30 "The John Davidson Show"
9:00 "The Goodbye Girl"
11:00 "Coming Home"

Home Box Office schedules in similar patterns:[3]

Wednesday P.M.

3:00 "The Buddy Holly Story"
5:00 "Robin and Marian"
7:00 "The Crazy World of Laurel and Hardy" (entertainment special)
8:30 "Steve Martin" (special)
9:00 "Wimbledon Tennis" (men's quarterfinals—delayed)
11:30 "Blackout"

Sunday P.M.
_____

2:30 "The Golden Age Of Buster Keaton" (special)
4:00 "The Apple Dumpling Gang"
6:00 "Silver Bears"
8:00 "Buck Rogers in the 25th Century"
9:30 "The Golden Age Of Buster Keaton"
11:00 "An Unmarried Woman"

Tuesday P.M.
_____

5:30 "Corvette Summer"
7:30 "Race For The Pennant" (sports, a look at series favorites)
8:00 "The Great Bank Hoax"
9:30 "Rich Little" (special)
11:00 "Buck Rogers in the 25th Century"
12:30 A.M. "Griffin And Phoenix"

Airing between seventeen and twenty new attractions each month (not counting final airdates from the previous month's premieres) requires scheduling four to five premieres each week, gradually integrating first-, second-, third-, and up to sixth-run presentations week by week so that the viewer has a constantly changing lineup of material from which to choose.

Counterprogramming broadcast network schedules is a strategic consideration. For example, on Monday nights, when *Monday Night Football* is a strong ABC attraction, Showtime tends to schedule a film with female appeal, such as "An Unmarried Woman." Preceding or following a popular broadcast network show with a program of the same genre creates a unified programming block (requiring a channel switch). Beginning programs on the hour as often as possible—especially during primetime from 8 to 11 P.M., makes it convenient for viewers to switch to and from pay-television.

Pay-television schedules are not designed for continuous viewing as in commercial television, but rather for selective viewing. **Promotion** stresses the values of convenience and choice in pay programming. For example, if pay-television viewers cannot see "Eyes of Laura Mars" on Sunday, July 22, at 9 P.M., they will have several other opportunities to catch it during the month, on various nights of the week and in different time slots.

Despite the "selective viewing" phenomenon of pay-television, the same pattern of **audience flow** that operates in commercial television is inevitably at work. A strong attraction early in the evening will create a larger audience for subsequent programs. Strong 7 or 8 P.M. **lead-ins** are strategic tools for maximizing viewing of all features during an evening, but strategies enhancing viewing over the period of a month are more important to pay-television.

Films and specials containing mature themes usually are scheduled at later hours than G-rated films, although pay-television is not bound by National Association of Broadcasters (NAB) codes or traditions. PG features are offered throughout the schedule. Parents are encouraged in monthly program guides to prescreen all films rated PG or R to decide which films are appropriate for their children to watch on subsequent airdates. Pay-television scheduling practices, through repeated telecasts, encourage parental control—which explains why there is little or no outcry from pay-television viewers about the content of R-rated films.

ENTERTAINMENT SPECIALS

Selecting performers to star in original pay-television **specials** and choosing properties to be adapted to the television medium require an intense examination of the cable subscriber's preferences and expectations. The commercial networks offer variety specials every week, and most leading entertainers can be seen either there or on the many talk/variety shows that are broadcast daily. It is vital, therefore, that every pay-television special offer something fresh and different: a performer who is well known but an infrequent network television guest, a performer often seen on network television but rarely headlining his or her own program, or a program that has a format or content not available on commercial television.

Pay-television has made a major asset of taping on location, offering its viewers a "front-row seat" at major theaters, nightclubs, and arenas around the world. A Las Vegas nightclub special provides the cable subscriber with the same performance that costs $40 per couple to see in person. Although there is no substitute for being there, the broadcast of a concert from Central Park or a country music festival in West Virginia makes the viewer in Cleveland, Ohio, or Agoura, California, a part of that one-time event. These are vivid reproductions of live performances, unlike conventionally packaged television specials. The integrity of a complete performance is maintained, without obligatory guest stars, dance numbers, and other forms of television window dressing usually employed to widen the audience base of individual commercial television variety programs. As with theatrical feature films, pay-television nightclub and concert specials feature material that commercial television does not provide and, in some cases, could not provide because of the unexpurgated content. Pay-television's time flexibility permits these programs to run their natural lengths, whether 1 hour and 11 minutes or 1 hour and 53 minutes, without the need to artificially compress the performances into 1 hour or 90-minute formats.

The Showtime schedule for July 1979 contained six specials, three premieres, and three holdovers from June. Five of the six rated as general entertainment and were suitable for entire families:

"The Juliet Prowse/Foster Brooks Special"—A pairing of music and comedy from the stage of the Desert Inn in Las Vegas: Juliet Prowse does her singing/dancing act and Foster Brooks his well-known brand of comedy monologues. Seven showings during calendar month (general).

"Andy Kaufman at Carnegie Hall"—The unconventional comedian, best known for his role in the hit television series "Taxi," was taped during his Carnegie Hall concert exclusively for Showtime. Six showings during calendar month (general).

"The John Davidson Show"—The Las Vegas Hilton is the setting for this popular singer to do his musical nightclub act. Four showings during calendar month (general).

"The New York Big Laff Off"—An original Showtime entertainment special featuring young comedians competing for prize money, hosted by Tommy Smothers. Two showings during calendar month (young adult).

"Charo"—An original Showtime entertainment special starring the bombastic Latin entertainer in her Las Vegas nightclub act. Two showings during calendar month (general).

"The Ben Vereen Show"—The multitalented TV and Broadway star does his nightclub act on the stage of the Riviera Hotel in Las Vegas. Two showings during calendar month (general).

Original programming may make up as much as 50 percent of the overall monthly schedule of pay-television networks by the close of the 1980s. Showtime spent between $6 and $7 million on original programming in 1979, entering into development deals with a variety of studios and independent producers. For example, Showtime instituted regular showings of Broadway and off-Broadway productions. Award-winning filmmaker Charles Braverman produced a magazine-format series called *What's Up America!* Playboy Productions produced its first show for pay-television and worked with Showtime to develop its first television series. Home Box Office is exploring new entertainment forms as well, with plans to include a "mini-docu-tainment" series and *Time Was,* hosted by Dick Cavett, exploring American history decade by decade from 1920 to the present. Home Box Office also produced a 1-hour consumer special in association with Consumers' Union, publisher of *Consumer Reports.*

In addition to licensing or cofinancing specials with the pay-television arms of suppliers such as Columbia Pictures, Warner Brothers, and Twentieth Century–Fox, pay-television networks have made a major commitment to the production of original specials in conjunction with various independent producers. Both Showtime and

Home Box Office work predominantly with outside producers; only a limited number of programs are produced by internal staff. This maximizes variety and flexibility in program development.

SPORTS

Sports programming creates a divergence of opinion in the pay-television community. Although Home Box Office regularly features national sporting events in its monthly lineup, Showtime has opted only to supply selected areas with sporting events of strong regional interest. Because of the commercial networks' financial strength and audience reach, they generally acquire the rights to most major sporting events. Pay-television therefore has to settle for events of lesser national interest. Nevertheless, an audience can be found for some sports not adequately covered by commercial television such as boxing (nonheavy-weights), regional college sports, and so-called minor sports like track and field, swimming and diving, soccer, and equestrian competitions.

The pay-television networks may be the ideal place to present sports as entertainment rather than to "cover" them in journalistic fashion. New formats may be created that focus on sports personalities or dramatize memorable past sports events, broadening the appeal of sports and offering an approach not characteristic of broadcast television.

PAY-TELEVISION'S CABLE AFFILIATES

As a national programming service, pay-television on cable must be conscious of the needs and problems of its **affiliates**, the local operators of cable television systems around the country. Programmers must keep attuned to current regional trends across America and keep an open ear to the affiliates who act as conduits for the demands and desires of their individual communities. Response to the programming desires of affiliates led to Showtime's addition of programs with strong nonurban appeal, such as concert performances by Willie Nelson, Crystal Gayle, Roy Clark, and Ray Stevens and a "Celebration of Country Comedy."

In the early days of pay-television, some cable operators expressed concern over programming of a controversial or adult nature. In response to these concerns, both Showtime and HBO created mini-program packages—abbreviations of the full monthly lineup that feature only G and PG attractions. However, these were not well received by the viewing public. In contrast, several local and regional programming services have had considerable success with **dedicated channels** offering only PG- and R-rated action/adventure series and spicy adult movies.

Pay-Television Rates

Pay-television networks set their monthly rates for cable operators based on each system's monthly subscriber charge for the pay-service and the number of basic cable subscribers in the cable system. This rate runs from 30 to 50 percent of the subscriber charge, averaging 40 percent. Each cable operator determines what the subscriber charge will be for pay-television services in the individual cable system. The average national retail subscriber rate for Showtime is about $10 per month and for Home Box Office about $9.

To receive any satellite services, pay-television channels, or free basic cable channels, cable operators must make an up-front investment by purchasing a satellite ground station or constructing a microwave interconnect. The Federal Communications Commission (FCC) in 1976 began to allow the construction of small (4.5 to 6 meter) satellite receive-only **earth stations**, which brought costs down from an average of $80,000 to as low as $12,000 to $15,000. Microwave interconnects, receiving signals from nearby cable systems with satellite receiving dishes, can cost from $20,000 to $50,000.

Other Satellite Programming Services

Most affiliates receive their pay-television "feed" via satellite. Using earth stations purchased primarily to receive pay-television signals, cable operators are exploring several kinds of satellite-distributed program packages. Systems offer these packages as part of basic cable service separate from the optional Showtime and HBO pay-channels. RCA Americom's communications satellite, which carried all pay-television programming available on satellite in this country as of January 1980, also transmits UA-Columbia's Madison Square Garden sports activities; Calliope, a children's programming service developed by UA-Columbia in cooperation with the Learning Corporation of America; Nickelodeon, a young people's entertainment service; and Star Channel, a movie service, both offered by Warner Amex Cable Communications, Inc. In addition, it transmits Newstime, United Press International's slowscan, 24-hour news service; the Entertainment and Sports Programming Network (ESPN), partially funded by Getty Oil; and three religious program services, Christian Broadcasting Network (CBN), People That Love (PTL), and Trinity Broadcasting Network (TBN). A cable industry consortium—the Cable-Satellite Public Affairs Network (C-SPAN)—provides gavel-to-gavel coverage of the United States House of Representatives. Cable operators generally are charged between 1¢ and 15¢ per month per subscriber for program services that become part of the basic cable service.

Four local independent commercial television stations are also available on satellite, offering syndicated television programming and local sports. The pioneer **superstation** is WTBS, Atlanta (formerly WTCG), owned by the colorful entrepreneur R. E. "Ted" Turner, who encouraged satellite distribution of his station's programming. Three other stations, WOR, New York, WGN, Chicago, and KTVU, Oakland, are also distributed by satellite companies. Small fees charged to cable operators for these superstations are collected by the satellite companies that deliver the signals as a **common carrier** service. The television stations collect no fee, although WTBS-TV has used its larger audience level to justify an increase in advertising rates. Superstation programming strategy is detailed in Chapter 13.

Additional services that will be available to cable operators in the 1980s are the Cable News Network—a 24-hour all-news channel operated by the Turner Broadcasting System; Cinemarcia 50+ Network—entertainment and public affairs aimed at persons over the age of fifty; and Galavision—films, sports, and entertainment features in Spanish.

In addition to various satellite programming services, many cable operators offer their subscribers a considerable amount of originally produced **local** programming—often covering local events in far more detail than local broadcast television stations. *Television Factbook* reports that in September 1978 there were 2,650 cable operators engaged in some form of local-origination programming—an increase of nearly 250 systems over the previous year and a half.[4] Much of this programming is automatic **alphanumeric** displays of news, time, weather, and stock reports.

However, almost 40 percent of these systems (1,035) were engaged in more ambitious kinds of programming. Many carry community, governmental, educational, and social service programs, ranging from two-way interviews at senior citizens' centers (as in Reading, Pennsylvania) to a telescreen version of classified advertising (as in Clinton, Iowa). New York's Manhattan Cable Television offers young filmmakers and video artists a forum for their experimental work, while the cable system affiliated with North Adams State College in Massachusetts regularly broadcasts classroom lectures.

THE PAY-TELEVISION AUDIENCE

Studies determining the makeup of the pay-television audience and its reactions to current programming philosophies are ongoing. Because cable television was used first to bring in more broadcast stations and to obtain greater channel coverage and clear reception, a great many areas currently served by cable are in suburban and rural markets where broadcast reception is poor. The customers in these areas tend to be 30 to 40 years old, mostly parents with teenage and younger children. This market is generally regarded as the "bedroom" community, where viewing habits are markedly different from those in urban markets. Urban viewers tend to be young, single, and apartment dwellers.

Because the urban 18 to 24 group constitutes the bulk of the theatrical movie audience, it is the prime target for most theatrical film producers. This creates a dilemma for the pay-television programmer whose prime source of material, the Hollywood motion picture indus- try, does not direct its efforts toward the same audience that cable reaches. Many families and older viewers, particularly in nonurban markets, reject the sexual depictions, violence, and youth-oriented sub- ject matter of many Hollywood films.

The character of the cable audience explains why the two largest pay-television services have made relatively large commitments to orig- inal production. Pay-television cannot continue to look to the movie industry for all of its programming when it has no control over the content. In fashioning original programming, pay-television services can gear each show toward desired segments of the audience or direct their energies to programming with broad-based family appeal. For example, original specials with such entertainers as Willie Nelson, Debbie Reynolds, Ben Vereen, Roy Clark, Monteith and Rand, and Tony Bennett can capture some of the viewers who will not watch films with significant doses of horror and violence such as "Damien" or "Midnight Express," while maintaining the youths and crossover viewers to whom both types of programming appeal.

The Audience-Measurement Problem

One of pay-television's greatest challenges is to establish a method of evaluating the success of each individual program in addition to overall viewer reaction to the total monthly package. This situation parallels the magazine business: it is difficult for an editor to know what each article or feature contributes to readers' satisfaction in each issue of a magazine. The monthly pay-television programmer finds difficulty in gauging the cause-and-effect relationship of specific programming choices. The A. C. Nielsen Company issued preliminary ratings for Showtime and Home Box Office based on audience measurement in a small number of pay-television homes during the February 1979 sweeps. If Nielsen continues to issue pay-television ratings on a regular basis, evaluating viewership quantitatively may become a standard pay- television practice.*

---

*Showtime research in 1980 has turned up two interesting statistics: in a community undergoing first-time cable sales (a newly installed system), of those people who decide to take cable service, 98 percent take pay-television; when HBO and Showtime are marketed as a package in a newly built system, 70 percent of people who take pay-television take both services.

Showtime researchers plan to improve their research model in the 1980s to provide a qualitative indication of subscriber response going beyond commercial television's purely quantitative rating systems. Pay-television must be concerned with how people liked each program, not merely if they watched. Another important factor is measuring the subscriber's "value perception" after viewing each program. Because they must pay for this monthly service, they must perceive a real value for what they have just seen.

Warner's **Qube** operation in Columbus, Ohio, has led the country in two-way cable communication, using a push-button device in each subscriber's home to let viewers talk back to their television sets. Uses for this device so far have included voting on a talent contest, answering consumer questions, program testing for Children's Television Workshop, and participating in various kinds of polls. Such a service would be the ideal method of answering pay-television suppliers' questions and determining accurate "ratings" for each pay-television program. One current form of pay-television audience measurement used by both Showtime and Home Box Office is the distribution of viewer surveys, encouraging comments from subscribers on every attraction.

PAY-TELEVISION PROGRAMMERS AND THE FUTURE

Because pay-television is so new, few people have extensive experience in the field. Most of the people who screen, acquire, produce, and program material for pay-television come from the commercial television or motion picture fields. All are engaged in a common learning experience. Producers, directors, writers, and performers find that pay-television welcomes new ideas and offers creative opportunities that commercial television cannot. Pay-television programmers are free from cautious advertisers who prefer to support programming formats with proven success. New program proposals are being made to major pay-television services every day, and as pay-television's programming appetite and budgets expand, so will the diversity of its product.

Isolating the winning trends in a field that changes constantly is difficult, but one trend is almost certain to dominate cable television in the coming years: specialization. Research results in the future may well demonstrate pay-television's current strategy to be impractical. With new channels and programming services being offered to viewers every year, the most logical move may be towards targeting channels to specific audiences. Separate channels may be devoted to children's programming, sports, cultural events, classic movies, action/adventure programs, or other specialized audience interests. Segmented programming is not new to television, but if undertaken by either of the largest pay-television networks, it would signal a new era in the television industry.

This is but one possibility for this ever-changing field. Effects of the burgeoning video cassette and disc industries are just beginning to be felt. Direct-to-home satellite distribution may bring other dramatic changes. FCC regulation and deregulation of various aspects of broadcasting will also play an important role in shaping pay-television's future. Rather than fighting new technologies as threats, broadcast television corporations are preparing to participate in new technologies to ensure corporate survival. ABC and CBS have created special divisions to produce and distribute programming for pay-television, and NBC executives have recently discussed publicly the possibility that the future may see several "NBC networks," targeting various audiences and distributed to television stations via satellite.

Satellites, coupled with cable television distribution, have indeed changed the structure and content of television. The innovative programming possibilities inherent in pay-television ensure an exciting future for America's television audience.

NOTES

[1]"Austin Furst on HBO's Programming," *Cablevision* cover story (February 26, 1979): 63–65.
[2]From Showtime's schedules for July 14, July 16, and July 31, 1979.
[3]From Home Box Office's schedules for July 4, July 15, and July 31, 1979.
[4]*Television Factbook*, September 1978.

ADDITIONAL PERIODICAL READINGS

"Austin Furst on HBO's Programming." *Cablevision* (February 26, 1979): 63–65.

Cover story of interview with HBO's vice-president of programming by Cablevision *editors.*

Baldwin Thomas F.; Wirth, Michael O.; and **Zenaty, Jayne W.** "The Economics of Per-Program Pay Cable Television." *Journal of Broadcasting* 22 (Spring 1978): 143–54.

Discussion of policies promoting the development of competitive pay-cable industry while maintaining the present "free" television program delivery system.

"HBO: Point Man for an Industry Makes It into the Clear." *Broadcasting* (October 17, 1977): 50–53.

Interview with Home Box Office's president and chairman on the company's current state and future plans.

Jeffries, Leo W. "Cable TV and Viewer Selectivity." *Journal of Broadcasting* 22 (Spring 1978): 167–77.

A before/after study of the effect of cable on the viewing behavior of subscribers.

Kaplan, Stuart J. "The Impact of Cable Television Services on the Use of Competing Media." *Journal of Broadcasting* 22 (Spring 1978): 155–65.

An investigation of the media-use behavior of subscribers to cable services.

"Nickelodeon: First Channel Programmed Entirely for Cable Is Aimed at Children." *TVC. Magazine* (April 1, 1979).

TVC staff report on the Warner Cable's children's channel.

Taylor, John P. "NCTA Convention Finds Cable System Operators Emphasizing 'Nonbroadcast' Programming." *Television/Radio Age* (May 21, 1979): 42 ff.

Analysis of the mushrooming growth of nonbroadcast cable programming and pay-cable, including implications for broadcast television industry.

"Warner Cable's Qube: Exploring the Outer Reaches of Two-Way TV." *Broadcasting* (July 31, 1978): 27–31.

A brief report on the potential of two-way cable covering Qube and an experiment in Reading, Pa.

Wurtzel, Alan. "Public-Access Cable TV: Programming." *Journal of Communication* 25 (Summer 1975): 15–21.

An analysis of public access programming on New York City cable channels.

13 Superstation Strategy

Sidney Pike

The superstation idea is an extension of the familiar cable/ television station relationship. A superstation is an independent that has its signal imported over much greater than usual distances without untenable costs. Originated by Ted Turner, president of Turner Communications Inc., the revolutionary idea of distributing a UHF independent's program schedule via satellite over a huge area of the United States for redistribution to homes by cable systems holds the potential for revamping the structure of the television industry. WTBS-TV of Atlanta (formerly WTCG*) was the first independent to become satellite/cable distributed and has been linked inextricably with the term superstation. *As vice-president and director of television operations of WTBS-TV, Sidney Pike has been a prime spokesman for the superstation concept. After a total of thirty years in television, starting as a producer/director for WBZ in Boston and later becoming director of program development for WHDH in Boston and station manager of WQXI in Atlanta, Mr. Pike joined Ted Turner's WTCG-TV as station manager in 1971. In addition to his present position at WTBS, he lectures at nearby colleges and represents the prosuperstation viewpoint on industry panels. In this chapter he describes the economics of the superstation concept, the role of common carriers, cable operators, and the programming strategy that has made WTBS the most widely distributed station in the country.*

THE NEW INDEPENDENTS

The end of television programming as now known will result from technological pressure and unsatisfied audience appetites. The commercial **network** practice of devoting major portions of **primetime** to hit formats (such as to westerns in the 1950s, police adventures in the 1960s, and family problems in the 1970s) is being resisted by a growing segment of the television audience that has recently gained program alternatives through cable service. The deregulatory fever in Washington hastens the inevitable changes.

Over the last thirty years, the television industry has acquired the dominant structure of three networks and roughly 600 **affiliates**. The

---

*A change of call letters from WTCG to WTBS was approved by the FCC in 1979.

emergence of **independent** stations was not resisted initially by the networks and their affiliates because independents generally did not compete effectively. They lacked success because of the absence of quality programming, the weakness of UHF channel allocations, and, in many cases, poor management. A few independents began to escape this treadmill about 1970. By the time the network affiliates woke up to the new competition, they found that these independents had provided substantial alternatives to affiliates' local news and syndicated programming in nonnetwork-filled time periods. In many markets independent stations have become number one or two in major time periods in which large amounts of advertising revenue are generated. The number of independents has grown rapidly, but local advertising dollars have increased at such a fast rate that the two or three affiliated stations in most markets have been able to afford to move over slightly to make room in the bed for a "little brother."

The **superstation** is an extension of the local independent station concept, capitalizing on two technological advances: cable television and satellite television relay transmission. A superstation comes into being when a **common carrier** company picks up an independent's broadcast signal, retransmits that signal by microwave via a "transmit" **earth station** to a satellite **transponder** (channel) leased for the purpose; in turn, the satellite redistributes the signal to "receive-only" earth stations (microwave receivers) maintained by local cable system operators. These operators **dedicate** one of their cable channels to the superstation signal, adding to the off-air and cable-originated material they provide on other channels to their subscribers. Cable systems pay the common carrier company a fee to receive the satellite signal, based on their total number of subscribers. As of 1979, cable operators paid about 8 cents per subscriber per month to common carrier companies for satellite reception of a superstation signal. None of this revenue goes to the superstation. But in order for a common carrier to risk the investment required for satellite distribution of an independent's signal, the cable industries needed a favorable climate for growth.

PROBLEMS OF CABLE GROWTH

Historically, restrictive Federal Communications Commission (FCC) regulations have been a major factor inhibiting cable growth. In particular, the 1972 regulations limiting the distance over which independent stations' signals could be imported by cable companies and rules that set a quota on the number of distant signals that could be imported restricted cable growth. These inhibiting regulations, combined with the high cost of building and maintaining lengthy terrestrial microwave relay systems for distribution of television signals, slowed expansion of the cable industry into new market areas in the late 1960s and early 1970s. Growth occurred only in areas close to major cities, such as near Chicago, where two of the city's independent stations were economically exported on a single microwave line to cable systems up to several hundred miles from the city.

Cable growth in the early 1970s—in total households—came largely through attracting new cable subscribers within existing cable communities who were willing to pay a basic subscription fee averaging $6 to $10 per month. The monthly base rate generally provided off-the-air television signals, signals from imported distant television stations, and locally originated services, such as scans of weather information and **alphanumeric news** channels. The addition of other programming services, not available over-the-air, lured some viewers without signal-quality problems into subscribing to cable service. **Pay-television** services, originated typically by companies owning several cable systems and offering unedited, commercial-free showings of recent motion pictures, came into being and were offered at an additional rate of $5 to $10 above the basic service rate.

During 1975–76 a series of events conspired to break cable loose from its relatively dormant state. In 1975 the FCC authorized the licensing of receive-only earth stations by cable systems to permit reception of pay-television programming offered via domestic satellite transmission by Home Box Office (HBO)—the first satellite-delivered service offered to cable systems. Under FCC regulations, the receiving antennas, or dishes, could not be less than 9 meters in diameter (to permit a "broadcast quality" reception of the satellite signal) and were priced from $85,000 to $125,000. Although expensive, the receiving antennas were purchased by a number of large cable systems that foresaw income potential from pay-television subscriptions.

In January 1976 the FCC dropped its distant-signal requirements ("leapfrogging rule") and permitted cable systems anywhere to receive any distant independent station from whatever sources.* In response, a common carrier company was formed—Southern Satellite Systems (SSS)—which became the first common carrier company to distribute a broadcast television signal via satellite to cable television systems. The signal they chose to distribute was WTBS, channel 17, Atlanta.

In December 1976 the FCC granted authority to SSS to transmit the WTBS signal.† At the same time, the commission reduced the re-

---

*In mid-1980 the FCC eliminated the ceiling on the number of distant signals that cable systems could import.

---

†In 1978 four companies—United Video Inc., Southern Satellite Systems Inc., American Microwave & Communications, and Midwestern Relay Company—were granted authority to operate domestic satellite channels carrying the signal of WGN-TV to various locations throughout the contiguous forty-eight states by the FCC. "Superstation Breakthrough," *Broadcasting* (October 30, 1978): 25.

quired size of receive-only earth station antennas to 4.5 meters, which had the immediate effect of reducing their cost to $45,000 to $60,000 and thus encouraged more cable systems to buy receive-only stations.

By the end of 1979, more than 2,000 cable systems had installed earth stations. Seventeen satellite program services were available. Earth stations of the receive-only type were for sale at prices as low as $8,000.* Existing cable systems had grown substantially in the number of homes served. And nearly every major city and many suburban areas were experiencing new cable system development. A cable revolution had begun, spurred on by the inexpensive access to satellite-delivered program services, among which WTBS was the single most desired service.

COMMON CARRIERS, INDEPENDENTS, SATELLITES, AND CABLE

SSS is a privately owned company not affiliated with WTBS or any other independent station. It contracts with cable systems to deliver the WTBS signal by providing an **uplink** facility in Atlanta and renting one of the twenty-four transponders (receive-transmit components on satellites, equivalent to "channels") on a satellite to transmit the WTBS signal to cable systems' own receive-only antennas.† The diagram of the distribution of WTBS by SSS depicts the process (Figure 13–1). SSS picks up the WTBS signal at a location just outside Atlanta. This signal is fed into an uplink dish which beams it to RCA's Satcom I satellite, about 22,000 miles above the earth. The signal then is retransmitted down to the many 4.5-meter **downlink** dishes operated by nearly 2,000 cable systems that pay SSS for the relay service.

Renting one of the transponders on the RCA Satcom I satellite and providing the uplink through RCA Americom's earth station costs the common carrier company about a million dollars a year. In 1979 SSS

---

*On October 18, 1979, the FCC approved voluntary licensing of receive-only dishes. However, users still must get permission from programmers to receive their transmissions. "Deregulating the Dishes: FCC Lets Loose Earth Stations," *Broadcasting* (October 22, 1979): 28.

---

†Other superstations are planned: Satellite Communication Systems Inc., a joint venture of Holiday Inns and Southern Satellite, applied in 1978 for permission to carry the signal of KTVU, Oakland–San Francisco, and Southern Satellite itself has applied to carry KTTV, Los Angeles and WPIX, New York. Eastern Microwave Inc. has applied for WOR, New York (with a switchover to WCBS's all-night local programming during WOR's off-hours), and WSBK, Boston. United Video also has asked to relay WOR and WSBK. "Superstation Breakthrough," *Broadcasting* (October 30, 1978): 25.

began operation of its own uplink, modifying these costs. SSS charges a cable system 10 cents per home per month for full 24-hour service or 2 cents per home per month for night-only service (1 A.M. to 6 A.M.), discounted when paid annually in advance. SSS receives all this money

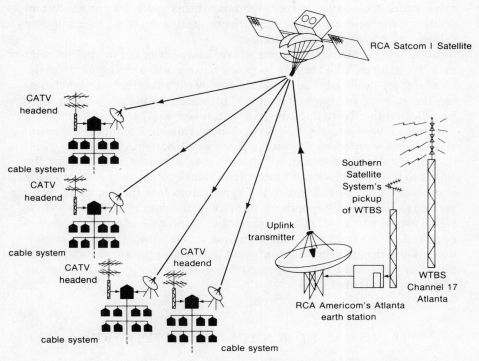

Southern Satellite System's transmission of programming from WTBS. Atlanta independent. to CATV system headends uses uplink in RCA Americom's Atlanta earth station. and transponder in Satcom I satellite SSS pickup of WTBS signal off the air is at site adjacent to the RCA's Atlanta earth station nine miles from indie's transmitter. Transponder retransmits signal direct to CATV systems' earth stations.

**Figure 13–1. Distribution of WTBS
via Satellite**

from the cable systems, and presumably the cable companies charge it back to their subscribers as part of their regular monthly fee or use the superstation's programming as an inducement to attract more cable homes.

SUPERSTATION ECONOMICS

Superstations receive no increase in revenues directly as a result of their superstation status. Their only source of additional compensation is increased rates for advertising to match increased audience size. However, this increase in rates challenges tradition. In the early days of cable, when the service was still quite limited, no one suggested to television advertisers that they should pay for increases in audience size resulting from cable coverage beyond the local market. Television station sales staffs and national representative firms gave the cable system audience increment to their advertisers gratis, referring to additional cable homes as the **bonus audiences**.

It is hard for superstations to break advertisers of the bonus habit even after the so-called bonus audience has become even bigger than the local station's direct-broadcast audience. Most advertisers resist changing the rules of the game. However, increased audience delivery must be reflected in advertising rates for two reasons: (1) superstations need increased revenue to provide services not available from local television stations but wanted by the public (such as 24-hour programming); and (2) superstation penetration of distant markets jacks up costs for the rights to transmit theatrical films, **off-network** series, and certain sports events. This happens because the **syndicators** fear their sales of those programs to other independents in markets reached by the superstation signal are jeopardized. However, as of 1979, no case of a failed sale had occurred. But syndicators still demand greater prices from superstations, knowing that the programs that they sell to the superstations will be received in markets far removed geographically, thus possibly eliminating potential sales.

VOLUNTARY AND INVOLUNTARY SUPERSTATIONS

The difference between a voluntary and an involuntary superstation is the difference between aggressive and passive promotion of a station's "super" status. Superstations carried by satellite did not exist prior to 1977, and the broadcasting industry as a whole feels potentially threatened by their existence. Their proliferation would subvert the privileged relationship between networks, their affiliates, and advertisers. Growth in the number of superstations continues to be a prickly legal and economic issue in the minds of many broadcasters.

WTBS is a voluntary superstation; it was the first of the superstations and actively promotes this attribute. WTBS encourages identification with the word *superstation* by incorporating it in its letterhead, using it over the air, selling it to advertisers, and proselytizing it to the industry and the public.

In contrast, WGN-TV, an independent in Chicago (the third largest market) is more reluctant to be labeled a superstation. Although its signal is indeed relayed by satellite and distributed to many participating cable systems, WGN did not actively seek superstation status. Its management is more impressed by the potential disadvantages of superstation identification than by the advantages. As the station sees it, one of WGN's main attractions is live sports, and wide distribution of these events might interfere with sales of rights by the owners of the teams to stations outside the Chicago market because of the loss in market **exclusivity**. Since WGN is an old, established, highly successful station in its market area, it lacks incentive to seek out controversial changes in its status.

Another reluctant superstation is KTVU-TV, Oakland. It has in fact been a land-carried superstation since the early 1960s. Although it concentrates on programming for the Oakland–San Francisco area, its signal has been imported up and down the coasts of California, Oregon, and Washington, as well as inland into California, for two decades. In many places along the mountainous coast, reception requires cable rather than over-the-air broadcasting, and KTVU is one of the few major independents available for cable systems to carry. The stations' signal is now picked up by a common carrier and redistributed to more distant locations via satellite, but the management of KTVU is concerned that becoming known as a superstation may imperil its ability to acquire programming, claiming that possible rises in the cost for films override any apparent benefit of superstation status. Consequently, KTVU does not cooperate with common carriers desiring joint **promotion** of its signal; it does not advertise its cable distribution in trade publications; and it does not assist cable companies in promoting its schedule.

Both WGN and KTVU can be called *involuntary* superstations since they did not initiate satellite distribution and do not actively promote their increased coverage. They have not altered their programming strategies to please audiences outside their local markets, but because those independents already program entertainment for a heterogeneous audience, their strategies appeal to distant audiences.*

SIGNAL COVERAGE

The programming strategy of an active superstation is necessarily affected by its coverage area. The commercial television broadcasting system, because of its dependence on concentrations of large audiences, fails to give adequate service to certain parts of the country—especially rural areas. Many of these areas have benefited from the introduction of

---

*As of 1979, WOR-TV, New York City, is also available to cable systems via satellite.

cable television service with concomitant superstation and other imported signals. Independents have their greatest viewer density in the
states surrounding their points of origination: WGN in the northern
portion of the Midwest, WTBS in the Southeast, and KTVU in the West.
However, cable markets tend to be scattered over the entire country
rather than grouped closely together. In consequence, superstation signals tend to leapfrog many populated areas, reaching more rural homes
than urban. It is in rural cable areas that promotion of superstation
programming succeeds best in luring new audiences.

However, it is conceivable that some superstations will become
more nationally oriented than others in the future. In addition to serving
the needs of its broadcast coverage area (as presently required by the
FCC), a superstation willing to invest in program development could
generate a much larger share of the total television audience, function-
ing much like one of the national television networks by providing a
schedule of first-run programs for its cable "affiliates." However, a
superstation, under present FCC rules, is licensed to serve only the
particular market reached by its over-the-air broadcast signal. It must
cater to that market's needs and must make a special effort to present
programs that serve the local community. Some portion of the broadcast schedule, as well as a portion of program development efforts, must
be devoted to this responsibility. However, WTBS's cable audience
exceeds its broadcast audience more than ten times over, and the station's management acknowledges an additional responsibility to that
audience.

The map showing the location of the cable systems distributing
WTBS's signal makes clear the wide availability of WTBS programming
(Figure 13–2). The WTBS signal is carried on cable systems in Alaska,
Hawaii, and Puerto Rico. This wide distribution could lend itself to new
programming strategies if permitted by the FCC. WTBS at present
programs largely for its own broadcast time zone, the eastern zone. It
cannot satisfy the needs of all the various time zones it is carried in
without disrupting service to its own local broadcast audience. For some
programs, viewing in different time zones is not a problem—for example, Midwest and West viewers may enjoy a favorite sport in the late
afternoon even though it originates at 7:30 P.M. in the East. But time zone
difference can create absurdities: *Romper Room*, a preschool children's
program, is aired at 8 A.M. in the East, but it is of little interest to viewers
on the West Coast at 5 A.M. when children of that age are asleep.

BLACKOUT RULES AFFECTING INDEPENDENTS

Under the law, stations in the top fifty U.S. markets have total
program **exclusivity** within their markets. Any syndicated program or

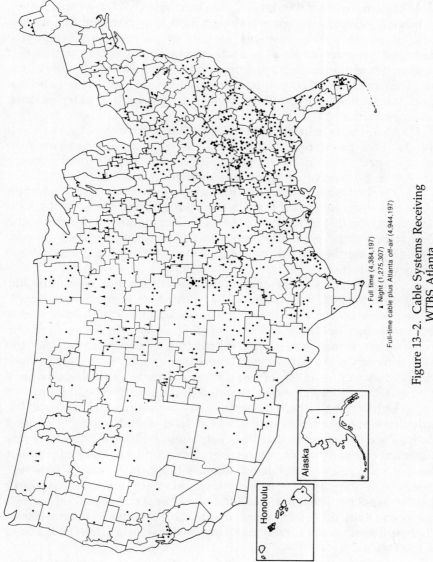

Full time (4,384,197)
Night (1,275,307)
Full-time cable plus Atlanta off-air (4,944,197)

Alaska

Honolulu

Figure 13–2. Cable Systems Receiving
WTBS Atlanta

film imported from a distant station when a local station also had the rights to that same program must be blacked out on written request of the local television station (or the syndicator in some instances) to the cable system. In other words, FCC **blackout** rules require a cable system to block a particular program or event from importation into a market from a distant station (network affiliate or independent) when that particular program or event is under contract to a station within that market. Protection of local program rights relates to the length of the program contract in the top fifty markets: for affiliates, contracts (and, consequently, protection) average five years; for independents, seven years.

Most markets in the United States have all three networks available to them through affiliates. The usual goal of cable systems is to bring in services not normally available—such as independent stations, pay-television, and other services distributed by satellite.

For the next fifty markets, the regulations are different. Protection of station program rights is for a maximum of two years. If the local station and the distant station show the same program in primetime, the local station can claim protection. If the distant station shows the program in primetime and the local station shows it outside primetime, no one gets protection.

No protection exists for markets smaller than the one-hundredth. However, the FCC has traditionally wanted to protect those small-market television stations from the financial injury of fractionalizing their audiences with too many competing signals. In them, only one independent signal has been permitted to a cable system (usually the local or nearby one), but blackout rules do not apply. However, in these markets, as well as in larger ones, if no station is available 24 hours a day, a 24-hour station may be imported during the **overnight** hours.

Debate on the blackout rules goes on within the FCC and the industry.* Some members of the FCC have felt that profits of local stations are sufficient so that they would not be harmed financially by increased competition. Other members have felt that the elimination of the blackout rules would harm local stations. However, a two-year economic inquiry by the FCC looking into program exclusivity and distant signal importation found little or no impact on broadcast stations from exclusivity or distant signals due to cable systems in their markets. These conclusions are supported by the Broadcast and Cable TV Bureaus of the FCC.[1]

In spite of these alterations in FCC attitudes, a superstation that is attempting to make its programs attractive to cable systems is wise to originate as much new or **unduplicated** programming as possible. Local sports are a good example of such unduplicated programming. Specials

---

*In mid-1980 the FCC eliminated the syndicated program exclusivity (blackout) rules, but it is likely that this decision will be appealed.

such as local rock concerts, public affairs, documentaries, and news are also invulnerable to blackout.

ELEMENTS OF SUPERSTATION STRATEGY

The success of the ordinary independent station is based on its ability to **counterprogram** the network affiliates in its market at specific peak-audience time periods of each day. However, the success of the superstation lies in providing alternative programming throughout the broadcast day. The usual independent carefully programs against the affiliate in each specific time period, but the superstation provides a plethora of alternate choices throughout the day. This means that the cable subscriber no longer has to wait days to watch baseball, football, basketball, or hockey. The availability of satellite-distributed sports events from superstations as well as local sports coverage greatly increases the chances of a viewer's chosen sport being on the air any night or afternoon the viewer chooses. Movies and specials are attractive alternatives to network comedies, **soaps**, and game shows whatever the time of day or night. The tools of superstation programming strategy are sports, program **specials**, movies, syndicated programs, telecourses, and news, scheduled 24 hours a day.*

Twenty-four-hour Service

For most television stations, 24-hour service is too costly, because the revenue generated by advertising in the early-morning hours is insufficient to defray feature film **amortization**, station labor, and operating costs. But for the superstation, although 24-hour service is a **loss leader** in its initial development phase, it later becomes a profit center once a wide audience is reached.

For example, some cable systems that do not have a 24-hour station available locally sign up with a common carrier such as SSS for nighttime service only. Providing 24-hour programming can be vital to the success of a cable system. It can be the "extra" that attracts enough additional cable subscribers to make the system profitable.

In addition, a 24-hour superstation offers programming attractive to shift workers who cannot watch television during regular programming hours. Many workers who are either on their jobs or sleeping during the normal television day, will watch daytime-type programming in the 1:00 to 6:00 A.M. period. Once advertisers realize that this new audience is available to them, even the early-morning hours can become a profit center for 24-hour superstations.

---

*Superstation programming comes to the cable operator in a fixed schedule—similar to that provided by a network during primetime or that provided by a pay-television supplier.

Sports

One of the biggest attractions of superstation programming is a heavy schedule of live sports events. For example, each year WTBS originates 100 Atlanta Braves baseball games, 40 Hawks basketball games, and 25 Flames NHL hockey games.* In addition, it covers occasional one-time sports specials such as the Annual Masters Water Ski Championship and the Pee Wee Reese baseball championship game. WTBS usually first broadcasts these events live. It repeats many of them on tape one or more times, but it is not desirable to delay a sport that receives wide press coverage since the winner will be known before the event is aired. Some professional sports events are repeated on WTBS for a new early-morning audience at 1 A.M. (EST). Viewers on the West Coast can enjoy the same games at 10 P.M.

ABC, CBS, NBC, and the independent national sports promoters sew up exclusive national rights to games. Nevertheless, a huge number of games originating on local market stations remains available and can attract large audiences when distributed by cable companies. It is crucially important that technical production quality match that of major network sports producers if viewer and advertiser interest is to be maintained. For this reason, WTBS owns three **remote** trucks with twelve top-of-the-line cameras. It can televise a complete golf tournament, one of the most technically demanding of sporting events. Owning their own remote equipment gives superstations flexibility in choosing the timing and maintaining the quality of their sports coverage.

Program Specials

The remote equipment used for sports telecasts can also serve for occasional **specials** such as rock concerts, holiday events, local children's or adults' theatrical performances, and important public affairs events. Many programs that serve the local community can provide unduplicated entertainment for a much greater region when distributed by cable. One of the main benefits of the superstation is its ability to produce unique specials of wide appeal that cannot be blacked out anywhere in the United States.

One particular type of program with lasting appeal that has nevertheless been phased out by the networks is the talent development or talent exposure program. The *Ed Sullivan Show*, the last example of this type of program in primetime, was discontinued in 1971. During its twenty-three year run, the Sullivan show gave many unknowns an opportunity to perform, introducing several present-day stars to na-

---

*Ted Turner owns the Atlanta Braves and Atlanta Hawks but not the Atlanta Flames.

tional audiences. The networks, in their rush for the mass audience, have closed this avenue for exposure. The public's continuing appetite for comedians, jugglers, magicians, and other stage performers goes largely unfulfilled. Local television stations, whether affiliates or independents, have been unable to capitalize on this opportunity because costs far exceed potential income on a purely local basis. Superstations, however, can fill this need cost-effectively because their audience reach justifies the necessary expense of producing programs having more than strictly local appeal.

Movies

Movies make up the largest single element in superstation programming as measured by air time. Particularly for the 24-hour station, an abundant supply of theatrical films is necessary. WTBS uses up to forty features per week—about 1,800 movies per year. To support this appetite, WTBS maintains a library of about 2,600 feature films, providing more rest for individual films than the once-a-year scheduling used by most television stations.*

These films are a mixed bag. Some are first-run off-network **made-for-television movies**, others are **reruns**, and some are old movies that have been around since the 1930s, 1940s, or 1950s. These films generally do not compete with the better **pay-cable** offerings since they are not box office giants, but they provide satisfactory escape for audiences. Eventually, it may become possible for superstations to participate in the production of their own made-for-television movies. More movies for theatrical showing are being produced now than ever before, but some, because of sexual content, cause problems for television markets.

Syndicated Programs

Independent television stations generally counterprogram network affiliates' news and adult programming with **strip**-scheduled mass-appeal **syndicated** shows. For example, scheduling programs that appeal especially to children in the early **fringe** time period is one key secret of success for most independent television stations. But superstations actually find the syndicated programs that form this most important staple of the typical independent their weakest programming strategy.

Syndicated programs are the most duplicated form of programming and, under present FCC rules, are frequently blacked out, especially in the top fifty markets where most advertising revenue is gener-

---

*The film library at KTVU, Oakland, has 1,500 titles with a value of nearly $30 million in the Oakland–San Francisco market.

ated. The newest, most popular series such as *Laverne & Shirley* and *Happy Days* are licensed to large numbers of television stations and are most likely to be blacked out on any signal introduced into a coverage area. The oldest syndicated series such as *Father Knows Best* or *Leave It to Beaver* are no longer as heavily distributed nationally and so do not have potential blackout restrictions when carried by a superstation.

Telecourses

Courses for college credit offered over television in the early-morning hours are an area for potential growth. Telecourses have had some success in finding viewers on both commercial and noncommercial television, but the most successful have had general appeal rather than being specialized subjects. Specialized telecourses could reach select viewers scattered over a wide geographical area if carried by superstations; consequently, subject matter appealing only to restricted numbers of people would then have an opportunity to reach sufficient viewers. Telecourses remain to be developed as an element in superstation strategy.

News

Superstations find both special opportunities and special hazards in dealing with news and public affairs programming. The wide regional coverage of the superstation makes the locally oriented news it prepares for its own broadcast market inappropriate for viewers in other markets. Nor can the superstation compete effectively with established local coverage by stations in their cable clients' own local areas.

The best strategy for superstations is to confine spot news to bulletins on fast-breaking regional and national events, saving most of their news departments' energies for documentaries and in-depth coverage of current public affairs issues. Here superstations can take advantage of the fact that the national television networks often treat subjects briefly only to drop them while they still have current interest. Superstations can capitalize on the original network coverage as a kind of promotion for their own subsequent in-depth treatments of such topics.

One example of this type of news follow-up was WTBS's in-depth treatment of new religious groups (cults) in a series called *In the Name of God*. Following the Guyana incident in 1978 (a shocking mass suicide/murder among members of a cult), WTBS devoted 10 hours in primetime to this subject. Hare Krishnas, Moonies, and Children of God were represented on the programs with the best known deprogrammer Ted Patrick as well as leaders of the conventional religious faiths and former cult members. In 1978 WTBS won an Emmy for a three-hour primetime special on the high cost of medical treatment. The station was nominated for the same award in 1979 for a special on abortion. Also in 1979 it won a local documentary award for "Sweet Auburn Avenue," a history of blacks in the city of Atlanta. These programs point up the fact that high-quality documentaries can have both purely local appeal and broad regional or national appeal as well.

The major event in WTBS's 1980 program schedule was participation in an interstate convention called Energy and the Way We Live: A National Issues Forum. WTBS used live television to coordinate forums in different parts of the country and produced a 9-hour telethon, five monthly specials, and five half hours of primetime programming as a part of the national energy "exposathon." One of the network-like facets of the superstation—its simultaneous carriage in many time zones— made primetime viewing of some portion of the energy "exposathon" possible for viewers in the East, Midwest, Far West, Alaska, and Hawaii. A superstation can afford to make large blocks of time available for such an event whereas the national commercial networks would find it too costly.*

TIME ZONE STRATEGY

Satellite distribution allows a television signal to reach from New York to Hawaii simultaneously. An East Coast superstation could carefully choose its programs to counterprogram network affiliates in the eastern time zone. However, there are six different time zones in the country, counting Hawaii. By the time a given superstation signal reaches Hawaii, the carefully chosen counterprogramming would be meaningless. For example, a children's program aired in Atlanta at 7 A.M. is received on the West Coast at 4 A.M., hardly a children's time period. Since specialized audiences disintegrate as signals leave the originating time zone, the logical scheduling strategy for superstations is to avoid special-audience programming, filling the bulk of any 24-hour period with programs with broad appeals for varied ages and audiences.

In other words, superstations cannot compete head-to-head with market-specific independents located out of their originating time zones; superstation successes are based not on specific counterprogramming, but rather on the ability to provide alternative program choices throughout the broadcast day. As an illustration, an 8 P.M. sports event from Atlanta might be welcome at 7, 6, or even 5 P.M. as an alternative to national and local newscasts in the central, mountain, or western time

---

*Turner Communications (not WTBS) leases a satellite transponder for delivery of a 24-hour continuous news service begun June 1, 1980. This news service is directed toward cable systems but is also available to WTBS.

zones. During the afterschool and **primetime access** periods, independents tend to program for children, capitalizing on the fact that children determine which channel will be turned on during those periods. This leaves predominantly adult households with few program choices, even in major markets, and reduces the HUT (homes using television) level at those times of the day. Superstations fill the gap by serving adults in central to western time zones with adult programming also designed to interest older children.

Superstations have introduced a third choice to the central through western audiences during the early afternoon as well. Without satellite service, viewers generally have a choice of only game shows and soap operas on the network affiliates and young children's cartoons on independents. Satellite service gives viewers the option of syndicated reruns designed for an older (over ten) audience, movies, or occasionally sports.

UNIQUE FUTURE POSSIBILITIES

Program costs will rise for superstations as their audiences grow. One possibility for the future is the creation of a temporary fourth network. A combination of four or five superstations could cover a third or more of the homes in the United States. By cooperative program funding in a manner similar to that used by Operation Prime Time (OPT),* such a group could produce major programs with high audience potential. The natural competitiveness of superstations would limit such coproductions, but even a single program concept intended for primetime in each time zone could be effective. This means an eastern superstation running the program at 8 P.M. would be blacked out at 5 P.M. in the West Coast major markets and vice versa. Commitment from individual superstations would depend on protection of their airings in predetermined major markets.

Another possibility is that production centers will evolve in other cities besides New York and Los Angeles. Chicago and San Francisco–Oakland are two likely centers; Atlanta could offer such an opportunity because it has the facilities and the motivation to generate national programs and could lead the way for superstations.

Cable television homes and audiences are increasing monthly nationwide; the amount of advertising money available increases along

---

*Operation Prime Time refers to a cooperative venture by a group of stations that pooled financial resources to finance some major program series independent of the networks. Other nonmember stations had an opportunity to purchase runs of the series if they were not in the market of a station that contributed to the financial pool.

with this growth. The three national networks and their affiliates along with the now successful independents would like to keep the broadcasting system the way it is so that advertising revenue is funneled only in their direction. If they succeed, not only will cable viewers suffer in areas unable to receive multiple-program signals, but also the creative talent of future producers, directors, writers, comedians, and musicians will have reduced program access. Superstations can increase opportunities for access to the television screen for a greater number of talented individuals. They will have added opportunities to develop their talents as the need for greater amounts of television programming grows. A growing population with increased average education will want better quality and more specialized programs. In addition, expanding advertising budgets seek new outlets.[2] There is a limit on how much the commercial broadcast stations can charge for spot commercials, so advertising pressure will need more outlets—resulting in more program sales opportunities and in a demand for talented people.

Superstations with their growing audiences can provide producers and distributors as well as advertisers the air time for new programming. In the end it is the viewers who benefit from superstations because of increased opportunity to choose programs that interest them.

NOTES

[1]*Inquiry into the Economic Relationship Between Television Broadcasting and Cable Broadcasting,* Docket 21284, 71 FCC 2d 632, May 7, 1979.
[2]John Dempsey, "Spots Selling Like It Was Gas," *Variety* (July 4, 1979): 1 ff.

ADDITIONAL PERIODICAL READINGS

"Is NTIA Superstation Plan Answer to Syndication Woes?" *Television/Radio Age* (March 12, 1979): 105 ff.

Article on the proposal to require cable systems to obtain consent from the originating station before retransmitting a signal.

"Superstation Breakthrough." *Broadcasting* (October 30, 1978): 25–26.

Discussion of the FCC's decision to allow "open entry" policy for resale carriers that feed local stations to cable television systems.

" 'Superstations' via Satellite Get Off to Dramatic '79 Start." *Television/Radio Age* (January 1, 1979): 43 ff.

Analysis of the possible effects of pickup of independent signals by common carriers and relay via satellites to cable systems.

Wahlstrom, Fred. " 'Superstations' Spur Growth of Cable TV," *P.D.Cue* (January 1979): 18–24.

An analysis of the influence of superstations, particularly WTBS-TV, on the growth in numbers of cable subscribers.

PART FOUR
Radio Programming Strategies

Part IV examines radio rather than television. It covers both commercial and noncommercial programming strategies for the rock and classical, news, and talk formats—often subdivided into "music" and "information" radio. Since the commercial radio networks play a minor role compared to the television networks, they are discussed as one set of programming resources inside chapters focusing on the strategies within program formats. The chapters on all-news and talk radio cover the commercial networks; the chapter on public radio deals with national public radio.

Differences between music and information formats and commercial and noncommercial operation are crucial to understanding program decision making and strategy in radio. Since music programming dominates the entire radio industry, Part IV begins with a chapter that takes the reader step by step through the process of selecting a music format in a hypothetical major market. Separate chapters are devoted to all-news and talk formats because these formats rely largely on local live production rather than on prerecorded material. Music formats, once selected, require few day-to-day strategic decisions. Frequently commercial music formats are purchased as a package from a format supplier, and the same successful format may appear in markets all over the country. In contrast, news and talk formats demand more personalized programming to fit local market conditions. Noncommercial formats tend to be highly individualized.

Chapter 14 details the process of choosing a commercially viable music programming plan for a given market—a format. The final selection of a rock format in this exercise is based on the author's wide experience in the radio industry. He has been general manager of several radio stations with music formats and has written several textbooks on radio. The strategies he presents are important because at least 90 percent of radio stations air music programming.

The next two chapters cover all-news and talk radio. Although these formats occur in their purest forms only in very large markets where a high degree of specialization can be supported economically, news and talk make up the bulk of nonmusic air time for small and midsized markets. All-news is advancing as an AM specialty in response to the shift of music formats from AM to FM. However, many of the concerns of the news programmer apply to 5-minute hourly interruptions inside music formats as well as to more lengthy newscasts. From his long-time connection with a major-market all-news station, the author of Chapter 15 provides an inside look at the business of radio news, its unique problems, and its on-air strategies.

Talk radio is the subject of Chapter 16. This format occurs in variations from all talk to sporadic interruptions of music programming when special guests become available or special controversies arise. Some stations have adopted a news/talk or talk/news format that they call "information radio," which includes elements of news, talk, and some music. Programmers of all the variations of the talk format must deal with the problems discussed in Chapter 16. The author, who directs both news and entertainment programming for a talk station in one of the largest markets, delves into the touchy issues of fairness and pressure from community groups which apply to any size market and to any format that deviates from "canned" material.

Chapter 17 deals with noncommercial radio. Out of more than 5,000 radio stations in the country, slightly more than 250 are noncommercial. They come in variations of five different formats and may be affiliated with National Public Radio (NPR). The author manages an FM station that zoomed from obscurity to national prominence when it was reprogrammed as a classical music station in 1976, becoming the most-listened-to public radio station in the country by 1978. The chapter includes a case study of that station and shows how public stations can compete head-to-head with commercial stations.

Radio programs appear to lack complexity when compared with television, but these chapters make clear that programming strategy is highly developed within music and information formats. Part IV completes an overview of programming strategy in the field of broadcasting that covers television and radio, station and network, and commercial and noncommercial operations.

14 Music Programming

Edd Routt

    As former general manager of three radio stations and author of three books on radio, Edd Routt brings a background of expertise in news, sales, and station management to this chapter on music programming. He creates a hypothetical market in which the reader goes step by step through the process of selecting a competitive format. After deciding on rock music, he details a system for song classification and delineates the role of research. This chapter draws on the author's experiences as vice president and general manager of WKRG/WKRG-FM, general manager of KLIF, general manager of WRR-AM/FM, and sales manager of WFAA/KZEW. In addition, he has taught station administration for six years at Southern Methodist University and written three books on broadcasting: The Business of Radio Broadcasting *(TAB Books, 1972),* Dimensions of Broadcast Editorializing *(TAB Books, 1974), and* The Radio Format Conundrum *(with McGrath and Weiss, Hastings House, 1978). His chapter exhibits depth and variety in its coverage of the strategies that suit rock music formats and the problem of news within music format schedules.*

MUSIC FORMAT STRATEGY

Some **stations** play country, classical, **beautiful music**, **ethnic**, or disco, but contemporary rock is the prevailing genre in music radio. More people listen to rock, in one form or another, than to any other style of music. There is no question that the passionate, relentless beat of rock is as firmly established in America as country, jazz, and classical. In creating and implementing a music **format**, station planners must consider five main factors: the technical facilities, as compared to those of the competition; the character of the local market; the delineation of a target audience; the available budget; and the potential revenue. Evaluation of these factors will determine which music format can win in the **ratings** in a given market.

Technical Facilities

The *best* facility has the *best* chance. AM's power and frequency and FM's power and antenna height are important for several reasons. Generically, these elements determine signal quality. A clear, undistorted signal is less tiring on the listener than one that is distorted, faint, or accompanied by natural or artificial interference. All other qualities of similar formats being equal, the station with the best signal will be the listener's choice. Emotional fatigue unconsciously sets in after a period of straining to hear a program through a noisy, uncomfortable signal.

An FM station with 100,000 watts of effective radiated power (ERP) with its antenna assembly mounted on a 1,000-foot tower is a much better facility than a station with the same power but with its antenna mounted on a 500-foot tower. The AM station with a power of 50,000 watts on a clear channel (820 kHz) is a much better technical facility than a station with 5,000 watts of power at 570 kHz. Usually the low-power station is at the mercy of the higher power station. A 5,000-watt facility with a country or beautiful music format may be very vulnerable to a station of the same format with 10,000 or 50,000 watts.

This rule of thumb does not hold in all cases. For example, a 10,000-watt facility at 1600 kHz might easily fall victim to a 1,000-watt station at 710 kHz. In AM, both power and dial position are important. The lower the frequency, the greater the range of the AM signal. A 1,000-watt station at 710 kHz might easily reach a greater population than a 10,000-watt station at 1600 kHz. In FM, tower height and power are the principal considerations. A low-power (Class A) FM station with a 1,000-foot antenna might cover more territory than a full-power (Class C) station with its antenna mounted 200 feet above average terrain. Having the best or one of the best facilities in the market is crucial to winning against competitors.

In the AM vs. FM competition, the victories since the early 1970s have been going to FM, where music competes against music. A beautiful music format on FM will win in ratings against a similar format on AM, simply because FM reproduces music with greater fidelity. This is true also of FM rock vs. AM rock and, lately, even FM country vs. AM country. In fact, in recent years, FM has scored greater gains in audiences than AM in virtually every music format.

The technical qualities of the facility play an important part in the initial decision to enter music programming competition. It would be aesthetically foolish and economically disastrous to pit, say, a daytime AM against a full-power FM in the contemporary rock field. Conversely, if the leading contemporary music station in a market is AM and the new facility is a high-quality FM, the AM will be extremely vulnerable to the new programming assault.

Market

In deciding on a radio format, the programmer's essential first step is to review the radio competition thoroughly. Television, cable, and newspaper competition can be ignored because television and newspapers will stay relatively stable no matter what radio does, and cable companies compete only for audience time, not for advertising dollars.

Format strategy can be examined by working through a hypothetical market—a metropolitan area of 500,000 inhabitants in which seventeen stations are heard, licensed either to the metro area or its suburbs. Further assume that a small group of radio enthusiasts are about to buy one of these stations and to design a program format from scratch. Here is a list of the stations in the market:

Station	Type	Format	Percent Share	Facility[a]
WAAA	AM day	Religious	1.0	1 K @ 1500 kHz
WBBB	AM day	Country	4.2	1 K @ 1600 kHz
WCCC	AM day	Talk	2.6	5 K @ 840 kHz
WDDD	AM day	Ethnic	4.8	1 K @ 900 kHz
WEEE	AM day	Local	0.9	1 K @ 710 kHz
WFFF	FM	Classical	1.1	100,000 @ 700'
WGGG	FM	Schulke	7.6	100,000 @ 600'
WHHH	FM	Bonneville	8.7	100,000 @ 540'
WIII	FM	MOR	0.8	3,000 @ 250'
WJJJ	FM	Ethnic	6.1	100,000 @ 540'
WKKK	AM	Country	9.9	5 KD/1 KN @ 970 kHz
WLLL	FM	Country	12.1	100,000 @ 700'
WMMM	AM	Rock	16.5	5 KD/5 KN @ 1480 kHz
WNNN	AM	News/Info	5.0	10 K @ 1010 kHz
WOOO	AM	Rock	0.6	1 KD/½ KN@1310 kHz
WPPP	FM	AOR	12.1	100,000 @ 540'
WQQQ	FM	MOR/Contemporary	4.9	100,000 @ 1,000'
Other	(Distant signals)		1.1	

[a]K = 1,000 watts; 5 KD/1 KN means that a station uses 5,000 watts in the daytime and reduces to 1,000 watts at night.

All stations are licensed in the metro area except for two suburban stations: WEEE, the daytimer, programs strictly for its local audience.* WIII, the low-power FM station, block programs its schedule, running three hours of country music followed by three hours of rock followed by an hour of gospel and so on. The station about to be sold is WQQQ in the metro competition with a 4.9 audience **share** of the market—not bad, but well behind the leaders.

One of the prospective buyers' first steps toward a purchase decision might be to make simple bar graphs of all stations' **demographic** profiles, to show what percentage of each station's total audience each of the six standard age groups represents. The bars in such

---

*The traditional practice of omitting AM after the call letters is followed except where needed for clarity; FM is added after station call letters except where redundant with immediately available information.

graphs display the age "leanings" of stations' audiences, suggesting the industry name of "skew graphs." Arbitron is the principal source of the data; the 6 A.M.-to-midnight, Monday-to-Sunday page of a ratings book breaks out all individual demographic groups. However, any service that provides demographic separation provides the necessary information. Table 14–1 shows skew graphs for two of the stations in the hypothetical market.

With skew graphs of all the stations in a market laid out before them, program strategists can quickly analyze which age groups are best served by which stations and therefore which stations represent major competition. The examples in Table 14–1 show only age, but sex break-outs would also be useful. For example, an AOR (album-oriented rock) operation might show 30 percent adults 18 to 34 years, but the males in the market represent the usual 60 to 70 percent of the total.

In going over the list of stations in the hypothetical market, the planners identify those with which they do not expect to compete seriously. The prospective facility is FM (a decided plus); it is full power (most desirable); and its antenna is on the highest tower in the market (bingo!). It is otherwise a dog. But, the *facility* is superior to anything in the area.

First, the planners can scratch all AM daytimers as potential competition. That takes care of five stations and cuts the field of competition from sixteen to eleven. Next, they can knock out any good music and classical operations (one in this market, WFFF-FM) as most markets can accommodate only a single classical station. That leaves ten. It would be foolhardy to tackle two beautiful music operations with **syndicated** programming by Schulke and Bonneville (program consultants and group station owners). They are two of the many companies providing taped music and program counseling. WGGG-FM and WHHH-FM are among the most successful beautiful music stations in the country, and two beautiful music stations should be quite sufficient for this market. Scratching these cuts the competitive field to eight. The suburban station (WIII-FM) can be eliminated since it will never be in competition with a high-powered FM; the latter certainly is not interested in duplicating WIII's limited and suburban-oriented format.

Two ethnic stations (WDDD-AM and WJJJ-FM) have a combined share of 10.9 The market shows a black population of only 25,000, or about 5 percent, and no other substantial ethnic population. It would appear that black-oriented radio is well represented by the two stations, which show a combined audience of twice the black population. Scratch one more (the FM ethnic WJJJ as well as WDDD which was already counted out as a daytime AM). The field is down to six, plus the proposed buy.

The three country stations have a total of 26.2 percent of the market, and need to be considered. If country were adopted, WQQQ

Table 14–1. Skew Graphs for a Hypothetical Metro Survey

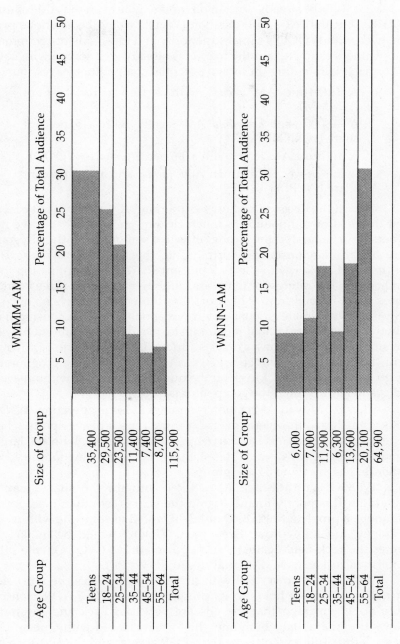

WMMM-AM

Age Group	Size of Group	Percentage of Total Audience
Teens	35,400	
18–24	29,500	
25–34	23,500	
35–44	11,400	
45–54	7,400	
55–64	8,700	
Total	115,900	

WNNN-AM

Age Group	Size of Group	Percentage of Total Audience
Teens	6,000	
18–24	7,000	
25–34	11,900	
35–44	6,300	
45–54	13,600	
55–64	20,100	
Total	64,900	

Source: April/May 1978 Arbitron. Used with permission.

(the proposed buy) could easily defeat the AM daytimer with the country format (WBBB, already written off) and maybe even the AM fulltimer (WKKK). But the FM country station (WLLL) would be a serious problem, even with WQQQ's signal superiority and top-grade programmers. The planners estimate that the market is already well served with country formats. Eliminating these two potential competitors leaves four:

> A full-time AM *rocker* with a 16.5 percent share (WMMM)
>
> A 10,000-watt *news/info AM* facility with a 5 percent share (WNNN)
>
> A full-time AM *rocker* with a 0.6 percent share (WOOO)
>
> A full-power FM with an *AOR format* and a 12.1 percent share (WPPP)

Even if the decision on how to program WQQQ is still not easy, at least the field of competition is much clearer, and the prospective new owners have separated the strong, effective stations from the also-rans. Here are the circumstances surrounding the final four stations: The full-time AM **rocker** with the 16.5 percent share is an old-line top forty that has held top ratings for ten years, although in the last three years its shares have slipped from a high of 20 to the present level. As an AM, WMMM is vulnerable to attack by a well-done FM rocker, using basically the same **formula**, that is, hit music, personalities, limited news, a few singing logos, games, contests, and a lot of community involvement. But this rocker will be a fierce competitor! No new programmer can go into a market and knock off the number one rocker without a long and costly fight, even if the competitor is an AM.

The 10,000-watt AM station is another old-line operation. WNNN holds affiliation with several news networks, has a heavy sports schedule, and generally attracts a 25 to 64 year old audience, with the largest segment being 35 to 64 years. This station is not competing for the young audience, just the 25 to 54 age group.

WOOO, the full-time AM rocker with the 0.6 share, may be written off. It is poorly financed, and the staff is less than mediocre. It will not be a problem to WQQQ unless it is sold to someone with plenty of money and know-how. Even then, WOOO would be unlikely to reenter the rock field against a high-powered FM (WQQQ), the other established rocker (WMMM), and the AOR (WPPP).

WPPP's full-power FM with the AOR format may be a problem but not as long as it holds to its present formula. The AOR plan is a "pure" one, meaning that the DJs are very laid back and the music follows the traditional album line; the format is laced with Queen, Dire Straits, Jethro Tull, and other known AOR artists, and the audience has a much larger proportion of males than other music formats. New artists are introduced weekly, and new product from known artists is almost automatic. This station might change formats if the new WQQQ (1) captures a substantial portion of the big AM rocker's audience and (2) cuts into the AOR station's predominantly male audience. These are the chances any programmer takes: sleeping giants are sometimes awakened when new people come to town beating drums and taking everybody's ratings.

Identifying Target Audiences

It is not enough to study skew graphs and other research data about the people in a market who may listen to radio. It is essential to go into the community to find out specifically what people are doing, thinking, and listening to. It is helpful to observe life-styles by visiting restaurants, shopping centers, gas stations, discotheques, bars, taverns, and other places where people let their hair down.

The 40-year-old lawyer who dresses in dark suits during the week and has lunch at a stuffy club may be found in the evenings wearing jeans and a T-shirt in a favorite disco. He's hip, married, has two children, and loves to go dancing with his wife. A potential listener to a new rock station? Absolutely! Are there more like him? They number in the thousands in most markets of the nation.

Formal research can be used to supplement personal investigation. Most cities have local survey research firms that can be hired to make special studies, and national firms such as Frank N. Magid Associates and McHugh-Hoffman specialize in broadcast station research. A study using lengthy, in-depth interviews either in person or by telephone might get interesting responses: too many commercials, bad commercial production, too much kinky music, too many contests, can't win contests, or **jocks** are idiots. As you can imagine, a station getting answers like these is ready for a major overhaul.

Many broadcasters employ university instructors and students to do summer studies that can be very beneficial. Later on, staff involvement in the community often provides feedback on how the community is reacting to one's programming strategies. Discos performed for students by DJs can provide an additional channel for input.

As an example of the kind of findings that prove useful, here is the experience of a station in Dallas. It identified its typical listener as male, about thirty years old, earning $25,000 a year, driving a Corvette, drinking a foreign beer, going out at least twice a week with a date to a good restaurant, and playing tennis. The station was able to sell this audience description to advertisers and to listeners. **Promotional** material stressed joining the "in" crowd who listened to this particular station.

In the hypothetical market, counting both ethnic stations with formats that are heavily disco, total contemporary listenership is about 45 percent. The AM rocker and the AOR-FM pull an inordinate portion,

28.6 percent. Three country stations combined have a 26.2 share of the market. There is only one news/information format station, but a market of 500,000 will barely take care of one such station, much less two. Also, people who listen to these adult-oriented all-news or news-talk stations are much older and spend their nonnews listening time either with the good music stations or the country stations.

In any area, the 18- to 49-year-old audience is the most desirable to most advertisers. It represents 56.1 percent of the hypothetical market, and teens make up another 15.1 percent. Altogether, 71.2 percent of this market may be available to tune in WQQQ-FM. That leaves a mere 28.8 percent potential for the adult-oriented stations. The target audiences of *most* advertisers are aged 18 to 34, 18 to 49, or 25 to 54 years. Rarely does an advertiser seek the 54 to 64 audience. Advertisers assume older people to be pretty well set in their buying habits; they are regarded as saving money rather than spending it, having bought about everything they are ever going to buy. But the youth market has money, responds to advertising, and can be induced to buy even if it means going into debt. Advertisers should readily buy time on a new rock station, which clinches the decision to buy WQQQ and rock.

IMPLEMENTATION

The program director's first step is to put out the word through personal contacts and the trade press that WQQQ is hiring top forty jocks, a production manager, and two people to handle the news. Since this station is going to rock, news will play a minor role. The program director will act as music director temporarily to initially structure the music, and later one of the jocks can take over those duties along with those involving research. The music director works for the program director, doing research, preparing proposed additions and deletions to the **playlist**. The program director usually makes the final decision; the music director does all the background work up to decision time.

The usual hit music operation requires six to eight **disc jockies**, along with a production director and, perhaps, a music director. In a market of 500,000, the program director may earn as much as $35,000 a year, the morning DJ probably gets $25,000; and the production director gets something in the middle. The afternoon drive DJ may cost $20,000. The other five or six jocks will average $12,000 to $15,000 per year. In the top ten markets, one may have to double or triple these salary figures to get the required talent.

In a medium market (500,000), television and billboard advertising might run $15,000 a month for good exposure. It may cost five times that in a Dallas- or a Chicago-sized market. Not only are unit prices higher in a large market, but there is usually also much more territory to cover. A 100 percent showing in one market may require 35 billboards, for example, while a similar showing in Dallas would require 125 boards.

Consultants are available to advise on every conceivable aspect of operations. Programming consultants help to find the market voids, to spot competitor weaknesses, and frequently even to assemble a staff to work up a specific format. There are legal, technical, personnel, and sales management as well as programming consultants, and all of these may be employed at one time or another. Consultation is expensive. An engineer may charge $300 a day plus expenses. A programmer may charge $2,000 a month on a three- to six-month contract. A complete service like Schulke or Bonneville, depending on market size, could run as high as $5,000 to $10,000 a month. Nevertheless, a neophyte licensee may be literally unable to start up without the use of one or more consultants. A great deal of highly specialized knowledge and experience must be brought to bear immediately once the Federal Communications Commission (FCC) has given the licensee authority to start operations.

Getting records is fairly easy. The program director makes contacts with friends in the record business (promoters, pushers) to get on their call schedules and mailing lists. This ensures that the station will receive all the current material immediately. Someone will have to dig for the "recurrents" and the "golds"—especially the latter. Because of their age, these records are scarce; distributors are often out of stock and pressings are no longer being made. It may take months to build the gold library, and these recordings should be kept under lock and key to forestall avid collectors among staff members.

The program director may decide to "cart" all music, that is, to dub it onto tape cartridges. This enables the station to play its music inventory without damaging the actual discs, whether albums or singles. Carting also introduces a control factor. The announcer who wants to "swing out" a bit simply will not have the opportunity, if all turntables are removed from the control room, if all music is carted, and if only the carts the program director wants played on the air are allowed in the control room. But carting is costly, time consuming, and risky. Some programmers believe that dubbing inevitably lowers quality.

When not busy interviewing potential DJs or talking to prospects on the telephone, the program director works on obtaining music and constructing a **hot clock**. A hot clock prepared by the program director (or consulting service) is a design, looking like a face of a clock, in which the formula for producing the planned station "sound" is visualized. It divides an hour into portions for music (by category), weather, news, **promos**, and commercials. Hot clocks are examples of **dayparting**, that is, estimating who is listening and what their activities are, and then programming directly to them. The morning clock includes news, for example, but the 7 P.M. to midnight clock does not. News is principally for a morning audience on a rock station. Figure 14–1 shows a morning clock: the hour makes room for 10 commercial minutes. There are only 8 in the evening period clock in Figure 14–2. *Gold, power,* and *recurrent* refer to kinds of music; *liners* are show comments by the DJ; and *PSAs* are public service announcements. Music stations generally use four

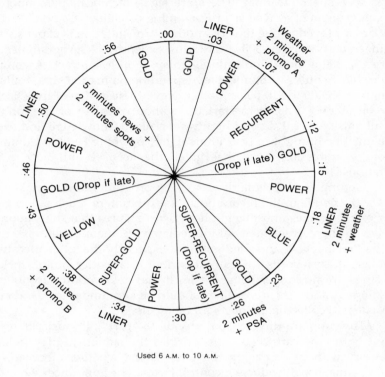

Used 6 A.M. to 10 A.M.

Figure 14–1. Morning Drive Hot Clock

clocks for weekdays and as many as two additional ones for weekends. Morning clocks apply to the morning drive period; midday clocks to the 10 A.M. to 3 P.M. period; afternoon clocks from 3 P.M. to 7 P.M.; and night clocks from 7 P.M. to midnight. Other clocks may be developed for certain weekend dayparts and days on which special events occur.

THE MUSIC

Jim Mahanay, the highly successful program director for WKRG-FM (Mobile, Alabama) and former program director for three years of WQUA (Moline, Illinois), developed a music system that is used

as this chapter's model. This system represents one plan for programming a rock format station. It evolved from Mahanay's association with
Jim Davis, former RKO programmer, and much research went into its
formulation. It is designed to achieve maximum attractiveness to the 18
to 34 (primary) and the 18 to 49 (secondary) demographic targets. There

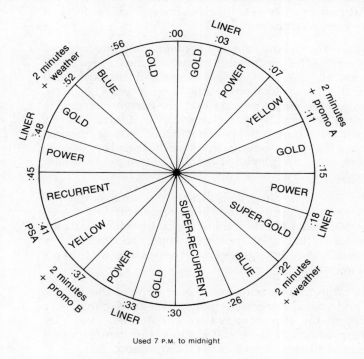

Used 7 P.M. to midnight

Figure 14–2. Nighttime Hot Clock

are seven major music categories in the system: power, yellow, blue,
super-recurrent, recurrent, super-gold, and gold.

    1. *Power*. There are eleven songs in the power category.
Four are played each hour. This means a turnover rate of 2
hours and 45 minutes—the time that elapses before the
cycle of eleven songs begins again. These are the most
important songs in the system and consequently receive
more air play than any other music presented on the station. They attain their status as powers by reaching a
combination of high national chart ranking, high local sales
ranking, high research status, and the unanimous verdict
as winners by the music selection board, usually composed
of the program director and music director. *Billboard, Radio*

& Records, and *Rudman* are three of the major sources for charts (or lists) of national rankings. They show the position of current hits this week, compared to last week. These publications chart the paths of hundreds of pieces of music each week and are consequently referred to as the "charts." Information on local sales comes from telephoning a dozen or more retail stores. In large cities, forty or more stores may be canvassed.

2. *Yellow.* The yellow category contains nine or ten songs that comprise the lower status records on the current chart. They are all up-tempo or fast songs and are positioned within the music clock so as to achieve a tempo balance. These may be either records that are currently rising in popularity to a power status or songs that have recently been withdrawn from the power rotation because research indicates that their popularity is declining. The yellow-category songs are played at the rate of two per hour and are recycled every 3 hours and 15 minutes.

3. *Blue.* The blue category is exactly the same as the yellow category except they are down-tempo or slow songs. In fact, the most important thing about the yellow and blue categories is that they are both tempo categories. They comprise the bottom eighteen to twenty songs on the current playlist.

It is important to note that the content of the power, blue, and yellow categories changes weekly to conform to changes in the current playlists. These three categories comprise what might be called "the core contemporary music marketing strategy" of the radio station.

4. *Super-recurrent.* The super-recurrent category contains fifteen songs that have recently been on the current list. To qualify as a super-recurrent, a song must have attained a number-one ranking in one or more of the trade magazines and absolute acceptance by the prime target demographic audience as measured by the station's own research. One super-recurrent song is played once an hour, creating a rotation pattern of 15 hours.

5. *Recurrent.* The recurrent category contains thirty songs that have recently been in the super-recurrent rotation. These songs are also played at the rate of one per hour. This category is designed to increase the amount of very recent popular music aired on the station. It creates the impression that the station plays more varied music than it actually does because one current (power, yellow, or blue) has to be cut to make room for play of a recurrent. This gives the listeners the impression that the station airs a

large range of music although only one song is added per hour. The recurrent songs are proven winners and contain no risk to the format attractiveness even though the whole list is heard only once in 30 hours.

6. *Super-gold.* The super-gold category contains fifty-three songs that have at one time climbed the ladder to the top and moved downward through the recurrent list. These are the "never-die" songs that will always be recognized by the target audience and immediately identified by them as classics. These fifty-three songs change periodically to make way for newer songs. The age of records in this category may vary from three months to two years, but they are the prime-core winners and are genuine enhancers of a music format.

7. *Gold.* The gold category completes the pattern of the formula. Gold songs are played at the rate of four to five songs per hour, depending on the daypart and the availability of audience with the desired demographics within each daypart. In order for a song to make the gold list it must be a proven winner. One source for many gold libraries is the *Miles Chart Display,*[1] which lists every song by its national chart status over several years. Other sources are available from which to compile the gold library such as *Billboard, Radio & Records, Gavin, Record World, Rudman,* and *Broadcasting,* but the credibility of national ranking in the *Miles Chart* cannot be overlooked. All gold records receive a daypart code as follows:

0—May be played any time in the 24 hours, any day in the week
1—May be played only in A.M. **drivetime**
2—May be played from 9 A.M. to noon
3—May be played from noon to 3 P.M.
4—May be played from 3 P.M. to 6 P.M.
5—May be played from 6 P.M. to midnight
6—May be played from midnight to 2 A.M.
7—May be played on weekends

Each song may have several codes, making it available at different times during the day. The recordings in the gold library are coded "A" or "B," meaning "recent" or "older." This designation ensures that each receives the right demographic exposure whenever played.

Depending on daypart, a station may use three A golds to two B golds. This formula is obtained by making a simple demographic curve of the target audience. For example, there are many more 18 to 24 year olds available during the 7 P.M. to midnight daypart than any other demographic group. Consequently, a station will expose more A gold in that period than B gold, achieving higher identification with the available audience.

Music Research

Most music radio stations employ one or more part-time assistants to the music director who handle call-out research and the assembling of statistics. The music researcher of a rock station determines the best-selling records currently on the playlist by compiling the names of the fifteen top-selling LPs and singles from the local record stores. The station researcher also keeps tabs on records that are not played on the station but are selling due to air play on other area stations and disco exposure. The researcher may be full or part time and usually works for the music director.

Trade publications such as *Billboard* and *Radio & Records* are studied to help in deciding on new music to add to a playlist. Each week the researcher compiles chart positions of the top thirty songs from each magazine and averages them to get composite ratings. The chart movements of newer songs and news regarding air play in other areas are also helpful in choosing the "adds." In markets with a sizable black population, the researcher keeps abreast of the soul charts as well as pop in *Billboard* and *Radio & Records*. The more objective information the researcher gathers, the easier it is for the programmer to evaluate the record companies' advertising and sales pitches. Record promoters will naturally emphasize their products' victories, neglecting to mention that a record died in Los Angeles or Kansas City. The station must depend on its own research findings to rate a piece of music reliably.

Call-out research gets reactions directly from rock radio listeners. There are two versions of the technique, referred to as "active" and "passive." In active call-out research, a list of active listeners is obtained from contest entrant lists. The passive version simply uses random names from the telephone directory. In either case, respondents are asked to listen to extracts from the songs being researched or lists of titles and to rate them on a scale running from one to seven as follows:

---

1 = "Never heard of it"
2 = "Dislike it strongly"
3 = "Dislike it moderately"
4 = "Don't care"
5 = "Tired of it"
6 = "Like it"
7 = "My favorite record"

When a sampling is completed (fifty to one-hundred calls is typical), the votes for each number on the scale are tabulated. The

various totals are then manipulated as follows in order to obtain interpretations in terms of ratios or percentages:

Total Votes for	Divided by Total of	Equals a Ratio That Measures
6+7	sample	Positive acceptance
2+3	sample	Negative rejection
5+6+7	sample	Positive recognition
2+3+5	sample	Developed dislike
4	sample	Burnout
5	sample	Neutral
6+7	2+3	Acceptance
6+7	2+3+5	Tolerance
1	sample	Unfamiliarity
2+3+4+5+6+7	sample	Familiarity

As an example of how the formula works, assume fifty calls are
made to contest winners within a week in which twenty-five records are
discussed. Ten listeners say they like song number four, and fourteen
say it is their favorite record. Twenty-four of fifty have given number four
a six or a seven. For the "positive acceptance" measurement, divide
twenty-four by fifty; the result indicates that 48 percent of the audience
want to hear number four played.

The top thirty or forty pieces on the current station playlist can be
compared to the rankings in the publications *Radio & Records, Billboard,
Gavin, Rudman,* and *Record World.* If song number four is number one in
Radio & Records, it gets thirty points. If it rates number two in *Rudman,* it
gets twenty-nine points; a rating of number three in *Record World* gives it
twenty-eight points, and so on. After charting each song against the five
trade publications, the researcher divides the total by five to get the
average ranking. Their rankings are developed from data supplied by
hundreds of "reporting" stations.[2] If the researcher finds from the
call-out test that number four is burned out locally but was nevertheless
still running in the top three or four nationally, the song would be
retained but assigned a lower rotation position.

NEWS

News has always been a problem on rock 'n' roll stations. Many
broadcasters do not want it, cannot afford it, and feel their listeners are
bored with it but think they must provide news to satisfy the unwritten
requirements of the FCC. They dutifully promise in their license applications to program a certain percentage of news and are stuck with their
commitments.

There are two conflicting views about listeners' attitudes toward
news on music stations. Frank N. Magid Associates, in a study of Los

Angeles radio, found that a large percentage of rock listeners were "turned off" by news.[3] These same listeners also hated commercials, PSAs, and anything else not related to music and fun. On the other hand, an Associated Press study published in 1978 found that *everybody* wanted lots of news on their music stations.[4] The Associated Press, which is in the business of selling news services to radio stations, is not likely to publish a study that indicates young listeners do not want to hear news. Consultants, however, are in the business of finding out what is wrong with radio stations and have a vested interest in finding things wrong that can be fixed. No definitive studies have yet resolved this issue.

Listeners have come to expect to hear news on the hour and the half hour. The radio networks still schedule news at those times. Knowing this, some programmers schedule news at odd hours (20 minutes after and 20 before the hour, for example), hoping to pick up new listeners when competing stations schedule their news more conventionally on the hour and half hour.

Some recent thinking on scheduling news hinges on the habits of some listeners and Arbitron's diary method of surveying listeners. The idea is to hold a listener for at least 5 minutes in any quarter hour by playing some music (even on a talk/news station) so the station will get credit in a diary being kept by a listener. This assumes listeners *are* turned away by news.

Having decided where to put news, the programmer also needs to decide how to handle it, whether to go the low road or the high road. On the low road, jocks **rip and read** news wire copy as it comes out of the machine. Some low-roaders satisfy the need for local news by simply stealing from the local newspaper (the news itself cannot be copyrighted, although specific versions of it can). Programmers who set higher goals for themselves do well to hire at least two persons to staff the news operation. One staffer does the air work in the morning while the other develops local stories, mostly over the telephone. The two news staffers reverse their roles in the afternoon. The morning person leaves **voicers** (stories recorded by someone other than the anchorperson) for use during the afternoon and evening newscasts, and the afternoon person leaves them for use early the next morning. This would be a relatively luxurious news operation for a music station, however. The typical full-time news staff in radio stations throughout the country is only one person.

Nonentertainment Programming

To get (or renew) a license, one must promise (according to the usual legal advice) the FCC that at least 6 percent of the station's total schedule will be nonentertainment programming. Once the promise is made, the station must live up to it or risk not getting its license renewed. There are four areas for concern: news, public affairs, other nonentertainment, and public service announcements. A typical promise might be news, 2.2 percent; public affairs, 1.8 percent; other, 2 percent. A station broadcasting 168 hours per week, or 10,080 minutes, would therefore be expected to air 222 minutes of news, 181 minutes of public affairs, and 202 minutes of "other." The licensee might promise 168 PSAs per week, representing an *average* of one per hour. It is important to realize that PSAs need not be of a specific length. They are counted in units and may be from 5 to 60 seconds in length. Most rock stations use 10- to 20-second versions, reading them live and fitting them into regular commercial and ID breaks. Sunday morning religious programming fills the "other" requirement.

The public affairs requirement is sometimes more difficult. This often takes the form of a Sunday evening talk show in which current events are discussed by one or more "experts," a moderator, and listeners who call in.

Another public affairs stratagem that has gained wide acceptance is for members of the staff, including news personnel, to record an hour or so of conversation about current events. Most of this sort of programming on rock stations is buried either early Sunday morning or late Sunday night when minimum audience damage will be done.

AIR PERSONALITIES AND DAYPARTING

In contemporary radio, there are SCREAMERS!!! And there are very laid back jocks who just talk conversationally when they open the microphone switch. Then, there are those "friendly" jocks who fall somewhere in between the screamers and the laid backs. Once there was also the big voice *boss* who told the listener this was a Big DJ, a know-it-all, but this style faded away in the early 1970s.

By and large, modern jocks are friendly or very, very laid back. They *relate* to the target audience. Morning jocks, for example, probably will talk more than jocks in other dayparts, because their shows are service-oriented. They have lots of time and temperature checks. They may chat with the newscasters before the news, may bring the traffic reporter on and off the air, and, in fact, sort of manage the morning team. Listeners preparing for work or school are keen on time and weather conditions. The larger the market, the more important traffic reports become. Reports of a pileup on one expressway give listeners a chance to switch their commuter routes—and the station a chance to earn a Brownie point.

One of the major strategic resources of the music station programmer is known as **dayparting**. The term comes from the radio audience research field, where audience size is usually reported not by individual programs (as in television) but by segments of time several hours in length. The day breaks down into several fairly clear-cut day-parts, during which the audience is engaged in characteristic activities. The programmer's challenge is to make each program daypart distinct and appropriate to the audience activities but at the same time to keep the overall sound of the station consistent. The most important ingredient in making daypart distinctions is the personality of the jock assigned to each time period.

Morning

On most stations the morning jock is the only performer who is permitted to violate format to any appreciable extent. Normally, morning drivetime personalities are also the highest paid. They have a greater responsibility than others on the team because there is more audience available in the 6 to 10 A.M. period than at any other time of day. As the saying goes, "If you don't make it in morning drive, you don't make it at all."

Midday

The midday jock is friendly, but the incidental services during this daypart are curtailed in favor of more music. Although there is considerable out-of-home listening in the 10 A.M. to 3 P.M. period, Arbitron data show that the majority of the listeners are homemakers. Many midday jocks capitalize on this female audience by being sexy, using **liners** (brief continuity between records) that have special appeal to women, and by talking about what the listener might be doing at home. Some jocks even get off-color at times. In sum, the midday jock is more laid back than the morning jock and tries especially hard to be warm and friendly.

Afternoon

The afternoon jock (3 P.M. to 7 P.M.) is more up-tempo, as is the music in this period if the station is dayparting. Teens are out of school at this time of day and adults are driving home from work, necessitating a delicate balance between teen-oriented music and music that suits the moods and attitudes of the going-home audience. Again, traffic and weather are important in this period but not as much as in the morning. The afternoon jock alludes frequently to evening activities—about how good it must be to finish work and to look forward to playing for a few hours, to taking your honey out, to being with your guy tonight, or to doing whatever else people are planning. This jock relates!

Evening

Many contemporary stations program their 7 P.M. to midnight slot much differently from the other dayparts. The music may become heavily disco, heavily black, or laced with teen-oriented pieces. Teens are more available to listen at night, than the 18 to 49 listeners. Evening jocks may be screamers with a special appeal to teens. They may talk with teens on the phone and air some of the conversations. They may open the request lines and play specific records for specific people. In major markets, and even in many middle-sized ones, this practice creates problems for the phone company. In Mobile, WKRG-FM asked the phone company to make a record of calls that did not get through to its four request lines. In one week, there were 65,000 such unsuccessful calls. Imagine what the number might be in Los Angeles or New York! In many major markets in the last decade the telephone company has been forced to appeal to station management to stop asking listeners to call the station.

At some top forty operations, the nighttime slot is regarded as a time for AOR music, but this stratagem has not been notably successful in highly competitive markets. The principal reason is that such a drastic departure from the format destroys consistency. A station should maintain *basically* the same sound in the 7 P.M. to midnight slot as it does in the other dayparts.

All-night

In the all-night period, from midnight to 6 A.M., the attitude of the jock is usually one of camaraderie. "We're all up late tonight, aren't we? We have to work nights and sleep days." This jock must commune with the audience: the taxi drivers, revelers, police officers, all-night restaurant and grocery store workers, insomniacs, parents up giving babies two o'clock feedings, shift workers at factories, bakers, and the many others who are active between the hours of midnight and 6 A.M. The commercial load is almost nil during this period, so the jock can provide listeners with a lot of uninterrupted music. Many stations use the period to beef up their PSA quotient, although the FCC has begun to question broadcasters' tendency to bury PSAs in low-listener hours.

Under a strong program director who is a good leader, a kind of "sameness" can be developed among all the jocks in a specified format. This does not mean the drabness or dullness normally associated with sameness. It means predictability. Listeners who tune the station at odd hours *expect* to hear the same basic station they heard while driving to work in the morning or home in the afternoon.

ADVERTISING AND PROMOTION

The modern radio station pays almost as much attention to advertising and **promotion** as to programming. They are essential to keep a station from simply disappearing into the crowd. Nowadays stations are even turning to television in addition to their traditional use of newspapers, billboards, bumper stickers, car cards, and other display media. Promotional stunts are the special province of radio and heavily involve cooperation of programming personnel. A national group owner who went into the Dallas market in 1977 was rumored to have allotted a $600,000 budget solely for promotion. Most top forty operations, seeking a general (mass) audience with emphasis on the 18- to 49-year-old group, might give away as much as $200,000 a year in cash!

The traditional promotional stunt is the contest, but the current trend is to drop this word in favor of the word *game*. People may not think they can win contests, but they like to play games. The contest approach tended to emphasize a super-prize of $25,000 or more. It can be offered only once or twice a year (during the Arbitron survey **sweeps**). And because the station cannot afford to risk losing it all on the first day of the game, the winning of a super-prize has to be made difficult.

Current games include "cash-call," in which the jock on duty makes one call-out per hour and offers the jackpot to any person who can name the exact amount of the jackpot:

Jock: Is this Mary Jones at 1212 Elm Street?

Listener: Yes, I'm Mary Jones.

Jock: Well, this is Jocko at Station WPPP, and if you can tell me the exact amount in our WPPP jackpot, you'll win!

Listener: Mmmmmm. Last I heard it was $485.

Jock: You win! You're right. Mary Jones, you've just won yourself 485 American greenbacks!!! You've ripped us off, you lucky lady you!!!

Listener: Oh, wow! I can't believe it.

The more exaggeratedly a listener responds to his or her victory, the better the programmer likes it. Later the station will air promos in which the listener's response is repeated and repeated. Hyperbole is the element sought.

Caution is needed regarding the recording and airing of telephone conversations. The law requires that the person being called be informed immediately, "This telephone conversation is being recorded, and I'm Jocko from WPPP." Then, the dialogue can begin. It is a troublesome law that ruins many such calls because the listener is immediately alerted and usually fails to respond spontaneously. Management should seek legal counsel on this question and should write specific instructions to programming personnel on how such games are to be handled.

Cash-call is but one of many games. The "people's choice" gambit provides a variety of prizes and allows the contestants to identify ahead of time the prizes they want in case of victory. Color television sets were determined by Magid's Los Angeles study to be very desirable prizes. A thousand dollars in cash was also popular, along with free trips to Hawaii. People are more likely to think they can win a small prize than to believe they can win a $25,000 treasure hunt or open a safe containing $50,000. With a super-prize, one person is made happy but thousands are disappointed. It is better to break up the $25,000 prize into $25 prizes and scatter them through the year.

Community involvement projects are as important as contests. The station must be highly visible at local events. Some examples that benefit both the station and the community are:

> The station's van (complete with disc jockey, albums, bumper stickers, and T-shirts) shows up at the entrance to the hall that features a hot rock group tonight.

> Two or three jocks take the van and disco equipment to the beach (or any public park) on July Fourth to provide music and "freebies" to listeners and friends.

> Jocks provide free music for high school and junior high school dances.

COMMERCIAL LIMITATIONS

More arguments stem from the question of **commercial load** than from any other aspect of programming a rock format. In earlier times, FM stations had few commercials because they had so few listeners. Researchers began hearing listeners say, "I like so and so because they don't play commercials" or "because they play so much more music than other stations." Lights flashed and bells rang throughout the industry. Listeners hate commercials! Schulke and Bonneville, two of the major radio programming syndicators, began to employ the strategy of "music sweeps" and "stop sets." A **music sweep** is an uninterrupted period of music; a **stop set** is an interruption of the music to air commercials or other nonmusic material, such as news headlines.

Herein lies conflict. Sales personnel must have commercial availabilities (unsold spot time) if the station is to make money. Programmers rightfully argue that, if the station is to score big in the numbers, it must limit its commercial load. The answer is compromise. Salespeople agree to raise rates, and programmers agree to provide 10 to 12 commercial minutes per hour instead of the 8 to 10 of other formats or the full 18 that the sales interests wanted. The FCC has no specific rule on the commercial load but expects broadcasters generally to adhere to the National

Association of Broadcasters (NAB) standard of 18 minutes per hour maximum, except during political campaigns and other local seasonal events when exceptions may be made.

Not only do many successful rock operations run with a reduced commercial load, but also they often program (and promote) commercial-free periods. Further, the quality of commercial production is critical. The design of commercials must complement the format, rather than clash with it. A commercial for a rock show coming to town shows how relatedness can be achieved: the commercial may open with a piece of the rock group's music, followed by a popular jock touting the show, and end with more of the concert group's music. Many rock stations refuse to advertise funeral homes, intimate patent medicines such as hemorrhoidal creams, and other products and services they believe will offend their listeners.

It is not uncommon for new formats to kick off with no commercial load whatever. KFJZ-FM (Fort Worth, Texas, known as Z-97) opened its campaign to win the mass audience with *three months* of commercial-free programming. It offered a $25,000 cash prize to listeners who could guess the time the first commercial would be played. The result was gratifying, to say the least. The station rose from obscurity to a 5 percent share of the big Dallas–Ft. Worth metro area in those three months.

Sayable Call Letters

Gordon McLendon, early innovator of the top forty format, was one of the first broadcasters to recognize the value of sayable call letters. His first big station was KLIF, Dallas, originally named for Oak Cliff, a western section of the city. The station call was pronounced "cliff." Then there is KABL ("cable") in San Francisco, KOST ("coast") in Los Angeles, and WWSH ("wish") in Philadelphia. In recent years, particularly with FM stations, a new twist that combines call letters and dial position has been invoked. KFJZ in Ft. Worth calls itself Z-97; WKRG-FM in Mobile is G-100; the RKO station in New York calls itself WXLO-99X. These are memorable and distinctive nom de guerres and are gaining in usage daily. When the Belo Corporation in Dallas developed a new format for WFAA-FM, the historic letters were changed to KZEW, and the station is now known as "the zoo." (Gagsters used to try to pronounce WFAA, and it came out "woof-uh.")

Jingles

The day of the old minute or half-minute singing-jingle ID is, sadly, gone. Nowadays, having a chorus of singers praise the station for a minute or half-minute is out of the question. That would take time away from music, for which people tuned the station in the first place. Now most stations either do not bother with jingles at all or they keep them very short and to the point.

FCC AND OTHER CONSTRAINTS

There are myriad rules, regulations, and guidelines of which radio broadcasters should be aware. To keep up, responsible licensees employ a Washington law firm, read trade journals, subscribe to membership in the National Association of Broadcasters (NAB) and the National Association of Radio Broadcasters (NARB). Programmers, too, have to be aware of legal constraints that may impose limits on their ingenuity.

Contests/Games

The principal point to remember about on-air contests and games is to keep them open and honest, fully disclosing to listeners the rules of the game. Conniving to make a contest run longer or to produce a certain type of winner means trouble. Perry's *Broadcasting and the Law* is useful for flagging potential difficulties.

Program Logs

Any announcement associated with a commercial venture must be logged commercial matter (CM). Frequently the program director receives albums from a distributor to give away to listeners ("Be the sixth caller and win the Bee Gees' new album!"). Every announcement of a give-away should be logged CM because the station, through its acceptance of the free albums, is profiting from the announcement. The announcement was made in exchange for the free albums. The same rule applies to free tickets to a fight or a football game. However, if the station purchases the albums or tickets, they may be given away without being logged as commercial matter.

Plugola, Payola

Announcers who "plug" their favorite bar, restaurant, or theater are asking for trouble for themselves and the licensees. Similarly, a jock who accepts a color television set from a record distributor in exchange for air play of a record is guilty of **payola**. Such practices eventually surface, leaving the people concerned subject to prosecution. The penalties may include loss of the station's license, a $10,000 fine, and jail. Most responsible licensees require air personnel to sign, usually once every six months, statements that they have not been engaged in any form of payola or **plugola**.

Sounds That Mislead

Commercials that open with sirens or other attention-getting gimmicks (such as "Bulletin!") unjustifiably cause listeners to believe they are about to receive vital information. Listener attention can be gained in other more responsible ways that do not offend FCC rules or deceive listeners. It is especially important to monitor locally produced commercials for misleading production techniques.

RADIO'S FUTURE

Music is the main course in radio, and FM does it better; FM will win over an AM facility whenever there is a showdown. A case in point is the sad story of the AM station in Dallas, KLIF, once the unquestioned national leader in rock radio. For twenty years KLIF held number-one position in the market and was respected nationally as *the* station to imitate. Since the mid 1970s, however, Dallas has been an FM market. KVIL-FM is the leading station and shows no signs of weakening. KLIF no longer even shows among the top ten stations. Of the top ten in a market with more than twelve stations, eight are FM. KRLD (AM) and WBAP (AM) number in the top three, but these are 50,000-watt stations on clear channels programming, respectively, news/sports and country music/baseball. This picture is being repeated in market after market across the country.

What lies ahead for AM radio? Not pop music, that seems certain. Country music? Maybe. MOR music? Perhaps. But in no case can an AM stand up to a well-programmed FM station. One strong and recurrent view is that AM must program information to older audiences, even though information is expensive and complicated to program. So news and talk become viable alternatives for AM radio.

For daytimers, religion has become a mainstay, along with limited-audience ethnic formats. However, the difficulties were illustrated by KKDA (Dallas), once a country music station. New owners launched a black-oriented format and quickly gained position in the market. When they then acquired an FM facility, virtually all of the AM listeners switched over to the FM station. The AM daytimer that once fared well was reduced to an also-ran. Frequently an FM will show 7 and 8 shares in markets with more than twelve stations, while an AM daytimer plods along with 1s and 2s.

Disco music is the latest and hottest thing in the music spectrum. WKTU-FM in New York zoomed to first place in one book, but broadcasters have been hesitant to predict that disco would be the sound of the future. Several years ago, someone conceived the idea of a solid gold format. One station in Detroit tried it, made good gains in the first book, then fell back into obscurity. Another station tried commercial-free radio for three months, soared in the ratings, then fell back into eighth and ninth place. Such formats are like the hula-hoop: a craze today, forgotten tomorrow. What works is consistency—in service, in music, in technical quality, in overall personality. The fast-buck artist does not stand a chance in the marathon race for big audience and big dollars.

This chapter has been able to touch on only the more obvious strategies involved in the fascinating art of programming a modern music station. To the uninitiated, all radio music formats may seem much the same. In actuality, each is replete with subtle and not-so-subtle variations. To program a formula successfully in today's competitive market requires never-ending ingenuity, insight, and professional growth. The name of the game is change, but it must be accomplished by consistency in the on-air sound. Radio programming is in a constant state of evolution, and for those who enjoy innovation, radio programming offers a rewarding challenge.

NOTES

[1]Daniel J. Miles, Betty T. Miles, and Martin J. Miles, *The Miles Chart Display of Popular Music: Volume II, 1971–1975* (New York: Arno Press, 1977).

[2]Peter Hesbacher, Robert Downing, and David G. Berger, "Record Roulette: What Makes It Spin?" *Journal of Communication* 25 (Summer 1975): 74–85.

[3]KHJ-AM audience study by Frank L. Magid Associates, 1976, reported by Chuck Martin, program director, 1979.

[4]"Radio News Listening Attitudes," conducted by Frank L. Magid Associates for Associated Press in 1977, abstract, 11b.

ADDITIONAL PERIODICAL READINGS

Abrams, Earl B. "Radio Robots Come to Life as Automated Formats Score Ratings Gains." *Broadcasting* (September 23, 1974): 33–41.

Special report on automated radio music formats.

"FM: The Great Leaps Forward." *Broadcasting* (January 22, 1979): 32–49.

Special report on FM's gains in audience, programming, and sales.

Hesbacher, Peter; Clasby, Nancy; Anderson, Bruce; and **Berger, David G.** "Radio Format Strategies." *Journal of Communication* 26 (Winter 1976): 110–19.

A case study that tests the theory of relationships between music programming and audience size and composition.

Jaffe, Alfred J. "Cox Study Sees Big FM Growth at AM's Expense." *Television/Radio Age* (September 13, 1976): 23 ff.

Major report on FM by a broadcast group owner forecasting AM deficits in the 1980s and increasing FM profits; examines relative profits of different program formats.

Lully, James T.; Johnson, Lawrence M.; and Sweeny, Carol. "Audiences for Contemporary Radio Formats." *Journal of Broadcasting* 22 (Fall 1978): 439–54.

Demographic profiles of radio audience listener types, showing the comparative uniqueness of audiences for several formats.

"Many Worlds of Radio." *Broadcasting* (September 27, 1976; July 25, 1977; July 24, 1978).

Annual reviews of local radio programming trends, sales, and technology.

Nielsen, Richard P., and Thibodeau, Thomas. "Applying Market Research Methods for Formatting Decisions for Radio." *Feedback* (Spring 1979): 19–24.

Aid to format decision making supplied by a format-market matrix comparing market shares across markets and formats.

"Radio Programming & Production for Profit." *Broadcast Management/Engineering,* monthly series, January 1977 to date.

Discussions of program formats, production, and promotion, along with reports on syndicated programs and features.

"Radio Station Managers Don't Trust Ratings, Survey Shows." *Television/Radio Age* (October 16, 1976): 30–32.

Results of survey questions on ratings asked of radio station managers; study conducted by Marshall University in cooperation with Television/Radio Age.

Sobel, Robert. "Radio Music Audience Fractionalization Continues to Rise: Disco Up, Top-40 Down." *Television/ Radio Age* (August 28, 1978): A3–A7.

Analysis of trends in popular music on radio.

15 *All-News Programming*

Don J. Brewer

This chapter deals with a highly specialized form of radio — the all-news station. At present, this format occurs only in major markets and is more practical for network-affiliated or group-owned stations than for independents. Don J. Brewer writes of the day-to-day strategies of all-news radio after eleven years with KYW News Radio, the nationally known Group W innovator in the AM radio field. Mr. Brewer is regional affairs director for KYW as well as food and wine editor for all seven Group W radio stations. He was a station manager for a Department of Defense radio station in Germany after World War II, civilian director of the American Forces Network, Europe, and program director of Radio Free Europe before coming to KYW as an executive producer. The wealth of concrete detail in this chapter comes from the author's unusual background and provides an inside perspective on radio journalism.

PREREQUISITES

All-news places strains on the infrastructure of current broadcasting establishments — whether **network**, **group**, or **independent** — because the cost commitment is high; this flies in the face of trends toward **automation** in other simpler **formats**. Consequently, all-news radio is limited to major markets. Even with large audiences and expanded sales potential, it is likely to be narrowly profitable. The same investment in another format could bring a much greater return. For the foreseeable future, all-news is a "prestige" format, practiced best by major network **affiliates** and group owners willing to absorb initial high costs and low **ratings**.

The heartening thing is that, once entrenched, all-news commands a fanatically loyal audience. If creatively programmed, all-news can capture a broad range of listeners attractive to advertisers. The basic caveat for any all-news programmer rests in one word: credibility. This must be maintained in every program element from headline to commercial, because credibility is one quality that ensures success of the enterprise. It is the only thing an all-news **station** has to sell.

In the mid-1960s, two major broadcast establishments laid the foundation for operating all-news radio stations as we know them today. The first was Group W, Westinghouse Broadcasting Company. It converted three AM stations: WINS (New York) and KYW (Philadelphia) in 1965; and KFWB (Los Angeles) was added in 1968. The Columbia Broadcasting System followed suit with WCBS-AM (New York), KCBS-AM (San Francisco), and KNX-AM (Los Angeles); later, WBBM-AM (Chicago) and WEEI-AM (Boston) were converted, and in 1975, WCAU-AM (Philadelphia).*

In 1974 NBC began an abortive experiment of providing an all-news network service called News and Information Service. Its demise in 1976 worked hardship on many medium- and small-market affiliates, most of whom subsequently dropped the all-news format or modified it to talk/news. The emergence of AP and UPI audio news services, plus major network news and information divisions such as the ABC Information Network, gave heart to the survivors. But what was a tough, tentative format for many in major markets became an impossibly costly burden for those on the economic fringe going it alone.

The product manager of an all-news station lives with a very forthright credo: "Communicate credibility by commitment." The unspoken C in this is cost. The resources needed to operate an all-news station are considerable; attracting an audience of sufficient size and loyalty is a formidable task; maintaining basic journalistic standards, coupled with programming innovativeness is constantly challenging. Top management awareness of these factors is crucial to format survival. No format demands more involvement from its managers.

FORMAT DESIGN

In all-news stations, the initial task of the programmer, in company with other department heads, is to create the **wheel** (see Figure 15–1). This is simply a pie chart of an hour, divided into segments denoting break points for commercial/public service announcement insertions. These are normally clustered in such fashion as to minimize **clutter**. The general, sales, and program managers start with agreement on just how confining or flexible the wheel is going to be.

Typically, within preset guidelines, each hour contains approximately 16 minutes of spot announcement material spaced out in 18 interruptions. This framework, or programming infrastructure, forms the skeleton on which hang the sections of **hard news**, **features**, sports, commentaries, editorials, et al. It also affects decisions about the **cycle**—the span of news flow between repeat points. The cycle is commonly structured as a 20-, 30-, 45-, or 60-minute sequence. Cycle length

---

*WCAU's format was modified to news and information in December 1978.

affects other basic factors such as headline placement, major story development, and sports and feature scheduling. There are advantages and disadvantages to all cycle lengths, depending on local market conditions and conditioning, staff capability, editorial supervision, and content elements.

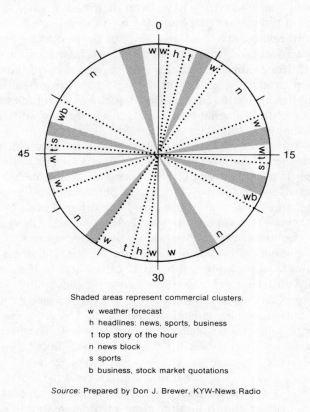

Shaded areas represent commercial clusters.

  w weather forecast
  h headlines: news, sports, business
  t top story of the hour
  n news block
  s sports
  b business, stock market quotations

Source: Prepared by Don J. Brewer, KYW-News Radio

Figure 15–1. Independent All-News
Station Wheel

Headlines are the handle to the cycle. Normally programmed at the top of the hour and at the half hour, their presentation style and substance need to be determined very carefully. If they **tease** or bear only a slight relation to the stories that follow, credibility suffers. The program manager who fails to define headline policy very carefully and who fails to oversee its application by the staff has a stuck zipper on the format.

For example, a typical tease headline might be written, "And, in Salem, Oregon, today, a wife who cried rape got an answer." This tabloid approach is damaging sensationalism. The ethical headline for an all-news format is more closely approximated as, "A Jury in Salem, Oregon, has ruled in favor of a husband, charged by his wife with rape while they were living together." The obvious is at question. If listeners are teased by the first kind of headline and distracted from hearing the follow-up story in detail, they have been deprived of valid information and will resent the station that half-informed them.

Closely related are the fine points of presentation. **Sound beds** (music backgrounds), gimmicky writing, or flash delivery tend to weaken both the credibility and the rhythm of the cycle. For example, one common practice is to repeat a single top story headline at the quarter- and three-quarter-hour points, usually as a prelude to weather, sports, or some other format basic. As a subtle form of audience attention reinforcement, it has wide acceptability.

Once the spot and headline placement parameters of the wheel are set, basic format components such as time, weather, traffic information, and sports can be keyed in. Sports is generally granted the quarter- and three-quarter-hour slots, with length determined by general interest, volume, time of day, and pressure from other news. Weather and time announcements gain in importance during certain **dayparts**, especially morning **drivetime**. Determining their frequencies is a pivotal decision. The same can be said of traffic information. If there is a time lag between on-site observation and actual broadcast, traffic information can seriously undermine the all-news station's believability.

For simplicity's sake, assume a format design based on a full-hour cycle. With announcement cluster, headlines, and basic format elements in place, eight fairly stable sections of news are left. The first and fifth sections, of necessity, contain the "meat" of headline extension. The second and sixth segments normally deal with news stories of less immediate importance. The remaining sections tend to incorporate some **soft news** and a mix of carefully selected features and news of local value. The fourth or eighth section often includes a station's editorial, meticulously identified as management opinion.

The format formula has variable mechanics; its strategy, however, is closely constrained. Many outside forces dictate the degree of the manager's flexibility within the format around the wheel. If it is a network affiliate, the program manager must work around prior commitments to network segments; consequently, local discretion diminishes. If the all-news station is an independent (that is, not network affiliated), choice is much wider. Other sources of program material often dictate placement. For example, sponsored segments may be sold as fixed positions in the wheel.* **Live-feed** items also interrupt the

---

*Some all-news stations sell 5- or 6-minute blocks of news time to a single advertiser, allowing identification of that sponsor with a certain feature or news segment.

rhythm of the cycle. Adjustment of program strategy within the fixed dimensions of the product base is a continuing process. It is the arena of decision in which the program manager will spend the rest of the available time and that will strongly influence reaction to new constraints such as cost considerations and staffing patterns.

Next to credibility, predictability demands primary consideration. The program manager may wrestle a long time with this one, because program elements such as time, weather, and sports are usually fixed within the cycle for the audience's ready access. But too many predictable items reinforce the canard that all-news is little more than endless repetition.

Program managers have to keep in mind that they and their staffs are "handling" rather than "manufacturing" the product. The placement and rotation of its basic elements become important, in a sense, inversely to momentum. In time periods in which local, national, or world news is a **critical information pile**, the cycle almost moves itself. In such a situation, the editor usually has multiple opportunities to choose among wire services, external story angles, and a variety of reaction sources. In effect, the story "runs itself." It is in the "slow" news spaces that product management becomes crucial, both in terms of conceptual planning and in very real operational impact on the audience's perception of it. This management takes the form of carefully watched story placement, creative rewriting of leads, and, in sum, the life span of the story.

PROGRAMMING ALL-NEWS CREATIVELY

The all-news programmer will find an unexpectedly wide range of opportunity for creative mix in the format. The major elements are

News	70.0%
Editorials	0.5%
Public Affairs	7.5%

(Commercials, public service announcements, and promotional announcements make up the average balance of time to add up to 100 percent. See Figure 15–1.)

News

Within this general category is included hard news copy; headlines and recaps; question-and-answer material from outside reporters by mobile radio, telephone, or in-studio interviews; news conferences; roundtable discussions; special **remotes**; and scheduled sports programming of scores and announcements from sports events.

Editorials

Most stations use an editorial director as writer, and the general manager often airs the material. The most common schedule for editorials, running a minute or slightly longer, is a 26 Plan (26 plays per week in all dayparts).* Depending on the number of editorials produced in a given week (usually three or four), they are salted throughout the run of schedule, Monday through Saturday, repeating no more than once in each daypart. Most stations stick to local issues.

Editorials are best scheduled in a section of the wheel farthest from the top stories, assuming that they are mainly local and that the editorials deal with local issues; this generally means editorials appear toward the end of a 60-minute cycle. Since editorials and commentaries can be easily confused in some listeners' minds, there should be at least 15 to 20 minutes between them, but one of each can be fit into a single 60-minute cycle. In any case, features should never be clustered, causing the listener to lose identification with the station as a hard news voice.

Public Affairs

This is the salt and pepper in the format. In most cases, the reports or programs are held to a length of between 1½ and 2 minutes. All-news stations that are totally independent have to create their own local commentators and feature editors or purchase **syndicated** material from production houses or network sources without market presence. Group all-news stations usually have their own mix of these; network affiliates, of course, share the popularity of established personalities. The 7 to 8 percent of public affairs segments in the mix usually fall into about six categories:

1. *Cultural segments* focus on area theater and movie reviews, food and wine shows, or reports on local galleries and exhibitions by someone from a major museum or art group.

2. *Features on science and medicine* are well received, particularly when zeroed in on personal health matters. This subject is handled either by a recognized local authority who is prominent in the medical community or by a national authority, who usually gives a lay summary of new material from leading publications for the professions.

3. *Business commentary* is another category frequently aired, going beyond stock market reports (which are basic

---

*The number 26 is an arbitrary industry norm that hangs over from traditional 13-26-52 week cycles of programming; editorials could be as readily run in 18 or 30 unit schedules, but 26 is most common.

news). They are provided either by a local brokerage house, a regional stock exchange, or a syndicator such as Dow Jones, AP, or UPI.

4. *Religious features* normally dwell on area judicatory meetings, plus church news of a social nature. But occasionally an all-news station will add a national commentator, usually syndicated, such as Norman Vincent Peale with his series of short homilies.

5. *Education features* are an important building block in the format, particularly since so much hard news erupts from the school systems nowadays. This is a delicate programming area. The programmer obviously can get burned by a controversial choice of commentator. Still, the material has to go beyond a recital of PTA meetings and social notes to be meaningful. Some risk-taking is necessary.

6. *Commentary* is authoritative personal opinion, as distinguished from station editorials, which reflect management policy and opinion. Commentaries and commentators are of themselves delicate tests of balance. Many all-news stations shy away from local commentary because it is too easily confused with the station's editorial policies. But, once a given format has matured, there is no real reason to steer away from local commentaries, as long as they are carefully scheduled far from editorial placement and have a distinctive character of their own.

Group and network organizations, plus a few syndicators, have stables of commentators. The trap here is that there are too few Sevareids and MacLeishes to go around, and not enough real shades of opinion that can be sustained. The station shirks its duty if it merely presents two or three of today's faddishly safe liberal commentators. Still, it is a horrendous chore to find a conservative who does not eventually get mired in ludicrous cant. There are dozens of "star" prosocial dilettantes, but the supply of disciplined thinkers in the mold of conservative commentators Elmer Davis and Will Rogers is short, to say the least.

Within the basic format design, programming priorities should be explicitly recognized. First, programmers must disabuse themselves of the idea that earthshaking news developments on a global or national scale are uppermost in the audience's notion of what is news. Since the morning drivetime is the peak period of audience interest and, therefore, the most viable period commercially, it is then that personal services should be most frequent and varied. Scheduling rules should go like this: time announcements at least every 2 minutes; weather information (both of the moment and forecast), no more than 10 minutes apart; traffic information (as valid and close to the flow as humanly possible), every 20 minutes, although the ideal will vary from market to market; plus interspersed allied information such as school closings, major area sports events, and so on. In other words, the top priority in any all-news format is personal service programming. The frequency of repetition slows down during the day and is stepped up during evening drivetime (4 P.M. to 7 P.M.).

SOURCES OF PROGRAMMING

The all-news program manager has a multitude of programming resources available. If the station is a network outlet, most of the basic feature input is supplied, often by prestigious, well-known people who are frequently television crossover names that lend a touch of glamour and extra authority. In most cases, these network features are line-fed at fixed times, and local program managers have little room for imaginative scheduling. In the network wheel in Figure 15–2 the Ns indicate live network feeds, which usually restrict the local program manager's options. The letter f refers to features that may originate at the network or locally. If the features can be tape-delayed, then they have space to develop their own matrices. In either case, programmers usually have a mixed bag of advantages and disadvantages in feature handling. The main support from a network comes in the form of network personalities, often from the television side, reinforcing "name" prestige through features, promos, and special series production.

The program manager connected with a group or chain of stations will probably have major story cross-feeds from sister stations and possibly a Washington or New York bureau on which to draw. A bureau provides foreign stories, analysis of national political and economic news, plus special events such as press conferences, United Nations developments, and personality interviews. Added to these highly professional programming sources is the capability of developing local resources. The degree of station independence varies considerably among group-owned stations, but scheduling is normally left to the local manager.

The important question, for any kind of station, is how much soft (as against hard, fast-breaking news) material is available? When? How often? What kind? Most soft material, based on an audience's natural interest in medical information, the entertainment industry, or hobby material, finds a catholic reception. Audiences vary, of course, in what they need and will accept.

Thankfully, radio in general seems to have recovered from the knee-jerk reaction to such fads as the consumer reporter. This phase degenerated quickly to the level of "If there are twelve eggs in the supermarket carton, you have a dozen." Hard news itself is so full of consumerism in all its manifestations that sensitivity to the subject by general-assignment reporters more than fulfills the need. The lesson of the consumer reporter fad is that when a special feature area tends to blur into the normal flow of news, the program manager should take a hard look at its value as a separate program item.

Scheduling features is a fine art in the structure of the format.

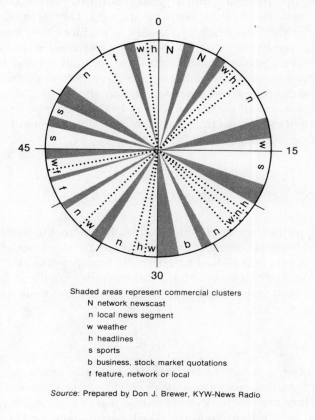

Shaded areas represent commercial clusters
N network newscast
n local news segment
w weather
h headlines
s sports
b business, stock market quotations
f feature, network or local

Source: Prepared by Don J. Brewer, KYW-News Radio

Figure 15–2. Network Affiliate
All-News Wheel

There is a temptation toward three pitfalls: scheduling repeats too frequently, scheduling material that requires more listener retention than they find convenient, or including irrelevant nonlocal material. For example, if a feature segment is aired on a Wednesday at 10:40 A.M., then aired on Thursday and Friday at the same time or within an hour either way, chances are the audience will be largely the same. Scheduling the repeat of a morning-drive feature in evening drivetime merely causes resentment in many drivers that catch both.

Another problem is that many feature contributors come from the print media and are not accustomed to writing material to be read aloud. A radio listener lacks a print reader's concentration span, and there is no rereading on radio. Each all-news segment must be as brief as possible; the giving of involved directions, recipes, and the like is an irritant.

A convenient trap for the programmer is **boilerplate** programming—the purchase of **canned** generic features. These are generally packaged and syndicated features such as *One Moment Please*, a boilerplate in the form of short morality talks. Since they have no local association, they usually are bland to a great degree and dilute the station's move-to-action motivation; they normally should be avoided by large-market all-news stations that have better alternatives. The program manager at a well-financed station should be able to generate local feature segments on the subjects of health, personal finances, local cultural activities, leisure time activities, and entertainment—prepared and announced by area talent.

CONTENT EXPANSION/CONTRACTION

The proper manipulation of basic format components such as weather and sports is most important. These are main personal service content elements that should be extremely flexible within the wheel. At times, of course, both become hard, major stories in and of themselves, such as during a major blizzard or when a local team wins a championship or fires its coach.

Weather

Weather is a key to an all-news station's prime programming periods. If a professional meteorology service is used, the station gains a special kind of credibility. Even in-house use of National Weather Service wires, area airport reports, Coast Guard data, or standard wire service reports should be calibrated to fit audience needs. Drivetime reports are usually short, immediate-area activity, with an occasional forecast addition to tell morning commuters what to expect going home and for the night to come. A significant number of boaters, private pilots, or farmers in the audience indicates that special reports at intervals are useful. And the long-distance business commuter should get at least a spot-check two or three times a day on weather in major cities served by available airlines. These reports can run from 30 seconds to 2 minutes and can be tied to a hard news story if conditions warrant.

Sports

Sports reporting is anchored to scores and area team activity but normally is expanded on weekends to cover many more games or contests at distant points—in the farthest reaches of Maine and California, there is probably a Notre Dame alumni association. Although weekday sports segments are usually held to about 2 minutes at the quarter- and three-quarter-hour marks, weekend sportscasts are easily expandable to 10 or 12 minutes.

In both weather and sports reporting, accuracy and timing are critical. A careful study of the market for various kinds of weather and sports information will dictate the validity of expanding or contracting the segments. As in all other news areas, being right is more important than being first. The program manager who neglects a sizable special-interest group will find the competition alert to fill the hole.

STAFFING THE ALL-NEWS FORMAT

When the nation's first major all-news stations initially adopted the format, management had a vague feeling that a supply of appropriate newspersons was bound to be available. As it turned out, nothing could have been further from reality. The first program managers were faced with a two-headed dilemma. News readers, or announcers, who could deliver copy adequately were available. There were also plenty of graphic journalists and wire service people willing to jump into the new medium. However, announcers, with rare exception, lacked the ability to write news, handle reportage, perform basic editing chores, and follow up on a running story. On the other hand, reporters and wire service types could not in most cases communicate effectively in sound. The all-news format created an urgent need for a new breed of electronic journalists.

It was difficult to break years of conventional radio management thinking that it could all be done with "whistles and bells." Such trappings as jingles, incompatible promotion techniques, personality delivery, and the constant adding and subtracting of gimmicks had to be sacrificed before an all-news station could be classed as truly professional. A partial, and only temporary, solution at some of the early stations was to "double-team" the program management. Dual positions were created with titles such as executive editor and executive producer, in an attempt to combine the talents of a print journalist and a broadcaster. Turning a news format into an air-worthy, professional service was a developmental hurdle for which management had little initial understanding.

Managers are also faced with the very real constraint of the union shops controlling production personnel in most major markets. The difficulty lies with the contracts with the American Federation of Television and Radio Artists (AFTRA) although many stations also have the dual difficulty of Newspaper Guild writers in-house. It boils down to contracts setting work rules, pay provisions, and exclusivity that can literally manacle an all-news manager. News *breaks*; it doesn't wait. If management cannot afford a story because complex costs surround its on-air repetition (from matching to union labor shifts, taped amplification and extension, or multiple-fee burdens of one kind or another), the story gets short shrift, if any attention at all.

These elements are all tied to working conditions in the various union contracts. There are contracts in which the repeat of a story in later shifts or dayparts carries a residual type of fee to the original reporter, writer, or anchorperson. Sometimes this kind of provision is designated as a "within-shift" rule that allows the story's use within the individual's scheduled shift, but adds a fee when it is used outside the particular shift. Added to that may be special tape-reuse fees or added costs for use by another station in the network or group. When reporters cannot edit tape, write their own extraneous wraps, or do simple editing because of contract constraints, delay becomes handicap. And handicaps create daily dissension and threaten the loss of cost control.

As is immediately obvious, especially in a union shop in which most positions are controlled by AFTRA or Newspaper Guild ranks, personnel costs take a big jump. The average all-news station in a major market starts with a program cast of twenty-five to thirty-five. Format evolution and union negotiations in the past several years have tended to tighten the staffing pattern, but all-news remains a labor-intensive format. Round-the-clock operations, living up to the slogan "All News, All the Time" (KYW, Philadelphia), leave little room for staff economies without compromising the promise of format.

Using taped segments on the **overnight** (1 A.M. to 4 A.M.) is widely practiced, and curtailed staffing on slower weekend shifts works reasonably well. Other options depend on availability of free-lance talent, overtime budgets, technical maintenance requirements, and a basic assessment of the needs of the market. For example, is there an appreciable audience in the wee hours?

COST AND QUALITY

Another vital C for the program manager pops up here: control. Control of product vis-à-vis control of cost requires a finely honed strategy. Cost control cuts in many directions, but it counts most when the opportunity arises to "own a story." A lack of budget reserve at those crucial moments leaves a manager unable to capitalize on strength and gives competition an audience edge hard to overcome.

The shrewd all-news program manager will be keenly aware of news themes that are being "ridden" in the market. There is a tendency for reporters and editors to follow on a story generated by a local newspaper or television station, such as a series on child abuse or auto repair swindles. If the theme is picked up and converted to a series of reports by an all-news reporter or team, it is not only duplicative (even when new material is exposed) but also drains budget. A local disaster, major storm, or original investigative project by the station staff then becomes an overbudget item of considerable magnitude. The prudent program manager hoards a portion of the operational budget for such opportunities and then goes all out to swamp the story from every possible angle, thus "owning" it compared to the competition. The dividend of this maneuver is that such an event is very likely to be an award winner in one of the several national or regional competitions sponsored by wire services, universities, and professional associations. Corporate management does like to see awards on the wall as visible indicators of status and enterprise.

In a 24-hour period the average all-news operation takes in about 400,000 words from all sources, including teletype; telephone; line-feeds from network, group, or contract services; **stringers**; and its own outside **beat** reporters. Of this data, somewhat less than half will be aired. Most all-news stations avoid the traditional "personality" cult of music formats or talk show announcing styles. During the average shift, the "product communicator" is on the air between 2 and 3 hours, doing some writing, collating, or ancillary production work in the off-air period.

If union contracts permit the prerecording of announcement material, rather than requiring it to be aired live, the program manager has a distinct advantage in achieving voice change and more efficient staff utilization. If this cannot be done, the anchorperson suffers from the constant stress of changing gears from hard news copy to often widely disparate, even frivolous commercial copy. A highly skilled announcer/ reader can manage this, but many come off badly in the process, and credibility takes a beating. The ideal tactic is to have the anchorperson totally involved in news preparation as well as in delivery and accompanied by supporting announcers at the microphone.

In building audience and meeting competition, one crucial decision is selection and assignment of outside reporters. If there is any one place for a program manager to spend money on the grand side, it is with this group. The determination of station outreach is critical, but merely advertising the station's coverage is quickly pegged as public relations sham if actual beat coverage is slighted or faked. Listeners are acutely (if often subliminally) attuned to their environment, especially the sound of it. Cold handouts, studio copy, voice cuts, sound effects cannot replace the presence of a live reporter. The program manager should study the station's formal ascertainment of community needs to understand the geographical extent of the station's commitment. Political centers such as city halls, statehouses, or county seats get staffing priority. Beats in education, transportation, health, crime, urban affairs (ethnic concentrations), suburban centers, and any special regional or local priority deserve close attention. A **correlator** (inside or telephone reporter) often can add a local dimension to a story, creating an **actuality**: the quick tape of a phone call can make the difference between a vaguely pertinent off-wire rewrite and a story with a local angle that has local audience impact and appeal.

INNER AND OUTER LIMITS

The all-news program manager, perforce, must operate within a number of constraints. These constraints often provide uncharted paths to creative opportunity—once the rationale for them is clearly understood. Constraints fall into two groups: internal and external. A lively sense of management techniques and a finely honed sense for convoluted interfaces are tools for internal strategies. Dealing with the external is a matter of understanding the nature of the audience and its fragmented responsiveness to the all-news concept.

All-news radio presents an almost Kiplingesque "if" situation: if the general manager is interested mainly in short-term corporate tactics; if the sales manager can muster a sales force that sells only radio and numbers rather than the all-news product; if the promotion manager has no appropriate promotion strategy; if the chief engineer sees fit not to apply maximum special support requirements; if, in other words, management regards the format as an ideological **loss leader** and insists on "yo-yo" format deviations to compete in the ratings scramble—then the all-news programmer is in deep trouble. All-news demands complete format support from all facets of the organization. Here are a few historical internal problem areas with which programmers must be prepared to deal:

1. *The incompatible commercial:* Many advertisers think it is just the thing to submit copy that sounds like a fake news bulletin, that contains verbiage that seems interwoven with hard news copy, or that requires an anchorperson to do dialects. Erosion of credibility is obvious.

2. *The jingle jokers:* Many in promotion and, sadly, even in programming feel that the all-news format is inherently dull and repetitious and, therefore, needs **hyping**. They try

to get in frequent jingle insertions unrelated to the basic format "sound package," promos that tease, and sensational headlines. They become especially frantic with those distractions during periods in which ratings firms are known to be gathering their listening data.

3. *The tech wreckers:* The demands of processing a heavy daily load of tape material, extra production requirements, and sudden, awkward remote broadcast assignments have forced more than one technician to the sanctity of the transmitter, resulting in sharp increases in "obligatory" meter readings and adjustments. Engineers will make themselves inaccessible if they feel they are being asked to do more than they think fair.

4. *The bottom line is all there is:* "You've blown the budget on the snowstorm, and we'll have to cover the capital hearings off the wire." This is what programmers often hear from general managers. Program managers have to be able to test this poor-mouthing for truth. This is, perhaps, their most dangerous confrontation with management. Many have fought with too little, for too much, at the wrong time, and over the wrong issues. The successful programmer finds out where the land mines have been laid before rushing into the fray.

A program manager without a disciplined philosophy about how to deal with external constraints makes the struggle more uphill from the start than it need be.

1. The initial cry from listeners when the format is introduced is "repetition." What the audience is really saying, however, is, "The way I listen to and use radio is not comfortable any more. You demand full attention, but I hear the same stories over and over." It takes a fair span of time before the audience begins to understand how all-news radio works.

2. The need to convey "bad news" creates another external pressure. All-news never provides calming background music for the routines of the day, nor will it offer a stimulating, continuous round of exciting rock music or spirited talk and debate.

3. Audience mail will complain that the station serves up horrid fascist ideals and reprehensible communist plots. If the volume of letters on each side is about even, the station must be doing about right.

4. Another powerful external pressure comes from civic groups and consumer bands bent on attacking the station's

license. These attacks can trigger enormous legal expense and create much inconvenience. However, the station that practices ethical journalism and uses sound broadcasting management has little to fear from these onslaughts.

MARKET DEFINITION

A concern of programmers nearly equal to internal constraints is the station's concept of its market. Often the market is treated as if it is limited to the city of license. However, a station's coverage area usually extends beyond city boundaries. The concept of regionalism is vital, not only from an audience outreach standpoint but also because it has a subtle influence on the opinions of the staff. The heart of urban society tends to beat overloud in the programmer's ears. The widened perspective gained from awareness of suburban and even rural attitudes toward social problems is invaluable. A regional thrust also tends to modify the program mix.

The contemporary ebb and flow of population between the city and suburbs dictate a broader set of programming value standards than ever before. All-news programming that concentrates on inner-city situations limits audience growth and surrenders competitive advantage. A case in point occurred a few years ago in a major eastern market. The executive editor of an all-news station received a proposal from a hobbyist to do a series of short reports on gardening. The idea was initially dismissed as lacking appeal for a mainly urban audience interested in more sophisticated activities. After a year or so of persistent application, the garden reporter was given a trial. The response was overwhelming and has kept up to this day. The program attracted a significant new subaudience from city and suburban dwellers alike. This experience gave the editor a new insight into the hundreds of small-town listeners the station had as well as making him realize that the "sophisticated" inner city was full of patio and window box horticulturists.

Setting up suburban bureaus, manned by outside reporters, ensures regional coverage. This strategy has to be balanced by obvious cost factors and areas of necessary concentration, but it works to great station advantage. When economic factors dictate, the use of **stringers** (per-story reporters) can often provide coverage of an entire geographic area without the expense of full-time staffing. This is especially useful for small- and medium-sized stations. The prime advantage of full-time reporters is the visible and audible presence of the station in the outlying areas. The major-market "bedroom communities" served gain involvement and empathy. If, however, population is sparse or mainly rural, this can be an unwarranted expense, and stringers are the alternative.

MEETING FCC OBLIGATIONS

By its very commitment to a basic tenet of "the public's right to know," an all-news station would seem to have an easy regulatory time of it. In reality, that commitment requires more attention to fulfillment than for any other kind of station. At the time of license renewal, the station must show a very real and comprehensive grasp of public issues, problems, and aspirations.

Public awareness of this commitment has heightened considerably in recent years, and challenges to all-news licenses are not uncommon. Most major stations employ outside research agencies—such as Media Statistics, Inc.—for community ascertainment and pay particular attention to minority and ethnic groups in the audience. Guidelines established by Federal Communications Commission (FCC) Docket No. 18774 ("Primer on Ascertainment of Community Problems by Broadcast Applicants")[1] is the basis for such research. Combined personal-interview and telephone methodology are normally used, with the addition of black and bilingual interviewing tied to a careful study of local demographic profiles. By simply paying attention to the daily flow of local news, the all-news program manager gains a pretty clear idea of what community problems are and draws up coverage plans accordingly. Ascertainment research results suggest appropriate coverage proportions of priority issues, which the program manager must balance with voluntary coverage of special areas of investigative reporting and major-event coverage.

A key to meeting FCC requirements accurately and responsively is keeping detailed records of coverage in every dimension. An all-news station that does not maintain a detailed monthly report system can find itself facing a horrendous information-retrieval job, tracking through logger tapes (as much as a four-year maintenance schedule) and bales of bound scripts.

AUDIENCE RESEARCH

Strategic use of audience research by the all-news program manager is important, but only if it is regarded as a single factor bearing on judgment of format suitability. It cannot be the governing force. Most stations subscribe to the monthly assessments of *Mediatrend* as a relatively current weathervane and (along with major advertising agencies) the highly detailed, quarterly reports from Arbitron. Other services tend to fall between these two and are marginally useful. From time to time, new services seek subscribers but emerge slowly. One is Burke Research of Cincinnati, relying on pure telephone research rather than on diaries. The sales keys are the October/November Arbitron reports on which most annual buys are made and on which most advertising agencies rely for guidance. A newspaper strike, severe storms, major sustained disaster stories, and so on, can all "wobble" a report book in an all-news station's favor. Such measurement devices as ESF (expanded sample frame—culls new and unlisted telephone respondents) may hurt or help as they fall. Format changes in the market, such as a new talk station or FM proliferation, can alter audience measurements remarkably. The temptation to "yo-yo" the format in response to such deviations is strong, and many all-news stations have learned to their sorrow that it seldom pays off in the long run. A frightening outcome is **plateauing** (leveling off) because it means that the audience and the station form a relatively complacent entity. Three or more Arbitron books with no share movement means that a station is not a growing entity in the market. Qualitative refinement, dogmatic as it sounds, is the manager's most valid response to counter a seemingly wild swing in the ratings.

Most all-news stations have a relatively easy time with the 50+ age group. Attracting and holding the 18 to 49 group and women present the greatest problems. The AQH (average quarter hour) span is another tough block in the audience-building scheme. The listener is in and out of the all-news audience. In contrast, a music station may hold some listeners over long periods, giving it a leg up on total listening time. The countermove is not to cater to random pressures but rather to choose the mix in as catholic a fashion as possible and "be there" with the steady diet of quality reportage at all times.

COMPETITION: ENDURANCE AND EDGE

A competitive pattern has emerged in the brief history of all-news stations: A well-operated one in a major market can count on something in the range of a 10 percent share of audience. If there are two all-news stations, they tend to simply divide the share of audience (given relatively equal effort and appeal). The format normally is not subject to radical swings in the ratings, perhaps because audience loyalty is readily identifiable.

All-news competition usually occurs between a network outlet and an independent station. The network-affiliated station programmer has the advantage of network resources but must air obligatory network news at key times. Thus, if the breaking story of the moment is local, the station may be running behind its momentum. Added to that is the gnawing feeling among the staff that they are second-class citizens, because the network voice automatically preempts their voices. The other side of the coin is that they must scramble to equal in professionalism the network's promotional and "name" weight.

A subtler form of competition for the all-news programmer arises from the drivetime news block confrontation. This usually comes from a well-established music station in the market with a fairly strong news department. To cope with the all-news intrusion into its audience, such a station will often expand its own news programming, particularly in morning drivetime. Since the music station can afford to compress its news staff effort into a 2- or 3-hour period, the facade of an important news effort can be erected. This, coupled with a well-regarded local **disc jockey**, can be formidable indeed. Pulling away from such a station over a stretch of time is not too difficult, however, because sustained, tight utilization of team strength will tell. Heavy use of well-founded and -programmed series, made up of short **vertical** or **horizontal documentaries** in morning drivetime, is one of the most effective countermeasures.

Differences in signal strength among stations are often mentioned as station advantages or disadvantages. These can be somewhat illusory, because far-flung signal strength can lead the all-news station into the trap of trying to spread its resources too thinly. For a network station this is not such a hazard, because the network base is broadly appealing without the constant need for as much local backup as the independent programmer has to muster. Concentrating on the smaller, but major, metro-area audience can be more rewarding for the independent station in terms of audience loyalty than trying to be too many things to too many persons at once. A prime example of this is the Los Angeles area. There, listeners are available and attuned in the L.A. primary-coverage zone to a 5,000-watt independent, while the 50,000-watt network outlet serves a much greater audience area. Power limitation, translated to automatic audience limitation, is an obvious *primary-area* audience constraint. It cannot be dismissed automatically, however, because the program manager must be aware that many in the metro audience relate to outlying population groups and want to know, in some dimension, what's going on out there. Still, the metro-limited station cannot afford to spread itself too thinly on the coverage of the fringe audience. Adding a metro general assignment reporter to the metro-limited station's staff will always pay bigger dividends than making a "spread" gesture of setting up a suburban bureau in an area not heavily listener populated. Suburban bureaus are for stations with wide-area signal coverage and adequate support budgets.

An important key to successful competition is well-thought-out promotion. Clever slogans, jingle packages, and spot promotion efforts are not enough; good promotion requires the sustained use of a valid theme underlying major programming and staff recognition of it. If the program manager's newsroom staff has no identification with a station promotion "theme," there will nearly always be weak communication of it to the audience. Amazing as it sounds, there is often little orientation or exposure by management to the staff on short- or long-range thinking behind a promotion theme or campaign. Overuse of "cute" promos dilutes the nature of material, and program managers and creative service or promotion managers have to work closely in harness to judge the total value of any external as well as in-house promotional theme or campaign.

A great weakness in most broadcasting entities is internal communication. This may be as simple as forgetting to tell the audience what comes next in the program. The solution is called "promoting off the desk." This means that the editor (with backup awareness by writers, correlators, and anchorpersons) must remember to create audience expectations for an upcoming special series, phone interview sequence, or other special item. This sort of promotion can be formalized to some extent. Foresight by the news director, editor, and, of course, program manager is vital.

Another aspect of maintaining a competitive edge is close monitoring of what goes on the air. A monthly review of script packages will show which writers and anchorpersons are "dogging it," that is, either using excessive pasteup of wire copy (necessary and permissible within reasonable limits on stories outside the station's coverage area) or simply using carbon copies of stories from previous news segments. This is an insidious tendency that eventually bores the audience and drives it away. Many program managers have become absorbed with seemingly vital future planning and have neglected this syndrome to their later sorrow. Keeping on top of script packages is a prime responsibility, and the competition will be quick to notice if a station fails to do so.

Last, programmers should not find themselves forced to play catch-up. They must listen to the competition regularly for the same reasons the competition listens to them.

FANATICS WERE YESTERDAY

Many practitioners of all-news radio remind one of Winston Churchill's definition of a fanatic: "He not only won't change his mind, he won't change the subject!" All-news programming tends to suffer from two extremes: those who periodically want to revolutionize the format and those who are so locked into a format concept that they will not consider change. All-news produces an evolutionary service, used by many different types of listeners at one and the same time. The programmer who does not dare to "dump the format" for an event that lends itself to another obvious form of coverage will lose crucial battles. The judicious use of format openings such as massive team reporting efforts from remote locations, proper invocation of telephone programming, and even the airing of play-by-play sports can have creative benefits. There is very little that touches the life of any major audience group that is not compatible with the meaning of the word *news*. Conversely, there are very few things an all-news station can attempt into which a satisfactory amount of straight, hard news coverage cannot be inserted.

One future opinion is all-sports radio, perhaps growing out of an established AM all-news station or an ancillary FM service. It would, at first, be limited to a few major markets. Many laughed at the idea of religious radio growth years ago but must acknowledge what is happening in that highly specialized field today. American sports fans are fanatics. Some fanatic broadcaster out there will respond. He or she needs to be a pragmatist to be a success.

It is doubtful from the present perspective that all-news can be either profitable or possible in a small- or even medium-sized market. Without sufficient personnel and money, all-news operations are almost bound to revert to the old **rip-and-read** practice of earlier days. To be sure, technology is cutting costs—slowly. ENG (electronic newsgathering) application in television is widening the audience's appetite for information that television alone cannot satisfy, ironically because of its own slavery to the old network radio formats, and, of course, its own cost problems tied to the personality cult. Thus, all-news has a somewhat limited future in the immediate sense, although the day of the **self-transmitting reporter** and the computer with **audio-speech capacity** is not far down the road as it applies to that portion of the product originating outside a station's coverage area. Creative format application and editorial judgment are the keys to the all-news product, and the opportunity for innovative development lies ahead in many yet untried forms.

NOTE

[1]"Primer on Ascertainment of Community Problems by Broadcast Applicants, Part I, Section IV-A and IV-B of FCC Forms," FCC Docket No. 18774, released February 18, 1971.

ADDITIONAL PERIODICAL READINGS

"All-News Stations Continue Successfully, Primarily as a Large-Market Phenomenon." *Television/Radio Age* (December 6, 1976): 42 ff.

Analysis of trends in all-news programming at station levels.

Bagdikian, Ben H. "Fires, Sex and Freaks." *New York Times Magazine,* October 10, 1976, pp. 40 ff.

Explanation of the appeal of all-news radio.

"Networks Offer More News to Listeners, Greater Flexibility to Affiliated Stations." *Television/Radio Age* (December 12, 1977): 38 ff.

Analysis of types and advantages of network news services from affiliate's point-of-view; reports on anticipated growth in services.

Powers, Ron, and **Oppenheim, Jerrold.** "The Failed Promise of All-News Radio." *Columbia Journalism Review* 12 (September/October 1973): 21–28.

Discussion of the content and programming methods used by all-news radio stations.

Sobel, Robert. "News-Oriented Stations, Syndicators See Radio Feature Field Showing Signs of Stability." *Television/Radio Age* (December 12, 1977): 42 ff.

Review of syndicated features and prospects for the future.

16 _Talk Radio Programming_

Bruce W. Marr

Bruce W. Marr is currently director of news and programming at KABC, Los Angeles. KABC is the AM station that initiated the talk format and is nationally known for its innovative leadership. Before coming to this ABC O&O, Mr. Marr worked for KFWB, a Group W AM station in Los Angeles; the Inland Broadcast Company in the Pacific Northwest; and WNRC (now WVOX), an AM in New Rochelle, New York, in a variety of capacities including newsman, disc jockey, and engineer. He lectures on radio programming at the University of Southern California at Los Angeles and serves as a director of the National Leukemia Broadcast Council. His chapter encompasses a spectrum of related formats ranging from all-conversation at one extreme to half-news/half-talk at the other, often called "information radio." The typical talk format includes live interviews with personalities, but its most distinctive feature is the telephone call-in show. One talk station stands out from another primarily on the basis of its proportions of interviews, call-ins, conversations, and news. Since nearly all stations at some time include elements of talk, the touchy issues of fairness and public pressure in this chapter have relevance for all programmers.

THE BEGINNINGS OF TALK

During the latter half of the 1970s radio broadcasting changed drastically. It was then that the hares of the industry—the AM broadcasters—paused to look over their shoulders at the tortoises—the FM stations. When they did so, they found themselves being overtaken. When they glanced forward again toward the finish line, they saw that some of the FM tortoises were already leading the race. By 1977 an entire generation of listeners had grown up with their radios permanently locked on the FM dial.

In 1978 a number of AM broadcasters assessed the situation and recognized that FM was becoming the music medium of choice for a substantial segment of the radio audience. To retain their audiences, several significant AM **stations** used the strategy of **counterprogramming**: They shifted their formats away from music to the spoken word. Information programming was born.

The format had been pioneered in 1960 by KABC in Los Angeles. The term _talk station_ came into being when KABC discarded its records and began airing nothing but the sound of the human voice. After that last record was played in 1960, KABC began filling virtually every minute of its 24-hour broadcast day with talk. The recordings that consume most of the air time on the great majority of radio stations disappeared. Each moment of programming was entrusted to the talent, skills, knowledge, and judgment of the on-the-air personalities, the management team, and the support people on the station staff. The station was originally promoted as "The Conversation Station." A 4-hour news and conversation program entitled *News/Talk* was instituted from 5 to 9 A.M. That designation later was adopted by KGO in San Francisco for its overall format. KGO used **news blocks** in both morning and evening drive periods and conversation programs throughout the balance of the day.

News/talk seems to have stuck and become the generic industry term for all stations that program conversation leavened with news during the drive periods. *Talk radio* includes the news/talk format as well as all-conversation programming.

PHILOSOPHY

Good talk radio is either broadcast journalism or very closely akin to it. As the format has matured, it has embraced more and more journalistic traditions. This introduces a conflict: professional newspeople filter out their own biases as they write and prepare stories. In live radio it is hard for the on-air person to examine personal points of view instantly and keep them in check. Management has to acknowledge that the members of the on-the-air team have their own biases and leave them free to express their stands on issues being discussed. Management can, however, expect them to treat guests with respect if the guests represent opposing sides of issues. This philosophy has grown slowly from the understanding that it is fruitless to ask on-air personalities to be unbiased. They are often investigators, sometimes advocates, and biases are doubtless part of their stock-in-trade.

STRUCTURE

The talk format provides the opportunity to maintain a constant framework yet remain fluid enough to respond to issues on a day-to-day basis and to reflect the mood of the community as it changes. All good broadcast personalities can judge the mood of the audience and respond accordingly, but the talk host is not hindered by limitations such as a music list and is free to change the tone of the talk appropriately. When an issue or news event is significant enough to color the outlook of an entire community or even the entire nation, the sound of the talk station will reflect the mood of the audience. Scheduled subject matter and previously booked guests should be and usually are preempted by significant events.

The November morning in 1978 when San Francisco Mayor George Moscone was shot and killed in his city hall office provides a vivid example of the responsiveness of talk radio. San Francisco's KGO radio had been planning to feature a psychological expert at 11 A.M. with a discussion on holiday loneliness and depression. Subsequent programs were to deal with taxation and alcoholism. When the city hall story broke, the entire Bay Area became numb. All of northern California wanted the details of a single story: the city hall shooting.

KGO's news team responded immediately, deploying its field reporters and assigning inside staffers to telephones. From the moment the story reached the station, the atmosphere within the station altered, and the change was reflected in the on-air product. Scheduled guests were canceled; talk hosts instantly became anchorpersons. Incoming reports filed by KGO's field staff mingled with reactions from civic officials gathered by inside newspeople using telephones. Comments by the audience were aired constantly. The station stayed with the city hall shooting story exclusively throughout the day, discarding its planned programming in favor of a strong response to its community's needs and concerns.

News

Because the talk format generally presents information, the audience readily accepts a break for a news bulletin. The interruption may be a bulletin from a network or a casual-sounding "visit" from a member of the station news staff who joins the talk host in the studio to break a story fresh from a wire service or a local reporter. The presence of the newsperson in the studio on such occasions provides the opportunity for questions and answers or conversation between the host and the newsperson. It is important to assure the audience that the news staff will follow the story and keep listeners up to date with return visits to the program as the story develops.

The resources and personnel of news departments vary substantially from station to station. But the station with even the most limited news staff can cover a breaking story using primary tools of their trade: the telephone and enterprising production people. Capitalizing on established contacts, ingenuity, and a **reverse telephone directory** (arranged by addresses instead of names), a **call screener** can put the talk host in touch with officials, eyewitnesses, and other involved parties even before a news crew can reach the scene of a story. During periods of disaster, the news/talk station can become a vital clearinghouse for information.

When wide-ranging brushfires swept through thousands of acres of southern California in October of 1978, KABC dealt with the disaster continuously throughout the day and evening—through reports from its news staff and through the liaison it established between those in need and those willing to help. One caller pleaded for safe pasture for his threatened livestock, and another listener responded with an offer. Other listeners, unable to reach their homes in the fire areas, heard reports by neighbors who called to report the status of the fire-fighting efforts. Temporary housing was offered on the air for evacuees. Those who had lived through other devastating fires in the brush country around Los Angeles called with tips on how to protect homes and property. Beyond the service provided to those threatened by the blaze, the station also delivered to its entire audience the story of the fire in very human and personal terms.

Conversation

The discussion of controversial issues is an integral part of talk programming. The question arises, in designing programming on controversial subjects, of whether it is wiser to invite representatives of each point of view to a single program and structure a debate or to invite individuals to express their points of view separately on consecutive hours of a single program or on successive programs.

Answers differ station by station, but the common denominator is *maintain control*. At a minimum, two persons participate in a telephone talk program: the host and the caller. If there is a guest on the program, there are three participants: host, guest, and caller. If two guests appear on the program, there are now four voices. Because it is radio, the listener has no visual reference and may not know who is speaking. If a debate is allowed to get out of control, the listener is subjected to a disjointed cacophony of voices, one speaking over the other. The best rule of thumb is to keep the number of voices few and easily identifiable.

PROGRAMMING SOURCES

Although music programmers can turn to a large number of sources to augment their locally produced programs or to program their entire broadcast day, talk programmers are largely on their own. Music stations can buy music tapes from a number of program services that will send an entire month's programming by mail. The music arrives at the station formatted and balanced by some of the nation's top programmers. **Syndicators** also offer music programming in segments ranging from 1 or 2 hours up to complete weekend-long specials. But the talk programmer has very few outside resources to call on. By its very nature, the talk format demands large blocks of timely, topical programming that no syndicator can offer.

The **networks** offer news, some **feature** material, and worthwhile public affairs programs but not enough to substantially diminish the burden on the individual program director. Only the Mutual Broadcast Network offers a large block of talk programming with its *Larry King Program,* which can be used to fill the overnight hours. In the foreseeable future, the radio networks will transmit their programming by satellite, enabling them to deliver five, six, or more programs simultaneously to their affiliates. Stations will be able to choose programs to fit their individual **formats**, and one or more networks can be expected to provide some talk programming.

Five-minute and 15-minute syndicated features are available from a growing number of companies, but these programs cannot provide the foundation for a talk station's daily schedule. Some programs are available from colleges and universities. These features often are highly informative but weak in production values.

TALK HOSTS

Conversation hosts are often generalists, as are most good broadcast journalists. They have developed the ability to grasp the essence of a broad range of subjects. The host of a general-interest talk program will discuss world and local affairs, politics, medicine, economics, science, history, literature, music, art, and sports trivia—often on a single program. The host will be an inveterate reader; some find a speed-reading course helpful.

A special kind of partnership grows up between the air personality and the program director in talk programming, involving a great deal of mutual trust. The program director is responsible for establishing policies that ensure high journalistic standards and operation within the bounds of good taste, Federal Communications Commission (FCC) law, and industry codes. Having established and communicated such policies, the program director must recognize that there will be day-to-day errors and deviations. The individual on the air has to make instant decisions and immediate responses. The conversation host is interacting with phone callers 2, 3, or 4 hours a day. Callers can be assertive, aggressive, and even downright belligerent. No format is easier to second-guess; the program director should therefore avoid calling air personalities to task impulsively. In almost every case, the personality is the first to know when something has gone wrong.

In fact, talk radio is radio waiting for something to go wrong. When things do go wrong, the first approach of the program director should leave an opening for the personality to say, "I know it was bad.

The reason was. . . ." The program director is responsible for determining that the air talent understands what happened but must then act as intermediary and arbitrator between management and air talents.

When a newcomer takes over an on-air slot on a talk station, a certain amount of audience turnover usually occurs. Many listeners and callers go elsewhere; new ones find and accept the new personality. Initial reaction is usually negative to the removal of the host who is being replaced, a natural response to a change that disrupts the listening habits of regular listeners. Even when ratings and other indicators confirm the need for a change, the followers of the departed personality will react vigorously enough to make programmers question their own judgments. The first programs of the new host will find callers responding timidly, as they would with a new acquaintance. It is to be expected that this introductory period will color the tone of the program for a time since the audience is an integral part of any conversation program.

AUDIENCE

The talk audience is as active as the station itself. Conversation stations are foreground stations, designed to be upfront in the awareness of the listener. Seldom do listeners use conversation radio as a background station the way they may a **beautiful music** station. This attribute represents an important sales advantage. Commercials are particularly effective within the conversation environment because they reach an audience that tuned in to *listen.* A commercial read live by an authoritative talk host has enhanced impact.

Another useful aspect of the talk audience is that it is above average in terms of affluence, education, spendable income, and many other categories that attract a broad range of advertisers. Investment and air travel commercials alone represent a substantial segment of regular talk radio advertising.

If a talk station is sufficiently involved in the community it serves, it attracts influential civic and business leaders, political figures, and thought leaders from all walks of life. It is not unusual, even in a radio market the size of Los Angeles, for public figures to call in response to the mention of their names on the air.

One disadvantage of the format is that it tends to appeal to an audience somewhat older than that of most music stations. The most optimistic target is the 25 to 49 year age group. Even when directed at this **demographic** group, the format will usually attract a substantial number of those 50 and over. Over the years, programmers have attempted to bring the average age of their audiences down into the more desirable 18 to 34 category but have had little or no success. KABC experimented on more than one occasion with youthful program hosts and content designed to appeal to the younger segment of the market. Each time the effort failed. The youthful approach not only failed to draw many young listeners, it also tended to alienate the older audience that was the hard core of the station's listenership.

Still, it is possible to manipulate a demographically top-heavy talk audience downward by rigid control of subject matter. The program manager and the air staff must construct each hour of programming to appeal to the key demographic group. Free-form (sometimes called "open-line") programs must be severely limited or entirely prohibited.

KTRH (Houston) aired a significant amount of free-form programming when it instituted its talk format in 1961 and found that it reached a predominantly older audience. The older listeners worsened the problem by dominating the air time. They felt free to dial the station at any time and discuss issues that were of interest to them but not to younger listeners. In 1975 the station imposed controls on the subject matter and was able to reduce the average age of its audience markedly.

One stratagem for forcing down the median age of an audience is the sports conversation show. Aired in late afternoon, such a program will attract a significant male audience younger than the normal 25+ target group without relinquishing the males 25 to 49 who make up the backbone of the station's potential evening drive audience.

GUESTS

Every talk program director receives vast numbers of audition tapes as job applications from potential talk hosts on which they interview nationally known celebrities; it follows that the applicants think these are their best interviews. Too often, however, celebrities have nothing new to say and contribute little to the program. The interviewers must feel that some of the celebratedness rubs off onto them.

The best audition tapes are those that give the program director an opportunity to hear the host's ability to probe substantive issues, to learn how well the individual prepares, and how agile his or her mind is. Celebrity interviews rarely offer such opportunities. Most of them include a few brief, pat questions from the host and lengthy answers from the interviewee. The person who stands to gain the most recognition from the interview is the celebrity.

Talk stations and hosts are constantly pursuing well-known names as guests, people who will bring "star value" to their programs. But often the best guest will be a local person whose name is unknown to the listeners. The local station in the small, remote community can program relevant topics without looking beyond its own coverage area. Stations that are far distant from the "talk show circuit" of the major markets need not avoid talk programming for lack of interesting guests.

An hour spent with a major movie star might better be spent with a mayor, school superintendent, game warden, newspaper publisher, football coach, or auto mechanic.

Stations can gain access to distant interviewees, of course, by using the telephone. A conference call permits local callers to participate in conversation with a distant guest. Programmers still prefer to have guests in the studio when possible, but the conference call is a practical alternative and permits the station to reach out across the world in search of guests who would not be available otherwise. Programmers would doubtless use conference calls more frequently if they were technically more dependable. Programmers across the country complain that guests are commonly cut off in midprogram, and audio levels and line quality fluctuate unpredictably.

Public relations firms representing nationally known figures deluge major-market stations with offers of appearances by celebrities. Those who are responsible for scheduling guests on such stations should consider carefully the relevance of the contribution of every guest, not merely the impact of the person's name.

Of all radio formats, the talk format shoulders the heaviest responsibility for preventing the intrusion of unscheduled commercial matter on the air. The terms **payola** and **plugola** are associated with the music industry, but the talk format offers the greatest opportunities for such abuses. An hour of friendly conversation presents endless opportunities for the on-air host to mention a favorite resort or restaurant or to comment on a newly acquired automobile. Moreover, the program host is often in the position to book as a guest a favored business acquaintance. The air personality therefore receives many offers, ranging from free dinners to discounts on major purchases. Policies aimed at preventing violations must be instituted and rigidly enforced. The on-air staff must be made aware that violators will be penalized severely by station management. Most stations have instituted affidavits showing that the law is understood, and some stations hire independent agencies to monitor programs for abuses.

However, it is fully appropriate for guests who represent commercial enterprises to appear on the station. It is appropriate, for instance, for a local travel agent to discuss travel in mainland China or for the proprietor of a health food store to present opinions on nutrition. And, obviously, personalities on the talk show circuit have something to sell—a book, a movie, a sporting event, a philosophy, and so on. Some mention of the individual's reason for appearing is appropriate because it establishes the credentials of the guest. An apt reference might be, "Our subject today is solar energy, and our guest is John Smith, author of a new book entitled, *The Many Uses of the Sun.*" Many stations prohibit more explicit information, such as "The book sells for $9.95 and is available at Jones Book Store."

Two criteria should govern the booking of all guests:

1. The guest must contribute to worthwhile programming.

2. Neither the station nor any individual in the station's employ may benefit from the appearance of the guest unless the remuneration is properly accounted for, and commercial references are logged and announced.

TELEPHONE SCREENERS

The **screener** or producer is a vital part of the talk radio staff because this person serves as the center who delivers the ball, in the form of the telephone call, to the on-the-air quarterback.

Screeners represent a substantial additional cost to station budgets, but only through careful screening can a station retain control of its own programming. Airing "cold" or unscreened calls can be compared to a **disc jockey** reaching blindly into the music library and airing the first record that comes to hand whether it be country, rock, classical, or a polka. Few program directors would relinquish control in that manner. The telephone call represents the **playlist** of talk radio. The screener constantly manipulates the lineup of incoming calls, giving priority to a more appropriate caller and delaying or eliminating callers of presumably lesser interest. The situation changes constantly as new calls come in, and the good screener orchestrates them to provide the most appealing program for the listener. If, for instance, the subject under discussion is the city fire department and ten callers are standing by to be put on the air when the fire chief calls, the chief's call obviously should move to the front of the pack and be aired at the first opportunity.

The screener filters out the "regulars" who call the station too frequently as well as obvious drunks and others not able to make a contribution. Callers thus dismissed and those who are asked to hold for long periods often complain of unjust treatment, but the screener must prevail, insisting on the right to structure the best possible sequence of talk. The best screeners do this with tact and graciousness.

Various systems are used to communicate between the screener and the on-air host to signal which incoming call has been screened and is due to be aired next. KABC uses a light system provided by the telephone company; it enables the screener to trigger one of a bank of lights directly above the keys on the telephone console in the on-air studio, which indicates to the host which call is to be aired next. Other stations use a simple numbered card system in which the screener holds up a card with a number printed on it indicating the number of the next telephone line to be aired. The screener keeps a log of the callers on hold for reference as the program moves along.

Virtually all talk stations use a device to delay the programming a few seconds between the studio and the transmitter to enable "dumping" profanity, personal attacks, and other unairable matter. The delay can be achieved by a tape loop that provides for recording the station's output at one point and playing it back a few feet later. The more modern digital delay units do away with the need for frequent replacement of tape loops to maintain air quality. The on-air host generally controls the "cut button" that diverts offensive program material, although the engineer should have a backup switch.

Because the program is delayed (generally 4 to 7 seconds before it reaches the air), the screener instructs all callers to turn off their radios before attempting to talk on the air. Failing this, callers hear their voices coming back at them some seconds delayed and find it impossible to carry on a conversation. Listening on the telephone they hear the real-time program material and can carry on a normal conversation with the host.

The conversation between the screener and the caller will generally sound something like this:

> Screener: Good morning. This is the *Joe Jones Program.* What did you wish to talk about?
>
> Caller: Well, Joe was talking about the energy crisis, and I would like to talk about alternative sources of energy.
>
> Screener: Fine, there are four calls ahead of you. Please turn your radio off and do not use your full name when you are on the air. I'll come back on the line and let you know when you are going on the air.

Most stations prohibit the use of the caller's full name in order to forestall imposters. There have been cases of callers identifying themselves as prominent people in a community and then airing false statements so as to embarrass the individuals they claimed to be.

CONTROVERSY AND FAIRNESS

While talk radio programmers get broad opportunities for creative expression, they also must devote considerable time to administration. Because the station deals almost constantly with public affairs issues, the programmer must always monitor the station's air for compliance with FCC rules and to avoid legal pitfalls such as libel.

Compliance with the **fairness doctrine** occurs naturally and without the imposition of daily evaluation by the program director as long as the on-air personality's calls actively represent a broad cross-section of divergent points of view. The input of guests and callers presents a whole range of additional opinions. Almost without exception, when the well-programmed talk station has been challenged by an outside party for failure to adhere to the fairness doctrine, it has been easy to show that all sides of controversial issues have been aired. Over the period of a month or two, so many points of view are presented on a single talk station that it is virtually impossible to identify any facet of an issue that has not been covered.

Nonetheless, a reporting system must be maintained by management to ensure compliance with the doctrine. The program director, acting as a part of management and representing the licensee, must be able to document full and fair coverage of controversial issues. Several steps are taken to ensure compliance:

1. Effective indoctrination of incoming on-air talent when they join the station staff. A primer prepared by the station's legal counsel on this and all legal restrictions can be given to all new programming employees.

2. At a bare minimum, annual meetings with the on-air staff to reinforce the FCC requirements. (Some station staffs meet every other month or more often.)

3. Monitoring of the station's output with ears well tuned to detect uncovered points of view or personal attacks.

4. A reporting system summarizing in writing the subjects that have been covered on each program and which sides of issues were discussed.

CONTROVERSY AND PRESSURE

Talk stations frequently find themselves the targets of pressure groups, activist organizations, and political parties trying to gain as much free access to the station's air as they can. While most deserve some time on the station, management must be firm in turning away those who seek inordinate amounts of time.

Political parties are well aware of the impact of talk stations and have been known to organize volunteers to monitor programs and flood the incoming phone lines with a single point of view. Politicians seeking air time have attempted to misuse the fairness doctrine. These partisans will frequently confuse the fairness doctrine with the **equal-time** provision for political candidates—sometimes through ignorance, at other times in attempts to confuse the program executive.

For example, in the late 1970s, a national group opposing the use of nuclear power objected to a statement made by Ronald Reagan on his nationally syndicated radio commentary. They claimed personal attack against the integrity of one of their members, Daniel Ellsberg, and demanded equal time from all stations that carried the original commentary. They submitted to the stations a tape-recorded comment of about 7 minutes duration, presenting the antinuclear position of their organization.

The group demanded equal time although the issue in fact involved a personal attack on a single individual. One station (KABC) disregarded the demand for time and instead scheduled an interview with Ellsberg. Because he is a well-known and controversial figure, the discussion was lively and informative, covering a wide range of topics. However, he declined to reopen the subject about which the personal attack had been claimed. Instead, he waived in writing any claim to further time to dispute the issue.

Because an effective talk station deals frequently with controversial issues, its management can expect threats of all kinds from irate members of the audience. A provoked listener will demand anything from a retraction to equal time and, on occasion, will support such demands with threats of legal action. Virtually all such threatened lawsuits vanish, however, when the management of the talk station explains the relevant broadcast law to the complainant.

Often the issue that draws the wrath of the audience is not the serious, controversial subject but the frivolous one. One recent statement that drew many shouts of righteous indignation was the opinion expressed by a Los Angeles sportscaster that Notre Dame's basketball team was superior to that of UCLA. That remark drew phone calls and letters demanding that the statement be retracted and the sportscaster be discharged. Such teapot-sized tempests, although not serious, make demands on the time of the programmer.

TAPE LOGS

A round-the-clock tape-recorded **log** is considered a necessity by most talk stations. Such a tape log makes it possible for the station to retrieve and reconstruct precisely what was said on the air in the event of threatened legal action. These tapes are made on special slow-speed monitoring recorders running at 15/32 inches per second. The program can be recorded on one track while a telephone company time check is recorded on the second track, thus providing the exact time of all on-air events. Such tapes are recognized as official FCC master logs and should be kept for at least three years.

Access to these log tapes by outside parties should be limited to those with a bona fide need. Many stations require a written request, which is examined by the station's legal counsel before the station complies. Such tapes have been requested as evidence in litigation that does not involve the radio station but concerns guests who have appeared on the station. In such cases, many stations require that the tapes be subpoenaed. Law enforcement agencies are also likely to request access to such log tapes. The Los Angeles Police Department once requested the aid of KABC in establishing the exact time a play occurred in a baseball game being aired on the station, information helpful to them in pinpointing the precise time of a crime. The station, of course, granted access to the tapes for that purpose.

THE COST AND THE REWARD

A primary ingredient in the recipe for success in a talk format is commitment at the top—station management level. A timely and innovative music format can catapult a station from obscurity to the number-one ranking during a single rating period. Talk stations and all-news stations, however, generally take years to reach their potential. But once success is achieved, the talk station enjoys a listener loyalty that endures while the more fickle music audience shifts from station to station in search of the hits.

The talk station generally is more costly to operate than is a music operation. Good talk personalities are often more expensive than disc jockeys, and they must be supported by producers, call screeners, and, frequently, extra administrative personnel. But the rewards in service to the community and in quality entertainment can be substantial for both programmer and audience.

The talk radio station of the 1980s will combine the news and conversation formats in a blend of programming characterized by live interviews, telephone **actualities**, and on-air audience feedback. It will have great journalistic flexibility and local responsiveness but will be most widely known for its colorful host personalities. Programmers will continue to use the strategy of control to draw younger audiences.

ADDITIONAL PERIODICAL READINGS

Avery, Robert K.; Ellis, Donald G.; and **Glover, Thomas W.** "Patterns of Communication on Talk Radio." *Journal of Broadcasting* 22 (Winter 1978): 5–17.

An analysis of the cycles of interaction between hosts and callers on talk radio programs.

Carlin, John C. "The Rise and Fall of Topless Radio." *Journal of Communications* 20 (Winter 1976): 31–33.

Discussion of the FCC rulings relating to sex on radio.

Kushner, James M. "KDAS(FM): Want-Ad Radio in Los Angeles." *Journal of Broadcasting* 16 (Summer 1972): 267–76.

Analysis of a unique experiment in radio programming, the all–classified ad format.

Saldan, Elena S. "Music Syndicators Expand Radio Station Offerings." *Television/Radio Age* (September 26, 1977): 25 ff.

Analysis of offerings of radio syndicators and programming services.

Surlin, Stuart H. "Black-Oriented Radio: Programming to a Perceived Audience." *Journal of Broadcasting* 16 (Summer 1972): 289–98.

Based on a study done with an NAB research grant; discussion of the problems of identifying black audiences.

Turow, Joseph. "Talk Show Radio as Interpersonal Communication." *Journal of Broadcasting* 18 (Spring 1974): 171–79.

Report of study of radio talk show callers to WCAU, Philadelphia in the spring of 1973.

17 Public Radio

Wallace A. Smith

Wallace Smith has been deeply involved in various aspects of public broadcasting, communications teaching, and university administration and counseling for more than a decade—first at Occidental College and then at the University of Southern California. A graduate of Waynesburg College and the Pittsburgh Theological Seminary (both in Pennsylvania), he holds a master's degree and Ph.D. in telecommunications from the University of Southern California. He is active in public radio locally, statewide, and nationally, as well as in the local cultural scene. As general manager, he has shepherded KUSC-FM through the transition from a low-powered student-run operation to its position today as one of the leading public radio stations in the nation. He is presently a member of the board of directors of National Public Radio and is serving his second term on the board of directors of the California Confederation of the Arts. He is chairman of the radio advisory committee of the California Public Broadcasting Commission, on the executive committee of the Association of California Public Radio Stations, and past president of Alpha Epsilon Rho, the national radio/television honor society. Mr. Smith's chapter focuses on the counterprogramming strategies of the public radio station, using KUSC's recent adoption of a classical music format as a case study. From this example it is clear that decision making in public radio programming is much like that of commercial radio, but that noncommercial status provides advantages for some formats.

PHILOSOPHY AND FORMAT

The purpose of noncommercial educational (public) broadcast licenses is intentionally different from the purpose of commercial broadcast licenses, but both licensees are challenged with using their channel assignments in the most productive manner to reach the largest possible audience given their program services. Even though **public broadcast stations** may serve a more diverse series of audiences with highly specialized programs, their overall objective is to reach as many listeners in their communities as possible. Commercial broadcasters want to attract large audiences to generate basic operating revenue and a substantial profit for their stockholders. Public broadcasters have the same objective but reinvest their profits (nonprofit revenue) in the program service.

The challenge to the public radio programmer is to design an alternative program service that differs significantly from program **formats** offered by other commercial and noncommercial stations in the market. The selected format must attract sufficiently large audiences to generate direct support of the station by its listeners and encourage individual philanthropists, government agencies, foundations, business, industry, and corporations to invest in the station. Motivating those individuals and agencies to support a given public broadcast station requires evidence that substantial numbers of people in a community use, want, and need the program service.

A unique sound is needed to capture the imagination of the potential listening audience. The programming must elevate the public station into a competitive position with other radio services. It is not enough to say, "We are public, therefore we are better," or to rely on the fact that there are no commercial announcements to build an audience. Localism is a key factor in unique radio formats. Radio is a flexible medium with lightweight equipment that enables it to respond quickly to spontaneous events. The more live local events and happenings included in a broadcast schedule, the higher the probability for success.

Public broadcasting's most valuable asset is the integrity and quality of its programs. Whatever format is selected, success is predicated on the delivery of a program service that will enhance the life of each listener and improve the quality of life in the community. Those are idealistic goals but create the margin of difference that will attract listeners to public broadcasting regardless of the station format. Commercial broadcasters are less able to give priority to such lofty ideals because of commercial demands that compromise even their most deliberate attempts to achieve excellence.

Public radio uses five basic formats: classical music and fine arts, news and public affairs, community service and public access, **eclectic**, and instructional. Americans are accustomed to selecting radio stations according to format. Nothing annoys radio listeners more than tuning to a news station for news only to hear classical music. Educating the public to accept more than one sound from radio is a slow process. Most public as well as commercial broadcasters therefore deliver expected formats.

Classical Music and Fine Arts

All-music formats in radio depend on prerecorded music for the majority of their broadcast schedules. Public radio stations that choose the classical music and fine arts format have a competitive edge over their commercial counterparts because they can broadcast long, uninterrupted performances of classical works. They can surround these performances with informational modules that enhance the listening experience of the audience but avoid the abrasive intrusion of advertisements. The ability of public radio stations to put aside time restraints contributes substantially to the quality of presentation of classical music.

The classical music format has become a staple in public broadcasting. Because it is considered a "safe" format, many social activists criticize managers who select it. Their criticism is usually a result of misplaced values. The priority for arts and music in our society is low: music and arts are tolerated, but most people have a limited understanding of their value. The size of audiences and financial support for the classical music and fine arts format in public radio is sufficient evidence of the need for such services among the various publics served by public broadcasting. Fine arts and music are frequently the stimulants to higher aspirations by individuals in society; a public radio format that feeds those aspirations is as important as any service that can be provided by public radio.

The classical music and fine arts format can take several forms. WNED-FM (Buffalo, New York) broadcasts all classical music with only the briefest interruptions for information about the performers.* KUSC-FM (Los Angeles), licensed to the University of Southern California, has a schedule that is 85 percent classical music. The other 15 percent includes fine arts modules on subjects besides music and programs about classical music.

News and Public Affairs

The news and public affairs format, although seemingly a natural for public radio, is a less-used format than one might expect. WEBR-AM (Buffalo, New York) is the sole example of an all-news station in public radio. The station is enormously successful, garnering the largest share of audience of any station in public radio. WEBR is also one of the few AM radio stations in public radio. The all-news format was introduced just as Buffalo was experiencing the first of its recent snowbound winters, and the need for news quickly established WEBR as a highly successful public radio station.

The Pacifica stations—WBAI-FM (New York), WPFW-FM (Washington, D.C.), KPFT-FM (Houston, Texas), KPFA-FM (Berkeley, California), and KPFK-FM (Los Angeles)—are a group of stations that pioneered the news and public affairs format for noncommercial public

---

*WNED-FM is one of three stations licensed to Western New York Educational Foundation. WNED-FM and WEBR-AM were commercial stations purchased by the foundation to be operated as noncommercial broadcast stations. The price of approximately $1.8 million is believed to be one of the highest outright purchase prices ever paid for a noncommercial radio station.

radio.* The Pacifica Foundation, licensee of the stations in this group, has a specific social and political purpose that influences their approach to news and public affairs. The listener has little difficulty recognizing the bias, and Pacifica is open about its philosophy. These stations were especially successful during the late 1960s when the nation was highly politicized over Vietnam and Watergate. They demonstrated the vital role of broadcasting that is free from commercial restraints in their reporting of the war and surrounding issues.

The differences between WEBR and the Pacifica stations lie in both their formats and their points of view. WEBR concentrates on **hard news** reporting and investigation, similar to all-news commercial stations. WEBR takes advantage of its noncommercial status to provide more complete coverage of news and events than is possible in commercial all-news operations. The Pacifica stations present a variety of news and public affairs programs in a somewhat eclectic format. One may hear an in-depth news report on Third World nations, followed by a program on automobile maintenance with a consumer emphasis, followed by a dialogue on Marxism, followed by a gay symphony concert, followed by a lecture on socialism. Listeners cannot predict what they will hear but can usually expect the ideas expressed and programs broadcast to reflect a nonestablishment, nontraditional point of view, whether the content is hard news reporting, commentary, news analysis, documentaries, or public affairs programs. Although the majority of program ideas are oriented to the political left, Pacifica recognizes its responsibility to present unrepresented right-oriented political philosophy. They tend to leave the broad middle, the traditional point of view, to other noncommercial and commercial broadcasters.

The disadvantages of the news and public affairs format are its expense and its lack of broad appeal. Moreover, raising funds to support a broadcast service that investigates and challenges the establishment is not easy.

Community Service and Public Access

Often considered the only legitimate format for public radio, community service and public access programming is essentially directed at the specific needs of unserved or underserved minorities. The programs are designed to provide basic information needed for social

---

*The Pacifica stations were founded in 1949 in Berkeley, Calif. All of the stations are qualified for financial support from the Corporation for Public Broadcasting, but only one—KPFT-FM in Houston—is a member of the national public radio system. Primary support for Pacifica stations comes from listener donations, and the stations generally refuse support from business and industry.

and economic survival and an opportunity for the public to use radio service to vent emotions or solicit support for opinions. KBBF-FM (Santa Rosa, California) is one of the few minority-owned public radio stations in America.* Its programming is directed primarily to Spanish-speaking and bilingual audiences in the Santa Rosa Valley. This station will soon become a major production center for a network of radio stations serving the Spanish-speaking farm workers in California and other special-interest constituencies within the Latino community.

KYUK-FM (Bethel, Alaska), licensed as a community station to Bethel Broadcasting Co., serves the special needs of its community with programs including the broadcast of personal messages to individuals who are isolated by climate and geography. KEDB-FM (Ramah, New Mexico) is licensed to the Ramah Navaho School Board and serves the special needs of the Indian reservation by providing instructional services and specific education in the culture and history of the Navaho Indians.

One of the best examples of a more diversified community service format station is KPBS-FM (San Diego). The station programs information of interest to and needed by citizens of San Diego. This station has led the nation in the development of bilingual programs for local and national distribution (National Public Radio's *En Folke Nacionale* is produced at KPBS); they developed a western regional weekly news magazine, *Pacific Weekend*; and they multiplex SCA subcarrier services for the print-handicapped.† Local programs include city council hearings and comprehensive local news coverage. Music programming is varied and includes folk, jazz, and classical. The current general manager of KPBS-FM has not only carefully designed the program service to meet needs of the community, but also led the public broadcasting industry in hiring women, minorities, and the handicapped as producers, engineers, and administrators. No matter how obvious the justification for selecting this format appears to be for public broadcast stations, few managers are able to successfully merge the components of community service and broadcasting to make it work. KPBS-FM is a rare example.

The community service and public access format is highly indi-

---

*KBBF-FM is licensed to the Bilingual Broadcasting Foundation. The station was established by support from the National Campaign for Decency of the Roman Catholic Church and was set free to develop its own support in the community. While the station struggles to survive, it has become a major training center for Spanish-speaking personnel for local public radio stations and National Public Radio.

---

†The FCC authorizes certain FM stations to provide multiplex services by transmitting two or more signals in the same channel.

vidualized. As such, it is often so highly specialized that it fails to serve the broader needs of the community. When a community can be defined as specifically as those cited, it is reasonable to use a public resource such as airwaves to deliver that service. The difficulty with the community service and public access format is that it frequently becomes the instrument of a vocal minority but often fails to reach the people who need it. People scream at people about a need that the people who are being screamed at already know exists. It accomplishes little beyond catharsis for the speaker. Those who could actually do something about the need listen to a different radio format, and those who are in need are likely to be so bored by discussion of issues they are already familiar with that they also listen to something else.

Eclectic

The most common format in public radio is the eclectic format, which is based on the premise that public radio should have a little something for everyone. Although these stations will occasionally emphasize one theme in their format, one can expect anything from a symphony concert to a school board meeting, to jazz, to cooking lessons, to folk music, to news, to soul music, to lectures on almost any topic. Increasingly, public radio stations are adopting a version of the eclectic format or the dual format. Many listeners enjoy the experience of turning on a radio station with the knowledge it might be broadcasting a concert, a lecture by Herbert Marcuse, a community forum, or a discussion of motorcycle riding. An essential requirement for this format is good quality and logic of program sequence. Listeners can develop a dependence on a program service that delivers a variety of programs as long as they can reconcile its logic and theirs in program sequence.

The key to a format with a variety of sounds is achieving continuity: making the diverse parts a whole. The eclectic is the most difficult to design of all radio formats. A logical program sequence is one that enables the listener to follow a diversified format from one program to another with a sense of appropriateness. This logic comes from carefully planned program blocks that lead from one set of ideas or listening experiences to another style of presentation. Listeners must be able to anticipate what they will hear when tuning to the station. The program manager of an eclectic station must satisfy that expectation by programming in such a way that listeners identify that station whenever they tune that frequency on the dial.

The critical difference between a successful eclectic format and an unsuccessful one is whether the listener can expect a logical sequence of diverse programs or a hodgepodge of programs that are put on the air at the whim of a programmer who is constantly attempting to keep the listener off balance. In communities in which commercial stations rely primarily on popular or **beautiful music**, the eclectic public radio service provides an interesting variety of options for listeners who will be attracted by the station's diversity.

KCRW-FM (Santa Monica, California) is one of the best examples of an eclectic format.* It programs significant segments of jazz, classical music, folk music, esoterica, coverage of local school board and city council meetings, Santa Monica College sports, political opinion, arts news, and music/talk mixes, such as its *Morning Becomes Eclectic*. Although this format may seem to be the hodgepodge for which public broadcasting is notorious, actually it is not. The manager of the station, Ruth Hirschman, one of the most brilliant programmers in public radio, achieves both continuity and diversity. People who listen to KCRW know what to expect when they tune to the station.

The manager of KCRW carefully selects the programs broadcast on the station to reflect the interests of Santa Monica and the various other beach communities on Los Angeles's west side. She also counter-programs other public radio stations. Working on the premises that the community served by KCRW has unique needs and interests and that the station can offer what is not available on other public radio stations, the daily schedule follows the rhythm of life of beach communities using counterprogramming for its anchor points.

The dual format appeared recently in public radio. This format is similar to the eclectic format but concentrates on two specific program forms—such as news and jazz. The dual format concentrates on building two distinct but hopefully comparable audiences for the station. WEBR-AM (Buffalo) is all-news during the day and jazz at night; no attempt is made to mix the two formats. WUWM-FM (Milwaukee) is also news and jazz. During the early morning and late-afternoon **dayparts** (**drivetime**), the station broadcasts news; late mornings, afternoons, and evenings are jazz. The manager of WUWM includes one or two jazz recordings in the news **wheel** to provide continuity and tries to maintain similarity in announcing style for news and jazz. Continuity of style and an occasional reminder of both formats during the news and music segments provide the essential glue for the dual program format.

Instructional

The instructional format was at one time the dominant format of noncommercial educational licensees. Some public radio stations licensed to school boards still use their radio stations to broadcast classroom instructional programs, but in-school programming has generally moved to public television to gain the advantage of visuals. WBEZ-FM

*KCRW-FM is licensed to Santa Monica Community College. The majority of staff are professional or community volunteers; however, some students work at the station for college credits.

(Chicago), KBPS-AM (Portland), and KLON-FM (Long Beach, California) are prime examples of the radio instructional format.* These stations broadcast other public radio program material but designate a part of their broadcast day for instructional broadcasts.

KLON, for example, broadcasts instructional programs for grades kindergarten through six. These broadcasts are designed for use by teachers as part of courses in literature, health, bilingual education, language arts, science, music, and social studies. They broadcast nine full series of programs for grades one to three and eighteen radio broadcast series for grades four to six. Instructional broadcasting is designed specifically to be used in the classroom. In-school radio programs provide support for the teacher but require a teacher to be in the classroom with a teacher's guide to coordinate the instructional programs being broadcast.

NATIONAL PUBLIC RADIO

Many public radio stations are members of National Public Radio (NPR). This system of more than 200 noncommercial, nonprofit radio stations broadcasts to communities in forty-seven states, Puerto Rico, and the District of Columbia. Each station, itself a production center, contributes programming to the entire system. Each station meets the distinct needs of its own community by mixing locally produced programs with those transmitted from the national production center.

NPR is a private nonprofit corporation serving the nation's individual public radio stations and is America's only nationwide interconnected system of public radio stations. As a national production center, it distributes informational and cultural programming to member stations daily. Funds for the operation of National Public Radio and for the production, acquisition, and distribution of radio programs come from corporate **underwriting**, private foundations, government agencies, the Corporation for Public Broadcasting, and member stations.

National Public Radio is a necessary part of whatever format is selected by its member stations because the program service of NPR provides radio stations with unique programming in news, public affairs, art, music, and drama. The quality of programs produced by NPR and by member stations for national distribution enhances the quality of local service provided by the individual stations. NPR's nightly news program, *All Things Considered,* is touted by journalists as one of America's outstanding news-journalism programs.[1] The live coverage of the

---

*WBEZ-FM is licensed to the Board of Education, city of Chicago; KLON-FM is licensed to the Long Beach Unified School District; and KBPS-AM is licensed to Burson Polytechnic School.

Panama Canal debates by NPR marked the first time that the United States Senate allowed live, gavel-to-gavel coverage of its deliberations.

NPR also provides stations with other special-audience program materials such as in-depth reporting on education, coverage of live music and arts events, bilingual Spanish news features, new radio drama productions, and live coverage of Senate and House committee hearings. The NPR program service will be greatly enhanced when earth satellite distribution provides better quality transmission of existing programs and multichannel capacity for four to twenty-four different programs in stereo or monaural sound (projected to begin in 1980).

Public radio stations are not required to use any given number of national programs. Each station selects the programs that most closely fit its format. The quality of national programs frequently entices stations to include programs from NPR that differ markedly from local station efforts. These programs are usually advertised as specials and justify interruptions in the normal schedule. Currently, live events such as the Senate hearings, live concerts from the White House, or opening-night broadcasts of the Los Angeles Philharmonic constitute the most impressive of NPR's offerings.

THE FINE ARTS/CLASSICAL MUSIC FORMAT: A CASE STUDY

The largest class of public radio stations in America is that licensed to colleges and universities. The emergence of public broadcasting generated a substantial dilemma for many of those institutional licensees. Traditionally, campus radio stations were training grounds for journalism and broadcasting students and assorted "radio freaks"— students who were interested in careers in broadcasting or looking for an extracurricular activity. When the Corporation for Public Broadcasting (CPB), under a mandate from Congress in 1969, began its campaign to develop a national public radio system, it found many of the most desirable noncommercial licenses were held by colleges and universities. CPB provided special grants to selected holders of educational and noncommercial licenses to explore the potential of the institution and the community to support a public radio service. The grant to the University of Southern California (USC) for $15,000 was given with the stipulation that USC would hire a full-time manager and an engineer to explore the potential of KUSC-FM.*

---

*The basic requirements for stations to qualify for CPB assistance has changed drastically since that time. Individuals interested in starting or upgrading public radio services should write to the Corporation for Public Broadcasting, 1111 Sixteenth Street, N.W., Washington, D.C. 20036.

The University of Southern California has held the license for KUSC-FM since 1946. Captain Alan Hancock—an oil wildcatter, marine biologist, and amateur musician—decided it would be nice to share the concerts of his string ensemble with the citizens of California, or at least those few with FM receivers in 1946. Over the years the station served as an outlet for Captain Hancock and variously as laboratory for the Broadcast Communications Department of the university and toy for any given generation of students. The station was on the air from 4 to 24 hours per day, and the budget seldom exceeded $4,500 per year. It was typical of most college campus radio stations, which fluctuated between ingenuity and disaster.

In 1972 USC hired the first full-time employee to manage its radio station. The original mandate for the general manager was (1) to provide continuity in management, (2) to work with the students who operated the station, and (3) to explore the potentials of the station for the University and the community. The students had great ambitions for the station and encouraged the manager to expand the service of KUSC to the broader public and to concentrate on building the station into a formidable public radio station in the then-fledgling public radio system. A chief engineer was hired, and these two full-time employees, working with a budget of $22,000 and about twenty-five loyal undergraduates, began building a full-service public radio station.

The first requirement was to convince the university to adequately fund the operating budget of the station and invest in capital improvements. Second, it was necessary to plan the transition of the staff from students to professionals. Third, a decision was required on a format that would have the greatest potential for success in a market already saturated by more than eighty-two radio stations, six of them public.

After four years of advocacy, the manager succeeded in persuading the university to invest $150,000 in capital improvements and to dramatically increase the operating budget from about $26,000 to nearly $100,000. CPB granted KUSC $775,000, and in December 1976 new facilities became operational. Two years later, in 1978, KUSC had thirty full-time professional employees, a budget of nearly $900,000, an audience that had grown from about 30,000 persons weekly (as measured by Arbitron) in 1976 to 224,000 in 1978, making it the most-listened-to individual public radio station in America.[2] The audience for the station nearly equaled the audience for its commercial classical music competitor and captured the imagination of both the broadcast industry and the public radio community.

Goals and Objectives

The strategies employed to achieve success in such a highly competitive business as radio are grounded in the basic nature of the medium. People listen to radio *stations,* not radio *programs.* They compare stations with stations, not programs with programs. Therefore, the successful radio broadcaster builds a sound image that distinguishes one station from all the others. KUSC's management set an ambitious goal of becoming the premiere fine arts and classical music broadcast station in America — the station that would set the standard against which all public or commercial classical music stations would be measured.

The format includes a significant number of nonmusic features and programs. The program service emphasizes quality in performance, language, and writing. A careful integration of high-quality news, cultural affairs, and modular features on the arts, drama, poetry, and literature enables KUSC to develop a consistent sound image with a variety of aural experiences. Although 85 percent of its programming is music, the format also needs local, national, and international news about the arts. Ara Guzelimian, director of arts and music programs for KUSC, believes that arts are not an escape from everyday life but rather a vital part of daily living. Toward that end, KUSC finds it consistent with the music and arts programs to include significant news and public affairs programs from NPR and plans the addition of local news and cultural events analysis teams to complement its national news programs.

An example of the interruption of KUSC music programming was the live broadcast of the Senate debates on the Panama Canal. The debate lasted for several days and was broadcast in the Pacific time zone from 6 A.M. to 2 P.M. each day. This significant event, the first Senate deliberations opened to full coverage by public radio, was too important to withhold from the citizens of Los Angeles no matter how great the protests from the classical music fans.

KUSC also interrupts music for presidential speeches (seldom available on commercial FM), congressional hearings that affect the lives of people who live in Los Angeles, and national events that feature live discussions of significant national and international issues (such as the National Press Club). Statewide coverage of events is provided by the radio news bureau of the Association of California Public Radio Stations, and local news will be added when appropriate staff members can be underwritten and hired. Part of the mission of KUSC is to present the arts in the context of the world from which they emerge. The connection between social and political events as presented in news and events coverage and the music and arts programs — still the primary substance of KUSC's broadcasts — is an essential ingredient of the KUSC program service.

Competition

There are more than eighty commercial and noncommercial radio stations in the Los Angeles market sharing a market of nearly ten million persons, the second largest in the United States. Establishing a new service in a market served by more than eighty radio stations and capturing a portion of that audience is a major challenge.

The primary competition for KUSC is a commercial classical music service with a long and well-established tradition as "the" classical AM and FM music source in Los Angeles. Changes in ownership over the years left the stations in the hands of individuals who did not take seriously the broadcast audience for traditional classical music. The quality of tapes, recordings, and equipment was poor. Little attention was paid to details of programming or an erratic **automation** system. Increases in the number of commercials compromised the integrity of the music programming. First shorter works, then movements of major works, then themes from movements of major works began to dominate the programming. A lack of respect for the music and an increasing number of tasteless commercials offended not only the dedicated classical music listener but also casual listeners.

AM and FM services were duplicated for as much time as the Federal Communications Commission (FCC) allowed under its nonduplication guidelines. The FM service included more broadcasts of complete works than did the AM service, but the maximum commercial load allowed (and capable of being sold by the stations) dictated the time left for music presentations.

KUSC decided to counter with a program service emphasizing quality in all aspects of programming. Quality of signal, quality of performance, quality of information about the music, and quality of nonmusic broadcast programs were stressed. The result was an apparent return to radio by many classical music listeners who had been alienated by the commercial AM and FM services. While KUSC's audiences grew from 30,000 to 230,000 in less than two years, the commercial FM station maintained its audience or grew slightly in listenership. This phenomenon suggests that KUSC shares a large part of the audience with the commercial FM classical station; that KUSC helps stabilize the audience for classical music radio by providing an alternative classical format for listeners to select if they are dissatisfied with a given program; and that listeners turned away from the classical format to another format such as beautiful music before KUSC emerged.

Another competitive element related to programming strategy was dial location. The FM commercial classical music station was adjacent to KUSC on one side of the broadcast band and KPFK—the Pacifica station that programmed a substantial quantity of classical music until the emergence of KUSC—on the other. The task of creating a sound image that would make it impossible for listeners to confuse KUSC with either of the other stations was enormous.

Since classical music listeners are usually highly critical, KUSC designed its music service to cater to the discerning tastes of the dedicated concert music listener. The programming of all classical works emphasizes complete and exemplary performances by the most respected musicians. Care is taken to place each work in the context of what precedes and follows it. The style and content of announcing are intended to lead the listener to new listening experiences. The audience should be able to recognize the difference in sound between KUSC and its commercial competition as easily as they can distinguish between a high-quality amateur performance and a performance by the premiere concert orchestra in America. The accomplishment of that objective requires not so much arrogance as dedication to quality and high standards of performance.

Staff

The transition from a completely volunteer staff (mostly students) to paid professionals was tedious and long lasting. Fortunately, students assumed the leadership in suggesting that a fully professional staff was needed to provide a high-quality, competitive public broadcast service. The process of developing a staff was further complicated by low pay scales and the fact that salaries for professional public broadcast employees of colleges and universities are tied to university faculty and staff pay scales. Public radio in general also has disproportionately lower salaries than public television.

Once the classical music and fine arts format was selected, the process of choosing staff members was aided by attrition and the need for students and volunteers to have specialized skills in order to remain on the staff. One rock-and-roll **jockey** who had no background in classical music determined that, if he were to have a future with the station, he would need to educate himself in classical music. He went to the library, checked out a bundle of books about music, and is presently one of the principal programmers and announcers at KUSC. Most of the others just resigned or disappeared.

The first staff under the new management combined volunteers, students, and full- or part-time paid employees. As the expectation for a high-quality broadcast service increased in the community, it was necessary to continually upgrade the professional experience and highly specialized skills of the staff. The demand for a more experienced, more professional staff became apparent from letters and comments of listeners. As the audience for KUSC increased in sophistication, the mail regarding errors and mistakes by KUSC employees increased in volume and intensity. Staff persons who were unable to meet the expectations of the audience for informed opinion, commentary, and programming were not retained. The emphasis on excellence in performance and broadcast content forced the station to search for personnel in all areas of operation who were knowledgeable about concert music. All of the persons presently working at KUSC know, understand, and love classical music. The receptionist is an excellent composer. The director of arts

338 Part Four: Radio Programming Strategies

and music programs is an established and respected music critic for the *Los Angeles Times*. The present consultant on new program development was director of public relations and musical adviser of the New York Philharmonic and held a similar position with the San Francisco Opera and the Los Angeles Chamber Orchestra. The first consultant was the former music director of the *New York Times* station, WQXR-FM. Administrative, clerical, and engineering personnel are expected to have a working knowledge of classical music and fine arts.

To achieve balance in a staff of creative, energetic people, it is essential to hire persons who have differing points of view. Managing a group of individuals to achieve harmony and unity requires enormous patience, discipline, and sensitivity. The result, however, is a highly satisfying experience for the listener. People are a major component of KUSC's strategy to achieve a sound image that will earn a competitive edge for KUSC over its commercial competitors. Many successful commercial and noncommercial radio stations employ as few as four or five employees. KUSC's thirty people are the margin of difference in its service, and the station makes a substantial financial and personal investment in its employees.

Promotion and Development

The critical role of **promotion**, advertising, and public relations in establishing a public radio service cannot be overemphasized. All the program strategies in the world are useless if people do not know that the program service exists.

A major public relations firm was engaged to develop the promotional and public relations programs for KUSC. The senior officers of this firm were fans of the station, believed in its potential, and agreed to handle KUSC at a rate far below charges made to commercial clients.

Their first assignment was to design and implement a graphic image to complement the sound image of the studio. Next they embarked on a campaign to get every inch of print copy and electronic media coverage possible. The judicious use of meager sums of money to purchase the best possible advertising space was helpful in introducing new listeners to the station. The radio editor of a major trade paper once commented that in his career with that trade paper, he had never seen any radio station get as much ink as KUSC.

KUSC eventually internalized its public relations department and staffed it with one officer from the public relations firm. An aggressive public relations campaign is still a major component of management strategy for the station.

Fund Raising and Accountability

Another major component of the KUSC strategy is fund raising. A fatal flaw in most public broadcasting entities is the failure to provide for a diversified financial base. The design and development of a sound fund-raising program requires time and professional leadership. KUSC established a fund-raising department to solicit support from individuals in the community, foundations, corporations, institutions, government agencies, and listeners. The success of the development director can be measured by the growth of financial resources for KUSC. Although institutional support from the University of Southern California has continued to grow from $100,000 to $300,000 annually, the ratio of that contribution to the total KUSC budget has decreased from 100 percent to about 25 percent. An effective, on-air fund raiser, held twice annually, generates more than 10,000 subscribers who contribute more than $300,000 per year. More importantly, a corporate giving program that began with a few corporations investing $100 to $500 has grown to include corporate donations of $1,000 to $56,000 and more annually. The aggressive campaign to build the financial base for KUSC has increased the budget from the $100,000 per year provided by USC in 1976 to nearly $900,000 in 1978 contributed by the university, the Corporation for Public Broadcasting, business and industry, and individual listeners.

The recitation of these successes should encourage all potential public radio managers to recognize the crucial role played by fund raising and the need for a strong financial base generated from the local community. Public broadcasting is a local service. The only justification for the success of any public broadcasting station is the commitment and support of the local community. The amount of support that can be generated by a station is relative to the size, wealth, support of nonprofit organizations, and pure pride of its community. But no community can expect to generate federal and state revenues if it does not demonstrate its willingness to invest its own resources in its public broadcast service. Full financial support by the licensee or its commitment to fund raising provides the financial base essential to a service of sufficient quality to capture the attention of the community and attract listeners to a public broadcast station.

However, some institutions prohibit fund raising by their public broadcast stations. Such a decision deprives the institution and its public station of funds that are essential to the station's growth and service to the community. Academic institutions are usually the most restrictive of the public broadcasting licensees. They are usually afraid that fund raising for the public broadcasting station will become competitive with other fund-raising activities. This attitude is shortsighted and fails to acknowledge that public broadcasting and education are distinct and separate businesses. Donors are able to make distinctions between gifts to a university and gifts to a public broadcast station that is licensed to the university.

The University of Southern California allowed and encouraged KUSC to raise funds. KUSC has been able to generate substantial funds for its operation, and the university adds nearly $600,000 annually to its income as a result of KUSC's efforts. Careful coordination between KUSC and the university's development office avoids embarrassing conflicts with potential donors.

Another word of caution: some corporations are unable to make more than one gift to an entity with the same tax exemption status. Likewise, it is often difficult for a corporation to justify adding a substantial gift to the radio or television station to its contribution to another academic or administrative unit of the university (such as to the school of pharmacy or department of engineering). Such dilemmas require ingenuity to resolve, but it is possible to discover ways of funneling the money for broadcast purposes through other entities. KUSC faced such a predicament when seeking underwriting from a major corporation that makes large annual contributions each year to the university. The executive staff of the corporation suggested they give the money to the performing organization to be designated by the organization as payment for the broadcasting performance rights and costs of KUSC's production of their performances.

Finally, a major failure of many public broadcasting entities is financial accountability. Public broadcasters often get so caught up in the design and development of their program service that they neglect the establishment of sound business practices, especially financial record keeping. Lionel van Deerlin, chairman of the House Communications Subcommittee, told a gathering of public radio managers attending the Public Radio Conference in San Francisco in 1978 that the state of financial record keeping in public broadcasting was appalling. Other government agencies, corporations, and foundations also show concern about the lack of sound business procedures in the administration and accounting practices of nonprofit organizations, including public broadcasting. Corporations and managers of successful nonprofit agencies have created special management programs to provide training for nonprofit agencies that deserve financial support but lack the essential management expertise to administer grants properly.

The call for accountability in public programs by consumer activist organizations, the reduction of tax revenues, and changes in tax laws greatly reduce the amount of revenue available for nonprofit entities. As a result, government agencies, foundations, corporations, and individual donors are increasingly interested in the best use of their investments. Financial accountability serves as one measure of the effective management of limited resources. It also provides additional security against wastefulness, duplication of services, and misappropriation of funds—matters of significant current concern in American society.

KUSC maintains its own business office along with the business offices of the university to assist the university and the station in accurate records of business transactions and the administration of financial matters. The decision by KUSC to include a full-time business manager on the staff has been repaid a thousandfold.

Evaluation

KUSC has established audience goals for its service and works to build a program service to fulfill those objectives. The station believes it should reach at least 0.5 percent of the available audience of 12 million people in southern California and should have a weekly cumulative audience of 750,000 persons within five years. Every scrap of available data is used to evaluate audience reaction to the program service. Mail response, telephone response, program-guide questionnaires, direct-mail solicitation, community ascertainment, personal contact, and Arbitron ratings are basic evaluative tools.

An example of the importance of audience data in program evaluation was provided by a radical change in listenership between one rating period and the next. During one year the station had a very high weekly **cume** rating followed by a rating period with significantly lower numbers. The staff noted several things contributing to the ratings decrease, and most of the reasons for change in audience were traced to programming. First, the commercial station broadcast a program that was unavailable to KUSC that greatly reduced the Saturday morning audience. Second, a special series of programs on a contemporary classical composer, Arnold Schoenberg, was aired over KUSC during the same ratings period. Because of the low audience appeal of experimental music, that program registered the lowest rating ever for a series on KUSC. Third, the afternoon classics program had a drop in ratings because the announcer had included more than the normal quantity of new and unfamiliar music.

The strategy for combating this in the future is to identify the few programs that the competitors have that are not available to KUSC. If it is not possible to secure rights to those programs, KUSC must broadcast stronger programs opposite them. Second, the station will not broadcast a series of programs that is likely to draw a limited audience during a ratings period. This is not to imply that only "safe" programs will be broadcast, only that the timing of the broadcast of programs that are likely to have small audiences will be more carefully selected. One can afford such programs when other programs are stronger and the overall ratings are higher. Third, the daily programming will be corrected to maintain the proper balance of familiar and unfamiliar music.

Some persons argue that public broadcasting stations should not attempt to attain high ratings. That is nonsense. Ratings provide a relative measure of success, and success is a desirable objective of public broadcasting. The more individuals who are served by public radio, the better. Although public broadcasters may rely less on the number of people they reach than on the delivery of alternative program services to special audiences, it is imperative that they strive to serve the largest possible number of individuals within those areas of special interest. To aim for less is to misuse a public trust and underutilize a scarce commodity—the broadcast spectrum.

TRENDS AND FORESIGHT

Because public radio has lagged far behind public television, the next five years will be years of dramatic growth. The market for talented young broadcast programmers and administrators will be substantial. The technological and regulatory developments that are threatening television and commercial broadcasting will have less impact on public radio. It is a locally based medium of communication that will continue to survive in the era of satellites and **superstations**—despite competition from additional broadcast stations. KUSC in Los Angeles will have to compete with programs imported from WGBH-FM (Boston), KSJN-FM (St. Paul), and WILL-FM (Urbana); those stations will have to compete with KUSC's programs in their markets. However, the major audiences for public radio are local, and the familiar personalities of local stations will diminish the threat from faraway program sources.

The chief threats to public radio are lack of funding and the government bureaucracies that manage the system. Public radio is relatively inexpensive. Because it costs less, it is often difficult to convince the persons and agencies that finance public broadcasting to allocate sufficient funds to accomplish the quality of service demanded by listeners to public radio. There is also a tendency for bureaucrats to consider radio and television as one. The subtle but substantial differences between radio and television are frequently denied by bureaucrats who reduce them to a single noun—*media*. This is as disastrous as expecting a basketball team to use a football because both basketball and football are sports that use a ball. If public radio is left alone to grow with its existing structure intact, the future for it is very great.

NOTES

[1]"Consider it a Gem," *Los Angeles Times*, November 1, 1978, p. II–6. ". . . and the result is the most refreshing display of unashamed and useful curiosity about events, large and small, and about what makes people tick, and why, *that reaches us through any electronic contrivance* [emphasis supplied]. The most modest statement that can be made about *All Things Considered* is that *it towers over all other radio journalism* [emphasis supplied]."

[2]Information based on a special CPB report of data collected by Arbitron in its October/November 1978 report of radio audience estimates for the Los Angeles market.

ADDITIONAL PERIODICAL READINGS

Josephson, Larry. "Why Radio?" *Public Telecommunications Review* 7 (March/April 1979): 6–18.

Addresses Carnegie Commission's request for justification of public funding of public radio; this issue of PTR focuses entirely on radio and includes several articles on the future of public radio in the 1980s.

Mullally, Donald P. "Public Radio: Options in Programming." *Public Telecommunications Review* 6 (March/April 1978): 8–13.

Discussion of the limitations inherent in block and format programming strategies.

Robertson, James, and **Yokom, Gerald G.** "Educational Radio: The Fifty-Year-Old-Adolescent." *Educational Broadcasting Review* 7 (April 1973): 107–15.

Facts and opinions on the state of educational radio gathered in the course of visiting every NPR (NER) member station in 1972.

Simkins, Tina. "Public Radio: Coming Out of Hiding." *Educational Broadcasting* 7 (May/June 1974): 15–19.

Overview of changes in public radio since 1967.

"Stations Add Professionalism in Programming, Technology," *Television/Radio Age* (April 9, 1979): M10–M18.

Report on improvements in classical music programming and challenges posed by new technology.

Abbreviations and Acronyms

Boldface terms are explained further in the Glossary.

ACT	Action for Children's Television
ADI	**Area of dominant influence**
AFTRA	American Federation of Television and Radio Artists
AID	Arbitron Information on Demand
AIT	Agency for Instructional Television
AOR	Album-oriented rock
AP	Associated Press (news service)
AQH	**Average quarter hour**
ARB	American Research Bureau
ASCAP	**American Society of Composers, Authors, and Publishers**
BMI	**Broadcast Music, Inc.**
CBN	Christian Broadcasting Network
CEN	Central Educational Network
CM	Commercial matter
CP	Construction permit
CPB	**Corporation for Public Broadcasting**
C-SPAN	Cable-Satellite Public Affairs Network
DJ	**Disc jockey**
DMA	**Designated market area**
EEN	Eastern Educational Television Network
ENG	Electronic newsgathering
ERP	Effective radiated power
ESF	**Expanded sample frame**
ESPN	Entertainment and Sports Programming Network
FCC	Federal Communications Commission
FTC	Federal Trade Commission
G	Movie code: general audiences
GPNITL	Great Plains National Instructional Television Library
HBO	Home Box Office
HHs	**Households having sets**
HUTs	**Households using television**
ID	Station identification
INTV	Independent Television Station Association

ITNA	Independent Television News Association
ITV	**Instructional television**
LULAC	League of United Latin American Citizens
MBS	Mutual Broadcasting System
MNA	Multi-Network Area Report
MOR	Middle-of-the-road (radio music format)
NAACP	National Association for the Advancement of Colored People
NAB	National Association of Broadcasters
NAEB	National Association of Educational Broadcasters
NARB	National Association of Radio Broadcasters
NATPE	National Association of Television Program Executives
NET	National Educational Television
NOW	National Organization of Women
NPR	**National Public Radio**
NSI	Nielsen Station Index
NTI	Nielsen Television Index
O&O	**Owned and operated station**
OPT	**Operation Prime Time**
PBS	**Public Broadcasting Service**
PDG	Program Development Group
PG	Movie code: parental guidance suggested
PMN	Pacific Mountain Network
PSA	Public service announcement
PTAR	**Primetime access rule**
PTL	People That Love (religious program service)
PTL	Public Television Library
PTV	**Public television**
R	Movie code: restricted
SCA	Special Communications Authorization (by the FCC)
SECA	Southern Educational Telecommunications Association
SIP	Station Independence Program (PBS)
SPC	**Station program cooperative**
SSS	Southern Satellite Systems
TBN	Trinity Broadcasting Network
TvB	Television Bureau of Advertising
TVPC	Television Programmers' Conference
TvQ	Television Quotient (ratings for television personalities and programs reflecting both popularity and familiarity to audiences)
UPI	United Press International (news service)

Glossary

Boldface words in the definitions also appear as defined terms.

Access: Public availability of broadcast time. In some communities, one or more cable channels reserved for public use requiring only fees to cover facility costs. *See also* **Primetime Access Rule.**

Action News: Television news reporting style emphasizing news film, rapid pace, and visuals; frequently includes informal dialogue among anchors.

Actuality: An on-the-spot news report or voice of a newsmaker (frequently taped over the telephone) used to create a sense of reality or to enliven news stories.

Adaptation: A film or video treatment of a novel or a short story.

Ad Hoc Networks: Temporary national or regional hookups among stations for the purpose of program distribution.

Adjacencies: A commercial or promotional spot next to a specific program or type of program. Also programs (usually compatible in type) in consecutive time periods.

Affiliate: A commercial radio or television **station** receiving more than 10 hours per week of **network** programming. Occasionally applied to individual cable operators contracting for **pay-television** or **superstation** services, or to public stations airing noncommercial programming from the **Public Broadcasting Service** or **National Public Radio.**

Alphanumeric News Service: Television news created on a character generator and distributed as lines of text to be displayed on television receiver screens.

American Society of Composers, Authors, and Publishers (ASCAP): An organization licensing musical performance rights. *See also* **Broadcast Music, Inc. (BMI).**

Amortization: The allocation of syndicated program series costs over the period of use to spread out total tax or inventory and to determine how much each program costs the purchaser per airing.

Area of Dominant Influence (ADI):   One of 211 geographical market designations defining each television market exclusive of all others; indicates the area in which a single **station** can effectively deliver an advertiser's message to the majority of homes. ADI is Arbitron's term; Nielsen's comparable term is **designated market area (DMA).**

Ascertainment: A two-part examination of local audience needs required by the FCC to retain broadcast licenses.

Audience Flow: The movement from one program or time period to another, either on the same station or from one station to another; includes turning sets on and off. Applied to positive flow encouraged by similarity between contiguous programs.

Audimeter: Nielsen's in-home television rating meter.

Audio-Speech Capacity: A computer able to create sounds representing human speech (not very natural sounding in present state of technology).

Automation: Use of equipment, usually computerized, that reproduces material in a predesignated sequence; includes both music and commercials and produces a **log** of airings acceptable to the FCC. Also used for traffic and billing and in some television production processes.

Availability: Spot advertising positions offered for sale by a **station** or **network**.

Average Quarter Hour (AQH):   Rating showing the average percentage of an audience that tuned a radio or television **station**.

Barter: Exchange by a **station** of commercial announcements for the use of a television program (the commercials usually are aired within the program being bartered but sometimes elsewhere in a station's schedule); purpose is to eliminate the exchange of cash and thus reduce the financial commitment of a station. *Hee Haw, Lawrence Welk, Mickey Mouse Club, Mike Douglas,* and *Phil Donahue* are bartered or partially bartered programs.

Beat: The geographic area or topic-related area in which a reporter gathers news (for example, White House, state government, northern suburbs).

Beautiful Music: A radio format emphasizing low-key, mellow popular music, generally with extensive orchestration and many classic popular songs (not rock or jazz).

Bicycling: Transfer of **syndicated** or **group** program tapes or films by means of wheeled delivery services or mail (in contrast to wired or microwave transmission).

Blackout: A ban on airing an event, program, or **station's** signal. Also FCC rules for blocking imported signals that duplicate other stations' programs.

Black Week: A seven-day period during which *no* network ratings were taken until the early 1970s; generally, the week before the beginning of the fall television season, Christmas week, and a week in April and in June; programs with low **ratings** (documentaries, **reruns**) usually were programmed during this time.

Blockbusters: Special programs or big-name films that attract a lot of attention and interrupt normal scheduling; used especially during **sweeps** to draw unusually large audiences; usually exceed 60 minutes in length.

Block Programming: Several hours of similar programming placed together in the same **daypart** to create **audience flow**. *See also* **Stacking**.

Boilerplate: Syndicated program packages using low-cost **formats**.

Bonus Audience: Generally, any audience coverage for which the advertiser does not pay; specifically, households increasing the total **households using television (HUTs)** for a program as result of cable distribution.

Bridging: Beginning a successful or highly promoted program a half hour earlier than competing programs in order to draw their audiences and hold them past the starting time of the competing programs.

Broadcast Music, Inc. (BMI): A music-licensing organization created by the broadcast industry to collect and pay fees for musical performance rights; competes with **American Society of Composers, Authors, and Publishers (ASCAP)**.

Buying: Renting by **stations** of programs from **syndicators**. *See also* **Prebuying** and **Presold**.

Call Screener: Person who screens incoming calls on telephone call-in shows and performs other minor production functions as assistant to a program host.

Canned: Prepackaged or prerecorded; commonly applied to **syndicated** minilectures, automated music, commercials, and other program elements that arrive at a station preproduced.

Checkerboarding: Scheduling five **stripped** programs alternately, one each day in the same time period, that is, five different shows five days of the week; used of **primetime access** programming on **affiliates**, in any **daypart** on **independents**.

Chromakey: The mechanism for inserting one picture on top of another by electronically eliminating background of a specific frequency (usually blue).

Clearance: Acceptance of a **network** program by **affiliates** for airing; the total number of clearances governs a program's potential audience size.

Clipping: Illegally cutting off the beginning or end of programs or commercials, often for the purpose of substituting additional commercials.

Clutter: Excessive amounts of nonprogram material during commercial breaks; includes credits, IDs, **promos**, audio tags.

Commercial Load: The number of commercial minutes aired per hour.

Common Carriers: Organizations that lease transmission facilities to all applicants; includes firms that provide **network** signal distribution by telephone, microwave, and satellite.

Composite Week: An arbitrarily designated seven days of program **logs** from different weeks, reviewed by the FCC in checking on licensee program performance vs. promise.

Contemporary: FCC radio **format** term covering popular music, generally referring to rock.

Core Schedule: Two hours of programs fed to PBS member stations for simultaneous airing four nights per week; begun in 1979.

Corporation for Public Broadcasting (CPB):   Government-funded financial and administrative unit of national public broadcasting since 1968.

Correlator: An inside or telephone reporter on radio who aids the editor; frequently responsible for **actualities** for news broadcasts.

Cost per Thousand: The ratio of the cost of a commercial spot to the size of the audience, reported in thousands; basis of comparison of advertising rates among media. Other bases are cost per point and cost per person.

Counterprogramming: Scheduling programs with contrasting appeal to exploit competitors' weaknesses and lure audiences.

Critical Information Pile: The quantity of important news breaking simultaneously that causes massive alterations in planned news coverage.

Crossover: Using characters from one program series in episodes of another series.

Cume: Cumulative rating; the total number of different households that tune to a **station** at different times, generally over a one-week period; used especially in commercial and public radio, public television, and commercial sales.

Cycle: Span of news flow between repeat points in all-news radio.

Daypart: Period of two or more hours, considered as strategic unit in program schedules (for example, morning **drivetime** in radio—6 to 10 A.M.—and **primetime** in television—8 to 11 P.M.).

Dayparting: Altering programming to fit with the audience's changing activities (such as shifting from music to news during **drivetime**).

Dedicated Channel: Cable channel restricted to a single type of program or aimed at a single audience (for example, sports' or children's channels).

Demographics: Descriptive information on an audience, usually the vital statistics of age, sex, education, and income.

Demo-Tape: Demonstration tape of a program, used for preview without the expense of producing a **pilot**.

Designated Market Area (DMA):   *See* **Area of Dominant Influence (ADI)**.

Disc Jockey (DJ):   A radio announcer who introduces records.

Docudrama: Fictionalized drama of real events and people.

Downlink: Satellite-to-ground transmission path, the reverse of **uplink**.

Drivetime: In radio, 6 to 10 A.M. and 4 to 7 P.M.

Earth Station: Ground receiver/transmitter of satellite signals; when receiving, the purpose usually is to redirect those signals to a broadcast station or cable head-end equipment; most are receive-only stations.

Eclectic: Mixed; applied to varied programming in radio incorporating several types of programs; a recognized **format** in public radio.

Equal Time: An FCC policy requiring equivalent air time for candidates for public office.

Ethnic: Programming by or for minority groups (for example, Spanish-speaking, American Indians, blacks).

Exclusivity: The sole right to air a program within a given period of time in a given market; imported signals can violate exclusivity agreements.

Expanded Sample Frame (ESF):   The base unit for a sampling technique that includes new and unlisted telephone numbers.

Extraneous Wraps: Reusable closings for radio news, prerecorded by an announcer or reporter for late on-air use.

Fairness Doctrine: A policy of the FCC upheld by the Supreme Court that **stations** provide air time for opposing views on controversial issues of public importance.

Family Viewing Time: A short-lived NAB code policy reserving the first 2 hours of television primetime—7 to 9 P.M. (EST)—for programs suitable for both children and adults; later determined to be illegal (if done at the FCC's behest) by a federal court.

Feature: Radio program material other than hard news, sports, weather, stock market reports, or music. In television, generally short for theatrical films used as features.

First-Run: The first airing of a program (not counting theatrical exhibit of feature films).

Flow: *See* **Audience Flow**.

Format: Overall programming design of a **station** or specific program.

Formula: The elements that define a format.

Fringe: The television time periods adjacent to **primetime**—from 5 to 7 P.M. and 11 P.M. to midnight or later; early fringe time includes the hour from 4 to 5 P.M.

Futures: Projected episodes in a series that have not yet been produced.

Group-Owned Station: Radio or television **station** licensed to a corporation owning two or more stations.

Hammock: The position between two successful programs; they support a new or less successful program by lending their audience to it.

Hard News: Daily factual reporting of national, international, or local events. *See also* **Soft News**.

Horizontal Documentaries: Multipart treatment of a news subject spread over several successive days or weeks. *See also* **Vertical Documentaries**.

Hot Clock: *See* **Wheel**.

Households Having Sets (HHs):   Ratings industry term for the total number of homes with receiving sets (AM or FM radio, UHF or VHF television, or cable hookups), that is, total potential audience.

Households Using Television (HUTs):   Ratings industry term for the total number of sets turned on during an **average quarter hour**, that is, actual viewing audience to be divided among all **stations** in the market.

Hyping: Excessive promotion of a program or airing of special programs in order to increase audience size during a **ratings** period.

Independent: A commercial television broadcast **station** that is not **affiliated** with one of the national **networks** (by one FCC definition, carries fewer than 10 hours of network programming per week).

Instructional Television (ITV):   Programs transmitted to schools for classroom use by public television or radio stations.

Jock: *See* **Disc Jockey**.

Kiddult: Television programs appealing to both children and adults.

Kidvid: Television programs for children.

Lead-in: Program preceding others, usually intended to increase **audience flow** to the later programs.

Liners: Brief ad lib comments by **disc jockeys** between records on music radio.

Live-Feed: A program or insert coming from a network or other interconnected source without prerecording and aired simultaneously.

Local: Programs or commercials generated 50 percent or more within a station's broadcast coverage area.

Log: The official record of a broadcast day, kept by hand or automatic means such as tape, noting opening and closing times of all programs, commercials, and other nonprogram material and facts mandated by the FCC.

Long-Form: Longer than the usual length of 30 minutes for most series and 60 minutes for **specials** (for example, a 60- or 90-minute fall season introduction to a new series) or playing the entire 2 or 3 hours of a film in one evening.

Loss Leader: A program (or **format**) broadcast because management thinks it is ethically, promotionally, culturally, or aesthetically worthwhile rather than directly rewarding financially; used in image building.

Made-for-Television Movie: Feature produced especially for television, usually fitting a 90-minute or 2-hour format with breaks for commercials.

Magazine Format: A television or radio program composed of varied segments within a common framework, structurally resembling a printed magazine.

Minicam: A small, portable television camera.

Mini-Doc: A short documentary.

Minimote: A small television remote unit.

Miniseries: Series shorter than the traditional thirteen episodes.

Music Sweep: Uninterrupted period of music on music radio.

National Public Radio (NPR):   The noncommercial radio **network** service financed primarily by the **Corporation for Public Broadcasting (CPB)**; serves **affiliated** public radio stations.

National Rep(resentative):   *See* **Station Rep(resentative)**.

Network: An interconnected chain of broadcast **stations**; refers to the administrative and technical unit that distributes (and may originate) preplanned schedules of programs (for example, ABC, CBS, NBC, Mutual, PBS, NPR, HBO, Showtime).

News Block: Extended news programming; in radio, the time immediately before and after the hour when most stations program news; in television, the period between 5:30 and 7:30 P.M. (varies with market).

Off-Line: Use of program elements as they are fed from a **network** or other source.

Off-Network Syndication: Selling programs (usually series) that have appeared at least once on the national networks directly to **stations** or **pay-television**.

Open-Entry Policy: Policy of the FCC permitting **common carriers** unrestricted access to commercial satellite channels. *See also* **Retransmission Consent**.

Operation Prime Time (OPT):   An association of **stations** and producers contributing funds on a prorated basis for the production of high-quality, **first-run** drama intended for **primetime** airing.

Overnight: Radio air time in the small hours, usually from 1 to 4 A.M.

Overnights: Television **ratings** from metered homes in major cities, available the following day.

Owned-and-Operated Station (O&O):   Broadcasting **station** owned and operated by a **network** or **group**. Number of stations licensed to a network is limited basically to seven television stations (five VHF and two UHF) and seven AM and seven FM radio stations.

Pay-Cable: Cable television programming service for which the subscriber pays an extra fee over and above the normal monthly cable fee. *See also* **Pay-Television**.

Payola: Illegal payment for promoting a recording, or song, on the air. *See also* **Plugola**.

Pay-Television: An umbrella term for any programming for which a fee is paid by viewers; includes **pay-cable** and **subscription television**.

Pilot: A sample first program of a proposed television series, often longer than regular episodes; introduces characters, set, situations, and style of the program; generally accompanied by heavy promotion when aired.

Plateauing: Leveling off in successive **ratings**; can characterize a single program or an entire **station's** or **network's** programming.

Playlist: Strategically planned list of records to be played on music radio.

Plugola: Inclusion of material in a program for the purpose of covertly promoting or advertising a product without disclosing that payment of some kind was made; penalties for violating **payola** or plugola regulations may be up to a $10,000 fine and/or a year in prison for each offense. *See also* **Payola**.

Positioning: Making the audience believe one **station** is really different from its competitors; especially important for **independent** television stations and music radio stations.

Prebuying: Paying for future airings of theatrical properties while they are still in production or being shown in movie theaters. *See also* **Buying** and **Presold**.

Preemption: Cancellation of a program by an **affiliate** after agreement to carry the program, or cancellation of an episode by a **network** in order to air a news or entertainment **special**; also applied to cancellation of a commercial sold at a special preemptible price to accommodate another commercial sold at full rate.

Presold: Series episodes or film idea sold before being produced (generally related to high reputation of the producer). *See also* **Buying** and **Prebuying**.

Primetime: Television **daypart**: practically, 8 to 11 P.M. (EST) six days a week and 7 to 11 P.M. Sundays. (Technically, any three consecutive hours between 6 P.M. and midnight).

Primetime Access Rule (PTAR):   FCC rule that, in general, limits evening **network** programming to three hours of entertainment material between the hours of 7 and 11 P.M.

Program Practices Department: **Network** department that clears all programs, **promos**, and commercials before airing; responsible for administration of network guidelines on such subjects as sex, race, and profanity. Also called "standards and practices" or "continuity acceptance department." Function also performed at every station.

Promo: A broadcast advertising spot announcing a new program or episode or encouraging viewing of a **station's** or **network's** entire schedule.

Promotion: Informational advertising of programs, **stations**, or **networks**.

Psychographics: Descriptive information on the life styles of audience members; includes attitudes on religion, family, social issues, interests and hobbies, and political opinions.

Public Broadcasting Service (PBS): The noncommercial federally supported interconnection service that distributes programming nationally to member public television stations; serves as a representative of the **public television** industry.

Public Station: Noncommercial **station**; prior to 1967 called *educational station*; licensed by the FCC as a *noncommercial educational* broadcast station.

Public Television (PTV): Overall term replacing *educational television* to describe noncommercial television.

Qube: Warner Communications' two-way cable system first installed in Columbus, Ohio.

Rating: Audience measurement unit representing the percent of the total audience (whether sets on or not) tuned to a specific program (**average quarter hour** periods).

Remote: Live production from locations other than a studio (such as football games, live news events).

Rep: *See* **Station Rep(resentative)**.

Rerun: Repeat showing of a program first aired earlier in the season or some previous season. Commonly applied to episodes of series.

Retransmission Consent: Control by originating station of right to retransmit that station's signals for use by cable systems; also a proposal to require agreement from copyright holder before programs can be picked up by resale carriers (**common carriers**); issue particularly affects **superstations**, cable operators, and writers/producers. (The distintegration of the 1978–79 Communications Act **rewrite** effort along with a key 1979 FCC decision permitting an **open-entry policy** for common carriers has tabled this issue, although inadequate 1978 Copyright Act retransmission provision remains.)

Reverse Telephone Directory: A phone book arranged by addresses instead of names; can be purchased from urban telephone companies.

Rewrite: Proposed redrafting of the Communications Act of 1934, introduced in early 1970s but dropped in 1979.

Rip and Read: Simplest form of newscasting; announcer rips copy from wire service and reads it on the air.

Road-Blocking: The simultaneous airing of a program or commercial on all three networks to gain maximum exposure for the content (for example, presidential addresses, political campaign spots, and commercial spots).

Rocker: Colloquial term for a radio station with a rock music **format**.

Royalty: Compensation paid to copyright holder for the right to use copyrighted material.

Run-Through: Staging of a proposed show for preview by program executives; often replaces script for game shows.

Screener: An assistant who pre-interviews in-coming callers or guests on participatory programs. *See also* **Call Screener**.

Second Season: Traditionally the thirteen weeks of episodes (of new or continuing programs) beginning in January; vitiated by practice of on-going program changes.

Self-Transmitting Reporter: One with a "lunchbox" or miniature transmitter; does not need telephone lines to reach the broadcast studios.

Semipilot: Sample videotaped version of a proposed game show with audience and production devices (such as music) but no finished set.

Share: A measurement unit for comparing audiences; represents the percentage of total listening or viewing audience (with sets on) tuned to a given station; total shares in a designated area in a given time period equal 100 percent.

Sit-Com: *See* **Situation Comedy**.

Situation Comedy: A program (usually a half hour in length) in which stereotyped characters react to new plots or altered situations.

Small Sweeps: *See* **Sweeps**.

Soap: *See* **Soap Opera**.

Soap Opera: A serial drama generally scheduled during weekday afternoons. Advertisers (such as laundry detergent manufacturers) targeting for homemakers, dominate their advertising time.

Soft News: Opposite of **hard**, fast-breaking news; consists of features and reports that do not depend on timely airing (for example, medical reports, entertainment industry stories, hobby material).

Sound Bed: Musical background; an instrumental beginning and ending for commercials, station identifications, or other on-air talk; applied especially to radio.

Special: One-time entertainment or news program with special interest; usually applied to **network** programs that interrupt regular schedules.

Spectacular: Older term for network television one-time-only programs interrupting regular scheduling. *See* **Special**.

Spinoff: A series using a secondary character from another series as the lead (for example, *Rhoda* was a spinoff from the successful appearances of the character Rhoda in episodes of *Mary Tyler Moore*).

Stacking: Sequential airing of several hours of the same kind of programs; similar to **block programming**.

Standards and Practices Department: *See* **Program Practices Department**.

Station: Facility operated by licensee in order to broadcast radio or television signals on an assigned frequency; may be **affiliated** by contract with a **network** (for example, ABC, NPR) or may be **independent** (unaffiliated); may be commercial or noncommercial (public).

Station Program Cooperative (SPC):   The vehicle for public station participation in choosing the national program schedule carried by PBS.

Station Rep(resentative):   Firm acting as sales agent for client station's advertising time in the national market.

Step Deal: Agreement to supply funds to develop a program idea in stages from expanded concept statement to scripts to **pilot** to four or more episodes.

Stockpiling: Preemptive buying of **syndicated** programs for future use that also keeps them off the market and unavailable to competitors.

Stop Set: Interruption of music on music radio to air commercials or other nonmusic material.

Stringer: A free-lance reporter paid per story used rather than by hourly or monthly wages.

Stripping: Across-the-board scheduling; putting successive episodes of a program into the same time period every day—five days per week (for example, placing *Star Trek* every evening at 7 P.M.).

Strip Run/Strip Slot: *See* **Stripping**.

Stunting: Frequent shifting of programs in schedule; also using **long-form** for a program's introduction or character **crossovers**; goal is to attract audience attention and consequent viewership; frequently used in the week preceding the kickoff of a new fall season combined with heavy **promotion**.

Subscription Television: Over-the-air **pay-television**.

Superstation: An **independent** television **station** that has its signal retransmitted by satellite to distant cable companies for redistribution to subscribers (for example, WTBS-TV, formerly WTCG, from Atlanta, Georgia).

Sweeps: The periods each year when Arbitron and Nielsen gather audience data for the entire country; the ratings base from a sweep determines the network and station rates for advertising time until the next sweep. For television, the four times are November (fall season ratings most important, becomes ratings base for the rest of the year); February (rates fall season again plus replacements); May (end-of-year ratings); and July, when a small sweep takes place (summer replacements). Radio sweeps occur at different times and vary from two to four to six annual occasions depending on market size.

Syndication: The marketing of programs on a station-by-station basis (rather than through a **network**) to **affiliates**, **independents**, or **pay-television** for a specified number of plays; *syndicators* are companies that hold the rights to distribute programs nationally or internationally. *See also* **Off-Network Syndication**.

Syndication Barter: Practice in which advertiser rather than **station**

buys rights to **syndicated** program and barters remaining spots to stations in exchange for free airing of its own spots in the program. *See also* **Barter**.

Tease: A very brief news item or program spot intended to lure potential audience into watching or listening to the succeeding program or news story; referred to as the "teaser" when used as the introduction to a program.

Tent-Poling: Placing a highly rated program between two series with lower **ratings** (often new programs), intended to prop up the ratings of the preceding and following programs.

Transponder: One of several units on a communications satellite that both receives **uplink** signals and retransmits them as **downlink** signals. Some users lease the right from satellite operators to use entire transponder (40 mHz bandwidth); others lease only a part of a transponder's capacity.

Treatment: Prescript outline of a new program (applied especially to **soap operas**); describes characters and setting of program.

Underwriting: Grants from foundations or private corporations to cover costs of producing or airing a program or series on public television or radio.

Unduplicated: Said of programming that is not available on any other local or imported station signal in a market.

Uplink: Ground-to-satellite transmission path; the reverse of **downlink**.

Vertical Documentaries: In-depth factual treatment of a subject in many segments broadcast on the same day. *See also* **Horizontal Documentaries**.

Voicers: Stories prerecorded by someone other than the announcer or **disc jockey**.

Wheel: Visualization of the contents of an hour as a pie divided into wedges representing different content elements; used in radio to visualize a program **format**, showing designated sequences and lengths of all program elements such as musical numbers, news, sports, weather, **features**, **promos**, PSAs, commercials, IDs, and time checks.

Bibliography of Books and Reports on Programming

This is a selective, annotated listing of books, guides, reports, theses, and dissertations on broadcast programs and programming. An item is included if it contributes unique or otherwise useful insights into the factors affecting television and radio program content and programming strategy. This bibliography emphasizes publications in the decade since 1970 and includes all books, guides, reports, theses, and dissertations cited in the text. Selected annotated articles from trade and research periodicals appear at the end of each chapter to facilitate reference use.

Abel, John D. *Television Programming for Children: A Report of the Children's Television Task Force*, vol. IV. Washington, D.C.: FCC, October 1979.

The fourth volume in a series contracted by the FCC comparing the amount and scheduling of children's television programs for two television seasons, 1973–74 and 1977–78.

Adler, Richard P. *All in the Family: A Critical Appraisal.* New York: Praeger, 1979.

Anthology of scripts and critical and descriptive articles about the 1971–79 program.

Adler, Richard, and Baer, Walter S., eds. *The Electronic Box Office: Humanities and Arts on the Cable.* Palo Alto, Calif.: Aspen Institute Program on Communications and Society, 1974.

Six contributed chapters on the potential of pay-cable as an alternate programming mechanism; includes a summary chapter on the Aspen Program Conference on the Humanities and the Arts on Cable.

Alvarado, Manuel, and Buscombi, Edward. *Hazell: The Making of a TV Series.* London: The British Film Institute, 1978.

The story of the compromises that went into the making of a British peak-viewing dramatic series.

Analysis of the Causes and Effects of Increases in Same-Year Rerun Programming and Related Issues in Prime-time Network Television. Washington, D.C.: Office of Telecommunications Policy, February 1973.

Analysis of the extent, causes, and effects of reruns during primetime on the networks, including useful statistical tables.

Andrews, Bart. *Lucy & Ricky & Fred & Ethel: The Story of I Love Lucy.* New York: E. P. Dutton, 1976.

Anecdotal narrative of the I Love Lucy *program of the 1950s.*

Arbitron Company. *Research Guidelines for Programming Decision Makers.* Beltsville, Md.: Arbitron Company, 1977.

Explains how to use Arbitron radio audience reports.

Armstrong, Ben. *The Electric Church.* Nashville: Thomas Nelson, 1979.

Informal history and discussion of current trends in religious radio and television.

Armstrong, Ben, and Sheldon, LaVay. *Religious Broadcasting Sourcebook.* Morristown, N.J.: National Religious Broadcaster, 1976.

Concepts of religious broadcasting, research, operations of religious stations, religious commercials and editorials, and programming; essentially evangelical point of view, presented in a series of article reprints.

Balakrishnan, Trichur R. "A Game Theory Approach to Programming Prime Time Network Television." Ph.D. dissertation, University of Illinois, 1974.

Mathematical model of network primetime decision making using game theory; focuses on decisions intended to increase ratings in order to increase advertising rates.

Barcus, F. Earle, with Rachel Welkin. *Children's Television: An Analysis of Programming and Advertising.* New York: Praeger Special Studies, 1977.

Compilation of three content analyses done for Action for Children's Television; ACT since has issued additional studies by Barcus.

Barnes, Rey L. "Program Decision-Making in Small Market AM Radio Stations." Ph.D. dissertation, University of Iowa, 1970.

Analysis of interviews with program decision-makers at twenty stations in five midwestern states.

Barnouw, Erik. *The Sponsor: Notes on a Modern Potentate.* New York: Oxford University Press, 1978.

Scholarly essay on the development and current influence of sponsors on programming.

Barnouw, Erik. *Tube of Plenty: The Evolution of American Television.* New York: Oxford University Press, 1975.

Based on his monumental History of Broadcasting in the United States *in three volumes, this is an anecdotal history of television and the influences on it.*

Barrett, Marvin. *Rich News, Poor News: The Sixth Alfred I. duPont—*

Columbia University Survey of Broadcast Journalism. *New York: Crowell, 1978.*

Biennial survey of trends in news programming at the network and local level.

Blakely, Robert J. *The People's Instrument: A Philosophy of Programming for Public Television.* Washington, D.C.: Public Affairs Press, 1971.

Discussion of the purposes and goals of public broadcasting.

Broadcasting and the Law. Knoxville, Tenn.: Perry Publications, 1972 to date.

Twice-monthly newsletter and supplements explaining findings of the Federal Communications Commission, courts, and Congress affecting broadcast operations.

Broadcasting Yearbook. Washington, D.C.: Broadcasting Publications, 1935 to date, annual.

Basic trade directory of radio and television stations and support industries.

Brooks, Time, and Marsh, Earle. *The Complete Directory of Prime Time Network TV Shows: 1946–Present.* New York: Ballantine, 1979.

Annotated directory of most network television programs with details on casts and content of the program.

Brown, Les. *The New York Times Encyclopedia of Television.* New York: The New York Times Book Company, 1977.

Descriptive and analytic comment on facts of network television programming, economics, and personalities in the 1970s.

Brown, Les. *Television: The Business Behind the Box.* New York: Harcourt Brace Jovanovich, 1971.

Detailed narrative analysis of the problems and policies of network television in 1970–71.

Cable Services Directory. Washington, D.C.: National Cable Television Association, 1978 to date, annual (title varies).

Annual directory of information on individual cable systems including amounts and types of local origination.

Cantor, Muriel G. *The Hollywood TV Producer: His Work and His Audience.* New York: Basic Books, 1972.

Unique study of working producers of primetime television programs based on interviews with eighty producers.

Clift, Charles, III, and Greer, Archie. *Broadcast Programming: The Current Perspective.* Washington, D.C.: University Press of America, 1974 to date, revised annually.

Facsimile reprints from trade and scholarly programming literature on ratings, network primetime programming schedules, network program types, local television programming, public broadcasting, radio programming, program regulation, and the role of citizen groups in broadcasting.

Cole, Barry G., ed. *Television: A Selection of Readings from TV Guide Magazine,* 2d ed. New York: Oxford University Press, 1980.

Compendium of reprints of TV Guide *articles from the 1970s.*

Cole, Barry G., and Oettinger, Mal. *Reluctant Regulators: The FCC and the Broadcast Audience,* rev. ed. Reading, Mass.: Addison-Wesley, 1978.

An analysis of the policies of the FCC and the constraints under which they are drawn. Revised edition is available only in paperback and includes index and updating chapter.

Coleman, Howard W. *Case Studies in Broadcast Management: Radio and Television,* rev. ed. New York: Hastings House, 1978.

Short case studies of problems in management decision making, many of them relating to programming.

Compaine, Benjamin M., ed. *Who Owns the Media? Concentration of Ownership in the Mass Communications Industry.* New York: Crown/Harmony, 1979.

Eight original articles providing tabular and text information on ownership of the major media, including radio, television, and cable.

Comstock, George; Chaffee, Steven; Katzman, Natan; McCombs, Maxwell; and Roberts, Donald. *Television and Human Behavior.* New York: Columbia University Press, 1978.

Substantial overview of the social and behavioral effects of television; summary of the research literature.

Cowan, Geoffrey. *See No Evil: The Backstage Battle over Sex and Violence in Television.* New York: Simon and Schuster, 1979.

The story of the legal battle over the family viewing hour written by one of the lawyers who took part.

David, Nina. *TV Season.* Phoenix, Ariz.: Oryx, 1976 to date, annual.

Annotated guide to the previous season's commercial and public network and major syndicated television programs.

Dessart, George. *Television in the Real World: A Case Study Course in Broadcast Management.* New York: Hastings House, 1978.

A simulated case study of a new VHF television station with sixty-five pages on programming issues.

Duncan, James. *American Radio*. Kalamazoo, Mich.: Gilmore Advertising, semiannual.

Reference source on Arbitron and Burke audience, programming, and sales statistics on both national and local market levels.

Ellens, J. Harold. *Models of Religious Broadcasting*. Grand Rapids, Mich.: Williams B. Eerdmans, 1974.

Discussion of programmatic approaches with many case studies of religious programming past and present.

Epstein, Edward J. *News from Nowhere: Television and the News*. New York: Random House, 1973.

A study of gatekeeping in the television news process at the networks based on 1969–70 research.

Federal Communications Commission. *Annual Programming Report for Commercial Television Stations*. Washington, D.C.: FCC, 1973 to date, annual.

Analysis of annual reports on programming filed by all commercial stations, providing national and per-market data on nonentertainment content noting proportion locally produced.

Fisher, Michael G. "A Survey of Selected Television Station Program Managers: Their Backgrounds and Perceptions of Role." M.A. thesis, Temple University, 1978.

Survey of 160 members of the National Association of Television Program Executives on personal experiences, background, and position in management hierarchies.

Gans, Herbert J. *Deciding What's News: A Study of CBS Evening News, NBC Nightly News, Newsweek and Time*. New York: Pantheon, 1979.

Sociological analysis of the journalists and their day-to-day decision making in developing a cohesive news policy.

Gates, Gary Paul. *Air Time: The Inside Story of CBS News*. New York: Harper & Row, 1978.

Gossipy "inside" review of the personalities behind twenty years of CBS domination of network journalism.

Gerrold, David. *The World of Star Trek*. New York: Ballantine Books, 1973.

Account of how the series concept was developed. Similar to The Making of Star Trek *by Stephen E. Whitfield and Gene Roddenberry, New York: Ballantine, 1968. See also David Gerrold's* The Trouble with Tribbles, *New York: Ballantine, 1973, about the creation, sale, and production of one episode of* Star Trek.

Gohring, Ralph J. "Influences on a Children's Program Decision-Maker on a National Commercial Television Network." Ph.D. dissertation, Ohio State University, 1975.

Analysis of one network's children's program decision making based primarily on participant observation and interviews with a network vice-president.

Halberstam, David. *The Powers That Be.* New York: Alfred A. Knopf, 1979.

Inside history of four of the largest media institutions in America including CBS; emphasizes the role of Paley and his influence on CBS's programming.

Hall, Claude, and Hall, Barbara. *The Business of Radio Programming.* New York: Billboard Publications, 1977.

Informal analysis of radio station management with focus on programming; includes verbatim interviews with key industry figures.

Head, Sydney W., ed. *Broadcasting in Africa: A Continental Survey.* Philadelphia: Temple University Press, 1974.

A survey of all broadcasting systems in continental Africa; over thirty authors.

Head, Sydney W. *Broadcasting in America: A Survey of Television and Radio,* 3d ed. Boston: Houghton Mifflin, 1976.

Basic analytic reference text on American broadcasting. (A 4th edition is anticipated in 1981.)

Heighton, Elizabeth J., and Cunningham, Don R. *Advertising in the Broadcast Media.* Belmont, Calif.: Wadsworth, 1976.

The economic underpinning of broadcast programming.

Johnson, Joseph S., and Jones, Kenneth K. *Modern Radio Station Practices,* 2d ed. Belmont, Calif.: Wadsworth, 1978.

Radio station programming from a practical management perspective.

Johnson, Nicholas. "Broadcasting in America: The Performance of Network Affiliates in the Top 50 Markets," 42 FCC 2d. (*Reports,* 1973): 1–72.

A case study of stations in three states—Arkansas, Louisiana and Mississippi—prepared as a statement of dissenting opinion by retiring Commissioner Johnson and his staff.

Johnson, William O., Jr. *Super Spectator and the Electric Lilliputians.* Boston: Little, Brown, 1971.

Book-length collection of five-part series from Sports Illustrated *(1969–70) exploring the impact of television on sports and vice versa.*

Katzman, Natan. *Program Decision in Public Television: A Report for the CPB/NCES Programming Project.* Washington, D.C.: National Association of Educational Broadcasters, 1976.

Statement on program strategy in national, local, and school public broadcasting.

Katzman, Natan, and Wirt, Kenneth. *Public Television Programming by Category: 1976.* Washington, D.C.: Corporation for Public Broadcasting, 1977.

Latest in biennial series on national and local programming trends in public television, including ITV; tables and charts.

Krasnow, Erwin G., and Longley, Lawrence D. *The Politics of Broadcast Regulation,* 2d ed. New York: St. Martin's Press, 1978.

Introduction to the five determining institutions in regulatory policy; includes five case studies, two of which deal with program content.

LaGuardia, Robert. *The Wonderful World of TV Soap Operas.* New York: Ballantine Books, 1974.

Details on a program genre.

Larson, James. "America's Window on the World: U.S. Network Television Coverage of International Affairs, 1972–1976." Ph.D. dissertation, Stanford University, 1978.

Empirical description of network coverage of international affairs, comparing coverage of Third World and developed nations and analyzing influence of technical structure on newsgathering.

Lichty, Lawrence W., and Topping, Malachi C. *American Broadcasting: A Source Book on the History of Radio and Television.* New York: Hastings House, 1975.

Collection of more than ninety readings and dozens of tables including 150 pages on programming developments.

MacFarland, David T. *The Development of the Top 40 Radio Format.* New York: Arno Press, 1979.

Reprinted doctoral dissertation on the philosophies and policies governing the development of the top forty format.

Mankiewicz, Frank, and Swerdlow, Joel. *Remote Control: Television and the Manipulation of American Life.* New York: Times Books, 1978.

Informed critical review of programming controversies.

Manning, Willard G., Jr. *The Supply of Prime-Time Entertainment Television Programs,* memorandum no. 152, Stanford, Calif.: Center for Research in Economic Growth, 1973.

An economic and policy analysis of program supply and domestic syndication, the competitiveness of supply, and prospects for cable.

Mayer, Martin. *About Television.* New York: Harper & Row, 1972.

Examines the decision-making process as one part of a review of the television industry.

McAlpine, Dennis B. *The Television Programming Industry.* New York: Tucker Anthony and R. L. Day, January 1975.

Analysis of costs to the networks of primetime programming since 1969; predicts a rise in fees paid by the networks to program suppliers.

Metz, Robert. *CBS: Reflections in a Bloodshot Eye.* Chicago: Playboy Press, 1975.

History of the CBS radio and television network from its inception to 1975 from an insider's perspective.

Metz, Robert. *The Today Show.* Chicago: Playboy Press, 1977.

Anecdotal narrative of an important television program.

Milam, Lorenzo W. *Sex and Broadcasting: A Handbook on Starting a Radio Station for the Community,* 3d ed. Los Gatos, Calif.: Dildo Press, 1975.

An antiestablishment guide for prospective station licensees providing useful information on management, regulation, and programming.

Miles, Daniel J.; Miles, Betty T.; and Miles, Martin J. *The Miles Chart Display of Popular Music: Volume II, 1971–1975.* New York: Arno Press, 1977.

Week-by-week graphs of the chart history of nearly 10,000 records and 2,300 artists; one of the bibles of music radio programming.

Miller, Merle, and Rhodes, Evan. *Only You Dick Daring! How to Write One Television Script and Make $50,000,000.* New York: William Sloane Associates, 1964.

Inside humorous account of the workings of television from the writer's perspective using one program proposal as a case study.

Morgenstern, Steve, ed. *Inside the TV Business.* New York: Sterling, 1979.

Eight chapters by outstanding industry figures on aspects of network programming.

NAB Legal Guide to FCC Broadcast Rules, Regulations and Policies. Washington, D.C.: National Association of Broadcasters, 1977. Regularly updated.

Loose-leaf one-volume compilation of selected FCC broadcasting regulations (many on programming) with analysis and commentary designed for station managers.

Noll, Roger G.; Merton, J. Peck; and McGowan, John J. *Economic Aspects of Television Regulation.* Washington, D.C.: The Brookings Institution, 1973.

Chapters on new technology and institutional impacts on FCC regulation of commercial, public, and cable television.

Owen, Bruce; Beebe, Jack H.; and Manning, Willard, Jr. *Television Economics.* Lexington, Mass.: Lexington Books, 1974.

Scholarly study analyzing the economic workings of the television industry with heavy emphasis on program supply using economic modeling.

Paley, William S. *As It Happened: A Memoir.* New York: Doubleday, 1979.

Personal reminiscences of an important figure in broadcast history; includes remarks on programming strategy with numerous annecdotal examples.

Pearce, Alan. *NBC News Division: A Study of the Costs, the Revenues, and the Benefits of Broadcast News* and *The Economics of Prime Time Access.* New York: Arno Press, 1979.

Reprints of a doctoral dissertation on the economics of news and sports programs telecast on NBC in the 1969–70 period, and an economic analysis of primetime prepared for the FCC.

Powers, Ron. *The Newscasters.* New York: St. Martin's Press, 1977.

An expose of the trends behind the scenes in television news; includes attack on the role of program consultants, influence of advertising, and encroachment into journalism of entertainment values.

Quaal, Ward L., and Brown, James A. *Broadcast Management: Radio, Television,* 2d ed. New York: Hastings House, 1976.

Structures and processes in broadcast management covering both local and network programming for radio and for television.

Quinn, Sally. *We're Going to Make You a Star.* New York: Simon and Schuster, 1975.

Revealing tale of a network's corporate lack of interest in their news anchors.

Radio Program Department Handbook: A Basic Guide for the Program Director of a Smaller Operation. Washington, D.C.: National Association of Broadcasters, n.d.

A booklet on small-market radio programming practices.

Read, William H. *America's Mass Media Merchants.* Baltimore: Johns Hopkins University Press, 1976.

Narrative description of American commercial film, video, and print media active overseas.

Report on Prime-Time Network Television, and *Report on Daytime Network Television*. New York: Batten, Barton, Durstine & Osborn, Inc., annual.

> *Booklet reports on the upcoming network season stressing details of interest to advertisers on program trends.*

Robertson Associates, Inc. *Local Station Utilization of PBS Programming: A Study for the TV Manager's Council of NAEB*. Washington, D.C.: National Association of Educational Broadcasters, 1977.

> *1977 study of public television station programming; reported in detail in Chapter 8.*

Routt, Edd. *The Business of Radio Broadcasting*. Blue Ridge Summit, Pa.: TAB Books, 1972.

> *Station operations and programming from a management perspective.*

Routt, Edd. *Dimensions of Broadcast Editorializing*. Blue Ridge Summit, Pa.: TAB Books, 1974.

> *Role, function, and practical aspects of editorializing for radio and television. See also Robert Vainowski's* In Our View, *Belmont, Calif.: Tresgatos Enterprises, 1976.*

Routt, Edd; McGrath, James B.; and Weiss, Frederic A. *The Radio Format Conundrum*. New York: Hastings House, 1978.

> *A wealth of detail on radio formats and factors affecting format decisions written from the point of view of the station manager.*

Scott, James D. *Bringing Premium Entertainment into the Home via Pay-Cable TV*, Michigan Business Reports, no. 61. Ann Arbor, Mich.: Graduate School of Business Administration, University of Michigan, 1977.

> *Program decision making by the pay-cable operator.*

Scott, James D. *Cable Television: Strategy for Penetrating Key Urban Markets*, Michigan Business Reports, no. 58. Ann Arbor, Mich.: Graduate School of Business Administration, University of Michigan, 1976.

> *Expansion of television into large cities by means of innovative programming.*

Shanks, Robert. *The Cool Fire: How to Make It in Television*. New York: Norton, 1976.

> *Anecdotal overview of how network television works, emphasizing producers and production but indirectly providing practical information on program decision making.*

Spence, Michael, and Owen, Bruce M. *Television Programming, Monopolistic Competition, and Welfare*, paper no. 9. Durham, N.C.:

Center for the Study of Business Regulation, Graduate School of Business Administration, Duke University, 1977.

Analysis of the biases in program selection arising under pay-television and advertiser-supported television using economic modeling.

Stedman, Raymond W. *The Serials: Suspense and Drama by Installment*, 2d ed. Norman: University of Oklahoma Press, 1977.

History of the serial dramatic form in film, radio, and television; useful case study of the development of a program genre.

Sterling, Christopher H., and Haight, Timothy R. *The Mass Media: Aspen Institute Guide to Communication Industry Trends*. New York: Praeger, Special Studies, 1978.

Includes fifty pages of historical statistics on content trends in all media with much material on radio and television programming, both public and commercial.

Sterling, Christopher H., and Kittross, John M. *Stay Tuned: A Concise History of American Broadcasting*. Belmont, Calif.: Wadsworth, 1978.

Chronological discussion of periods of radio and television history, with detailed information on programming trends for each period, including statistical tables.

Sugar, Bert Randolph. *"The Thrill of Victory": The Inside Story of ABC Sports*. New York: Hawthorn Books, 1978.

Anecdotal narrative of the people and programming of network television's most successful sports operation.

The Television Audience. Northbrook, Ill.: A. C. Nielsen Company, 1959 to date, annual.

Trends in television programming and audience viewing patterns.

Television Broadcast Policies: Hearings, serial 95–60. U.S. Senate, Committee on Commerce, Science and Transportation, May 1977.

Wide-ranging analysis of network program policies for both entertainment and journalistic material.

Thompson, Lawrence D. "Trends and Issues in Commercial Prime Time Television—An Analysis of Network Programming, 1966–1976." Ph.D. dissertation, Michigan State University, 1977.

Analysis of the trends at the three networks in primetime programming using an eight-program typology.

Tuchman, Gaye. *Making News: A Study in the Construction of Reality*. New York: The Free Press, 1978.

Sociological analysis of print and broadcast journalism process and product.

Tuchman, Gaye, ed. *The TV Establishment: Programming for Power and Profit.* Englewood Cliffs, N.J.: Prentice-Hall, 1974.

Critical anthology of journalistic and research articles on news and entertainment network programming.

Veith, Richard. *Talk-Back TV: Two Way Cable Television.* Blue Ridge Summit, Pa.: TAB Books, 1976.

Informal assessment of pay-cable and interactive cable emphasizing technology and content.

Virts, Paul H. "Television Entertainment Gatekeeping: A Study of Local Television Program Directors' Decision-Making." Ph.D. dissertation, University of Iowa, 1979.

Analysis of types of programmers based on strategies used in purchase and retention of a hypothetical syndicated program series, by twenty-eight midwestern station programmers.

Wakshlag, Jacob J. "Programming Strategies and Television Program Popularity for Children." Ph.D. dissertation, Michigan State University, 1977.

Quantitative analysis of the characteristics that predict children's program popularity with other children.

Warren, Edward A. "Programming for a Commercial Station," in *Television Station Management,* ed. Yale Roe. New York: Hastings House, 1964.

Collection of seventeen articles by professional broadcasters emphasizing programming and sales management; this chapter covers commercial television station programming practices.

Wolf, Frank. *Television Programming for News and Public Affairs: A Quantitative Analysis of Networks and Stations.* New York: Praeger, 1972.

A research study of factors affecting the quantity and proportion of news and public affairs programming on commercial television stations.

Wolper, David L., and Troupe, Quincy. *The Inside Story of TV's 'Roots.'* New York: Warner Books, 1978.

Network television's most-watched special series, showing planning, production, and network decision-making stages.

Yellin, David G. *Special: Fred Freed and the Television Documentary.* New York: Macmillan, 1973.

Study of the late NBC executive producer's day-to-day decisions and influence.

Index to Program Titles

This is a guide to specific television and radio programs, episodes, and films mentioned in the text.

General Index

Networks (continued)
news, 205, 290; nonprimetime programs, 189–205; owned and operated stations, 68, 107–109, 111, 112; pay-television, 221–240; primetime programs, 101, 167–186; promotion, 45, 101, 111, 172, 185; public radio, 315; public television, 92, 151, 152, 158, 207, 219; radio, 262, 315; regional, 23, 152–153, 211; relations with reps, 130–131; second season, 172; selection and evaluation of programs, 23–24, 170–175; specials, 181–182; sports, 73; Standards and Practices Department, 199–200. *See also* ABC; CBN; CBS; Commercial television networks; MBS; NBC; NPR; PBS; PTL; TBN

New York Times, 9, 12, 45, 178

News: affiliates, 57, 93, 95, 97–99, 102, 134–135; all-news radio, 13–14, 289–309; bulletins, 9; cable, 237, 257; consulting on, 126, 134–137; counterprogramming, 139; features, 290–292, 294, 296–298; hard news, 290–291; independent stations, 78–80, 97; local, 24–25, 127, 135; network, 23, 97–98, 205; newscasts, 135, 139; on music stations, 26, 267, 276–277, 306–308, 331; production elements, 136–137; and public affairs, 23, 25, 57; public television, 160; reps, 135; sports, 290–293, 299, 309; superstations, 256–257; on talk stations, 93, 313–314; teasers, 291; traffic, 292; weather, 292, 293, 298–299

Newspaper Guild, 300
Newsteams, 99
Newstime, 236
Newsweek, 193
Nickelodion, 236
Nielsen, 74, 85, 93, 128, 175–178; audimeters, 132, 177; *Multi-Network Area Report* (MNA), 178; *Network Programs by DMA,* 133–134; Nielsen Station Index (NSI), 134–135, 175–177; Nielsen Television Index (NTI), 132, 175–177; nonprimetime ratings, 190; NSI-Plus, 134–135; overnights, 132, 177–178; pay-television, 238; public broadcasting, 217; rep package, 133; *Report on Syndicated Programs,* 34, 133

Noncommercial broadcasting. *See* Public radio; Public television
Nonentertainment programming. *See* Federal Communications Commission
Nonprimetime network television, 189–205; children's programs, 189, 197–202; clearances, 190; daytime, 189, 194–197; early morning, 189, 190–194; late night, 189, 202–205

NOW, 85
NPR, 262, 325, 329, 332–333, 335

Obscenity, 60, 62
Off-network films, 230
Off-network series, 15, 37, 75, 84, 126, 139, 248
Off-network syndication, 15, 24, 74–76, 113, 114
Olympic games, 113
On-air promotion. *See* Promotion
Operation Prime Time (OPT), 86, 131, 258. *See also* Mininetworks
Overnights, 132, 177–178

Pacific Mountain Network (PMN), 153
Pacifica Stations, 327–328
Paley, William S., 16, 38–39, 44–45, 171, 175
Paramount Television Sales, 76, 77
Pay-cable. *See* Pay-television
Payne, Ancil H., 115
Pay-television, 141, 164–165, 221–240; affiliates, 235–236; audiences, 222–224, 232, 237–239; counterprogramming, 232; definition of, 221–222; demographics, 225–226; licenses, 229–230, 234; movies, 225–233; networks services, 223, 236, 237, 239, 221–239; off-network films, 230; off-network reruns, 15; promotion, 232; rates, 224–225, 236, 245; scheduling, 223, 224, 230–233; specials, 233–235; sports, 235; subscription television, 222

PBS, 92, 149, 151–152, 158, 207–219; audiences, 149, 217–218; children's programs, 198, 209, 210; core schedule, 209–210; lack of budget, 211; member stations, 208–210; politics, 208–213; Station Independence Program (SIP), 214; Station Program Cooperation (SPC), 149–150, 152; strategies, 209, 215–217; underwriting of programs, 156, 213. *See also* Public television

Personalities, 136, 139, 278–280, 301, 312. *See also* Disc jockey; Hosts
Pierce, Frederick S., 38, 171
Pilots, 131, 174–175, 196, 201
Playlists, 27, 32, 269
Pocketpiece, 176–177
Political candidates, 14, 59, 62
Positioning, 72–82
Post-Newsweek, 64, 68, 107, 114, 119
Preemption, 37, 38, 90, 95, 96, 101–102, 118, 175. *See also* Cancellation
Pressure Groups, 321–322. *See also* Action for Children's Television
Prime Time Access Rule (PTAR), 35, 59–60, 97, 126. *See* Federal Communications

Reps (continued)
  sweeps, 133; syndicated programs,
  131–135; TeleRep, 118; time zone
  strategies, 140
Reruns, 94, 97, 116, 126, 131–132; daytime
  networks, 196–197; late night, 194,
  204–205; primetime, 15; syndicated, 24
Research: attitudinal studies, 136; audience
  flow, 134–135, 139–140, 217; audience
  studies, public, 149, 160;
  computerized, 134–135; duplicated
  audiences, 127, 135; independent
  stations, 72, 84; network audiences, 38;
  overnights, 132; program tracking, 138;
  psychographics, 127, 136; radio, 28–29,
  275–276, 305–306, 336, 341; by reps,
  127–128
*Research Guidelines for [Radio] Programming
  Decision Makers,* 28–29
Retransmission consent, 63–64
Reynolds, John T., 115, 117
Rice, Crawford P., 114, 115
RKO General, 68, 117, 118, 125, 272
Robertson Associates, 144–145, 148–161
Rock music, 263–286
Rudman, 276
Rule, Elton, 171, 198

Sales, 4, 6, 71, 83; avails, 24, 77, 90, 112;
  manager, 41, 84, 302; radio, 290; reps,
  26, 128, 140, 141
Satellites, 9, 23, 63, 79–80, 115, 141, 151,
  210, 218–219, 221, 236–237, 333, 342.
  See also Cable; Earth stations
Scheduling: daytime series, 11; fall
  schedule, 169–175; nontraditional, 72,
  78–80; radio, 270–271, 290–293,
  295–298, 331; pay-television, 223–224,
  230–233; primetime series, 11, 37, 167;
  programs canceled, 169–170, 172;
  public television, 157–159; strategies
  for, 5, 10, 11–13, 112, 125, 160–161. *See
  also* Commercials
Schwartz, William A., 114, 115, 119
Science-fiction programs, 103
Scripts, 14, 45, 172–173, 196, 199–201
Second season, 172
Self-regulation. *See* Codes
Series. *See* Drama; Miniseries; Primetime;
  Programs; Situation comedies
Shares, 74, 75, 99, 133–134, 140, 265, 306
Showtime, 222–239
Silverman, Fred, 15, 16, 39, 45–46, 96, 163,
  171, 175, 178–179, 184
Situation comedies (sitcoms), 94, 97, 104,
  135, 138–140, 179, 196, 243
Skew graphs, 265–266
Small market stations, 4, 6, 27–28
Soap operas, 24, 59, 76, 95, 194–196

Social impact, attributes of, 9–10, 20. *See
  also* Prosocial content
Sources: of audience information, 26–27; of
  programs, 23–26, 150–157, 293–294,
  296–298, 314–315
Southern Educational Telecommunications
  Association (SECA), 152
Southern Satellite Systems, 245–247. *See
  also* Common carriers; Superstations
SPC. *See* Station Program Cooperative
Specials: local, 127; network, 12, 131, 173,
  175, 181–182; pay-television, 233–235;
  public television, 216, 217–218; sports,
  25, 72–73, 75, 80–81, 102–104, 111, 113,
  115, 127, 131; superstations, 252,
  254–255
Spectacular, 182
Spinoffs, 15, 39, 181, 183–184
Sports: independents, 80–81; network, 113,
  131, 181, 183, 197; news, 290–293, 299,
  309; pay-television, 235; radio,
  290–293, 299, 309; superstation, 254
Stacking, 77–78
Standards and Practices Department, 61,
  184, 199–200. *See also* Censorship
Star Channel, 223, 236
State television agencies. *See* Public
  television
Station Independence Program (SIP), 214
Station manager, 126, 128, 299–300, 334
Station Program Cooperative (SPC),
  149–150, 152, 214
Station representative, 26, 68, 125–142. *See
  also* Reps
Stations: affiliated, television, 71–86;
  all-news radio, 289–309; commercial,
  strategy of, 16; FCC commitment, 141;
  group-owned, 107–120; independent
  television, 89–105; music, 263–286;
  public, 16, 143–162, 325–342;
  representatives, 26, 68, 125–142;
  superstation, 243–259; talk, 311–323.
  See also stations listed by call letters
Step deal, 173
Stockpiling, 37
Storer Broadcasting, 68, 109
Strategies: audience flow, 13, 29, 134–135,
  139–140, 169, 217, 232; block
  programming, 13, 77, 138, 179, 265;
  blockbusters, 12, 178, 180, 216, 225;
  carry-over, 161; checkerboarding, 11,
  139; commercial television stations
  counterprogramming, 36–37, 72, 73,
  75, 78–79, 93, 99, 101–102, 126, 139;
  crossovers, 12, 180; hammocking, 13,
  179; lead-in, 34, 74, 96, 111, 133, 135,
  140, 179, 180–181, 232; long-form, 12,
  102, 182–183, 216; loss leaders, 34, 253,
  302; lynchpin, 179–180; network

DATE DUE

APR 2 6 1983		
APR1 0 1985		
29 july 88		
APR 0 2 1990		
APR 1 7 1990		
APR 1 6 1990		
APR 1 7 1991		
12-30-93		
NOV 0 2 1997		
NOV 1 9 1997		
MAY 2 7 2010		
GAYLORD		PRINTED IN U.S.A